The Hyphenate in Recent
American Politics and Diplomacy

The Hyphenate in Recent
American Politics and Diplomacy

by

Louis L. Gerson

The University of Kansas Press

Lawrence, 1964

PRINTED IN THE U.S.A. BY THE UNIVERSITY OF KANSAS PRESS

TO SAMUEL FLAGG BEMIS

PREFACE

Hyphenated Americans—those immigrants and their descendants who, either of their own choosing or as a result of outside pressure, link their American nationality with that of their ancestral lands—have received ever-increasing attention from American politicians and political analysts. This study is an attempt, first, to describe the factors which have caused many of these Americans of foreign origin to be susceptible to the statements of purpose and the propaganda of their ancestral lands, as well as to the manipulations of many American political leaders who use these ethnic attachments to win votes. Second, this study tries to measure the effects this susceptibility of the hyphenates has had on some traditional principles and objectives of American foreign policy and on their own political assimilation into the American political milieu.

Personal experience gave me my original interest in the subject: I am a naturalized American myself. I came to the United States at the age of seventeen. In the armed forces during the Second World War, and subsequently in academic life, I have had no difficulty in identifying myself as an American. I have been constantly aware, however, that great numbers of other immigrants and their descendants were increasing their identification with their native and ancestral lands. My continuing puzzlement over this difference between us was, in the end, the stimulus for a detailed study of ethnic political behavior. As a student of American diplomacy and foreign policy, I naturally paid particular attention to the effect which ethnic groups have had on these matters.

Since I emphasize the hyphenate factor as a significant one in shaping the course of our diplomacy and foreign policy, I am well aware that an impression of imbalance—a "side effect" usual in studies like this which highlight one factor out of many and perhaps even at the expense of many—is very nearly inevitable. But I believe the hyphenate factor *is* a significant one.

There are two limitations or restrictions which affect this study. One, beyond my control, is caused by the varying availability of sources. I have had to treat a few topics rather briefly simply because sources were not available in the quantity and quality the student might wish for. The other limitation is deliberate: I have restricted the study primarily to three periods of time.

For the most part, I have confined my inquiry to the years from

vii

1890 to 1956, with special emphasis on the periods 1914-1924 and 1933-1956. These restrictions may be justified on a variety of grounds. First, by 1890 American society had developed a relatively stable and distinctive institutional pattern. Moreover, by 1914 the United States had become a power whose prestige and influence were recognized throughout the world. Second, it was only in the last years of the nineteenth century that immigration reached its peak and became an important, often self-organized, channel of influence. Third, the outbreak of the First World War increased the nationalistic and patriotic sentiment of the ethnic groups which, because of their closely knit organization, were able to make their demands felt by the American government. Finally, reliable information about ethnic pressure on the government is available for this period. This is particularly true for those ethnic groups which were encouraged, by Woodrow Wilson's principle of self-determination, to work for the re-establishment of their ancestral lands. The end of mass migration to the United States came with the rigid immigration laws of 1924.

The second period of the study, 1933-1956, encompassing the Second World War and much of the Cold War, has similarities to the first period, but also shows some significant differences. Axis domination and later Soviet control over many European nations deeply moved the ethnic groups in the United States and motivated their attempts to influence foreign policy. Source materials in the Franklin D. Roosevelt, Harry S. Truman, and Yale Libraries, the Library of Congress, the National Archives, the files of governmental agencies and political parties, and interviews and correspondence with those who figured in the events of this period furnished a rich background for its assessment. I also consulted the Roper Public Opinion Research Center at Williams College and studied published poll data. In most instances, questions had not been formulated to assess the ethnic factor; when they had been, the samples were too small to be meaningful. I found the information about public opinion that was determined through private surveys made for the Nationalities Committees of both parties to be the most useful, because it had served as a basis for policy decisions by the committees.

Within these limits I have attempted to appraise the nature and scope of ethnic-group activity—particularly as it affects and is affected by the American political parties—and its impact on the formation and execution of foreign policy.

I wish here to express my thanks to the many officials, elected and appointed, of the government of the United States, who granted me long and unhurried interviews, made available some of their pertinent papers, and facilitated the gathering of documentary material.

I am particularly grateful, also, to Dr. Philip C. Brooks, Philip D. Lagerquist, and James R. Fuchs of the Harry S. Truman Library; to Dr. Herman Kahn, Dr. Elizabeth Drewry, and Robert L. Jacoby of the Franklin D. Roosevelt Library; and to Dr. Howard Gotlieb of the Yale University Library.

I am indebted to the following scholars who read my manuscript in its entirety or in part, and who gave me the benefit of their criticisms, suggestions, and encouragement: Dr. Thomas A. Bailey of Stanford University, Dr. Robert H. Ferrell of Indiana University, Dr. George L. Anderson of the University of Kansas, Dr. Richard L. Walker of the University of South Carolina, and Dr. Eugene Davidson; and to these of my colleagues at the University of Connecticut: Dr. G. Lowell Field, Dr. Curt Beck, Dr. Karl Bosworth, Dr. I. Ridgway Davis, Dr. Maurice Farber, Dr. Norman Kogan, Dr. Fred Kort, Dr. B. O. J. Linnevold, and Dr. Kenneth Wilson.

I should like to record, too, my appreciation to the Simon Guggenheim Foundation for awarding to me one of its honored fellowships, and to the administration of the University of Connecticut for facilitating and administering other grants-in-aid.

Betty G. Seaver has been invaluable in assisting me in research and in the preparation of the manuscript for publication. The astute editorship and many kindnesses of the Editor of the University of Kansas Press merit special attention.

My acknowledgments would not be complete without an expression of gratitude for the continuing inspiration of my first-generation wife, Elizabeth Shanley Gerson; of my children, Elliot, William, and Ann, who are paternally first-generation and maternally second-generation Americans; and of my fellow-immigrant father, Morris Gerson.

–L. L. G.

Storrs, Connecticut

CONTENTS

FOREWORD

By G. Lowell Field
Professor of Political Science
The University of Connecticut

When a democratic polity seeks to assimilate large culturally alien blocs, considerations of propriety and expediency greatly impede the frank discussion of many issues. A danger to the national interest in the external allegiances to which culturally divergent elements seem inclined is strongly felt by persons basically assimilated to the core culture. Yet the goal of the ultimate assimilation of the divergent groups and the sensitivity of such groups seem to require that the responsible public leader make no reference to any such concern. It appears necessary in practical politics both to pretend that important special loyalties to external cultures and causes do not exist and at the same time to make prudent appeals, as may seem expedient, to what are assumed to be the special loyalties of politically unassimilated peoples.

An element of pretense that allows disunifying appeals in the supposed interest of a practical unity of national purpose clouds political discussion by all immediately responsible actors on the political stage. Because of the necessity imposed upon political leaders to face these questions with something less than intellectual honesty, here is an area in which the contributions of scholars have a specially important place in the clarification of political thought. While political leaders cannot be expected to pick up and repeat the more disturbing statements which scholars may feel free to make on this topic, there can hardly be any question that by many such leaders a frankness of expression by those free to indulge in it may be welcomed as a clarification of a pressing problem.

Through much of its history the political system of the United States has been affected by the problem of assimilation of alien peoples in a manner that is perhaps without strict historical analogy. Cultural division has, of course, affected many historical states in ways more obviously determinative of political practice and constitutional structure than in the case of the United States. Examples are Canada, Austria-Hungary, and Switzerland. These, however, are states in which the divisions have characteristics that tend to insure their permanance and that preclude the goal of assimilation as a practical policy. Cultural divisions in these cases are rooted in the pattern of geographic settlement, particular ethnic groups dominating either distinct regions or numerous scattered enclaves constituting complete local communities. The various ethnic communities in these cases, moreover, have social structures so stratified as to embrace all levels of education, well-being, and status except perhaps a limited top stratum. They are thus, at least conceivably, viable in isolation from other culture groups.

The alien elements in the population of the United States have never had these two characteristics that tend to prevent the adoption of assimilation as a goal. There have been no ethnically distinct regions for any length of time and no significant body of ethnically distinct local settlements. Moreover, with minor local and temporary exceptions the waves of immigration upon our shores have thrown up only decapitated ethnic societies. In general, persons sufficiently educated or well-off to be able successfully to claim high status do not participate in mass emigrations. When they emigrate as individuals they are rather promptly assimilated. Realistically they form no part of the kind of ethnic divisions to which we refer. Thus inevitably the foreign stocks in the United States have depended to a large extent upon persons more or less completely assimilated to the core culture for the provision of the higher-status functions of social organization—employment, education, professional services, and (beyond a petty level) political leadership. In a less democratically oriented culture than that of the United States, such decapitated ethnic groups could hardly have failed to turn into a permanent depressed class.

The combination of two factors has caused the deep impact of the presence of unassimilated peoples on the political system of the United States. First, these peoples through social decapitation and lack of dominance of particular territories formed unstructured masses almost necessarily destined to assimilation to the core culture. Second, their great numbers and their constant intimate association with members of their own culture groupings insured that the successful completion of such assimilation would be delayed for decades if not centuries. If the statement is put more bluntly and expressed within the practical time-span of interest to the politician, the ethnic minorities could be referred to as assimilable but could practically be regarded as unassimilable. This convenient and, in a practical sense, almost unavoidable ambiguity allowed practices to be condoned that could never have been tolerated on practical grounds if the ethnic minorities had been seen as in the process of rapid assimilation and that could never have been tolerated on patriotic grounds if these minorities had been seen as permanent. For an American political leader to appeal to Irish immigrants as if to "Irishmen" or to Italian immigrants as if to "Italians" is ridiculous if such groupings are rapidly becoming American, and verges on the treasonous if such groupings are really foreign. The confusion of the practical view of the matter obscures both standards of judgment.

The crude experience of politics has not provided, and cannot in the foreseeable future provide, unambiguous perceptions of American ethnic groups that would of themselves clarify the basic ambiguity with which they are viewed by politicians. Obviously the "facts" of assimilation are facts only as to particular local and special situations. Different ethnic elements were added to the population gradually over many years. In some cases, like that of the Irish, most of the immigration occurred many years ago. In other cases, like that of the Italians, it is relatively recent. Conditions in different localities, moreover, have allowed ethnic separateness to be preserved in different degrees. Moreover, assimilation has many levels. In a significant sense in relation to attitudes to job-holding, personal consumption, and perhaps recreation almost all second-generation and older ethnic groups are assimilated to the gross features of American culture. In every generation, moreover, some upwardly mobile persons have passed into higher-status roles. For the definition of these roles the decapitated ethnic society has usually preserved no relevant tradition. Such persons in the areas of work experience are necessarily completely assimilated to the core culture and in many cases also they pass largely into a total social environment regulated by the core culture.

By this very process, however, the decapitated character of the ethnic residue tends to be emphasized. Except perhaps for the Negroes and Orientals in certain localities, the decapitated ethnic societies (by virtue of the assimilation of their most successful members) show no serious tendency to regrow their absent strata and to become complete societies. To those who do not obviously move out, as a result of especial personal success, into the general area of the core culture, the ethnic society—however attenuated its cultural distinction from American standards may actually have become with time—still forms the area of friendship, family relationship, and "home." Since it consists only of persons who seem not to have experienced the fullest possible personal success, the ethnic society as it persists after a generation or two is a society vaguely conscious of a grievance. It adopts the same ambiguity in reference to itself that the politician has found expedient in relation to it. For some purposes it adopts a pose of belligerent Americanism. For others it professes an artificial and sentimentalized affection for the old country—a feeling which its first-generation forebears in most cases probably lacked.

To preserve the separate consciousness of the more or less fully assimilated ethnic societies of the second and later generations requires some deliberate efforts. This circumstance opens the way to "professional ethnics," persons who make a career of representing ethnic groups in such capacities as newspaper editors and officers of special ethnic associations. It is with these persons that the politicians have at the national level of politics come to deal.

The relation of the ethnic representative and the political parties has become in the present century the central mechanism by which the presence of ethnic minorities affects the American political system. In fact, it is the activities of the professional ethnics that give the ethnic societies tangible form as political interest-groups in the mid-twentieth century, when direct immigration has long been negligible. The professional ethnic claims to speak for a distinct voting bloc. The politician cannot risk a test of the validity of this hypothesis and instead makes such concessions to the claims and wishes of professional ethnics as other considerations appear to permit. Thus the professional ethnic in turn is maintained as a person of importance by the deference which politicians accord him. The practical structure of ethnic blocs in this way becomes an appendage of the social complex made up of those persons active in the organizations of the two major parties. A circular mechanism thus works against the full assimilation of many groups which, in superficial aspects of behavior at least, are largely Americanized.

The real prevalence of ethnic political consciousness and of bloc voting by ethnics is unknown. Gerson in connection with the present study has examined the voluminous record of scientific opinion polls that might be relevant to these questions. None was so structured as to give statistically valid conclusions as to the reality of the supposed political behavior of ethnics that constitutes the stock in trade of professional ethnics in their dealings with politicians. The conduct of an opinion study having serious relevance to these questions would be exceedingly expensive. Moreover, there is no reason whatsoever to suppose that the "reality" underlying the belief in ethnic voting would be revealed as having any clear and succinct general character. The problem is not one of fact but of moral analysis. To what degree and in what forms is the recognition of residues of ethnicity by public leaders and particularly by the political parties beneficial or harmful to the national interest and to the personal and social adjustment of the ethnics themselves? We shall return to this question after summarizing some historical processes. Under these the way in which political organizations reacted to the presence of unassimilated masses determined features of American political culture which by a feed-back mechanism produce the moral confusion now prevalent in this area.

Historically, the assimilation problem began to affect the American political system on a purely local level in the slum areas of cities in which large bodies of immigrants had congregated. It was only certain portions of the immigrant stream that eddied into these backwaters. English or Scottish immigrants always passed smoothly into the core culture, which differs only in superficial ways from their own. By and large, German or Scandinavian immigrants had resources or skills that allowed them to spread over the countryside and so to avoid the urban concentrations which long isolated other ethnic groups. Initially—that is, during the middle nineteenth century—it was mainly the Irish who constituted obviously isolated and unassimilated masses in the larger cities. Later a variety of nationalities from eastern and southern Europe tended to replace them as the typical "foreign" masses of the cities.* In some areas the Italians or the Poles or both reached the point so long occupied by the Irish of constituting locally dominant ethnic blocs.

It was around the poverty-stricken immigrant concentrations in the cities that the practice of "machine" politics became habitual in the middle nineteenth century with spreading effects partly on overt political behavior in other areas but more significantly on the moral evaluation of politics in American culture. In its typical and now more and more obsolete form "machine politics" allowed the total

---

* Today, outside the area around Boston the Irish hardly constitute an ethnic minority in the usual political sense. There are, in fact, interesting tendencies among leaders of Irish identification to support the liquidation of the practices of "ethnic" politics. This suggests that well over a century is required (given the ethnic-oriented habit in American politics) for the practical assimilation of a once distinct ethnic minority to the point where the politicians begin to accept such assimilation as a fact.

dominance of the governmental organs of a city or urban region by what amounted to a firm or syndicate that, by providing minimal personal services to the isolated and unassimilated immigrant electorate, could with their votes determine the outcome of local elections. The machine politician was hardly in any ordinary usage of the word a politician at all. He had little need to concern himself seriously with issues of public policy and none at all with serious argument and propaganda. There was really no "politics" within a machine-dominated area. The machine was in essence an informally structured business firm dominated usually by some single "leader" to whom was subordinated in more or less feudal fashion a large body of local "leaders" that spent their time and made their living by operating informally job-finding, counseling, welfare, and recreational services for the benefit of the immigrant poor in their assigned territorial "fiefs." The income of the machine came in at the top level in the form of payments exacted from business firms to whom governmental contracts were let and more generally from businesses (legal or illegal, including gambling and prostitution) dependent upon licensing or other forms of governmental permission or tolerance. Portions of such income were filtered down through the levels of subinfeudation within the organization, the leader of each lower level deriving therefrom his personal income, as well as the funds necessary to maintain the services rendered to the indigent immigrant voters. Since only the machine offered to the average immigrant family in a slum area any kindly aid in adjustment to American life, to cast votes in elections as directed by their benefactors was a small and wholly acceptable price. To higher-level political organizations of the political party with which the machine was nominally affiliated, the machine sold its support in the nomination or election of candidates in return for some elective and appointive patronage in the state and federal governments and for tolerance of its own more or less illegal operations and those of the businesses constituting its source of income.

To what extent Americans in general during the nineteenth century (mostly living in rural areas) were aware of the political machines dominating the cities is questionable. All higher political leaders, however, must have known them well, since the votes which they could deliver were essential elements in political calculations in national elections and in those of most states. Machine politics in the cities was by the beginning of the twentieth century so completely habitual that its practitioners hardly recognized the illicit character of their operations and in many cases would discuss them without restraint with interested outsiders. This naïve attitude of many machine-politicians made possible the literary movement called the "muckrakers," which in the first decade of the twentieth century flooded the consciousness of literate Americans with the sordid details of the "shame of the cities."

Thereafter the pristine simplicity of machine operations vanished. Like other politicians inclined to unethical practices, the personnel of the American city machines had to divert energy to the concealments and subterfuges necessary to stay out of jail. Moreover, mass immigration terminated with World War I. By a generation later the type of population on which the machines had depended was no longer prevalent. More and more often machines were defeated in elections by politicians who exploited issues. In the nineteen-thirties the neighborhood services rendered by the machines were largely made superfluous by governmental employment exchanges, social insurance, and welfare agencies.

The effect of the long prevalence of machine politics on the ethical evaluation of political activities in American culture has been profoundly deleterious. It is impossible to maintain in an important activity ethical standards much higher than those re-flected in forms of conduct that are known to be widely practiced with impunity. It was not the neighborhood services of the machine to immigrant groups which presented the serious defiance of ethical standards, although these activities did involve plentiful irregularities in tempering the impact of the law on the poor and improvident. Nothing but votes came to the machines from its immigrant pro-tégés. Rather the obvious offense to morals lay in the fact that the whole income of the machine came from the sale of privilege to major business interests, the sale of exemption to businesses classed as illegal, the sale of mere justice to the wide variety of businesses subject to inspection and licensing, and the concealed draining of the public treasury by the inclusion of "kick-backs" to the machine in fees paid to contractors and salaries paid to officials.

That these practices were commonplace in urban areas through-out the later nineteenth century could not fail to have effects on practice within the political system as a whole. While true machines (as total organized entities) rarely operated beyond the cities, the individual forms of illicit income frequently occurred in rural areas, in state administration, and probably more rarely (except for kick-backs to the political parties from officeholders) at the level of federal administration.

The existence of machine politics and of the practices spreading outward from the true machine-controlled areas during the nineteenth century led to a pervasive if ambiguous disvaluation of political activity as a respectable field of endeavor. Persons with standing in the business, social, or professional levels of society could not in many localities without serious compromise of reputation participate at the local or grass-roots level of political organization, though they could, and often did, enter politics at more exalted levels as candidates for high office or as appointees to important positions in the federal administration. In such capacities, however, they were powerless to alter the moral tone of the lower levels of organization on which they depended for electoral support. Moreover, the democratic ethos served to prevent any direct attack upon the systematic recruitment of local political workers from levels of society where reputation is not a perishable commodity. One could not argue that local politics was excessively open to the ne'er-do-well and the shady character without appearing to argue that politics should be restricted to persons of patrician background. At a later stage, as ethnic groups began to provide the core of local political organization in the areas where they had congregated, one could not argue that political posts should not go automatically to particular ethnic categories without appearing to argue that such posts should necessarily go to "wasps" (white Anglo-Saxon Protestants).

The pervasive suspicion of the moral rectitude of the politician (with exception usually made for prominent candidates for exalted offices) and the consequent failure to expect any high level of public rectitude from political practitioners was not replaced by any constructive alternative viewpoint as a result of the revelations of the muckraking era. Rather, the general reaction of the educated was further to disvalue what was called "politics" as such. The Reform Movement which over the years has gradually altered the administrative structure of American government so as to make more and more difficult the older irregularities was itself in intention a "non-political" movement. Every effort was made to dispense with the usual forms of partisan organization. Many men and women of social position participated in "citizens' associations" which tried to displace the regular partisan organizations entirely in municipal elections and to render their role less significant at higher levels by such devices of "pure" democracy as the direct primary, the initiative and referendum, and the election of local officials and sometimes even of state legislators without the partisan endorsement of candidates. Thus the essential personnel of partisan organization at the local levels continued to be drawn, as before, from persons with little reputation to lose. It is only in the last few decades that some evidence of the penetration of local organizations of the parties by persons not dependent upon such activities for upward social mobility is beginning to come to notice.

The low expectation of serious political purpose from politicians, which itself stemmed in large measure from the successful organization of the immigrant vote by the city machines, opened the way to the second stage of the adjustment of the American political system to the presence of large masses of voters presumed to be only partially assimilated to the core culture. The early city machines had placed many immigrants on the governmental payroll as laborers. With the passage of time the machines themselves became largely ethnic (initially Irish in most cases). Persons of ethnic background thus appeared prevailingly in municipal office in many machine cities. Beyond the strictly machine-controlled areas ethnic "recognition" now became a recognized pattern of political appeal. The party ticket on the state-wide level must contain a certain proportion of ethnic names. While it might long seem necessary in a particular state to run a "wasp" for governor, the various subordinate administrative offices, which are popularly elected in most states, could easily be made the means of rewarding or attracting to the party the supposed ethnic voting blocs on which the city machines had earlier built their support. The open practice of the "balanced ticket," in which partisan nominations to various offices are apportioned among persons of different ethnic affiliations according to some temporarily agreed-upon local standard of allocation, reflects the low level of serious political purpose tolerated by cultural standards created by the previous long acceptance of machine politics as a fact.

It is not, in this matter of the recognition of ethnic status in political nominations, the overt actions of the political leaders but rather the attitudes and styles accompanying these actions that reflect the ethical disvaluation of politics in American culture. To find reasons for advancing certain persons from locally numerous ethnic groups would merely indicate the elementary shrewdness which any politician should have. To put up such candidates openly merely because they will presumably attract votes from their co-nationals—to allow it to be publicly understood that a "Pole" will get the Congressmanship-at-large and an "Italian" the treasurership—is in effect to admit that the party organization exists merely to win elections.*

That active politicians should wish to win as many electoral contests as possible is just as natural as that any particular worker should wish the wages for his own work to be as large as possible or that a businessman should wish for the most profits possible out of a given operation. These, however, are not interests that anyone else unconditionally shares. They are personal and private incentives to action which, properly speaking, are not shared by any persons upon whose behavior such outcomes may depend. While a customer may accept the fact that a businessman would like to make a substantial profit on a sale, he would regard the businessman as an idiot if he seemed to act on the assumption that the customer had any inherent interest in his making such a profit. Similarly, no worker may expect an employer to wish to pay him more than is prudently necessary to secure his continued services. He knows that his unqualified personal enthusiasm for his own economic well-being cannot rationally be shared either by his employer or by customers who would ultimately foot the bill. The case is altogether similar with respect to the interest of a politician or political organization in winning elections insofar as politics is respected as a serious pursuit. Under an ethic that takes political activity seriously the politician must offer reasons other than his own desire for success for soliciting public support. To indulge in obvious vote-getting tricks is as profitless within an electorate that takes political activities seriously as are transparent and crude tricks of salesmanship to a reasonably experienced body of customers. Openly to put up ethnic candidates for the sake of getting ethnic votes is one aspect of American politics that reflects the cultural disvaluation of politics. A politician can run a candidate merely because he is a "Pole" or an "Italian" only because he assumes that the public holds him to no serious standards of publicly useful behavior.

---

* These practices are not, of course, analogous to those in some countries where ethnic groups determined not to be assimilated have parties of their own and run candidates from their own membership. This style of politics is entirely different from that of the nominally all-inclusive American major parties.

When political organizations directly and openly solicit votes by the calculated inclusion of ethnic candidates on a ticket of nominees, it is a small step to the soliciting of votes by offering policy concessions to ethnic minorities. There is, however, usually no way to offer policy concessions to ethnic groups as such except in the realm of foreign policy, and in this area only by claiming to tie American policy to the interests of the ethnic's home country. Here also the lack of high cultural standards for political behavior (itself the offshoot of the early machine practices induced by the presence in the cities of large bodies of immigrants) allows an open trafficking in direct appeals for ethnic votes.

It has long been customary for the platform committees of the major parties immediately before the quadrennial sessions of their national conventions to hear at length the proposals of professional ethnics, with a view to the competitive phrasing of specific appeals to the groupings which such professional ethnics represent. At this level of policy it is obvious that vote-getting considerations are not exclusively applied. Somehow a line is drawn between open commitments of national policy that would be obviously absurd or disastrous and tendentious statements of sympathy with some foreign cause that will please some minority while probably falling short of such disastrous effects. This straddle is obviously difficult to make and to invite the competition of ethnic leaders for recognition by influencing the phrasing of party platforms is to invite pressures that will be difficult to resist. That the difficulty is openly invited by the customary behavior of responsible agencies of the major parties illustrates the lack of standards imposed by the culture upon the behavior of politicians.

Thus American foreign policy has long been clouded by professions of sympathy and aversion for foreign causes, professions whose major motivation lies in detailed considerations of domestic vote-getting. Occasionally expressions of sympathy are later translated into effective action. Thus, as Gerson's earlier study shows, the re-creation of the Polish state after World War I might not have occurred except for the interest which President Wilson and some of his associates had previously shown in the effective cultivation of the Polish-American vote.* In this case there proved to be no effective obstacle to carrying out a foreign action whose ultimate motivation lay in American domestic politics. It is easy for foreign governments

---

* *Woodrow Wilson and the Rebirth of Poland, 1914-1920* (New Haven, 1953).

to assume that such will always be the case. The disastrous conflict within the Western Alliance at the time of the Suez crisis might not have occurred if British and French diplomacy had not assumed that American policy was bound by the presence of the "Jewish vote" to actions favorable to Israel. When the chips are down, however, no President or Secretary of State will risk national survival in an effort to honor a campaign pledge to an ethnic minority. We do not liberate peoples when we cannot. No more than any other power do we involve ourselves in major conflicts on purely sentimental considerations. Thus appeals to ethnic groups are likely to turn out to be insincere. Not policy but the mere promise of policy was traded for votes. The ethnic whose effective weight in American politics seems to be assured by a success in influencing the phrasing of policy in favor of his foreign sympathies thus finds himself a dupe. Gerson's treatment of the "liberation" theme in the 1952 campaign and subsequent policy developments illustrates perhaps the major instance in which politicians recklessly used the technique of encouraging ethnic groups to see themselves as playing a legitimate role in American politics by seeking commitments whose fulfillment was in fact impossible.

From the foregoing argument it does not follow that the American experience with the assimilation of ethnic minorities has, on the whole, been a tragic one. America needed people. Immigration provided these people. For the most part, they improved their opportunities in life by coming here. For the most part, over a reasonable period of time they were assimilated. They became Americans. The values and goals of the American tradition were, on the whole, successfully transmitted. The immigrants of yesterday or their recent descendants are, for the most part, the Americans of today. All this has been sufficiently celebrated in the customary public rhetoric. This book is concerned with some of the inadequacies of the assimilation process and with the residual problems which these inadequacies have left for the American polity.

As has been said, these inadequacies in the assimilation process have had their primary effects in the political system. Given the American democratic ethos, they were perhaps inevitable. Only the long-term exclusion from the political process of the immigrant masses would have protected politicians from the temptations to purely expedient tactics in vote-getting which lowered the cultural standards for political activity. But to exclude the immigrants from political rights would have been, in effect, to exclude the poor and the unfortunate. Under any other ethos assimilation could hardly have been as adequate as it was. While the great immigration plus democracy has left us with impaired standards of political ethics, the great immigration plus a non-democratic ethos would presumably have left us with permanent ethnic minorities constituting a depressed caste.

The problem of ethnic politics in the United States of the mid-twentieth century may therefore be an inevitable residue of a certain historical problem handled under a certain historical ethos and may well be less harmful than would have been the residue from the same problem handled under a different ethos, but it is nonetheless a serious problem. The attainment of world-power status by the American nation has made it such. Our foreign policy is no longer a matter of mere gestures of primary concern only in our own neighborhood. In every corner of the world any commitment of American power or influence is taken in deadly seriousness. Nothing we do is without effects, but these effects cannot be sufficient simply to make over the world to our own liking. As a nation, we live precariously in a world that is half hostile and a quarter potentially hostile. Great as is our power, we have no leeway for its improvident or ill-calculated exercise. Prudently exercised, the power that we have should be sufficient for our national survival and even for a tenuous world leadership. It is, however, insufficient to be exerted carelessly with impunity.

It is upon the prudence of the exercise of such power as we have over the course of world events that the present careless appeal of politicians to ethnic loyalties has the most harmful effect. It is very simply the lack of concordance between domestic ethnic forces and the power relations that prevail in portions of the world from which these ethnic forces come that makes the playing of the game of ethnic appeals dangerous to national survival. Israeli power in the Middle East is balanced, if not clearly overbalanced, by Arab power, but there are many Jews and practically no Arabs in the United States electorate. Descendants of all the many nationalities of central and eastern Europe are numerous in America and, by and large, they will all favor a freeing of their traditional homelands from Russian dominance, but in the world as a whole Russia is the one power besides the United States possessing the means, or very nearly the means, in modern armaments to destroy all civilization in a sufficiently earnest military engagement. While an apparent commitment that is clearly inexpedient to the extent of threatening national disaster will in all probability not be seriously implemented by any administration in office, its existence has prior and far-reaching effects in crippling normal diplomacy. We broke the Franco-British power play in favor of the Israeli and against the Arabs at Suez in 1956 in spite of the fact that we depend most heavily upon the British and French as allies. Apparently the state of our domestic politics made it impossible to convince them in advance that we would take such action. Similarly, we could not effectively tell the rebellious Hungarians in the same year that in view of the actual line-up of power in the world our sympathy for their aims could not possibly be translated into useful support.

Yet serious as are the problems raised by the current appeals of politicians to ethnic sympathies, these problems lie precisely in the realm of the ethics of individual behavior more than in the realm of institutional forms. There is only one concrete measure of organizational policy which Gerson urges as a contribution to meeting the dangers which the artificial cultivation of ethnicity now raises in the American polity. This is the disbandment of the Nationalities Divisions of the two major parties. While such a development would have directly some effect upon the cultivation of ethnicity by the recognition which the parties now give through these divisions to professional ethnics, its main effect would be symbolic. It obviously could not occur except on the basis of a consensus among political leaders that the deliberate cultivation of ethnicity is harmful to the nation. It would symbolize such a judgment.

Institutional and legal remedies for the curse of ethnicity in American politics are not available because the standards of conduct needed are not capable of crude prescription. The law does not reach the fine points of human behavior. These lie in the realm of individual ethics supported by general assumptions of the culture. To say that an American of Polish descent should feel no sympathy for the misfortunes of Poland is morally ridiculous. To say that a politician should avoid encouraging persons and organizations of Polish descent to think that they have any special right to say what American policy toward Poland should be is precisely the kind of ethical discrimination which responsible persons expect from other responsible persons. In a free regime persons may not be denied the expression of opinions merely because they are interested parties in the matters to which these opinions relate, but in any responsible exercise of decision-making power it is necessary for those whose special interests might overwhelm their judgment of the general interest to disqualify themselves or to be disqualified from participation.

Aside from its mere historical interest, the importance of Gerson's study lies precisely in the way in which it highlights the danger to prudent national decision-making of the special affections of ethnic groups and of the special interests of persons active in ethnic organizations and of politicians accustomed to appeal to particular ethnic groups. This is precisely a question of moral orientation, a matter of seeing the facts of a situation and of recognizing the moral problems which they raise. It may be hoped that this book will lead toward a general recognition by public leaders of the dangers to national survival involved in the current easy and open cultivation by politicians of special ethnic clienteles.

Such a recognition of the moral problem could not properly lead to attempts at formal regulation of the rights of individual and organizational action by persons of special ethnic identification except as association with foreign governmental agencies might be involved. It could and should lead to the general recognition by political leaders that foreign policy is not legitimately bargainable piecemeal for votes. It should lead to suspicion and ostracism aimed against any political leader who obviously directs special appeals for the support of particular foreign policies to ethnic groupings with an undue emotional involvement in such policy commitments as are proposed. In a proper moral climate ethnic groups should themselves be embarrassed if subjected to this kind of appeal, just as a judge would be embarrassed by efforts to get him to participate in the decision of a case involving a close relative. It is entirely legitimate that such ethnic groups should wish and hope that American policy might assist the legitimate aspirations of their homelands. It is quite illegitimate to set up or to tolerate situations—like those in which foreign-policy hearings are conducted by the major parties before their national conventions—in which it appears that the feelings of ethnic minorities are legitimate grounds for deciding whether or not such intervention by American power is possible or desirable.

Part I

INTRODUCTION: THE HYPHENATE AND AMERICAN POLITICS

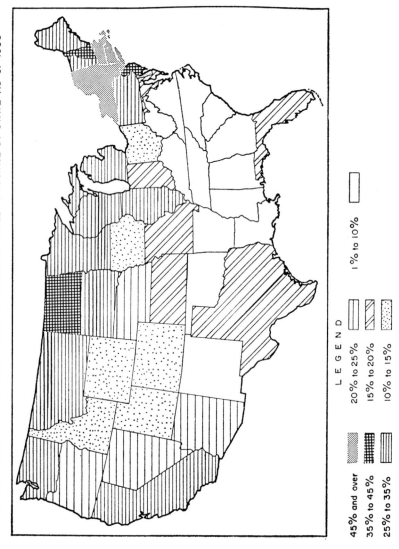

CONCENTRATION OF THE NATIVE WHITE OF FOREIGN OR MIXED PARENTAGE BY STATE AS OF 1950

LEGEND

45% and over

35% to 45%

25% to 35%

20% to 25%

15% to 20%

10% to 15%

1% to 10%

Chapter I
THE BIRTH OF THE HYPHEN

We are all tattooed in our cradles with the beliefs of our tribe;
the record may seem superficial, but it is indelible.
                                    —Oliver Wendell Holmes, *The Poet*
                                    at the Breakfast Table.

From its first hour of independence the United States has been the hope and asylum for hungry, oppressed, and persecuted peoples. It has had and continues to have a most powerful attraction to peoples of all nations, all races, and all creeds. No other country of modern times possesses such magnetism.

Since its beginnings the United States has accepted some forty million representatives, including at least some from almost every nation on earth. From early in the nineteenth century to 1930 approximately 60 per cent of the total world migration flowed to America.[1] In 1950 there were nearly eleven million foreign-born persons in the United States and almost twenty-four million whites of foreign or mixed heritage. These figures only suggest the ethnic composition of America.[2] In sheer numbers this movement of peoples has been one of the most impressive aspects of nineteenth- and twentieth-century history—a fact basic to an understanding of American foreign policy.

The mighty confluence of immigrants inevitably affected both domestic and foreign affairs, enriching and invigorating the culture and economy and at the same time impinging upon and affecting political development. A great majority of the immigrants became citizens; as voters and potential officeholders, they exerted a power felt directly by the government. Frequently they roused cultural, social, economic, or political issues which tended to divide the nation. Immigration itself was often a subject of heated national or state debate, with a bearing on both domestic and foreign policy. Then, too, increasing American prestige and strength in the international field fostered pressures from the immigrant population under indigenous and foreign leaders. Ethnic pressures have been applied not only in specific situations, but, perhaps more important, on the fundamental principles guiding the foreign-policy objectives and actions of the United States. Of all the traditional prin-

3

ciples, isolationism—keeping America separate and unentangled from loyalties to foreign nations or nationalistic movements—was the one most affected.

1

At the turn of the century the majority of immigrants came from Europe beyond the Elbe, an area with myriad cultures and languages. Unlike the "old" immigrants, they arrived in larger waves and in a shorter period of time. During the five decades from 1870 to 1910 the total foreign white stock (including foreign-born white and native white of foreign or mixed parentage) increased from 10,817,980 to 32,243,382—an increase of 21,425,402. In the decade 1861-1870 the percentage of immigrants from Southeastern Europe was 1.5, that from Northwestern Europe 87.8. In the decade 1901-1910 the percentages were almost reversed: 70.8 and 21.7.[3]

Fear for future American homogeneity and culture began to show itself with the high tide of immigration. "As I watch the formation of the new society," wrote Henry Adams to Charles Francis Adams, Jr., on November 10, 1911, "I am more and more impressed with my own helplessness to deal with it, and its entire unconsciousness that I, . . . or George Washington ever existed. Therefore we had better do our epitaphs and do them quick."[4] Few of the arrivals were Protestant; most were unskilled laborers and tended to settle in already overcrowded urban centers. They were not the immigrants whom the historian and political scientist Woodrow Wilson, before he became President, considered best for America.[5] His fear mirrored the anxieties, as well as the ignorance, of his contemporaries.

The large-scale immigration from Southern and Eastern Europe and the Orient came during the very period when racial theories derived from Social Darwinism were gaining adherents by the thousands. It also coincided with the change in the nature of revolutionary movements—from the liberal movements of the 1840's to the radical, communist, anarchist, or socialist movements of the first quarter of the twentieth century. The great influx of alien peoples fanned the popularity of Social Darwinism and threatened to revive the anti-foreignism of the Know-Nothing movement of the 1850's. The American historian John Fiske, the constitutional lawyer and political philosopher John W. Burgess, and the Reverend Josiah

Strong became the champions of the superiority of the Anglo-Saxon peoples, who, they believed, had an "extraordinary genius for self-government." To Henry Adams the "Aryans" were the creators of civil law. Woodrow Wilson thought it was significant that democracy was found only in countries "begotten of the English race." Even progressive reformers like David Starr Jordan and Edward Alsworth Ross, who repudiated important elements of Social Darwinism, were nevertheless in accord with the racial theories of its most rabid adherents. The most eminent political thinkers of German birth in the United States, Carl Schurz and Francis Lieber, also paid homage to the idea that the Anglo-Saxon race was divinely ordained. The early belief that all immigrants were capable of becoming good and loyal Americans began to fade by the end of the nineteenth century.[6]

2

By 1914 ethnic Americans had become strongly interested in their native countries; this concern invariably influenced their attitudes toward American politics. Significantly, many of the immigrants who had not experienced the intoxication of nationalism in their homelands discovered it in America. One must bear in mind that the wellspring of immigrant nationalism is to be found not only in affection for the native countries, which is often absent at the time of emigrating, but perhaps even more in the compressed ghettos where group consciousness was fostered by loneliness, poverty, prejudice, and periodic attacks from nativists and other ethnic groups.

Before the outbreak of the First World War the immigrants from Eastern and Southern Europe came mainly from those strata of society in which the national consciousness was not fully developed. A relatively small proportion came from educated and middle classes. Dukes, as the saying went, do not emigrate. The levels of education and technical skills were exceedingly low. Only a very small minority of the Polish immigrants, wrote Thomas and Znaniecki, had "any training in rational social cooperation." For most of them the "Polish national ideal" had little meaning.[7] Indeed, in Poland, as well as in Ireland in the 1840's, the more representative circles saw in the emigration of thousands of countrymen a threat of depopulation, with a "consequent weakening of any revolutionary activity."[8] Polish patriots, unable to stop the emigration "among the more passive part of the nation in which the national interests were relatively weak," were forced to accept it as a "necessary evil"; at the same time they favored "temporary instead of permanent emigration" and tried "to keep at home the most valuable part of Polish society."[9]

In the United States many immigrant groups who, in their homelands, had been restricted in the use of their language, customs, and religion, found the first opportunity for self-expression and freedom to practice their faith and way of life. Paradoxically, it was this very freedom in their adopted land that led to the ethnic-group identification and solidification which also set them off from the dominant group. In the countries of their origin, the Italians, Slovaks, Slovenes, Croatians, Ruthenians, Byelorussians, and many others had considered themselves more as citizens of distinct localities and adherents of certain churches than as members of national states. In their homelands loyalties had been local rather than national. For many, ethnic nationalism and patriotism toward the old country emerged only after their arrival in the United States.

One of the first concerns of the immigrants was the transplanting of their church. More than any other factor, perhaps, the church united and transcended old-country attachments and identification with local villages or regions. The church became the strongest link with the past and the first bridge to the future. It was to be expected that the non–English-speaking immigrants, in particular, would demand clergymen of their own stock, and would insist that their own language be used in their churches. Many American churches of the same denomination as that to which immigrants belonged either refused outright or were reluctant to allow the establishment of foreign-language subdivisions. This attitude encouraged the immigrants to set up their own churches, with their own ministers and priests. Thus, in the early days of the Republic, the refusal of the Methodist Church to fractionize itself led to the formation of German Methodist bodies. Thus, too, Congregational Armenians established their own church, and the Luthern Church split into German, Norwegian, Swedish, and Finnish synods.

The same problem, but in a more severe form, confronted the Catholic Church. In the United States it has been almost entirely made up of successive waves of immigrant groups, each of which insisted on services in its native tongue and priests of its nationality.

The resulting conflict, which began with Irish resentment of the "anti-foreignism" of the then strongly entrenched French clergy, continued when the Irish, once they were the majority in the hierarchy, balked at the requests of newer arrivals. It was this reaction to the antipathy of the older immigrant groups, as well as the uncompromising insistence of the various ethnic groups on their native languages, their own priests, their own parishes, and control of their own parochial schools, that led to the development of intense ethnic nationalism among American Roman Catholics. Thus the Catholic Church in the United States, itself a universal church, unable to withstand these pressures from its multi-lingual adherents, became, unwittingly, an important factor in the rise of ethnic nationalism.

In general, religious conditions in America made for the emergence of ethnic-group solidarity. Indeed, the first differentiation was on religious lines. The parishes and churches of distinct nationality organized, regulated, and preserved the ethnic cultures and in so doing fostered the group consciousness which in time turned into ethnic nationalism. Even when cultural, social, and political assimilation began to make heavy inroads among second, third, and fourth generations, the old religion continued to keep its adherents together. Religious affiliation and religious beliefs continued to serve after language and culture were forgotten or lost.[10]

Other primary preoccupations of newly arrived immigrants were economic and social. The immigrants' lack of training made it difficult for them to obtain decent wages. This enabled many Americans to feel superior to the unskilled and uneducated newcomers. At the same time, however, native workers began to fear them as a potential threat to their own livelihood. Immigrant reaction to these attitudes was inevitable. Low social status and the sense of being both exploited and resented led to the development of an inferiority complex and heightened ethnic feeling.

In their search for social and economic security, the minority groups—of primarily peasant backgrounds—began to insulate themselves in urban "pocket states"—Little Italys, Little Hungarys, Little Polands. Living in these colonies led to an accentuation of national consciousness. It was here in the tenements that attachment to the native village or province was transformed into a strong identification with the native land. Here the Pole, the Slovak, the Hungarian, the Latvian, the Lithuanian, the Italian, and many another gained a stronger ethnic sense than he had ever had before. It was here, as he met compatriots and immigrants from neighboring lands, that his new nationalism burgeoned, only to be manipulated by native or foreign-born leaders and American politicians. As Emily Balch says in her excellent pioneering study: ". . . to many an immigrant the idea of nationality first becomes real after he has left his native country; at home the contrast was between village and village, and between peasants as a class and landlords as a class. In America he finds a vast world of people, all speaking unintelligible tongues, and for the first time he has a vivid sense of oneness with those who speak his own language, whether here or at home." Miss Balch further observes that ethnic political leaders take "advantage of this heightened racial feeling and of the freedom of the new world to teach their people patriotism as they understand it." Here in the adopted land, she continues, "Polish leaders indoctrinate their people with Polish enthusiasm and hopes of a future free Poland, . . . the Slovak is taught . . . to interest himself in the struggle for national existence in Hungary. In the same way . . . the Irish, and later the Syrians, Armenians and other oppressed and burdened peoples have found in America, where liberty and prosperity give them room, a national recruiting ground for patriots."[11]

Years later a perceptive student of American politics described a similar process among Italian-Americans. Italians were strongly attached to their native villages—"an attachment that can reach as far as the province or the region," wrote Max Ascoli. They considered themselves Sicilians, Neapolitans, or Pugliesi. In the United States, he concluded, "they were unified into a 'national' block by the other Americans with whom they came to live and who called all of them Italians—or rather 'Wops.' "[12]

The economic, political, and cultural conditions in the homelands of nationality groups at the time of their emigration had an important effect on the extent of change necessary for their political integration in the United States. Memories of economic misuses and political sufferings in the old country could not be easily erased. The stronger their sympathy for their native country's welfare, the deeper was their emotional attachment to its internal and international politics.

A majority of the newcomers, particularly those of the last two dec-

8

ades of the nineteenth century, were ill-prepared, if at all, to understand the nature of democracy and its processes. In their native lands
suffrage had not extended to the emigrating segments of the population; the art of self-government was unknown to them. It took awhile
for many an immigrant to discard his belief that government was simply a tax collector, a crime punisher—"The farther it was removed
from the people—the better." The immigrants, James Bryce recalled,
knew little about American institutions, statesmen, political issues,
and methods of free government.[13]

Settling in densely populated ghetto-like areas where their social
and economic position was subordinated, the immigrants tended to
remain aloof from American political life.[14] With no experience to
guide them, they were not ready to participate at all, let alone to act
intelligently, in politics. Many of them, particularly before the
passage of the Immigration Act of 1917, were illiterate. Great numbers, through their immigrant organizations and the foreign-language
press, learned to read their mother tongues only after arriving in
America.[15] The isolation of the immigrant urban dwellers was further compounded by the transplanting of Old World hatreds and
mutual distrusts. Historic grievances and wrongs were bitterly aired
when Ukrainians, Poles, Czechs, Slovaks, Lithuanians, Latvians, Jews,
Armenians, Russians, Germans, Irish, Italians, and the many others
found themselves living in the same city blocks. These enforced contacts revived rivalries and fostered pride in the homelands even in
those who had previously rejected outright any kind of affiliation.
Wounds that had never properly healed were reopened. Much of the
immigrants' energy was thus dissipated in fruitless antagonisms.[16]

The revival in Russia, at the end of the nineteenth century, of
virulent anti-Semitism—and its importation by many of the non-
Jewish Russian immigrants, one may add—helped to extend Zionism
among many American Jewish groups which had formerly rejected
the appeals of Jewish nationalistic movements. Zionism originated
in the desire of the Jewish masses to put an end to national and
social inferiority and economic persecution. It was to find, particularly during times of persecution, many influential adherents
in the United States.

Even the Americanization movement itself, which followed the
rise of anti-alienism at the turn of the century, tended in some of its
phases to hinder the process of political assimilation. Those Ameri-

canizers who sought speedy conversion of the immigrant to the New World's culture often achieved the opposite effect—a more complete withdrawal. Those who wished to protect the immigrant from the New World's pressures gave support, though unintentionally, to the view of a fractionized nation even at the cost of weakening the country's efforts to defend its existence. The later attempts of Nazi Germany and Fascist Italy to gain control over their former nationals in the United States forced "even the most liberal wings of the Americanization movement" to question whether the "traditional tolerant attitude toward the immigrant could be maintained without seriously undermining" national solidarity.[17]

Always sensitive to criticism and aware of their inferior status, the immigrants most of all yearned for respectability. Immigrant leaders, foreign governments, and party strategists were quick to sense this "soft spot in immigrant psychology." More often than not, they took advantage of it by approving and, indeed, recommending ethnic nationalism. Michael Davitt, an astute Irish leader, showed his understanding of immigrant feeling when he advised a large Irish-American audience at Cooper Union in 1880: "You want to be honored among the elements that constitute this nation, as a people not coming from a paupered land; and in order that no sneers be cast on you when you stand for any position . . . you want to be regarded with the respect due you, that you may be thus looked on, aid us in Ireland to remove the stain of degradation from your birth and the Irish race here in America will get the respect you deserve."[18]

Ethnic nationalism did not aspire so much to the winning of power in the United States, or to the championing, exaltation, and preservation of lands of origin, as it did to the achievement of dignity, equality, and respectability in the adopted land. At times, however, this aspiration—based as it often was on the revival, strengthening, and support of ancestral aims—has strayed into ethnic chauvinism.

3

The growth of ethnic nationalism served to accentuate the hyphen. But of all the factors contributory to hyphenization, the American party system ranks first. The majority of the newcomers, one should remember, came to the United States for economic reasons. Their first efforts went into finding employment and making the many adjustments to the new environment; these naturally overshadowed political concerns and delayed the immigrants' education in democracy. In time the picture began to change. From their midst emerged important individuals who, through adaptability or longer residence, had learned the ways of the New World. Such men became their spokesmen, counselors, and "middlemen." And it did not take long for some politicians to recognize the value of those who had the confidence of their fellow-immigrants.[19]

The very concentration of immigrant groups in strategic urban centers was a latent political force which had to be reckoned with. At first, through the spokesmen, the "immigrant" boss bought and sold large blocs of votes, grasping thereby control of local government. "Incompetent to give an intelligent vote," observed Bryce in 1895, but soon realizing their votes had value, they fell under party domination. "Such a sacrifice of common sense to abstract principles has seldom been made by any country."[20] A half-century later, Edward J. Flynn, the Democratic boss of the Bronx, New York, recalled, "The immigrants, . . . being human, wanted friends, jobs, the chance to become citizens. Tammany was smart enough to offer them all three, in return for a lifetime and often second-, third-, and fourth-generation fealty to the party. It was as simple and as obvious as that."[21] Large segments of the unwitting immigrant population were readily exploited by political strategists and by their own leaders.

Rather than emphasize aspirations common to all Americans, party leaders in their quest for votes stressed the uniqueness of the immigrant. In consequence, hyphenism became a badge of discomfiting pride, a symbol of attachment to their homelands, to a great many newcomers and their descendants. Continued stress upon the diversity of the American people tended to enhance a feeling among those of foreign origin that they were inferior second-class citizens and that their status as hyphenated Americans would be permanent.

Almost always the immigrant wants to be a good and patriotic American, but the society in which he finds himself usually does not allow him complete adjustment to his new environment. He is forced, often against his preference, to bolster his self-respect by rediscovering and strengthening his ties with his people, their heroes, and "superior" culture. Thus the power and prestige of Mussolini brought to many Italian-Americans a solacing sense of *grandezza* even though they may not have approved of the means used to achieve that end for them.[22]

11

At the turn of the century immigrants of more than forty years' residence, as well as second- and third-generation descendants, became more and more aware of their origins. It is no accident that with the trend toward hyphenization a large number of reminiscences and immigrant histories began to appear. The various alliances, organizations, foundations, lodges, and leagues which had been originally organized for economic, social, cultural, or religious purposes began to show an interest in politics. By 1914 these associations were playing an ever-increasing role in national politics. In time, leadership in some immigrant organizations passed to individuals whose main concerns were their native lands. Indeed, the very status of many of these leaders depended on keeping the groups separate from the main stream of American life. Many of them, whether indigenous or foreign, were often allied with, and sometimes even controlled by, various patriotic movements in the lands of their origin. As their hold over fellow immigrants strengthened, so did the immigrants' susceptibility to the propaganda and the avowed purposes of their native lands.[23]

Roughly until the beginning of the twentieth century, the immigrant "boss," whose political status depended on the foreign-born, rarely experienced revolt. His power was independent of the many domestic issues which divided the electorate, such as the tariff, cheap money, or progressivism, all of little interest to the immigrants, who, isolated from the many issues vital to the United States, were led to follow the party lines unquestioningly.[24]

Party methods for controlling the immigrant vote began to break down after 1900—a fateful coincidence with the emergence of America as a world power. Outright selling of votes had become impractical; new methods were devised to capture the allegiance of the immigrants. Successful attempts were made to organize ethnic social and religious clubs, lodges, and associations and affiliate them with the parties—sometimes directly, sometimes through the individuals controlling them.

Whenever the United States has been at war or been threatened with war, ethnic Americans invariably have been subject to the influences of foreign governments or foreign nationalistic or ideological movements. Through consular officials, ambassadors, or secret agents, parent countries or exile governments have overtly or covertly set up or sought to transform ethnic organizations in order to bind

12

the immigrants to themselves. Some, like Nazi Germany and Fascist Italy, expanded the conception of nationality to include those of their nationals who had emigrated.[25] Using ethnic organizations and the foreign-language press, at times secretly subsidized, they made their appeals to their "nationals"—naturalized American citizens and the descendants of immigrants. Thus, by exploiting already party-aggravated immigrant grievances, suspicions, self-consciousness, inferiority complexes, and sentiments the foreign governments hoped to frustrate or defeat American foreign policies. The Nazi government is a case in point. Since it had been unable to make large inroads in the German-American community, it did not hesitate to ally the pro-Nazi German-American Bund with anti-Semitic or Ku Klux Klan organizations in its attempt to divide the American people. This practice has also been used by those foreign governments which have not contributed many immigrants to the United States and consequently could not count on significant support. For example, the Arab League, concerned over what it believed to be powerful Jewish influence on American foreign policy, sought help after the Second World War from the very same groups the Nazis and Fascists had found so useful in the late 1930's.[26]

At times foreign governments have attempted to consolidate the organizations of one nationality group and also to unite the organizations of several nationality groups under one "roof" organization. The most recent instance of the latter occurred during and immediately after the Second World War when the Soviet Union, with the help of American Communists, brought together in the American Slav Congress many unsuspecting Slavic nationality groups—Poles, Czechs, Slovaks, Ukrainians. It was Stalin's hope to use this "roof" organization as a means of defeating avowed foreign policies of the United States.

4

During most of its history, and particularly in peacetime, the United States has been tolerant of the political activities of refugees and immigrant peoples. Premature, abortive, or successful liberal, royalist, Communist, or Fascist revolutions have brought exiles and refugees to its shores from almost every nation. From the time of America's own war for independence to the present, Latin-American juntas have planned, plotted to overthrow governments, supplied arms for co-revolutionists, and occasionally invaded their countries as "liberators" from United States bases. Here in the nineteenth century Irish-Americans were recruited and openly drilled by the Fenians, who led them in an attack on Canada while the government of the United States showed a bemused indifference to the invasion. Here in America Zionists have worked and sold bonds for an independent Jewish Commonwealth in Palestine. Here in the "asylum of the oppressed" the nationalist aspirations of the Poles, Czechs, Lithuanians, Latvians, Ukrainians, and many others have received powerful support from their American compatriots. Here future prime ministers and presidents of resurrected or newly established nations—men like Ignace Jan Paderewski of Poland, Thomas G. Masaryk and Eduard Beneš of Czechoslovakia, Chaim Weizmann of Israel, Eamon de Valera of Ireland, Karlis Ulmanis of Latvia, and many Latin-American dictators or presidents—have fanned the smoldering nationalistic spirit and learned how to use the voting power of their immigrant peoples. Here American Negroes have supported an Africa for Africans. Here hundreds of Italian-American women sent their wedding rings to help finance Mussolini's Ethiopian expedition; for their "spirit and sacrifice" an official of the Italian consulate in New York blessed the iron substitutes provided by Il Duce.[27] Here Japanese-Americans sent money to help Nippon's war effort. Here the American Chinese dug deep into their pockets to aid Chiang Kai-shek fight the Japanese and, later, the Chinese Communists. Here, too, there have been White Russian, Little Russian, Great Russian, Bulgarian, French, German, Lebanese, Spanish, Italian, Chinese, and Japanese Fascists, monarchists, Communists, Socialists, and liberals. Indeed, it is difficult to believe that this "Nation of Nations" was ever neutral or hoped to remain neutral.[28]

Only when war was imminent or already a reality, or when national interest was clearly involved, did the American government show concern over these political activities. Then it was often too late to rectify the conditions resulting from its tolerance. Promises and pledges in the form of platform planks or presidential statements—which had been made when it seemed politically safe both domestically and internationally—came back to haunt many a President and Secretary of State. Once the United States became engaged in war, the agitations of the nationality groups forced the government into taking drastic measures to curb their political activities, often inspired by foreign governments or movements. Measures were taken to prevent exiled political leaders from controlling immigrant groups. Under the direction of the Department of State, the Department of Justice, the Federal Bureau of Investigation, and the Office of Strategic Services, nationality groups were quickly classified as either "patriotic" or "subversive." The foreign-language press was painstakingly scrutinized for evidence of foreign direction. Leaders were investigated for possible subversive activities and, at times, their freedom of occupational choice was severely restricted. Special propaganda agencies were established because of fears that many nationality groups would not coöperate with or whole-heartedly support the war effort.

During the First World War George Creel's Office of Public Information devoted itself to inculcating patriotic Americanism among the immigrant population. Under its direction Loyalty Days were organized to give ethnic Americans an opportunity to express their love for their new home. These "days" proved so successful and popular that they are still being observed—a boon to some politicians whose stock in trade it is to cater to the ethnic vote.[29] The Office of Public Information's emphasis on, and praise of, the diverse origins of the immigrants more often than not underlined for them their uniqueness and hyphenate status, with the result that many withdrew even more into ethnic isolation. As Hungarian-born Lajos Steiner said in reply to Senator Overman's questioning about Creel's activities among Hungarian-Americans, "I am awfully sorry that the bureau did more for the Europeanization of the immigrant than his Americanization. The old country was glorified and its national anthem was sung."[30]

The wartime practice of dividing Americans of foreign origin into "subversive" or "patriotic" categories has seldom proved satisfactory. In no way has it been fair to the great loyal majority. When the United States entered the war against the Axis, those Americans of enemy stock were thereby automatically rendered suspect and placed under surveillance; those whose native lands had been overrun by the German, Italian, and, later, Russian armies were not only considered "patriotic," but were encouraged to strengthen their efforts in behalf of the homelands. At times naturalized citizens who came from enemy countries have been treated as permanent aliens, with their privileges curbed to such an extent that they became "citizens of inferior grade." One shameful episode in American history occurred during the Second World War when entire Japanese-American communities were uprooted from the West Coast and herded into camps in the interior.[31]

Rarely has such classification taken into account the existence of intra-group conflicts. No ethnic group in the United States has ever been unified under one leadership; all have been divided into rival factions and associations reflecting social, political, economic, and ideological orientations. It has been this inability to agree among themselves and coöperate with one another that has accounted for many of their failures to influence American foreign policy at the right moment. Most recently bitter conflicts have divided the immigrants who arrived between 1890 and 1925 and the émigrés of the same national origins who arrived after the Second World War.[32] During their first months in the United States, the émigrés openly avoided any relations with ethnic groups, a fact which did not endear them to the leadership of ethnic organizations. As a whole, they were impatient to free their homelands. As time went by, the neglect of the liberation promises of the 1952 campaign and the growing emphasis on coexistence following the Geneva conference caused the émigrés to lose hope of returning. They began to make friendly overtures to ethnic leaders. At first the latter resisted, but more and more coöperation is becoming noticeable; this is true particularly in the foreign-language press wherein young exiles have been given editorial positions. A majority of the émigrés has either joined ethnic organizations or leans heavily on them as a medium of political activity.

To be sure, the State Department has been aware at times of schisms within a given ethnic community. After some scrutiny, the Department has reluctantly yielded to political pressure and endorsed one group over the others. This involvement has rarely cleared the air. On the contrary, it encouraged the group endorsed by the government agency to try to discredit, weaken, or destroy the rival factions. There has been a "tendency on the part of some elements," Louis Wirth observed, in some minority groups to take advantage of war "to settle old quarrels of a factional sort or of a personal sort by denouncing their rivals to the government agencies."[33] Thus, during the First World War one Polish-American group which had received the favor of the State Department accused other Polish-American groups of disloyalty, pro-Germanism, or socialism, with the hope that the government would stop their activities and that control of the whole ethnic community would fall to it.[34] During the Second World War, to cite one example, there were two Free Rumanian groups in the United States. One was pro-King Carol, the other anti-King Carol. In order to obtain the aid of the majority of the Rumanian immigrants and the blessing of the American government, the pro-Carolists labeled the anti-Carolists as Communists; the anti-Carolists branded the pro-Carolists as Fascists.

At times foreign governments have been able to influence the decisions of the American government in its endorsement or classification of ethnic groups as "loyal" or "disloyal." In 1941 Yugoslav diplomats of pan-Serbian orientation convinced the State Department that many American Croats should be classified as enemy aliens. "Under such pressures," wrote Bogdan Raditsa, "American Serbs and American Croats, who had lived as good neighbors for centuries in Europe and for decades in North America, turned against one another."[35]

With few exceptions, the American immigrant has always been loyal to the land of his adoption. Rarely has he knowingly joined a subversive or even questionable movement. Having come from nations intolerant of subversive groups, he has naturally assumed that none of the organizations which have asked for his support or membership is un-American. This belief that the United States would not allow subversive movements to exist is well known to many an aspiring ethnic leader. Time after time foreign or indigenous organizers have been able to infiltrate or control existing organizations or even establish new organizations by the simple method of obtaining endorsements from unsuspecting Presidents, Secretaries of State, and other prominent Americans. Under pressure from politicians with large ethnic constituencies, many Chief Executives have sent laudatory statements to leaders of immigrant organizations. Not infrequently presidential candidates have spoken before such groups, thus legitimizing and enhancing the power of their leaders. More than that, the appearances lent weight to the leaders' claims that their activities serve American national interest. Often a merely routine and indifferent letter of courtesy from an important government official acknowledging receipt of a request for a commemorative address or statement to an ethnic conference has been taken for an official credential or endorsement by the government of the United States.[36] The Communist-inspired American Slav Congress became a "legitimate" organization through the success of its president, Leo Krzycki, in securing favorable statements from Secretary of State Cordell Hull, Federal Security Administrator Paul V. McNutt, Mayor Edward J. Kelly of Chicago, and others. Armed with these statements, Krzycki had them printed for distribution to Slavic-American organizations in a colorful brochure emblazoned with the American flag and portraits of General Douglas MacArthur and other famous Americans.[37] The irony of it was that some prominent ethnic leaders, among them Judge Blair F. Gunther, censor of the Polish National Alliance, did not suspect until it became quite obvious that the American Slav Congress was a Communist-front organization.[38]

5

It might be assumed that immigrants' activities on behalf of their native lands, accompanied as they have been with inevitable internal dissensions, would weaken the hold of the American party boss. On the contrary, he has brought the immigrant closer to the machine. Many politicians, some of them without thought or hesitation, some reluctantly, have catered to persistent ethnic nationalistic sentiments in the hope of ensuring party loyalty. At times the national committees of both parties have interfered in the internal struggles of the ethnic organizations by endorsing for leadership persons considered "safe." At one time or another, both parties have profited from the immigrant vote. But profiting most were those who claimed to be the spokesmen of the ethnic groups, speaking for all their peoples.[39]

Thus a belief that Americans vote on the basis of national origin began to be perpetuated in the American body politic. In the decade preceding the First World War, local efforts to secure the Irish, German, Polish, or Jewish vote were common. Soon these tactics spread from city government to state government, thence to the national arena.

"United we stand, hyphenated we fall," observed the *Toledo Blade* at the outbreak of the First World War. "When two flags are hoisted on the same pole," said Theodore Roosevelt, "one is always hoisted undermost." At about the same time Woodrow Wilson, also aware of this weakness, subtly hinted to Americans of foreign origin that "some Americans need hyphens in their names, because only part of them has come over; but when the whole man has come over, heart and thought and all, the hyphen drops of its own weight out of his name."[40] The hyphen, however, did not drop easily.

Roosevelt's 1900 prognosis that within two or three generations most descendants of non-English immigrants would be "absolutely indistinguishable from other Americans and share their feelings exactly"[41] seemed then to be a reasonable forecast of the twentieth-century course of hyphenism in politics. Surely, with the cutoff of large-scale immigration in 1924, the growth of technology tending to standardize American life, and increasing internal migration, the United States should have experienced that amalgamation of its citizenry. Yet such is not the case. "We are a Nation of Nations," declared *Fortune* after America's entry into the Second World War. "Our foreign stock's emotions and dreams bear on this country's stamina and driving power. Their weight is momentous at home and even more so abroad."[42] Hyphenization, explained Walter Lippmann in 1952 in a series of lectures on American foreign policy to British audiences, is a "morbid experience."[43]

With justification and pride the American people project the image of the United States as a melting-pot nation. Yet beginning with this century the electorate has divided itself on the basis of origin, race, and, at times, creed, during the presidential campaigns. A threat of war or war itself has a catalytic effect; in such times of stress even many nationality groups which have shown tendencies to blend into American political life during times of domestic and international repose begin, under the influence of their leaders and politicians of both parties, to separate and withdraw. Hyphenism lay more or less dormant from 1920 until the middle 1930's, reappearing forcefully as Axis-Soviet power struggles foreshadowed an era of international tension.

Chapter II

THE HYPHEN IN POLITICS

How do ethnic groups go about trying to influence American foreign policy? What are the sources of their pressures? Where are their pressures felt?

Traditionally a pluralistic society, the United States has always admitted a variety of cultures and ways of life. It has continuously recognized their right to exist and given them freedom to flourish within its social framework. Ethnic organizations are active today within the contexture of American democracy. They possess the rights, privileges, and obligations of any citizen or lobby group and as such are a part of the American society. In permitting ethnic groups to act politically, the government has accepted and, indeed, given formal recognition to the concept of group differentiation rather than assimilation. Ethnic groups are becoming stronger, and they exert a multiplicity of pressures in various directions and on all political levels—local, state, and national.

The political and constitutional structure of the American society offers excellent ways for ethnic groups to exert pressures on Congress, the major parties, and the presidency. The parties are primarily loose federations of state parties which seldom submit themselves to central discipline. This diffusion affords a variety of opportunities for ethnic groups to work through the party leaders. The formulation and execution of foreign and domestic policy is a complex process. The manifold influences of diverse nationality groups affect that process, particularly because their influences are directly reflected in the working of the political system. Because nationality groups often have a strong interest in some special aspect of foreign policy, they have been able to exert, for varying periods, disproportionate pressures in that field.

Leaders of immigrant groups have relied upon many direct and indirect channels to reach the government. One of these is the ballot. The threat to employ this power often brings results, especially for those groups which are well organized. Politicians respect and exaggerate the power of the nationality vote, particularly since many citizens of foreign extraction live in strategic electoral districts or states.

20

It is ethnic political organization which gives force, direction, and purpose to the diverse ethnic elements. The American political structure and the minority character of immigrant groups—often politically divided—have made it impossible for an immigrant party to take root. Ethnic political groups have functioned only within the major parties. Participation is organized usually through local clubs, with a state league or federation as the higher body.

As of September, 1959, according to the American Council for Nationality Service (this organization is the result of a merging of the Common Council for American Unity and the American Federation of International Institutes), there are 500 leading—"national in scope; branches in many states"—nationality organizations in the United States.[1]

Nationality organizations have been both an integrating and a disruptive force. As mutual aid or benefit societies, as social or cultural clubs, and as religious fellowships, they have been useful in helping the immigrants to adjust to the New World. As political organizations catering to national consciousness, foreign ideologies, and foreign leadership, they have been divisive even within the ethnic communities. Party leaders in their quest for votes have often stimulated and encouraged the transformation of purely social ethnic societies into political units. Unlike many labor organizations which trained and educated immigrant workers for citizenship, the parties had no such conception of their role "in the larger field of citizen-training."[2]

There is scarcely a nationality group in the United States which does not concern itself to some degree with politics on an international, national, or state level. In recent years ethnic minorities have instituted new approaches to political activities—one being the merging, under joint directorships, of such activities by organizations of those Americans whose native lands have come under Soviet domination. It is worth noting that the Nationalities Divisions of the political parties have welcomed and aided this development, hoping to facilitate thereby contact with representatives of these groups.

Soon after the onset of the Second World War numerous exile organizations appeared in the United States. Their main functions were to act as unofficial governments and to work for the eventual liberation of their homelands. In 1949 there were ten committees

21

of Iron Curtain exiles. Many of these committees along with other refugee and exile organizations have been very active in calling the attention of the American government and people to their particular causes.

On September 20, 1954, exile representatives submerged their mutual historic hostilities and organized a common forum, the Assembly of Captive European Nations, for the purpose of restoring freedom to their enslaved lands. Undoubtedly coöperation exists between the foreign-exile groups and the indigenous leaders of ethnic organizations.[3]

In April, 1956, after the failure of the Republican administration to fulfill campaign pledges to liberate the "Captive Nations" and to repudiate the "Yalta Betrayal," the National Confederation of American Ethnic Groups was organized in Washington, D.C. Its purpose has been to seek direct representation of its views in the decision-making bodies of the government, by-passing both parties. Its stated aim is to unite nationality groups into one "giant confederation," thus enabling eighty-six million ethnic Americans, according to its calculations, "to become a dominant and constructive force on the American scene."[4]

2

Another force which maintains and enhances group unity and affects the voting behavior of ethnic citizens is the foreign-language press in America. It is an impressive instrument of communication. The foreign-language press, like the nationality organizations which it complements, has two aims: to promote Americanization and to preserve ethnic identity. As a medium for Americanization, it has, through the dissemination of American news, advertisement of American products, and discussion of American problems, prepared its readers for citizenship. Millions of immigrants who could not have been reached until they learned English were thus apprised of the American way of life.[5] As an instrument for the preservation of ethnic identity, the foreign-language press has, at times, fostered life in isolated ethnic communities, kept alive old-country disputes, evoked pride and nationalism for the lands of origin, and spread propaganda that often had nothing to do with America. At the turn of the century, particularly, it openly attacked Americanization and encouraged antipathy toward American cultural, social, or political values. Frequently it has been used by foreign governments, exile leaders, refugees, and politicians who hoped to exploit its potential power over its readers' political behavior.[6]

With one hand summoning the immigrant to America and the other tying him to his homeland, the foreign-language press has produced confusion—particularly as to its exaggerated claims of effectiveness and group identification. Indeed, this may account for the inability of many of its newspapers, journals, and magazines to sustain themselves over long periods. High birth and mortality rates are a characteristic of the foreign-language press. Some students of immigration who have been concerned over its divisive effect on the ethnic population have been prone to dismiss its influence on the ground that its demise is imminent. During the First World War the foreign-language press reached a peak of 1,350 publications in thirty-six languages. After the war, and especially after the passage of the immigration law of 1924, which severely restricted the flow of immigrants, when many publications ceased to exist, this prophecy seemed warranted. In 1933 Albert Parry wrote an epitaphic article on the foreign-language press appropriately entitled "Good-Bye to the Immigrant Press."[7] The obituary was premature, since in 1940 1,047 newspapers and periodicals were still printed in foreign languages. One year before the United States entered the Second World War a comprehensive article on the effect of the large number of immigrant papers printed in thirty-eight languages appeared in *Fortune*.[8] It discounted as "purely academic" the then-prevalent idea that "abolition of the foreign-language press would speed up the process of Americanization, . . . for this press won't live much longer anyway." The 1956 circulation of the 838 publications of the foreign-language press (dailies, weeklies, periodicals, and others printed wholly or partially in thirty-nine foreign languages) was estimated to be over ten million. According to the 1958 *Directory of Newspapers and Periodicals* the circulation of those foreign-language publications reporting figures, 508 out of a total of 916, was over six and one-half million.[9] The foreign-language press, like the hyphen, did not die.

The slowly descending numbers of foreign-language press publications—from 1,350 in 1917 to 1,047 in 1940 to 838 in 1956—show that the decline has not been so rapid as has been generally supposed. Also, the figures are misleading in that they do not take several factors into account. The rise and fall of the foreign-language press reflects not only the flow of immigration but also America's involvement in world affairs. Many immigrant publications spawned during the heightened nationality activities of the First World War ceased to exist when the United States withdrew into isolationism. The economic depression undoubtedly contributed to this diminution too. The foreign-language press stirred with new vigor, however, when the possibility of America's participation in the Second World War revived nationalistic hopes, fears, and agitations among ethnic groups. Later, the Cold War gave a new lease on life to the press of those groups whose native lands were Communist-controlled. In 1956 there was no appreciable decrease among the Slavic papers.

The figures indicative of decreasing numbers of foreign-language publications do not reveal the growing tendency of many nationality groups to print newspapers and magazines in English in order to reach the third- or fourth-generation descendants who have either forgotten or never learned the mother tongue of their immigrant forebears. It is also worth noting that several nationality organizations have been publishing scholarly and semi-scholarly periodicals which are distributed to universities, government agencies, and opinion leaders. The expanded role of the United States in world affairs has stimulated the growth of foreign-area institutes which concern themselves with areas hitherto given only glancing attention by American social and political scientists. Many recent exiles and émigrés have been recruited to staff these institutes, giving an opportunity to the intellectual refugee to influence American scholarship and, through it, the opinions of the government officials and the public.

The immigrant press has been clinging tenaciously to ethnic Americans. Its publishers and editors, like the nationality leaders, generally need their jobs and savor the prestige, the glory, and the illusion of their influence. Through numerous consolidations, publication of English sections, and chain-ownership, many of them have been able to put the remaining papers on a more solid footing—this is also true of the American press. Those who have been unwilling or unable to make changes have clung to their mastheads hoping for better times. The continuation of the Cold War and the politicians' perennial pursuit of the ethnic vote would seem to justify this sanguine expectation.

24

Foreign-language radio broadcasts are another medium of ethnic communication. In 1942 it was estimated there were 205 radio stations broadcasting in twenty-six languages to a potential audience of fifteen million persons—three million of whom neither spoke nor understood English.[10] In 1956 the Common Council for American Unity reported 576 stations broadcasting 1,157 programs each week in thirty-five languages.[11]

A 1941 survey of foreign-language broadcasts emphasized their low cultural level. Most programs, it said, were directed toward older persons unacquainted with English and emotionally involved in their native lands. Little effort was made to interest the younger people born and raised in America. The programs typically conjured up a "rather anachronistic picture of the home country."[12] Another study on the relationship of foreign-language radio and the Second World War gave evidence of the effect of anti-democratic propaganda on the thinking of immigrant groups. It noted "shocking cases of treason and sabotage" due to the prejudices and whims of local advertisers who were able to influence the owners of small stations to become "more or less willing channels of anti-American agents in the United States."[13]

In addition to domestic radio broadcasts in foreign languages, there have been a long series of short-wave broadcasts from abroad that were aimed at immigrants in the United States. Before the Second World War these emanated from Germany and Italy; after the war, from the Soviet Union.[14]

3

Potentially, the best sphere for ethnic pressure is Congress—the embodiment of the vast and varied sentiments of the American people. Since 1945 Congress has gained a greater prominence in foreign affairs; this is particularly true of the House of Representatives. Logically enough, then, ethnic pressures to advance the interests of the lands of origin are directed toward Capitol Hill.

A Congressman's short term of office makes him especially vulnerable to lobby groups. While he may doubt that an ethnic leader can "deliver the vote," his uncertainty permits no disregard of either leader or group. As Adlai Stevenson observed, "Congressmen are bound to be concerned primarily with the demands of their constituents. . . . Any foreign-policy measure can be held up or killed by any sizable group in Congress. Our wheat growers can strain our traditional relations with Canada, . . . Zionists can complicate our relations in the Middle East. And a single Congressman in a strategic position can mess up our immigration laws or cripple our overseas propaganda operations."[15] The United States Senator enjoys a more comfortable position than does his colleague in the lower chamber. His six-year term renders him less likely to be affected by demands or threats from pressure groups. It is for these reasons, probably, that the House and its Committee on Foreign Affairs rather than the Senate and its Committee on Foreign Relations have been the arena for concentrated ethnic-pressure activities.

Ethnic organizations develop and foster close relations with members of Congress through formal and informal personal contacts. Written communications are an important link with these public servants; letters and petitions are continuously submitted. Often this material takes the form of resolutions demanding the unification of Ireland, an investigation of Yalta, condemnation of the Soviet seizure of the Baltic states, or the liberation of conquered countries. Often, too, it may be a request for a proclamation for the observance of an ethnic "week" or some other objective with the aim of enhancing the prestige of a nationality organization and apprising the people of the existence of a special group and its particular interests. Congressmen and Senators rarely ignore these communications. They readily insert much of the material, which numbers hundreds of pages, in the *Congressional Record*—most of it appearing in the Appendix. Often individual legislators make available reprints from the *Congressional Record* for distribution by ethnic leaders.

At times the Congressional zeal to pass joint resolutions requested by ethnic leaders has produced conditions adverse to the interests of nationality groups, as well as to the interest of the United States. On July 17, 1959, Congress unanimously passed Senate Joint Resolution 111 which asked that the President issue a proclamation "designating the third week in July 1959 as Captive Nations Week" and "to issue a similar proclamation each year until such time as freedom and independence shall have been achieved for all the captive nations of the world."[16] There was little Congressional discussion. No one questioned the long list of the "subjugated nations," which included Poland, Hungary, Lithuania, Czechoslovakia, Latvia, Estonia, White Ruthenia, Rumania, East Germany, Bulgaria, mainland

China, Armenia, North Korea, Albania, Tibet, Ukraine, Azerbaijan, Georgia, Idel-Ural, Cossackia, and Turkestan. To the members of Congress this was but another innocuous resolution; it was not even sent to the Senate Committee on Foreign Relations for approval. "The Judiciary Committee," wrote syndicated columnist Henry R. Taylor, "churned it out, along with other casual holiday proclamations, such as National Hot Dog Month."[17] The reluctance of Congressmen to vote against an anti-Communist resolution is understandable. Less understandable is the lack of opposition from the State Department "even though it was foreseen that this might embarrass" Vice-President Nixon during his visit to the U.S.S.R. On the very day of the passage of the joint resolution, July 17, President Eisenhower acceded to the wishes of Congress and issued a proclamation declaring a Captive Nations Week beginning July 19. The tone of the President's proclamation, however, was considerably different from that proposed in the resolution. It did not say which nations were subjugated or which desired liberation; nor did it promise action to liberate them. It merely urged Americans "to study the plight of the Soviet-dominated nations and to recommit themselves to the support of the just aspirations of the peoples of those captive nations."

Captive Nations Week probably would not have caused much stir were it not for Premier Khrushchev's using it to taunt Nixon during his Russian tour, which was coincident with its observance, and, also, the August third announcement of an impending exchange of visits between Eisenhower and Khrushchev. To allay Khrushchev's sensitivity, Nixon explained, ". . . Actions of this type cannot, as far as their timing is concerned, be controlled even by the President, because when Congress moves, that is its prerogative. Neither the President nor I would have deliberately chosen to have a resolution of this type passed just before we were to visit the U.S.S.R. . . ."[18] The sponsors of the joint resolution, as well as the ethnic leaders who had hailed it as a "firm determination to stand behind the campaign promises of President Eisenhower in his 1952 campaign," were caught in a dilemma. While it is true, as many admitted, that the timing of the resolution was poor, it dramatically symbolized, particularly in the light of Nixon's implied apology, the fruitlessness, futility, and deleterious effect of such resolutions.

"The monotony of repetitive declarations by America on the

plight of the captive nations of Europe," Representative Charles A. Vanik of Ohio declared, "imply objectives which our Nation seems unable to promote. They create false hope which can fester only into bitterness in the hearts of people who have been friendly to America. . . ."[19]

Members of Congress are frequently asked to speak before conventions and meetings of nationality and exile organizations. Politicians have welcomed these invitations in the conviction that such appearances are an effective vote-getting device. Speeches and comments made at these gatherings are printed in the foreign-language press, frequently in the American press, and most certainly in the *Congressional Record*. At times, they are broadcast over Radio Free Europe, giving an erroneous impression of official approval of the nature and aims of these groups.

Ties between ethnic organizations and members of Congress are sometimes quite intimate. Many members are of foreign extraction; some are members of ethnic organizations. Indeed, it is these very facts that frequently account for their election and re-election. Occasionally men who have been active in the foreign-language sections of both parties' Nationality Divisions have been endorsed and helped by party leaders to obtain nominations for Congressional seats and other important political offices. In August, 1942—to cite one example of an attempt to gain this kind of support—William Petrus, president of the Federation of Slovak Clubs of New York, appealed to President Roosevelt to use his "good offices towards securing" Edward Vaczy's nomination for Congressman at Large. Vaczy's qualifications, according to Petrus, were that he had "been connected with the Foreign Language Divisions at the Democratic National State and City Campaign Committees for nearly thirty years" and was "well known to the leaders of the various Nationalistic Groups."[20] The recent chairman of the House Committee on Foreign Affairs is another case in point. At the time of Thomas S. Gordon's election to the chairmanship of that committee, a *New York Times* biographical sketch emphasized his ethnic background as a salient reason for his elevation to the position.

Some leaders of ethnic groups have a thorough understanding of the procedures of Congress. Congressional hearings are an important political instrument available to ethnic groups, for it is there that representatives of nationality organizations—many of whom are registered lobbyists—can meet the important committee members who will draw up measures in which they are interested. There, too, they may present directly to the legislators their points of view, provide information, and discuss proposed legislation.

Organized pressure groups have also been concerned with chairmanships, memberships, and the jurisdiction of Congressional committees. By bringing pressure on party leaders a group may influence the selection of members. When Representative Gordon was asked to account for his being put on the Foreign Affairs Committee in his freshman year, he replied, "I suppose because there had never been a Polish member on the committee."[21]

In some areas, particularly where large concentrations of one or more ethnic groups exist, the political organization of the major parties on the local level has come under the control of ethnic groups. This facilitates the elevation to political office of some of their members. Congressional districts with large concentrations of Americans of foreign origin are often represented in Washington by members of those ethnic groups. This is especially true of New York and Illinois. In Connecticut it has been a practice of both parties to nominate a Polish-American for the office of Congressman at Large. Indeed, this seems to be one of the most important qualifications.

Not always is it necessary for an ethnic group to air its cause. The mere existence of a group concentrated in a strategic area forces political leaders to take note of the group's interests. In eight key states with 213 electoral votes there are over 5,500,000 foreign-born voters. New York leads in this respect, with California next in importance. The next-ranking states are Illinois, Pennsylvania, Massachusetts, Ohio, New Jersey, and Michigan. Foreign white stock in leading cities is roughly as follows: New York, 4,445,000; Chicago, 1,630,000; Detroit, 765,000; Philadelphia, 738,000; Los Angeles, 677,000; Boston, 422,000; and Cleveland, 409,000. Approximately the same order obtains for white foreign-born.[22] If a constituency is such that one ethnic group predominates, politicians will cater to it, stimulate its latent attachment to its native land, and, what is more significant, anticipate the wishes of the group.

"Big Bill" Thompson, mayor of Chicago, in a bid for Irish approval promised to "punch the snout" of the King of England should he set foot in the city, and, in order to endear himself to German-Americans, refused to receive Marshal Joffre during the First World

War. More recently, New York's Mayor Robert Wagner would not welcome the King of Saudi Arabia, who, of course, could hardly be popular with Jews. These chief magistrates were probably not asked by their Irish-American and Jewish constituents to take those positions, which they anticipated would gain the votes of certain groups.

Genuine issues of presidential campaigns have often been blurred by tactics used in courting the ethnic vote. In the campaign of 1920, for example, politicians did their best to capture or hold the German, Irish, and Italian vote, thus seriously obscuring the main issues of the campaign. German-Americans were told that the Treaty of Versailles was a "base betrayal of the Fatherland." Millions of Hibernian-Americans were reminded of Wilson's refusal to affront Great Britain by pressing for Irish independence at Paris. Italian-Americans, dissatisfied with Wilson's course regarding Fiume, were pleased to find in Senator Henry Cabot Lodge a champion of their cause. By inserting dozens of such ambiguous and platitudinous issues which were calculated to bewitch and captivate the hyphenates, the politicians obscured some of the important issues for the American people.

Often politicians whose constituencies are composed of diverse ethnic elements find it desirable either to avoid expressing themselves on foreign policy or to blur, rather than define sharply, specific issues of foreign policy. Paul Scott Mowrer in *Our Foreign Affairs* related a conversation with a certain Senator who told how impossible it was for him to take an interest in foreign policy because of the diversity of ethnic population in his state. No European question could be touched, the Senator said, without arousing "some element in America." He added that it was more profitable to confine discussion to Japan because harmony of opinion would be certain; since the Japanese in America control no votes, members of Congress would lose nothing politically.[23] During the 1916 presidential campaign, the *St. Louis Post-Dispatch* noticed Candidate Charles E. Hughes's difficulties. "To satisfy the pro-Germans," it said, "he must quarrel with the pro-British, who demand war with Germany. . . . Mr. Hughes dare not have a policy, because to have a policy is to antagonize one element or another of his followers."[24]

More recently, during the 1948 presidential campaign, the Republican candidate, Governor Thomas E. Dewey, aware of the dif-

30

ficulties of championing the causes of one nationality group in a nation of many, did not expect any political involvement when he told a delegation of Italian-Americans that he favored giving Italy control of its former African colonies. After all, no other ethnic group in the United States had any real interest in Africa. To Dewey's chagrin, he soon found otherwise, for the American Negro press immediately attacked him.[25] The challenge from Carl Murphy, president of the *Afro-American,* impelled him to emphasize that the control he favored would be "under a United Nations trusteeship." The clarification did not put an end to the repercussions. Paul E. Fitzpatrick, chairman of the New York Democratic State Committee, labeled Dewey a "meddler and blunderer," recommending that President Truman "capitalize" on Dewey's mistake "as it should be capitalized." ". . . the duplicity and double-talk of Dewey," wrote Fitzpatrick to the Publicity Director of the Democratic National Committee, "is something that should be given nationwide publicity and can be properly handled only by President Truman himself." Fitzpatrick was convinced that Dewey's "methods to attract votes" would destroy the confidence of the American people "in his ability to handle intelligently the complex foreign situation." In the ensuing campaign the Democrats did not allow Dewey to forget his statement.[26]

4

The major parties have consistently and actively sought the support of ethnic groups. This persistent attention to the immigrant vote, markedly accelerated with the arrival of large numbers of the Irish in the 1840's, has undoubtedly affected the very nature of the American political system. The Republican and Democratic National Committees began organizing Nationalities Divisions in the 1880's and retain them still.[27] Though the titles of the divisions have changed often in a bewildering profusion of political nomenclature, their purpose has remained constant. Through these divisions, which are devoted exclusively to capturing the ethnic vote, both parties continuously reinforce the ethnocentricity of the American of foreign origin—an ethnocentricity originally cultivated by churches and social or fraternal orders. Passage of time and the decreased flow of immigration since the turn of the century have not diminished the activities of the Nationalities Divisions. On the contrary, their

31

organizational machinery has been vastly improved and their operational methods strengthened through the use of ever-increasing experience in the field of political propaganda.

The Nationalities Divisions of both parties are continuously at work, even between campaigns. During the months preliminary to the final formulation of party platforms, they hold conferences to assist legislators of ethnic origin and those representing strongly ethnic constituencies in preparing planks designed specifically to attract the vote of the ethnic American—these planks to be later considered by the platform committees for inclusion in the parties' official statements of policies and principles. Non-voting has been prevalent among ethnic Americans; their unused and uncommitted ballots are the target of registration drives regularly sparked by the divisions. In preparation for the biennial political contests, field men of the Nationalities Divisions travel extensively in those states wherein a high percentage of the ethnic vote is concentrated in order to sound out the sensitivity of foreign-language groups to present or future policies. They also consult with leaders of nationality groups for ideas and suggestions on how best to appeal to ethnic Americans. Both Nationalities Divisions frequently designate state, regional, or national chairmen for many separate ethnic groups, working thereafter through volunteer committees recruited by these chairmen.

Directors and chairmen of Nationalities Divisions pay diligent attention to struggles over leadership of ethnic groups. At times they have been successful in helping certain contenders—generally those who are active in party work or those who have, or seem likely to have, an ability to influence votes—to take over control of organizations.[28] This is usually accomplished by the simple expedient of making it possible for the favored person to receive the endorsement of an important political leader—occasionally even the President himself.[29]

During the political campaigns of the early 1930's, the Foreign Language Citizens' Department of the Democratic National Committee and the Division of Naturalized Citizens of the Republican National Committee exploited the ethnic American's concern with economic and social issues. In 1932 and 1936 their appeals were based on depression-related problems. Under the direction of Bernard Richards, the emphasis of the Democratic Nationalities Division was placed on a line from President Roosevelt's acceptance speech,

"Liberty requires an opportunity to make a living."[30] This sentence and expository material were translated into all the major languages, including Chinese.[31]

In the late 1930's as foreign-policy issues began to dominate the attention of the American people, the Nationalities Divisions exploited the ethnocentrism of ethnic Americans by appealing to their reviving emotional interest in ancestral lands which were or might become affected by Nazi and Fascist ambitions. This transition was best exemplified by the strategy of the Republican Nationalities Division. In the October 4, 1936, Sunday edition of the *Westliche Post* (St. Louis), its advertisement appealed both to German-American concern over economic problems in the United States and to heightened interest in the *Vaterland*. Roosevelt was described as a frivolous spender who had been born rich and never learned the "true value of a dollar." It asked the voters to decide between economic stability and ruin. In a most curious but nevertheless revealing attempt to benefit from German-American attitudes toward thrift and toward Germany as well, the Nationalities Division saw, or thought it saw, or at least wanted German-Americans to see, a relationship between Roosevelt's fiscal attitudes and his feeling toward German-Americans. In proof, this quotation from the pro-Bundist New York weekly *Deutscher Weckruf und Beobachter*, July 30, occupied a central position in the advertisement: "Mr. Roosevelts [*sic*] feelings towards the German citizens are laid down in documents. . . . When he was in 1920 candidate for the office of vice-president he referred to German-Americans as disloyal elements and boasted that as assistant secretary of the navy he expended $40,000,000 for guns without authorization of Congress, long before the severance of diplomatic relations with Germany in 1917. For this he would have been liable, as he stated in an address at the Brooklyn Music Academy, to a penitentiary sentence of 999 years."[32]

Until the beginning of the Second World War, roughly, the Democratic National Committee devoted less time to ethnic groups than did the Republican. A great majority of the ethnic and religious minorities had been under the strong local control of Democrats who knew how to handle the relationships between the groups and the National Committee. The historic alignment of the groups tended to allay any incipient fear that some might bolt the party. The first sign that hitherto loyal and submissive ethnic groups were weakening in their allegiance appeared in 1938. Party reports were ominous. German-, Italian-, Polish-, and Ukrainian-Americans, along with other "foreign groups," were, as one county committee chairman put it, "definitely off the reservation."[33]

In 1948 and especially in 1952, the Republican party made a concerted effort to challenge Democratic control of minority groups. It is significant that the Republican decision to try to capture the ethnic vote coincided with the beginning of unrestrained American peacetime involvement in world affairs.

In the 1952 campaign each of the Nationalities Divisions prepared and made available lists of dates important to foreign-language groups so that the "proper felicitations might be made." They also supplied candidates with guidebooks giving pertinent data on the history of various nationality groups and problems of current interest to them. A 1952 guidebook for Republican candidates read: "There are some six million Americans of Polish origin in the United States who are vitally concerned as to our foreign policy toward Poland, the country of their fathers and forefathers. It is imperative for any Republican candidate who desires the friendship and support of these people to have a working knowledge regarding Poland." According to another guidebook, "It is estimated that there are thirty eight million Americans of mixed German origin in the United States, of these there are about five million who are active in German-American organizations and parishes. They are vitally concerned as to our foreign policy toward Germany, the country of their fathers and forefathers." Yet another guidebook called attention to some 150,000 "Americans of Japanese origin in the United States who are concerned as to our foreign policy toward Japan," and advised the Republican candidates of the vital importance of gaining their friendship and support.[34]

In addition to these guidebooks the Nationalities Divisions print campaign literature in various languages for the candidates who wish to distribute it. Ethnic organizations are almost always taken into account whenever a political program is planned in areas where they are entrenched. Following are some of the recommendations on how to develop political programs among ethnic organizations which the Republican National Committee supplied to its candidates in 1952:

1. Establish a continuing special section in your political organization to

gather information and develop a program dealing especially with the ethnic group organizations in your political area.

2. This special section should consist of an over-all director and a director for each ethnic group found in your political area.

3. The special section should undertake the following:

   a) Determine which are the major ethnic groups in your political area by finding out what churches, schools, clubs and organizations these ethnic groups have established.

   b) Seek out the clergymen of the churches, the executives of the organizations and the business leaders. Visit each of them at his or her home.

   c) Learn all there is to know about the ethnic groups—the way they live, what they think and how they vote. . . .

   d) Determine what political issues are of burning importance to each group by putting questions (separately) to a significant number of leaders of the various churches and other organizations.

   e) Develop campaign material on the basis of what these people are concerned with. Be sure that the material is so put as to not alienate any of the ethnic groups.

   f) Contact the non-English language newspaper editors and publishers in your political area. Send them press releases and also give them consideration in your advertising budget.

   g) Contact directors of the non-English radio programs with political news and with spot announcements.

4. Your political organizations should invite the peoples of all ethnic backgrounds to become politically active—ask them to fully participate in the affairs of the party. Let them become party workers and seekers of public office as well as voters.

5. Allocate adequate funds for the operation of the special section.[35]

During the 1956 campaign the Republican National Committee split the activities of its Nationalities Division among three distinct organizational units: nationalities, ethnic, and minority. The nationalities section concerned itself with such groups as Armenian-, Czech-, Hungarian-, Italian-, Lithuanian-, Polish-, and Russian-Americans; the minority section with Negroes; and the ethnic section with Jews. It is worth noting that the Republican party inserted a plank in its 1956 platform advocating, for the first time, renunciation of restrictionist immigration policies.

The Democratic party also expanded, in 1956, the activities of its Nationalities Division under Governor G. Mennen Williams of Michigan, the chairman, and Michael Cieplinski, a New York City

Polish-American, its director since 1948. In the campaigns of 1956, 1958, and more particularly of 1960, the party strove determinedly to bring ethnic Americans back into its ranks. Following the Second World War ethnic defections from the Democratic party, which had begun in the late 1930's, became more numerous for several reasons. One was disenchantment on the part of those whose native lands had fallen into the Soviet orbit; Republican charges of a Democratic "Yalta betrayal" made a strong impact on them. A second reason was Republican accusations that the Democratic party was "soft" on Communism. A third was what Samuel Lubell characterized as "politics of revenge" by Italian, German, and other ethnic groups who were unable to forgive or forget the Democratic administration's bringing the United States to war against their native lands. Still another was growing prosperity.

The loosening of ethnic ties to the Democratic party gave wider scope to party rivalry for ethnic support. Stimulated by party strategists and ethnic leaders and nourished by the Cold War, the intensity of ethnic political involvement was unprecedented for peacetime. Ethnic Americans were conspicuously splitting their tickets; shifting allegiances left a residue of uncertainty for political strategists.

"A singular display of Democratic statesmanship" occurred during the 1958 campaign when, according to the *Reporter,* the National Committee decided to adopt the 1952 Republican liberation policy. Governor Averell Harriman berated President Eisenhower for having forsaken the issue and demanded that the United States "keep raising the question over and over again." Thomas K. Finletter declared as "the beginning of a hope" that the "freeing of the people of Eastern Europe is a definite and unshakable part" of American foreign policy. "When the Republicans ran as a me-too party in domestic issues," the *Reporter* observed, "they at least had something to imitate. Now in foreign affairs the Democrats are diligently collecting the policies that the Republicans have proclaimed and then dropped."[36]

In April, 1958, the Democratic Nationalities Division held a conference at which representatives of twenty-six ethnic groups from every state heard party leaders discuss organizational methods. Some observers believed this to be the first political effort directed at geographical concentrations of nationality groups; previous efforts had been on a nationality-by-nationality basis. Governors G. Mennen Williams of Michigan and Averell Harriman of New York exhorted the representatives to "greater efforts to organize ethnic branches" within the party. One person who had worked with nationality groups in the successful campaign of Governor Robert Meyner demonstrated a "unique electronic device about the size of a breakfront that revealed by a variety of colored lights on a map of New Jersey the location and numerical density of the various ethnic groups." Stanley H. Lowell, assistant to Mayor Wagner, sounded the only warning note. Lowell said that the mayor had always provided "prompt and resolute action in response to the needs of ethnic groups," but nevertheless cautioned against " 'the beginning of a trend' in government to recognize foreign language groups by classifying certain jobs by nationalities."[37]

During times of war or threats of war the foreign-policy planks of both party platforms have reflected the emotions, desires, and hopes of ethnic peoples of the United States. This has become more evident during the last decades. The Cold War and the coincidental emergence of the newer ethnic groups as powerful political forces in American society have made ignoring the multi-ethnic heritage of the American people virtually impossible. While foreign-policy planks may not be specific in regard to "ethnic issues," they certainly do not ignore them. In politics, especially as a result of the parties' continuing pressures, half-buried ethnic loyalties and prejudices keep playing a sizable role. Care is taken in the drawing up of foreign-policy planks in order not to win one group or please none in particular at the cost of alienating another.

Since both parties solicit advice and statements from various ethnic groups,[38] it becomes increasingly difficult for either to take a stand much stronger than the others. While the Republican party charged the Democratic party with betrayal at Yalta, the Democratic party subsequently condemned the Republican party for dishonoring its liberation pledges. Because the 1960 Democratic convention preceded the Republican, the only course open to ethnic spokesmen who hoped to influence the Republican platform was to press for promises more specific than those the Democrats made at Los Angeles.[39] In this they did not succeed. In the end, both parties' planks touching upon issues of ethnic interest were remarkably similar.

Both parties have worked closely with the foreign-language press.

Even with little knowledge of the immigrant press, politicians early realized its potential influence in politics. At first they attempted to control it through the placement of advertising. An outstanding example of this occurred in the decade just before the First World War. In 1904 the Republican National Committee procured the services of Louis N. Hammerling, a recent immigrant and illegal citizen, to handle the campaign in the foreign-language press. Hammerling soon sensed the possibilities offered by the position. Utilizing his political connection, he established, in 1908, an advertising agency, the American Association of Foreign Language Newspapers. Through this efficiently run organization he shortly became a prominent political figure—an "immigrant middleman" with the ostensible power to influence more than seven hundred immigrant newspapers with a circulation of over seven millions and twenty million readers. According to Hammerling's testimony before a Senate committee, the Republican party, convinced that "it pays to advertise," spent more than $100,000 during the 1912 campaign for space in the foreign-language press. Hammerling, who continued to work for the Republican party through the 1916 campaign, became an undisputed "authority" on that press. With no one to challenge his *expertise* or to question the value of advertising in the foreign-language papers, Hammerling was able to secure an almost complete monopoly in the field. His influence over editors and publishers was so great that politicians and foreign governments began to believe that he exercised absolute control. Hammerling's lucrative business came to an end when the government of the United States learned that foreign governments, particularly those of Germany and Hungary, used his influence to deliver the editorial and other support of some of the foreign-language newspapers in their behalf.[40]

To be sure, the present methods which both parties use to sway the foreign-language press are not so crude. Nevertheless, newspaper advertisements in the foreign-language press during political campaigns continue to reflect party attention. In 1956 a Democratic advertisement in the Polish *Nowy Swiat* "juxtaposed Eisenhower's 1952 promise to work for the liberation of the captive nations with Dulles's 1956 statement that Russia's dispatch of troops to Poland did not violate international law; this was cynical, the advertisement said, and endangered not only Hungary's and Poland's freedom but also our own. 'The Republicans killed the investigation of Katyn.

In Geneva Eisenhower forgot about Poland. Vote for yourself, vote for your home folk, for our friends and the friends of Poland.' " A Democratic advertisement in the Slovak *New Yorksky Dennik* said, "Vote for men who will do everything in their power for the sake of your homeland"; similar advice was carried by the Estonian *Vaba Eesti Sona*. Stephen S. Scopas, chairman of the Greek Division of the Independent Citizens Committee for Wagner, signed a statement which appeared, in part, in the Greek *Atlantis:*

> Americans of Greek Descent are Urged to Vote for Wagner. . . .
>
> 1. Robert F. Wagner is a proven Philhellene. He has been a dues paying member of Ahepa (American Hellenic Educational Progressive Association) since 1951; he has attended all our important religious, patriotic and fraternal functions, has demonstrated his sincere friendship for our people and visited Greece last year where he was conferred with honorary citizenship of Athens.
>
> 2. He has actually served as a member of our Justice for Cyprus Committee. . . .
>
> 3. He has pledged to extend the Refugee Relief Act and the Orphans Program, scuttled and bungled by the Republicans.

A Republican advertisement in the Hungarian *Amerikai Magyar Nepszava* stated, "The truth is that Eisenhower's purposeful and vigorous foreign policy has shaken the tyrannical rule of Moscow to its foundations, thereby promoting the oppressed peoples' fight for freedom and reinvigorating their faith in the ultimate victory of liberty." The *New Yorker Staats-Zeitung und Herold* carried an advertisement in German hailing Eisenhower as "the man who led America out of the Korean War . . . and who has made the new Germany our friend . . ." and characterizing the Republican party as "a friend of Germany, the liberator of the Iron Curtain countries and a free Germany." The New York *Irish Echo* ran an advertisement for Jacob Javits which read: "Send a friend of Ireland to U.S. Senate. Has fought and will go on fighting for 1. unification of Ireland and end of partition 2. help in building up Ireland's industrial future 3. help to promote the tourist trade to Ireland and aid its economy 4. voted for the Fogarty resolution." Later 1956 appeals for Italian and Polish votes reflected the political coming of age of these two groups. Addressing "Americans of Italian Origin" in *Il Progresso Italo-Americano,* the Democratic party recorded Italian-American officeholders appointed by Wagner and claimed itself to be "the sole party that has provided the possibility for so many Americans of Italian origin to climb the ladder of success. . . ." In *Nowy Swiat* the Democratic advertisement for an Assembly candidate described him as the "only candidate of Polish extraction in metropolitan New York." Even the usually politically quiescent Asian-American population began to stir. In New York the Japanese American Committee for Stevenson—Kefauver—Wagner advertised in the Japanese-language *Hokubei Shimpo,* and the *Chinese Journal* carried a plea for the votes of "citizens of Chinese ancestry" from the Democratic candidate for the state's Supreme Court.[41]

During the campaigns the Nationalities Divisions work directly with the editors and publishers of the foreign-language press. As a result of this coöperation, editorials and feature stories with photographs of Presidents, Senators, or Congressmen and ethnic leaders appear with some regularity. At times, prominent editors and leaders of nationality organizations with large memberships are invited to the White House to pose with the President for pictures of supposed mutual benefit—prestige for the nationality spokesmen and added emphasis on the Chief Executive's interest in the ethnic groups for the party. In 1956 the Democratic Nationalities Division worked with more than five hundred foreign-language newspapers with the hope of enlisting the support of their readers.[42]

Of course, many editors of the foreign-language newspapers welcome the concern of the parties. Because of this interest, some papers within a given nationality group may become pro-Republican or pro-Democratic, depending on the issues, personal promises, or political expectations. In this they are akin to the American press in general. However, there is one difference, at least, which may have escaped the notice of the Nationalities Divisions of both parties. A foreign-language paper may extol one party's principles and expose the other's broken promises, but in support of party candidates—the real purpose of the party attentiveness—it may have a less faithful policy. A 1956 *Atlantis* editorial suggested that its readers not "lose sight of the fact that in these elections a number of young American-Hellenes are candidates for high office. . . . It goes without saying, then, that all 'Greek votes' must be cast in favor of 'Greek candidates,' even though such a voting procedure will require the crossing of party lines. . . ."[43] During the 1958 campaign the Polish *Dziennik Chicagoski* reminded its readers several times of the duty of Polish-Americans to vote for Polish-American candidates of both parties. When an American of Polish extraction enters the voting booth, the paper advised, the first thing he should do is to look for a candidate with a Polish name or a candidate of Polish origin and then vote for him. In the editorial "Let Us Remember Polish-American Candidates," the newspaper informed its readers that Polish candidates were on the voting lists of both parties; the Democratic party "with whom the Polonia in Chicago has been traditionally bound for many years," had eighteen Polish-American candidates, while the Republican party, "which had only recently begun to show an interest in Polish votes in Cook County and Chicago," offered eleven Polish-American candidates. The editorial went on to say that voting for Polish-American candidates of both parties in no way should be construed as an espousal for separatism—after all, various nationality groups had been doing it without any harm to themselves. *Dziennik Chicagoski* failed to tell its readers what to do when both parties had nominated Polish-Americans for the same office. This problem, evidently, was not important for consideration. The editorials would seem to indicate that with the re-entry of the Republican party into competition with the Democratic party for the ethnic vote, nationality groups could expect that more of their members would be elected to state or national offices. At the end of the 1958 campaign the Polish-American press proudly hailed the election of thirteen Americans of Polish descent, the largest number yet, to the Congress of the United States.[44]

5

The President, an elected official and head of his party, is seldom free from ethnic pressure. Recently, it has become a practice to bring special advisers on ethnic problems to the White House. As Chief Executive and final decision-maker, the President is of prime importance to the spokesmen of ethnic organizations. Congress, the party system, and various executive agencies are primarily the means through which attempts are made to influence the President, although frequently direct pressure is used.

The First World War brought into being conditions which demanded a change from the traditional American principle of isolationism to one of responsibility in world affairs. This was bound to produce tensions, particularly among Americans of foreign origin.

41

Thus, with the birth of American responsibility there was also born the "morbid experience" of hyphenization.

When Wilson proclaimed the principle of self-determination as the capstone of American foreign policy during the First World War, he was immediately hailed by many ethnic leaders in the United States as one of the greatest champions of mankind. Either directly or through Colonel Edward M. House, his confidant and personal friend, Wilson encouraged and incited the nationality groups to believe that his principle of self-determination applied to all their homelands. To the Poles it meant a free Poland; to the Irish, a free Ireland; to the Zionists, a Jewish Commonwealth in Palestine; to the Germans, a just and honorable peace for defeated Germany; to the Italians, the incorporation of *Italia irredenta* into Italy; to the Croats, a free Yugoslavia; to the Czechs and some Slovaks, an independent Czechoslovakia; and, to many Slovaks, a free Slovakia.

Wilson's first realization of the dangers of championing the causes of hyphenated Americans came during the campaign of 1916 when he was disturbed by the efforts of ethnic Americans to influence American foreign policy in the interests of their homelands. Significantly, he attacked only those hyphenates like the Irish-Americans and German-Americans who were against his program of preparedness. His real awakening occurred during the peace conference, when he was made acutely aware of the political embarrassments of having aligned himself with a few minorities in a country of many.

Presidents, like Congressmen, are importuned to honor historic ethnic heroes, to speak before nationality organizations, to endorse the aims and objectives of those groups, and to proclaim special nationality "days" for the purpose of focusing the attention of the American public.[45] The pressures to do so, it should be noted, have come from party leaders who are always concerned over the ethnic vote.[46]

With the participation of the United States in world affairs after 1941 pressures from ethnic groups were applied again with full force. Presidents Roosevelt, Truman, and Eisenhower found themselves in almost the same position as Wilson. Demands have been made—often backed with threats to withhold the ethnic vote if they are not met—for a Jewish national home, for liberation of nations under Soviet control, for various aids to newly established nations, for other ethnically oriented goals. No President or presidential candidate since the turn of the century has been completely immune from these persistent pressures and harassments from leaders of ethnic groups and the politicians who cater to them. Yet, it should be noted that Presidents have resisted these pressures even though in so doing they were led to believe they were jeopardizing their support. Some who succumbed to campaign demands have, after being elected, spurned or contravened their pledges when in their judgment the national interest required it. Nevertheless, in most cases the course of American diplomacy has been affected.

Part II

THE WORLD WARS AND THE HYPHENATE

Chapter III
THE EMERGENCE OF THE HYPHENATE

At the end of the nineteenth century, in widely separate areas of the globe, three new great powers were born: Germany, Japan, and the United States. To Great Britain, ranking power of the nineteenth century, this momentous and unprecedented multiple birth constituted a formidable challenge. In order to retain her role as a balancer, she allied herself with Japan in the Far East and edged ever closer to the United States. To gain the support of the former, she tacitly assented, at Russia's expense, to Japanese designs in Manchuria, Korea, and China; to gain American friendship, she began to withdraw from the Caribbean in return for a joint hand in the Pacific and in hope for common action to secure the Atlantic from German ambition.

While Great Britain quickly understood the significance of the new order, the United States, as Samuel Flagg Bemis put it, "did not realize it fully until the First World War."[1] Some of her citizens, however, soon were appreciative of its import—a perceptible movement toward closer Anglo-American relations. Two major nationality groups, the Irish and the German, sensed the possibility and were determined that it should not come to pass. To the Irish-Americans, even the idea of either an informal or formal alliance with Great Britain was enough, as Thomas Bailey recounted, to make them "apoplectically profane";[2] to the German-Americans, it was beyond conceivability.

2

Before the final quarter of the last century, the Germans in America had emigrated from several states which had not yet become one nation. In 1870, Bismarck, the "Iron Chancellor," brought about unification, and Germany emerged as a European power. The wars which had led to unification stimulated the consciousness of German-Americans and effected a cohesion within the various German elements in the United States.[3] German-Americans, including the great majority of the liberal refugees of 1848, jubilantly greeted Germany's stature; who led the German people was of small moment. As did Italian-Americans during Mussolini's Fascist regime, German-Americans basked in the ascendancy of their native land.

47

During the first four decades of the nineteenth century, the German-Americans had been neither particularly attentive to nor active in American politics. Nor did they have a desire to influence major American policies. Until the 1850's, theirs had been only a sporadic interest, occasioned principally by movements such as temperance and sabbatarian crusades. The arrival of German forty-eighters—a group with a liberal core—stirred latent German-American political consciousness. But it was the nativist movement, perhaps more than any other force, which brought them into politics; a factor, according to John A. Hawgood, "extremely unfortunate . . . for it brought them in as Germans, feeling as Germans and as aliens," and thus at a most "crucial time postponed for decades a co-operation in American life and politics. . . . In many ways this is the great tragedy of German-America."[4] Significantly, this political awakening was contemporaneous with the first real signs of nationality bloc voting.

It was not long before the politicians began to cater to the German-American vote, which, beginning with the 1856 campaign, played an increasing part in state and national politics. Indeed, although debate on the decisiveness of the German and foreign-born vote in the election of Lincoln continues, general scholarly opinion is that the forty-eighters—under the leadership of such men as Carl Schurz—and nativism stimulated German-Americans to vote for Lincoln, thus producing in the new administration a sense of obligation to recognize them in the distribution of political spoils.[5]

The unification of Germany in 1870 accentuated the hyphen among German-Americans. Bismarck's policies found ardent partisans in them. German-American leaders and the German-American press supported the German position that the Franco-German war was an unjust one, forced upon the new nation by Napoleon III. They argued that it was in the interest of the United States to support Germany and that Germany had been pro-Union during the Civil War, while Napoleon III with the aid of the French army had challenged the Monroe Doctrine by putting Maximilian of Austria on the throne of Mexico. When American newspapers showed a preference for France by reminding the American people of their debt to Lafayette, the German-language press dismissed this as "cheap attempts to win the Irish Catholic vote."[6]

German military victories of 1870 and 1871 were publicly celebrated in many American cities. The *New Yorker Staatszeitung*

48

and prominent German-American leaders "proposed a national society to foster better relations between America and Germany, increase the political influence of the German-American group, and preserve German culture and the German language in America." From Milwaukee went a message to the Reichstag "pointing out that Germany's victories were won 'for the Germans in the United States also.'" One theme, according to Carl Wittke, was central to all these activities: "To show Americans what Germans could do when they are united."[7] The voicing in the United States of fears, protests, or criticism of Prussian arrogance made no impression in Germany and almost none upon German-Americans.[8]

With Germany's increased prestige came a diminution of her emigrants' sense of inferiority. Her expanding power was lessening their political and social isolation. Those German-Americans who had minimized their origin began to feel it to be an asset. "Germany had ceased being 'the Cinderella among the nations,'" Wittke wrote; German-Americans felt they had been called "Dutchmen" long enough.[9]

The first and perhaps the most dramatic incident which foretold German-American reaction toward conflict between the United States and Germany occurred during the presidential campaign of 1888. Urban German-Americans had voted strongly for Cleveland in 1884; they are credited with having contributed to his defeat in 1888. This reversal came as a result of the clash of American, British, and German interests in Samoa. (This clash was resolved by a tripartite condominium which many students and observers characterized as a departure from the historic principle of non-entanglement.) The strained relations between Germany and the United States were reflected in the voting of German-Americans who thus provided a telling overture to their future political behavior.[10]

As the United States and Great Britain grew closer, many German-Americans discounted the possibility of a real alliance. Several years before the outbreak of the First World War, Dr. William Weber, a Pennsylvania clergyman writing for a serious Berlin review, advanced two factors as prohibitive: historical considerations and the balance of power held by German-Americans. Weber felt that the German-American National League's two million members, largely Republican-voting citizens, could prevent such an alliance. Although the league, by Weber's admission, represented anti-prohibition interests, it stood also for " 'all the German ideal aims to which a loyal American citizen of German extraction may, and naturally does, cling.' " Its workers and propaganda funds could be decisive in absolutely enforcing the demand that " 'under no circumstances an alliance with England against Germany' " be signed. Neither did Weber assess the Democratic party as being capable of following a policy favorable to Great Britain. Its majority in the northern states was Irish-American, and they were as numerous as German-Americans. Their hatred of the British assured their determined opposition toward anything which would " 'secure any special privileges to their hereditary enemy.' " Furthermore, Irish-American leadership had assured the German-American National League of their immediate support should the question of an Anglo-American alliance against Germany arise. For these reasons Weber was confident that the German Empire need not have the "slightest reason to be concerned about the attitude of the United States in a war conjured up by England."[11]

The reasoning of Weber and others made an impression on German official thinking. By 1914 there were more than eight million foreign-born and first-generation German-Americans. The German-American community was well organized on all political levels and had an able and aggressive press. Its principal organization, the National German-American Alliance which claimed a membership of two million, was convinced of its power, prestige, and influence. Soon after the war broke out, German-Americans raised hundreds of thousands of dollars for German war relief, bought millions of dollars worth of Imperial bonds, and put pressure on pro-Allied newspapers for a "fair showing" of "the German side." Many German-American leaders worked hand-in-glove with German agents and did not shy away from generous financial assistance proffered by the German Embassy in Washington. "Indeed," wrote Arthur S. Link, "it does not seem farfetched to say that the German Americans were as united in support of the Fatherland as were the Kaiser's most loyal subjects."[12]

German-American thinking, "uniform and unsophisticated," German-American loyalty to the Fatherland—fanned as it was by German sympathizers, German agents, the German propaganda agency in the United States (German Information Office)—as well as Irish-American support, convinced the German Foreign Office that through these hyphenated citizens it could affect American foreign-policy decisions. In January, 1916, the United States ambassador to Germany, James W. Gerard, wrote Colonel Edward M. House that Alfred Zimmermann, German minister of foreign affairs, had protested American arms sales to the Allies and had warned that, were the extent of the sales known, it would cause war. According to Gerard, Zimmermann "spoke of 500,000 trained Germans in America joining the Irish and starting a revolution to upset our present Government!!!" In a letter to Woodrow Wilson the same day, Gerard referred to the Zimmermann conversation: "I thought at first he was joking but he was actually serious." In February, 1916, Gerard cabled that the United States ambassador to Turkey, Henry Morgenthau, who was of German birth, had been asked by Zimmermann "if it was not true that German Americans in the United States would rise to rebellion if trouble should occur between Germany and America."[13]

In the fall of 1914 Wilson himself, it seems, showed concern over mounting German- and Irish-American agitation. "We definitely have to be neutral," he is reported to have said, "since otherwise our mixed populations would wage war on each other."[14] German- and Irish-American attacks on the administration became especially noticeable when, as Link put it, "it became increasingly apparent that neutrality as the President practiced it meant American acquiescence in British control of the seas and the outpouring of munitions and war supplies from the United States to the Allied countries." German- and Irish-American leaders advocated "true neutrality," which meant, as Link correctly defined it, "doing everything possible to prevent the British from enjoying the advantages that accrued to dominant sea power."[15] In the Congressional elections of 1914 these German-American attitudes manifested themselves more concretely. "There is a great deal of feeling among the German-Americans," Secretary of State William J. Bryan acknowledged to Walter H. Page, "because we allow the sale of contraband. The fact that Germany cannot take advantage of this opportunity enables those friendly to Germany to appeal to those who sympathize with that country. We lost a good many votes on this account in German-American communities."[16] The German ambassador to the United States also did not fail to note the voting behavior of German-Americans. "As the statistics prove," Johann von Bernstorff reported to the German Foreign Office, "the Democratic party was beaten in the last elections in all districts where the German and the Irish votes were the decisive factors."[17]

In November, 1914, Professor Hugo Münsterberg of Harvard sent Wilson a letter critical of American neutrality policies. He warned of "political upheaval" among German- and Irish-Americans, of "the firm decision of the hyphenated vote to turn away from an administration to which it would otherwise be bound by many ties," and of German- and Irish-American feeling accurately expressed by the editor of *Fatherland:* "It is time to reassert our declaration of independence." The President forwarded Münsterberg's letter to Acting Secretary of State Robert Lansing with the suggestion, ". . . perhaps it would be wise to take very serious notice of it." The State Department's memorandum on it, requested by Wilson, took strong issue with Münsterberg and vigorously denounced him and other German sympathizers for attempting to "separate American citizens of German nativity or descent from the general body of the American people" and for arousing the "spirit of racial allegiance to use this great body of citizens . . . as a political machine . . . to threaten the Administration into showing special favors to Germany and Austria in the performance of the neutral duties of this Government." Upon receiving the memorandum, Wilson, who only ten days earlier had suggested "very serious notice" of Münsterberg's criticisms, wrote Lansing, "I did not mean to have you take Münsterberg's letter quite so seriously as you did."[18]

While Wilson's fear of a possible German-American "political upheaval," if, indeed, it had ever been real, soon receded, the British government remained apprehensive over German-American influence on American policies. The Foreign Secretary, Sir Edward Grey, was aware of the large number of German- and Irish-American voters and disturbed by reports that organized pressures had been influencing executive, Congressional, and public opinion against the Allied cause.[19] In August, 1915, Grey informed House that he was being urged to set up pro-British committees in the United States and to investigate, and perhaps try to direct, Irish-American feeling. Grey wondered if he should accede and thus interfere "with the natural course of public opinion. . . ."[20]

How successful was German propaganda in the United States? What effect did German-Americans have on the course of American neutrality? Until the summer of 1915 both German propaganda and German-American activities achieved results, but the very measure of their success created the illusion in Germany that the ethnic composition of the United States rendered the nation impotent to help the Allied cause. German-American leaders and German agents, by appealing to the traditional American principles of isolationism and neutrality, had been able to win over many uncommitted Americans. (They were also able, at the same time, to take advantage of Irish animosity toward Britain and Jewish hatred of Russia.) Their cogent arguments, based as they were on the American experience, did not necessarily raise the spectre of dual allegiance. After mid-1915 controversy over submarine warfare embittered relations between Germany and the United States and made difficult the use of "American" arguments to support pro-German sympathies. Then, too, the blundering of German agents and the concomitant success of British propaganda turned opinion against Germany and even produced bewilderment and consternation among German-Americans as well. (Following the outbreak of the Second World War the German-American community was to undergo an almost similar experience.) Without the support of the general public—now more sophisticated and increasingly aware of the problems involved—German-American leaders could not build up enough pressure, even with the aid of Irish-Americans, to force Congress or the President to do their will.[21]

From 1855 until 1915, Germans in America, wrote John A. Hawgood, did not live in the United States, "but in German America, and lived and wrote for German America, in very many cases, rather than for the United States of America."[22] As the United States grew more closely aligned with Great Britain and finally entered the war on her side against Germany, German-Americans were forced to reëxamine the nature and meaning of their loyalties. This was an unfortunate and unpropitious time to resolve their problem, fraught as it was with deep perplexities and emotional anxieties.

3

Until the 1890's, German-American interest in the Fatherland had, with the exception of the Samoan incident, little effect on American foreign policy. Relations between the United States and Germany were routine; no conflict of interest arose which would bring the problem of divided loyalty into focus. The serenity which characterized German-American attitudes toward American foreign policy was not a quality of the Irish-American. The Irish, a majority of whom came to the United States after the 1840's, carried with them a vindictive hatred of Great Britain. The animosity continued strong and unabated, inevitably affecting their political behavior. Throughout the nineteenth century, and more particularly until the seventies, strained relations between the two governments made it possible for these immigrants to sustain their animosity without a sense of ambivalence.

Unlike the German-Americans, the Irish were unhampered by language difficulties. They were eager to plunge into political activity and soon allied themselves with the Democratic party. They had an affinity and seemingly natural capacity for political organization. Unlike the Germans, too, they congregated in urban areas, politically important eastern cities where they soon held the balance of power in state and national elections. From the moment of the Irishman's arrival, American politicians "fawned over the Irishman to woo his vote."[23] This overwhelming and flattering interest developed in the Irish-Americans an exaggerated sense of their political importance and influence.

Unlike the German-Americans who witnessed but did not participate in the rapid events that led to the unification of Germany, the Irish-Americans until 1921 had a cause: the independence of Ireland. Because it raised the possibility of a clash with Great Britain, American territorial expansion into the Southwest, the Northeast, Oregon, and the Caribbean had a natural appeal for the Irish-Americans. Irish-American leaders were perennially hopeful that through Anglo-American conflict Irish independence would be won. Throughout this period they championed any enemy of Great Britain, be it the Russians or the Boers, showing no reluctance to advocate that United States support of these nations was in the national interest. England's danger was Ireland's opportunity.

American politicians were, of course, quite aware of Irish-American bitterness toward the British. To try to win the Irish vote was irresistible; the desirability of the prize outweighed their fear of it. The politicians continuously highlighted British-American relations and even encouraged the Fenians to think they favored Fenian designs for military attack on Canada. In so doing, they made Irish-Americans believe that anti-British feeling in the United States was synonymous with pro-Irish sentiment.

Sir Cecil Spring Rice, after a close study of the Fenian agitation at the end of the Civil War, observed in 1887: "So there is a large amount of absolutely unreasonable hostility which time and a judicious treatment of political questions will soften down; and all this finds expression in a virtuous indignation at the wrongs of Ireland, in the same way as whenever Russia becomes unpleasant to us, we used to be in the habit of pointing out that the oppressor of Poland was without the pale of civilisation."[24]

In March, 1867, Sir Frederick Bruce, British minister to the United States, having attentively surveyed the activities of the Irish Fenians and the efforts of American politicians to secure the Irish vote, reported to his government that the "hostile character" of Irish-Americans constituted a "serious and increasing danger to peaceful relations" between the United States and Great Britain. Bruce perceptively analyzed the conspicuous Fenian organization, which attempted to channel the unquenched Irish-American hatred of the British, as a force which could have weakened the influence of Irish-Americans on American policy toward Great Britain. It tended, he wrote, "to separate the Irish from the American." Bruce prophesied the influence of the Irish in America would become "far more dangerous" when they learned to adapt their hostility to Great Britain by pursuing "objects which would appeal rather to American interests than to American sympathies."[25] The forecast threatened to become a reality a quarter-century later.

As long as Anglo-American relations were strained, Irish agitation against the British did not constitute too serious a problem. But when, after the Civil War, American-British relations began to improve, the situation drastically changed. Rapprochement between the United States and Great Britain both threatened the Irish cause and militated against the continued popularity of strong anti-British propaganda.

In the campaign of 1888 both parties made a determined effort to win the Irish vote. Aroused by the British attitudes on the fisheries question and interested in a high tariff, the Republicans sought Irish-American and New England's support by stirring traditional prejudices against Great Britain and also by accusing the Democrats of being tools of "free trade" England. Anglophobia mushroomed. Because election-conscious Republicans did not want the Democrats to take credit for settling the fisheries issue, the Republican-controlled Senate killed, in August, the pact which had been signed in February by Cleveland's Secretary of State, Thomas F. Bayard, and Joseph Chamberlain of Great Britain. "Selfish partisanship," writes

Allan Nevins, "has seldom entered into our diplomatic relations in a more sinister way."[26]

Cleveland's surprising call for retaliatory anti-British legislation following the rejection of the treaty delighted the Irish-Americans whose vote was to be the prize in the parties' tug of war. But their jubilation and Cleveland's probable satisfaction with his coup over Benjamin Harrison, the Republican candidate, was short-lived. California Republican George Osgoodby, sensing in Cleveland's message the possibility of an ingenious electioneering device to fool the Irish-Americans, undertook to expose it. Writing under a pseudonym to the British minister to the United States, Sir Lionel Sackville-West, he asked whether the naturalized citizen of English birth which he represented himself to be should vote for Cleveland: "I am unable to understand for whom I should cast my ballot, when, but one month ago, I was sure Mr. Cleveland was the man. . . . I apply to you privately and confidentially for information which shall in turn be treated as entirely secret."[27] Sackville-West rose to the bait, replying that he believed Cleveland the better choice because the President would "manifest a spirit of conciliation in dealing with the question involved in his message."[28] Osgoodby gave the Sackville-West letter to the Republicans, whose release of it just before the election provoked a predictably explosive public reaction. The Democratic National Committee telegraphed the White House that the Irish vote was slipping from its hands. In a last-minute effort to mend the damage, Bayard, under instructions from Cleveland, informed the British government that the usefulness of Sackville-West had ended. When Lord Salisbury did not recall the indiscreet minister, Cleveland dismissed him. In Thomas A. Bailey's estimate the Sackville-West affair "may have cost Cleveland the election, but there can be no doubt that it further embittered Anglo-American relations."[29]

Their "success" in the 1888 presidential election encouraged the Republicans to pursue similar efforts in subsequent campaigns. In 1896 they openly solicited Irish-American support for their candidate William McKinley with a pamphlet appealingly entitled "How McKinley Is Hated in England."[30]

A year after the Bryan-McKinley campaign, the arbitration treaty between the United States and Great Britain which followed the Venezuelan crisis met with Senate disapproval. One of the most important factors leading to the rejection was Irish-American opposition. Arbitration meant peaceful settlement; this was the last thing that Irish-American leaders wanted. Fearing it as a forerunner of a British-American alliance which would make it more difficult to bring about American pressure to free Ireland, they worked hard to defeat it. Michael Davitt, Irish nationalist in the British Parliament, lobbied against it in the Senate. Irish-Americans naturally took pride in the role they had played. The *Boston Pilot* exclaimed: "Had Irish-Americanism anything to do with the failure of the English arbitration treaty? We trust so, and believe so. We should be very much ashamed of our fellow citizens of Irish blood if they had not done their utmost to baffle the attempt to place this republic before the world as a mere colony of Great Britain."[31] "The rejection of the treaty," said Bailey, "came as a blow to peace lovers, even though the debate did much to popularize arbitration."[32]

In 1920 the Irish and other hyphenated Americans were to play a similar role in helping to block American entry into the League of Nations. This also was a disappointment to "peace lovers," even though the debate did much to publicize the idea of the League.

Until the turn of the century the American politician could find common cause with the Irish-Americans by appealing to their hatred of Britain. To inflame Irish-American emotions was a cheap price to pay for the Irish vote; it involved only periodic statements which indicated anti-British attitudes. After 1900, when America and Great Britain began to move closer to each other in defense of shared interests, this tactic became increasingly difficult to employ. As the United States and Great Britain grew more allied, the question of a free Ireland became a "hot potato" for the Democratic party. By this time Irish-Americans were learning that the anti-British feelings of the catering politicians were not necessarily pro-Irish sentiments at all.

By 1900 American policy-makers, including many who had previously encouraged Irish agitation against Great Britain, were showing irritation that the rapprochement between the two powers was being threatened by that agitation. "There is such a mad-dog hatred of England," Secretary of State John Hay wrote to a former secretary, "prevalent among newspapers and politicians that anything we should now do in China to take care of our imperiled interests, would be set down to 'subservience to Great Britain.' . . . Every Senator I see says, 'For God's sake, don't let it appear we have any understanding with England.' "[33]

On the eve of the Boer War, Hay, in emphasizing the American "duty of neutrality," observed, "Whatever we do, Bryan will attack us as a slave of Great Britain. All their State conventions [Democratic] put an anti-English plank in their platform to curry favor with the Irish (whom they want to keep) and the Germans whom they want to seduce. It is too disgusting to have to deal with such sordid liars."[34]

4

By the turn of the century Irish- and German-American leadership as well—which by that time politicians had convinced of their voting power—on the basis of American interest, found no difficulty in championing abstention from European involvement. There was no need to invoke the memory of Irish martyrs in the fight for Irish freedom. There was no need to support or apologize for German imperial designs. All that was needed was to invoke the revered memory of George Washington and Thomas Jefferson, the architects of the traditional principle of noninvolvement in European affairs. And when, despite their efforts to keep the United States aloof, America entered the war and Wilson proclaimed self-determination as the capstone of American foreign policy, Irish-Americans more legitimately than ever could support this principle as being in the national interest of the United States. This they did. But the animus toward Britain and Wilson, compounded as it was by internal dissension among their leadership, made it difficult to bridge the exclusive Irish efforts in behalf of Erin with general American sympathy and national interest. Would more judicious and restrained pressure on Wilson have helped the Irish cause? In all probability it would have eased Wilson's diplomatic burdens during the war, but not in its aftermath. At the peace conference Irish-Americans—no matter how they had previously behaved—would have learned, as they did learn, that Wilson's espousal of the right of peoples to determine their governments did not apply to the people of Ireland. What Wilson had in mind when he spoke of self-determination was self-determination for those peoples dominated by enemy nations, not those controlled by Britain.

On June 28, 1914, Gavrilo Princip, a young Bosnian revolutionary, assassinated the Archduke Francis Ferdinand of Austria. The shots fired at Sarajevo echoed among the oppressed nationalities of the Habsburg, Russian, and Prussian empires, reëchoing among the millions of their first- and second-generation compatriots in the United States. This ominous event quickened the hopes of many revolutionary leaders who until then had been able only to pray for a universal war to liberate their peoples.[35]

The outbreak of the First World War heightened the nationalistic fervor and aspirations of the subjugated peoples in Austria-Hungary, Russia, and Germany and found ready support among their former nationals living in America—a great majority of whom had come within the three decades previous. The war in Europe produced a "hyphenated uproar" in the United States. The melting pot, the symbol of the transforming of the immigrant into an American, had failed. "No reverberatory effect of the great war has caused American public opinion more solicitude than the failure of the 'melting pot,'" wrote Randolph Bourne. "The discovery of diverse nationalistic feelings among our great alien population has come to most people as an intense shock. It has brought out the unpleasant inconsistencies of our traditional beliefs."[36] Had there been no war, Americanization, the powerful catalyst in the melting pot, would in all probability have helped dissolve the hyphen. The war, however, acted as an inhibitor and crystallization set in.

To be sure, for many decades before the war American politicians had catered to the "foreign vote" and in so doing enabled it to play an important role in politics. It seemed to occur to neither Democrats nor Republicans that they countenanced dual loyalties. The public watched the game with tolerance. The war in Europe caused a belated awakening and brought acknowledgment of the presence of the hyphenated American; there was no longer just the Irish- or German-American. There were Swedish-, Italian-, Jewish-, Polish-, Latvian-, Lithuanian-, Ukrainian-, Hungarian-, Armenian-, Russian-, Slovenian-, Serbian-, Macedonian-, Turkish-, Finnish-, and many, many other-Americans.

As the war progressed, the stimulation for active American participation in behalf of the nationalist aspirations in Europe and elsewhere increased. Stirred and incited by indigenous and foreign leaders, ethnic groups began to demand that the United States—a powerful neutral but also a possible belligerent—should desist from involvement, should participate actively, or should use its weight to bring about the fruition of their dreams. The hyphenate clamor was not lost upon the Democratic and Republican parties. A real battle began between them either to hold or to win over the ethnic groups. This open competition further accentuated the hyphen and persuaded the ethnic leaders in America, as well as in the native lands, of their power to influence American decisions.

Before the First World War the foreign-language press and the various nationality organizations and societies were concerned primarily with social, cultural, and material interests. The war caused a change in orientation. Immigrant leaders from war-torn Europe, lay and ecclesiastical, began to concern themselves with the large question of nationalism and to encourage their followers to help win or regain national independence.

It is not surprising that the outbreak of the war increased the nationalistic and patriotic sentiment of nationality groups. Ethnic organizations became more closely knit and fell under the influence of nationalistic leaders. Within a short period, state organizations united to form national bodies; as such they were able to make their demands felt by the government. With the appearance of this political force which aimed to influence national and international issues, an additional obstacle to national unity in the United States materialized. German-, Irish-, and a great majority of Swedish-Americans who championed neutrality, isolationism, and anti-preparedness were confronted by other ethnic groups who saw in American entry into the war the realization of their hopes.[37] Soon the latter began to operate with growing vigor. The birth of new nations and the reëmergence of old were helped to a large degree by the existence in America of active colonies of those nations. Under the active leadership of their spokesmen, often without any real control by the groups themselves, these colonies kept alive the ideal of independence, offering financial support and applying political pressure at critical moments.

With mounting interest and responsibility in world affairs, the American people became more concerned with foreign-policy issues. The immigrant groups were the first to sense the impact of the new era. Professor Marcus Hansen, an outstanding student of immigration, observed that unlike the American press generally, the foreign-language press was not ignorant of the portentousness of pre-1914 European happenings. He wrote that each of the diplomatic crises preceding August, 1914, formed the basis of news and editorial comment that almost always reflected the opinions prevailing in the countries of origin. Consequently, many Americans of foreign derivation "were almost as prepared for war, psychologically," as were the Europeans.[38] When the conflict did come, the entire foreign-language press and a majority of ethnic organizations, depending on the fortunes of their native lands, turned either for or against American principles of neutrality and isolationism, creating thereby many of the internal and external problems which were to plague the nation from then on.

Chapter IV

WOODROW WILSON AND THE HYPHENATE

Woodrow Wilson was one of the first Presidents to feel and react to concentrated hyphenate pressures on American foreign policies. In 1912 Wilson was elected on domestic issues and regarded himself "as being fully prepared only in regard" to internal problems.[1] Before assuming the Presidency Wilson commented, "It would be the irony of fate if my administration had to deal chiefly with foreign affairs."[2]

It was, however, Wilson's fate to meet a new world situation which demanded the adaptation of the traditional American principle of isolationism to one of involvement in world affairs. This was bound to produce tension, particularly among Americans of foreign origin, the majority of whom were recent and not yet assimilated immigrants. On the eve of the First World War approximately one-third of the total population of the United States—32 million out of 92 million—was either foreign-born or first-generation American. Of these, almost 11 million came from Germany and Austria-Hungary; more than 3 million from the United Kingdom; more than 4½ million from Ireland; approximately 3 million from Russia, and more than 2 million from Italy.[3] It was the campaign of 1912 that brought to Wilson an awareness of the potential voting power of ethnic groups.

In 1902, Wilson, as an historian, had had harsh things to say about immigrants from Southern Europe in *A History of the American People*: ". . . but now there came multitudes of men of the lowest class from the south of Italy and men of the meaner sort out of Hungary and Poland, men out of the ranks where there was neither skill nor energy nor any initiative of quick intelligence; and they came in numbers which increased from year to year, as if the countries of the south of Europe were disburdening themselves of the more sordid and hapless elements of their population, the men whose standards of life and of work were such as American workmen had never dreamed of hitherto." Nor did Wilson stop here. He went on to contrast favorably the Chinese and the "new" immigrants: ". . . yet the Chinese were more to be desired, as workmen if not as citizens, than most of the coarse crew that came crowding in every year at the eastern ports."[4]

In the pre-convention months of 1912 studious political opponents uncovered Wilson's uncomplimentary remarks about Polish-, Hungarian-, and Italian-Americans of a decade earlier. On May 27, the *New York Evening Journal* stated: "Professor Wilson is on record as an advocate of Chinese labor. He has declared over his own signature that he considers the Chinaman, with all his vices, preferable to white immigrants from Southern Europe—Italians, Hungarians, Poles, et cetera."[5] Wilson's intemperate rhetoric was thoroughly publicized by the Republicans. The Jewish, German, Italian, and Czech press reprinted the damaging paragraphs from his work. Propaganda leaflets urging Americans of Polish and other origins not to vote for Wilson "the slanderer" were widely distributed. In Congress, Representative William A. Rodenberg of Illinois attacked Wilson for his attitudes. Stimulated by the propaganda, Polish and other ethnic societies began the organize vociferous opposition to Wilson. "As Mr. Wilson has shown that he is narrow and unjust in his attitude toward the Poles," read the resolution adopted by the United Polish Societies of Manhattan, ". . . we, Polish American citizens of the United Polish Societies, strongly and unanimously oppose his possible nomination."[6]

Fearing that the hostility of these ethnic groups might hurt his chances for nomination by the Democratic party, Wilson took steps to explain away his earlier animadversions. He wrote various nationality leaders that he greatly admired and respected the new immigrants. Wilson's reaction nerved a Polish-American group to suggest that he insert an erratum slip in his book retracting his aspersions, that he rewrite the passage in the next edition, and that he make public apology to Americans of Polish, Italian, and Hungarian derivation. "There was a time," Arthur Link wrote, "when Wilson would have hastened to rebuke such 'impudence'; now, however, he was a politician and quaffed the bitter draught."[7] Wilson neither apologized nor inserted the erratum slip, but he did promise " '. . . that it would be best for me at the earliest possible moment to rewrite the passage referred to in my history.' " Wilson informed his publishers that he wished to consider rewriting certain passages "in order to remove the false impressions which they seemed to have made."[8] After his election in 1916 a new edition of his multi-volume history appeared; the passage under attack stood unchanged.[9]

It was not until 1915 that Wilson began the discussion of "hyphenism." It should be noted, however, that his first attack on hyphenated Americans was directed at the German- and Irish-Americans. The German-American press retaliated by charging that the President had singled out the German element for special insult because it "insisted upon strict impartial neutrality and had the temerity to challenge the 'pro-British' sentiments of the administration in Washington." Wilson was sarcastically labeled "the servant of John Bull." Americans were advised to reread Washington's Farewell Address—an admonition against entanglement with Europe.[10]

With the outbreak of the war ethnic political behavior became an important consideration to the American politicians. German- and Irish-American leaders were looking forward eagerly to translating their grievances against Wilson at the national convention and in the subsequent campaign. By the middle of 1916, Carl Wittke wrote, the German-American press was "virtually unanimous in its hatred of Wilson." Although Wilson's renomination in St. Louis was certain, German-American editors believed that they had the power still and, as Wittke said, "the temerity to propose more acceptable candidates."[11]

Convention leaders were certainly aware of the German- and Irish-American antagonism toward Wilson. Joseph Tumulty, Wilson's secretary, Henry C. Campbell, an editor of the *Milwaukee Journal,* and Frank Polk, Counselor of the State Department, agreed not to truckle to the hyphen. Senator Paul O. Husting of Wisconsin, whose constituency was heavily German-American, courageously recommended accepting "the challenge from the German-American Alliance" by including a plank in the Democratic platform on the problem of hyphenism. Tumulty concurred. In the middle of June he brought to Wilson's attention a *New York World* editorial which called the hyphenate vote " 'a definite factor that cannot be discredited' " and suggested that the Democratic party "set forth its position on this vital matter in no uncertain terms." Tumulty urged Wilson to express his views immediately and to reiterate his principles of neutrality to defy those who were seeking to " 'debase our politics through the creation of the German vote in the United States as a power.' "[12]

The President's "fighting" telegram concerning hyphenism to the Democratic Committee on Resolutions was incorporated in the plank of the platform entitled "Americanism" which averred that the role of the United States in international relations turned upon national preparation and character. Summoning those "of whatever origin or creed who would count themselves Americans, to join in making clear to all the world the unity and consequent power of America," it ringingly concluded:

We therefore condemn as subversive . . . the activities and designs of every group or organization, political or otherwise, that has for its object the advancement of the interest of a foreign power, whether such object is promoted by intimidating the government, a political party, or representatives of the people, or which is calculated and tends to divide our people. . . . We condemn all alliances and combinations of individuals in this country, of whatever nationality or descent, who agree and conspire together for the purpose of embarrassing or weakening our government or of improperly influencing or coercing our public representatives in dealing or negotiating with any foreign power. We charge that such conspiracies among a limited number exist and have been instigated for the purpose of advancing the interests of foreign countries to the prejudice and detriment of our own country. We condemn any political party which, in view of the activity of such conspirators, surrenders its integrity or modifies its policy.[13]

While the Democratic party took a strong stand in its platform against hyphenization, the Republican platform was silent. Indeed, in his keynote address to the Republican convention delegates, Warren G. Harding criticized Wilson's stand against hyphenism and flattered the foreign-born in an obvious attempt to win their votes. Charles E. Hughes, the Republican presidential candidate, stood for "undiluted Americanism"; he did not raise the issue of hyphenism during the campaign. German-Americans seemed content. "We do not want to Germanize America," the Milwaukee *Germania-Herald* claimed. "We want to Americanize it, and therefore we have to de-Briticize it."[14] Throughout the entire campaign, according to Wittke, the German-language press "discussed little except Wilson's alleged partiality for the British." German-Americans had an almost "pathetic desire" to accept Hughes as the "German-American candidate" but this proved difficult. Many had serious misgivings about Hughes's views on foreign policy, particularly if he was to be dominated by men like Theodore Roosevelt, who had endorsed him. Indeed, numerous German-American papers pleaded in vain for Hughes to "muzzle" Roosevelt, "the wild man from Oyster Bay," who assailed hyphenism with such characteristic force that they feared German-American voters were frightened away from the party.[15]

In 1916 Democrats viewed the coming presidential election apprehensively. Signs that Wilson's prestige was ebbing encouraged party leaders to voice their criticisms of their standard-bearer. The Republican party, divided in 1912, was reunited in 1916. With Roosevelt's endorsement of Hughes, the breach between the stalwarts and progressives was ostensibly mended. This unity gave the Republicans a distinct advantage and made more formidable the task of the Democrats.

Soon after the nominations, the campaign strategy of both parties became apparent. The West, the politicians were convinced, held the key to victory. Sure of the East, where the trend of public opinion was against Wilson, the Republicans turned their attention toward capturing from the Democrats western progressives and independents. Throughout the campaign the Republicans exploited the antipathies of German- and Irish-Americans toward Wilson; the Democrats cultivated those Americans of foreign origin whose native lands had been overrun or were controlled by Germany and Austria-Hungary.

In the battle for the German-American vote Wilson was actually helped by Roosevelt's speeches. During the height of the campaign Roosevelt warned the electorate against false and vociferous leaders of immigrant groups. Like Wilson, he singled out German-Americans. "No good American, whatever his ancestry or creed," he warned, "can have any feeling except scorn and detestation for those professional German-Americans who seek to make the American President in effect a viceroy of the German Emperor," who act "purely in the sinister interest of Germany," and who are ready to "sacrifice the interest of the United States whenever its interest conflicted with that of Germany." To Roosevelt they represented "adherence to the politico-racial hyphen which is the badge and sign of moral treason to the Republic." By setting these men apart "for specific denunciation" Roosevelt felt he gave ample proof that Hughes was "incapable of being influenced" by their "evil intrigues."[16]

Roosevelt's vigorous public addresses attacking German-Americans embarrassed Hughes. The Republican candidate did not openly or flagrantly cultivate German- or Irish-Americans, but neither did he repulse them. Hughes's predicament was obvious to the Democrats. "It would be beneficial for the President," Daniel C. Roper, chairman of the Democratic National Committee, wrote to House, "to refer again to what he means by hyphenated Americans and draw his former distinction clearly between them and others of foreign birth or extraction, and in this connection refer to Roosevelt's position in the campaign as the spokesman of Mr. Hughes, in which he practically denounces all Germans, and defends the 'Americanized' Germans, which is the great body of them, against Roosevelt's sweeping aspersions...."[17] It is entirely possible that Roosevelt may have cast adrift many German-American votes which might naturally have found refuge in the Republican harbor.

Soon after Wilson's renomination, worried reports of the party's weakening position among Irish-Americans began to arrive at the White House and the national headquarters. The Reverend Edward Flannery informed Tumulty that "beyond a doubt" the Irish Catholic vote in "New York, New Jersey, Delaware, Indiana, Connecticut, Montana, and Massachusetts had been alienated by Wilson's foreign policies." The Republican victory in Maine prompted Jeremiah O'Leary, leader of an organized movement against Wilson, to write the President an offensive letter predicting his defeat. Wilson reacted to the injudicious remarks by inviting O'Leary and all "disloyal Americans" to vote against him.[18]

Irish-American animosity toward Wilson was further heightened by the events antecedent to the execution by the British of Sir Roger Casement, leader of an abortive invasion of Ireland which coincided with the Easter Rebellion of 1916. Irish-American pressure on Wilson to intervene in behalf of the doomed Casement met with his refusal because such a move would be "both inexcusable and embarrassing." Wilson's reasoning was not that of the United States Senate. With an eye to the Irish-American vote, it passed, on July 29, a resolution requesting that the British government exercise clemency. Though the resolution was sent immediately to the executive offices, the State Department did not receive a copy until three days later—the day before the execution. The State Department cable forwarding the resolution to the British Foreign Office arrived after the execution. Irish-American bitterness over the delay ran deep. Although the administration pointed out that the British cabinet had been apprised of the resolution after its passage by the British ambassador to the United States and had nevertheless "concluded that it could not grant clemency," Judge Daniel Cohalan and other Irish-American leaders adjudged Wilson remiss. Anti-Wilson hysteria continued.[19]

Democratic party regulars, worried by German- and Irish-American defections, convinced Wilson that the antidote lay in attracting Slavic and other non-German and non-Irish ethnic votes. In the fire of the campaign the uprighteous and condemnatory "Americanism" plank went up in smoke. The climax of Wilson's activity to win ethnic votes came on October 26 when he reminded Poles abroad and Polish-Americans of their weakness in being "unorganized." In the same speech the President invited Americans of foreign birth to come to the White House to explain for him and the American people the problems and issues of Europe: "I venture to say that America is the only country that understands the other countries of the world. Men of our citizenship can interpret for us all of the countries of the world."[20] Wilson, no doubt under the influence of his political advisers, wanted to organize Polish-Americans and other nationality groups for his reëlection. The President, bitter foe of hyphenism, was suggesting that the "coarse crew"—and its descendants—which had been crowding in at eastern ports at the turn of the century organize itself for political purposes.

The outbreak of the First World War increased the patriotic sentiment of immigrant groups in America toward their native lands. This natural interest in the fate of the old home countries was grist for the mills of party strategists. In the 1916 campaign politicians began strategically to appeal to the deeply ingrained traditions, attitudes, and experiences of Americans of Slavic and other origins. By raising certain issues they were able to play upon emotional and cultural attachments. More than that, they encouraged effective political organization within nationality groups. In so doing, they also facilitated the not always altruistic purposes of native or foreign leaders. By appealing to the ethnic vote Democrats may have gained in 1916, Republicans in 1920. But the returns were greatest for the ethnic leaders, who, once in control of a group, were able to use their power to make demands of the American government.

It was perhaps no mere coincidence that in the election year 1916 Wilson began to show a great interest in the descendants of the "new" immigration. Soon after his nomination, Wilson took a stand against requiring literacy tests of immigrants. He made strong representations to the Central Powers for the relief of the starving

Poles and other peoples in ravaged Eastern Europe. He designated special days for the Americans to give aid to Armenians, Syrians, Lithuanians, and others. Wilson's humanitarianism and ethical considerations merged with his political ambitions. They also laid the foundation for sympathy for the nationalist aspirations of the submerged nationalities in the Turkish, Prussian, Russian, and Austro-Hungarian empires.

Ethnic organizations sensed a significance in Wilson's new attitudes. The leaders endorsed his actions and paid tribute to his unselfish zeal and interest. The president of the Polish-American Democratic League praised him for having "solidified the great Polish-American vote" through his "fair treatment of all American citizens of foreign extraction," adding that the differences of opinion of 1912 were "practically wiped out" and that the majority would vote solidly for him.[21]

Some Polish-American newspapers, perhaps to measure the extent of the change in Wilson's thinking, began to investigate his appointments to federal offices for the frequency of Polish-Americans. At the instigation of Representative Adolph J. Sabath of Illinois, Wilson ordered a survey which brought out that his only Polish-American appointee had been born "en route to United States from Poland."[22]

After the election the Democratic National Committee provided House with tabulations of the Polish-American vote. House, who had made a special effort to cultivate the Polish-Americans and the man he considered their spokesman, was pleased with the picture of fidelity drawn by the committee's statistics. From Congressmen of Ohio, Wisconsin, New York, Indiana, and Massachusetts, House learned of thoroughgoing Polish-American support for Wilson. According to Senator Gilbert M. Hitchcock, the Polish-American vote in Nebraska for Wilson was 85 per cent. Missouri reported that 90 per cent of its approximately 300,000 Polish-Americans voted Democratic and meaningfully pointed to Wilson's state plurality of 28,659. North Dakota, where Wilson's plurality was 1,735, reported that Polish precincts gave him an "overwhelming majority." Ohio, which was Wilson's by a plurality of 90,408, estimated the Polish-American vote for him "as high as 90 per cent" out of nearly a half-million.[23] The "evidence" of the Polish-American vote for Wilson undoubtedly persuaded Democratic strategists that it was important and, further, that Polish-Americans voted on the basis of their national origin.

Wilson's solicitude for American citizens of East European background greatly encouraged the leaders of the Polish, Czech, Serb, Croat, Slovene, Slovak, Zionist, and other movements. Soon after the outbreak of the war, representatives and adherents of those movements began arriving in the United States seeking moral, financial, and political help from their former nationals. In March, 1915, representatives of Serb, Croat, and Slovene organizations in the United States and Canada meeting in Chicago passed a resolution "calling for the 'union of all Yugoslav lands of the Austro-Hungarian Monarchy and the Serbian Kingdom into one state unit.' "[24] The convention, like all similar gatherings of nationality organizations, did not completely unite all American Serbs, Croats, and Slovenes, but it nevertheless did produce a "basis of cooperation among the majority of them."[25] Soon thereafter a Yugoslav National Council, affiliated with the London Yugoslav Committee, was established in Washington under Don Niko Grškovič for the purpose of informing and influencing the American people, recruiting volunteers for the Macedonian front, and raising money for the Yugoslav Committee.[26]

Of all the ethnic groups active in the United States, Polish-Americans benefited most. In 1914 Polish immigrants outnumbered those from any other East European area.[27] Their number made them important in American life. Moreover, they enjoyed special advantages. One was the pro-Polish tradition which had grown out of America's gratitude toward Thaddeus Kosciusko and Casimir Pulaski—Poles who had fought for American independence during the Revolution. Another was American sympathy for the Poles because of the injustices of the eighteenth-century partitions and because of the heroic but unsuccessful revolutions of 1830, 1848, and 1863. In addition, the Polish cause had an extraordinarily able and skillful spokesman—Ignace Jan Paderewski, world-famous pianist. Under the active leadership of Paderewski and Roman Dmowski, representative of the Polish National Committee, Poles in America throughout the war kept alive the ideal of Polish independence, offering financial support and political pressure at critical moments. Paderewski came to the United States in 1915 as the unofficial representative of the Polish National Committee. America was of the utmost importance to the Polish cause; in no other country outside Poland were there so many Poles. No other country could supply so much money to relieve devastated and war-stricken Poland and to help the political activities of the committee. Paderewski and Dmowski, perhaps more than any other Slavic leaders, were first to recognize that the voice of America would have weight with other countries.

Paderewski was admirably fitted for his work in the United States. He was the best possible emissary the Poles could have found to present their case to the American people and their leaders. After he arrived, he lost no time in cultivating prominent Americans. In November, 1915, he met, through industrialist Robert Wooley, the key man for his purposes—Colonel Edward M. House, confidant, adviser, and close friend of Wilson.

It was House who did his best to keep the President in line for the Polish cause during the war and the peace conference. Paderewski's brilliant propaganda and his successful uniting of divergent factions and organizations within the Polish-American community was enormously assisted by the support of this "providential man," as the pianist called the enigmatic Texan.[28]

House took for granted that Paderewski was the spokesman of the Polish-Americans. When John Dewey and others pointed out to Wilson and House that Paderewski did not wholly represent Polish sentiment in either Poland or America, House disregarded them.[29] House recorded that his interest in Poland "had been fanned to one of admiration" by Paderewski. "I had such confidence in his integrity and fairness of mind that I did not hesitate to take to the President any statement he gave me as a fact. I thought in helping Poland, I was helping civilization and was furthering democracy in Europe."[30] Years later House wrote, "It was solely through Paderewski that I became so deeply interested in the cause of Poland, and repeatedly passed upon the President Paderewski's views which I had made my own. That was the only real influence that counted. . . ."[31] It was House, more than anyone else, who swung the idealism of the President behind Paderewski's efforts to bring about a large, independent, free, and united Poland and to safeguard it during its first years. And it was largely because of House that the United States government allowed Paderewski and the Polish National Committee to recruit Poles in America who were not subject to the draft to fight in the interest of a Polish independent state.

The publicity attendant upon prominent exiles like Paderewski increased their status in the eyes of the American people and government. To Americans, these men, rather than the stay-at-home leaders of the nationalistic movements, were the personifications of their native lands. Indeed, their activities in America detracted from the domestic revolutionary movements. ". . . The Poles when thinking of America, thought of George Washington, and Americans when thinking of Poland thought of Paderewski."[32] The military achievements of men like Josef Pilsudski, Polish revolutionary hero who led Polish legions against Germany, Russia, and the Habsburg empire, were to a great extent eclipsed by the political industry of their compatriots in the United States. Nevertheless, at the end of the war Pilsudski, in spite of the efforts of Paderewski and Dmowski to supplant him—even with the help of the government of the United States—gained control of the new Polish government. While the peace conference was still in session, while there was need for American relief for the starving Poles, and while there was some evidence of popular support in Poland for Paderewski, Pilsudski consented to the inclusion of Paderewski in the cabinet as prime minister. On December 7, 1919, Paderewski relinquished his premiership and voluntarily exiled himself.[33]

Chapter V

WOODROW WILSON AND SELF-DETERMINATION

Self-determination is not a mere phrase. It is an imperative principle
of action which statesmen will henceforth ignore at their own peril.
—Woodrow Wilson, February, 1918.

You have touched on the great metaphysical tragedy of today. . . .
When I gave utterance to those words, I said them without the knowl-
edge that nationalities existed, which are coming to us day after day . . . .
—Woodrow Wilson, June, 1919.

The entry of the United States into the First World War had a
marked effect on the liberation of East Central European peoples
and the rebirth of their nations. With the diplomatic and decisive
military involvement of America in the affairs of Europe came the
triumph of the idea that every nation should be free to govern
itself and that such freedom is an essential condition of a lasting
peace. In accordance with this principle, there followed, at the end
of the war, the establishment of a new political order in the large
region of Europe between the defeated Germany and the newly
established Communist state of Soviet Russia, together with re-
affirmation of the pledge of a Jewish homeland in Palestine—then
a part of the crumbling Ottoman Empire.

The First World War did not start as an ideological crusade.
When war broke out in 1914, none of the belligerents was in favor
of liberating oppressed nationalities or of extending democracy.
"Alas," admitted Georges Clemenceau, "we must have the courage
to say that our programme, when we entered the War, was not one
of liberation!"[1] There were two powerful deterrents to any formulation of a policy of liberation. One stemmed from the very alliance
of the Western powers with Tsarist Russia; the other from the unwillingness of the Entente powers and the United States to dismem-
ber the Habsburg empire. So long as there was hope of separating
Austria-Hungary from Germany, the Allies and the United States
did not wish to alienate that empire. In 1917, Tsarist Russia, de-
bilitated by revolution, collapsed. By that time too, other belligerents were near physical exhaustion. To win the sympathy and
to strengthen the sagging morale of their peoples, governments re-

73

sorted to ideology. Psychological warfare, as it was called in the Second World War, became a vital element in the conduct of the war from the time of the Russian Revolution and American military participation in the war.

The Bolshevik Revolution of 1917 and especially the negotiations at Brest-Litovsk forced the United States and the Allies to present to the world a complete outline of their war and peace aims. A program which would rally liberal opinion in the world, restore and strengthen the determination of the Russian people to continue in the war, and, among other things, induce national or political groups in the enemy countries to support the Allied cause, was a necessity. The inherent appeal of Soviet propaganda in behalf of nationalities at Brest-Litovsk was undeniable. Secretary of State Robert Lansing was impressed with the adroitness of the Bolsheviks, but felt it would be unwise to try to answer their demand that all belligerent nations grant self-determination to their peoples in Europe and in their colonial territories.[2] However, by proclaiming the principle of liberation of nationalities, the Bolsheviks threatened to capture the psychological offensive. To them, self-determination was primarily a tactical device of exploitation in the struggle for power. Like most political phrases, self-determination had a different meaning for the Bolsheviks and for the West; the former interpreted it as applying to the proletariat of every nation rather than to peoples or nations.[3]

Bolshevik policy toward nationalities was misunderstood by the West as well as by many leaders of nationality groups in Europe. To many, the Soviet Revolution transformed the war into a crusade for the liberation of subject peoples. The democratic terminology of the Bolsheviks inspired confidence and hope in the hearts of some patriots, labor leaders, and liberals; conservatives everywhere were aghast at the consequences of the collapse of the Tsarist government. The former cheered the disintegration in Russia; the latter, believing Communism to be a temporary disease, attempted to restore the empire so that it might continue to play a role in the European balance of power. Neither alternative held out any real prospect of autonomy.

It was both natural and expedient that Woodrow Wilson become the champion and apostle of self-determination in the first months of 1918. The Bolshevik bid for leadership in the movement in behalf of nationalities menaced not only the Allied cause but also the future character and composition of the Russian, German, Austro-

Hungarian, and Turkish empires' succession states. Moreover, Communist propaganda which appealed to the hungry, tired, and disillusioned for the purpose of destroying Western civilization had to be fought and countered. It fell to Wilson to stand up to the challenge and compete with Lenin for the minds of men. On January 8, 1918, without the previous knowledge of his own State Department, Wilson proclaimed his Fourteen Points.[4] This political program became a cornerstone for a new liberal world. It attracted whole nationalities to the Allied side; it spelled out hope for a defeated Germany; and it promised a new international order.

Wilson's championship of self-determination was rooted in both realism and idealism.[5] Before 1918 the American President had not been deeply interested in the fate of East Central Europe and the Middle East. But by then these areas confronted him with problems of a magnitude demanding ideology and action. Unhesitant, he enthusiastically based his foreign policy on the principles of the "New Freedom" which he had sought to apply at home: faith and morality as a foundation for action; a belief in the capacity of people to govern themselves. Wilson had, as well, a conviction in the mission of America to broaden the area of peace and prosperity. In 1918 the logic of reality seemed to be in accord with Wilson's logic of ideas. Then he could say with evident sincerity, as he did on February 11, "Self-determination is not a mere phrase. It is an imperative principle of action which statesmen will henceforth ignore at their peril."

Wilson's greatness lay in his ability to project what he believed to be the American political tradition into a liberal international faith. He did so eloquently and well. In order to hasten the last stages of the war, the Western powers reluctantly committed themselves to self-determination. Under pressure from Wilson, they went further than they had originally intended. To Wilson, self-determination was popular sovereignty—an embodiment of democratic theory. "Even if he belonged to the generation that had accepted the Union," observed Alfred Cobban, "as a Virginian and Southern Democrat he had the right of secession in his bones." Whenever Wilson spoke of self-determination he spoke as if it were an "absolute principle of international right."[6] It has been said that the main weakness of Wilson's international order lay in the generalities of his principles, particularly that of self-determination. As cogent and efficacious propaganda, however, the principles were unequaled. The President, commented Thomas Bailey, "deliberately reduced his war aims to these pithy placard paragraphs, so that they could be used to seduce the enemy, unite the Allies, and inspire the home front."[7]

Quite possibly Wilson was seduced by his own eloquence and did not fully appreciate the explosive power carried by the principle of self-determination. Not so his Secretary of State: Lansing felt that Wilson's program was contradictory and impracticable as a universal tenet; he described the phrase "self-determination" as "loaded with dynamite": "It will raise hopes which can never be realized. It will, I fear, cost thousands of lives. In the end it is bound to be discredited, to be called the dream of an idealist who failed to realize the danger until too late to check those who attempt to put the principle in force. What a calamity that the phrase was ever uttered! What misery it will cause!" Lansing pointed out the inconsistency with historical events of advancing self-determination as an American principle and postulated its likely effect on subject peoples like the Irish, Indians, Boers, and those of the Mediterranean area.[8]

Colonel House, an active participant in the formulation of the Fourteen Points, soon had many misgivings himself. In April, 1919, when Edward Beneš asked his "good offices" in behalf of Lusatian Slavs in Germany who desired the right of self-determination, House wrote, "It has become a craze and in many instances ridiculous."[9] Ridiculous though it may have seemed to House, it was not viewed in that light by the Irish, Lithuanian, Estonian, Lett, Rumanian, Greek, Bulgarian, Finnish, and Ukrainian representatives who sought his help—with little success—toward achieving their nationalistic aspirations.[10]

The partisans of Poland, however, were not given short shrift by House. His diary entry for February 18, 1919, reads, in part: "I am exceedingly anxious to do for Poland all that is good for her, but I am afraid like other countries of Europe, she wants the impossible and will be dissatisfied with less. However, I am so much concerned in her welfare that I shall try to meet the wishes of her people wherever possible."[11] Nevertheless, in rendering momentous service to the leaders of the movement for a free Poland, House—though unaware of it at the time—also helped other nationalities. By promising and working for Polish independence on the basis of self-determination, he strengthened the demands and claims of all.

Despite its weakness, self-determination became the foundation upon which the new, reborn, and transformed states were to be built. As its proponent, Wilson was viewed as a Messiah by captive nationalities everywhere. Arthur Hugh Frazier wrote that to the subject peoples of Austria-Hungary Wilson represented "a moral force entirely free from any vestige of ulterior motives; his conceptions of liberty and the self-determination of nations are accepted by them with unquestioning confidence and they look to him as a guide in political as well as in spiritual matters. It would be difficult to exaggerate this phenomenon."[12] With more insight into the realities of European politics on the part of the President and with more good will on the part of the European allies, the Republican party leaders, and the newly emerging states themselves, Wilson's program could perhaps have been better adapted to the conditions then existing.

In the Fourteen Points Wilson did not entirely commit himself to the idea of self-determination; the time was not propitious. The President was sensitive to the risks in advocating a principle which, if narrowly and specifically defined, could easily have defeated his whole peace program. Points X, XI, and XII testify to his prudence. "The peoples of Austria-Hungary," Point X states cautiously, "whose place among the nations we wish to see safeguarded and assured, should be accorded the freest opportunity of autonomous development." Point XI, dealing with Rumania, Serbia, and Montenegro, merely asks that "relations of the several Balkan states to one another [should be] determined by friendly counsel along historically established lines of allegiance and nationality. . . ." Point XII, which concerns itself with the liquidation of the Ottoman Empire, pleads that the non-Turkish nationalities should be "assured . . . an absolutely unmolested opportunity of autonomous development. . . ."

The outright and unqualified commitment to an independent Poland in Point XIII highlights the ambiguous application of the principle of self-determination in the three preceding points. More than that, it demonstrates the uniqueness of the Polish cause in the Wilsonian program. Poland was the only nation of East Central Europe accorded individual attention. It should be further noted that the President and his advisers recognized that the nationality and religious conflicts which would accompany the rebirth of Poland would be in no way less intense and chaotic than those which would follow the breakup of the Dual Monarchy.

Wilson's espousal of a free Poland was a blend of realism and idealism. In a sense, in 1918 it required no particular boldness to advocate the re-creation of Poland; the political process which led to the revival of the Polish state had by then already begun. Driven by the exigencies of the war, Russia, Germany, and Austria-Hungary had each made rival concessions to Polish nationalism. It must be remembered, however, that by "Poland" Germany and Austria-Hungary meant the Russian portion of Poland in union with them; Russia meant the Poland under her tutelage. After the collapse of the Tsarist regime, the provisional government came out in favor of a free Poland, "in a free military union" with Russia, the boundaries of which would be settled by a Russian constituent assembly. The Bolshevik Revolution, even though it embraced self-determination, brought no declaration for a free, united, and independent Poland. To some extent Point XIII was a reiteration of promises—albeit dubious—already in existence. But more surely it stemmed from Paderewski's unique influence on House and his and Dmowski's ingenuity in marshaling Polish-American pressure on Wilson and other Democratic leaders.

It was only when the United States entered the conflict that Poland had, for the first time, a wholly disinterested force at work on her side—one whose commitment to self-determination for Poland had no strings or reservations. As Paderewski acknowledged in his last speech to the Polish parliament on May 22, 1919, "Without the powerful support of President Wilson whose heart has been won to our cause by our best friend, Colonel House, Poland would undoubtedly still remain an internal question of Germany and Russia...."[13]

While the reaction of the Poles to the Fourteen Points was enthusiastic, that of the subject nationalities of the Austro-Hungarian empire was one of angry foreboding. Wilson, the eloquent champion of self-determination in general and of Poland in particular, had betrayed them. The President was against the liquidation of the empire. Wilson neither advocated the liberation of its peoples nor demanded the creation of independent national states within it. Their resentment was justified. The memorandum of the Inquiry—a committee of experts on international problems which House had organized in the summer of 1917—upon which Point X was based, had not envisaged the destruction of the Dual Monarchy. The document, dated December 22, 1917, suggested that United States policy must consist "first in a stirring up of nationalist discontent, and then in refusing to accept the extreme logic of this discontent, which would be the dismemberment of Austria-Hungary."[14]

The month of May, 1918, was a critical and momentous time for patriotic leaders of the submerged nationalities in the Habsburg empire in general and for Czechs and Slovaks in particular. By the end of that month, the significance of events in Austra-Hungary, Siberia, and the United States converged upon the policy-makers in Washington, demanding their immediate attention and action.

It was not until May 29 that the United States took the initial step toward a decision for dissolution of the Habsburg empire. On that day, with Wilson's approval, Lansing made public an announcement which he believed "would have a very great influence upon a large body of our population." Taking cognizance of the proceedings of the Congress of Oppressed Races of Austria-Hungary which had been held in Rome in April, it declared that the United States had followed "with great interest" the "nationalistic aspirations of the Czecho-Slovaks and Jugo-Slavs" and expressed "earnest sympathy." Upon releasing the announcement, Lansing cabled Ambassador Thomas N. Page in Italy requesting him to "explain confidentially and orally" to the Italian government that the announcement "would result in benefit both to the Czecho-Slovaks and Jugo-Slavs, to the cause of the Entente in general and to that of Italy in particular, since it was thought such an announcement would give great encouragement to the Czecho-Slovaks and Jugo-Slavs in the United States on their support of the United States in this war, would encourage and greatly increase enlistments in this country for the Czecho-Slav Legion now acting in Italy with Italian Army, and would encourage the Czecho-Slovaks and Jugo-Slavs in Austria in their efforts to hamper the Austrian military operations against Italy."[15] "The Declaration of May 29," as Victor S. Mamatey rightly observed, "was a timid venture into psychological warfare." In no way did it commit the United States, but it did awaken American interest in the subject nationalities and was accepted "as another proof of the democratic and idealistic purpose of American policy." In consequence, the State Department "lost the complete freedom of action which it previously enjoyed"; to back away from what the public assumed to be a new position, and an admirable one, would not have been easy.[16]

Earlier in May, Thomas G. Masaryk, Czech nationalist and

world-renowned scholar, arrived in Washington. Charles R. Crane—manufacturer, philanthropist, and friend of Wilson—gave Masaryk access to the administration. Representative Adolph J. Sabath, Bohemian-born Democrat from Illinois, paved Masaryk's way in Congressional circles. Sabath and Senator William H. King began sponsoring resolutions favoring the establishment of an independent "Bohemian-Slovak State." The resolutions, similar to those passed by a convention of Czech and Slovak organizations in 1915, did not, however, come to a vote. Americans gave the subject only cursory attention. "At the time," wrote Mamatey, "the American public was not only uninterested in the fate of the Czechs and Slovaks but, with rare exceptions, completely unaware of their existence."[17]

To focus attention on the Czech cause and to bring about the administration's recognition of his leadership of that cause, Masaryk embarked on a tour of the United States. The tumultuous welcomes afforded him by Czech and Slovak immigrants caught the eye and ear of the nation; his purposes were being realized. Throughout the rest of his stay Masaryk lobbied vigorously in behalf of independence for his people, strengthened the interest of Czech-Americans in their native land, and successfully cultivated important government officials.

On May 30, 1918—the morrow of the American declaration of "sympathy"—leaders of Czech and Slovak organizations meeting in Pittsburgh signed the famous and still controversial agreement which promised the Slovaks some degree of autonomy in the future Czecho-Slovak state. Pittsburgh was hailed by many as the birthplace of an independent Czechoslovakia; later scholarship was to call this a myth. The agreement witnessed to there was "designed, in part," wrote Mamatey, "to influence American policy"—a cogent argument to be used in support for a Czechoslovak state in discussion with Wilson.[18]

Four days after the Pittsburgh meeting Masaryk was received for the first time by Lansing; less than three weeks later he was invited to the White House. Significantly, the first official recognition of Masaryk's status as president of the Czechoslovak National Council coincided not only with the declaration of May 29 but, even more important, with heightened public interest in the dramatic progress into Siberia of some 50,000 Czechs and the American government's decision to intervene there. Plans to send an expeditionary force to

Siberia to encourage anti-Bolshevik elements in Russia and, as Secretary of State Cordell Hull later revealed, to prevent Japanese expansion, were rapidly maturing. The relief of the Czech legions, which practically controlled Siberia and were in no real danger, was a convenient pretext for the contemplated action.[19]

The change in the official attitude of the American government toward Czech aspirations is best revealed in Wilson's decision to meet with Masaryk. From Charles Crane and others Wilson had formed a favorable opinion of the Czech statesman which antedated his arrival. Masaryk, "a professor, not a businessman," George Kennan has observed, "fitted Wilson's image of the positive and constructive political figure." Despite unrelenting pressure from Crane, and so long as Masaryk's ideas and hopes did not agree with his own approach toward the problems in Russian and Austria-Hungary, Wilson refused to grant an interview. Not until June 19, about six weeks after he reached Washington, did Masaryk see Wilson. "From the movement of Masaryk's meeting with the President on the 19th," wrote Kennan, "the American intimacy with the Czechoslovak cause grew apace."[20]

Wilson made the final decision on dismemberment of the Habsburg empire on June 26. By then conditions in Europe seemed to be in accord with his principle of self-determination. Emperor Charles' peace offers had ended in failure and Great Britain and France had committed themselves to Czechoslovak and Yugoslav leaders. On June 25 Lansing submitted to Wilson a "Memorandum on the Policy of the United States in Relation to the Nationalities Included within the Austro-Hungarian Empire" which recommended support of the aspirations of those nationalities. ". . . we should be perfectly frank with ourselves," Lansing wrote, "and admit that, as long as there was a chance of entering into a separate peace with Austria-Hungary, it was wise and expedient to attempt to do so, even though it was contrary to the just claims of the nationalities within that Empire which sought independence." He asserted that it had become "useless to pursue further a policy which would be ineffective and in no way beneficial in winning the war."[21] The next day Wilson replied, "I agree with you that we can no longer respect or regard the integrity of the artificial Austrian Empire. I doubt if even Hungary is any more an integral part of it than Bohemia." Evidently Lansing's had not been the only influence, for

Wilson continued, "I have made this judgment in part upon a very interesting and illuminating conversation I had a month or two ago with a group of Magyar Americans who spoke plainly to that point."[22]

Even so, it was not until the fall of 1918 that Wilson acknowledged the Czechoslovak National Council as a *de facto* government. In August Senator Henry Cabot Lodge, forceful critic of Wilson, injected the problem of Yugoslav and Czechoslovak aspirations for independence into the Congressional campaign. His somewhat sudden interest in behalf of nationalities was to become a more potent factor in the 1920 elections and would be used against Wilson's peace program. The success of Masaryk in obtaining American recognition of the Czechoslovak National Council stimulated other nationalities to work for acceptance of their committees or demands. Unfortunately for many, intra-group dissensions and inter-group differences in America and in the native lands were disabling handicaps. Most had no well-known émigrés of Paderewski's or Masaryk's stature; their leaders in almost all cases were minor personalities who dissipated strength in personal rivalries. Their immigrants were less numerous. Their organizations were not sufficiently well established within the United States to aid in the struggle for national liberation. It was difficult if not almost impossible, therefore, for them to form politically effective roof organizations capable of exerting pressures in Washington at strategic moments.[23]

That Wilson's principle of self-determination was not a tenet of universal application but primarily a war measure became especially evident to Irish-Americans and the Irish who for many decades had yearned for freedom from British rule. On June 11, 1919, when Frank E. Walsh, a former chairman of the National War Labor Board and delegate to the peace conference of the American Commission on Irish Independence, reminded Wilson of his earlier declaration on the right of self-determination, Wilson answered: "You have touched on the great metaphysical tragedy of to-day. . . .When I gave utterance to those words, I said them without the knowledge that nationalities existed, which are coming to us day after day. . . . You do not know and cannot appreciate the anxieties I have experienced as the result of these many millions of peoples having their hopes raised by what I have said."[24] Three months later, Wilson further clarified his meaning: "It is not within the privilege of the conference of peace to act upon the right of self-determination of any peoples except those which had been included in the territories of the defeated empires."[25]

While Wilson felt that the question of self-determination for the Irish was outside the province of the peace conference, he reasoned that because Austria-Hungary and Germany were enemy nations and Russia was in the hands of Bolsheviks, self-determination for the Poles, Czechs, Slovaks, Serbs, Croats, and Slovenes was a justifiable item for the Paris agenda. He concurred in the promise for a Jewish national state because it had originated with and been supported by Great Britain.

2

The stimulation of the group self-consciousness of ethnic Americans by the First World War did not except the Jews. Unlike that of other groups, their ethnocentrism was not provoked by patriotic attachments to the lands from which they had emigrated, but rather by the effects of the war on their co-religionists and by their animosity toward Russia, the land of pogroms. By the turn of the century the American Jewish community, which had been principally of German origin, was considerably increased by a large emigration from Russia and its occupied territories in East Central Europe. Hatred and fear of Russia latent in these recent refugees from Tsarist persecutions flamed anew with the outbreak of the war. They disliked the Triple Entente and tended to support Irish- and German-American efforts to keep the United States from allying itself with Great Britain and France—the partners of Russia.

To the American Jews of German and Russian origin, the war was primarily a struggle between barbaric, autocratic Russia and civilized, enlightened Germany. Great Britain, declared a Jewish newspaper in September, 1914, "had no business allying herself with an Asiatic barbarian"—a theme repeated in other major Jewish publications. "The Jews support Germany because Russia bathes in Jewish blood, . . ." the *Yidishes Tageblat* editorialized. "Who will dare say that it is a crime for Jews to hate their torturers, their oppressors and murderers? . . ." Two years later another Yiddish paper, commenting on the suppression of the Irish Easter Rebellion, cited it as proof that "the British lion's nails are as bloody as the Russian bear's." Prominent American Jews like Jacob H. Schiff, successful banker and philanthropist, openly announced their partisanship for Germany. Henrietta Szold, founder of the American women's Zionist organization, Hadassah, voiced her belief that the Allies were not fighting "in favor of the principle of smaller nationalities." Until the March, 1917, revolution in Russia and the American entry into the war a month later, American Jews of various origins and political orientations—radical, conservative, or Socialist—remained predominantly pro-German.[26]

While the outbreak of the war united the American Jewish community in a common desire to keep the United States from joining the Entente powers, it created disunity in, and indeed menaced, the embryonic world Zionist movement which sought to obtain international support for the foundation of a Jewish state in Palestine. As Europe separated itself into two combatant groups, communication among the Zionist leaders, citizens of the different nations at war, was disrupted. The leadership was divided in its opinion as to the eventual victors: some expected the fruition of their dream to come from Germany; others were most trustful of British help; and there were some who looked toward Turkey to satisfy their aim. A great many, however, declared their neutrality. These men, uncertain of the war's outcome, were unwilling to rely exclusively on any nation or group of nations; they were concerned lest open support of one belligerent might jeopardize the Jewish population of another. These attitudes and outlooks were not unlike those of the leaders of the submerged nationalities in East Central Europe, who until the last years of the war were at variance in their beliefs as to which nation or group of nations offered the best hope for liberation.

Another disruptive factor within Zionism was that Jews, like other patriotic nationals of different religious beliefs, devoted themselves to the war efforts of their native lands. This was true even in Russia. While Russian Jews in the United States ranked themselves against Tsardom and desired its defeat, many Jews in Russia publicly supported the Tsar and worked for his victory. Zionist leaders in the United States were clearly aware of these complications. At the Rochester convention in December, 1914, and the Boston convention in June, 1915, the Federation of American Zionists (established in 1897) passed resolutions calling attention to the fact that Zionists were "citizens of every embattled state" and as such were "fighting with the utmost courage and loyalty in every army" and performing civil and military duties even to those states which were *"false to their own solemn obligation"* toward Jewish soldiers and their families.[27] Although the federation called itself neutral, it left no doubt that its membership was overwhelmingly pro-German.

As the war progressed new factors arose which outweighed those threatening the Zionist cause and counterbalanced the division and frustration among Zionist leaders: the Jewish-American relief program; the entry of Turkey into the war and the concomitant burden of giving aid to the Jews in Palestine; British imperial policies and concerns in the Middle East and in Europe which sought to use Zionism as an instrument of war propaganda; and the friendship of Justice Louis D. Brandeis, a Zionist leader, with Wilson.

The reaction of the American Jews toward the war was based primarily, if not solely, on their great anxiety over the fate of their fellow Jews in the war-affected countries; Zionist aspirations were not a noteworthy consideration in the early years of the war. During the 1914-1917 period of neutrality, Jewish-Americans organized their efforts to assist and relieve the suffering in Europe and Palestine. Soon the United States became the world center for such philanthropic activities. The fact that the government sanctioned and encouraged their work served to erase Jewish misgivings about Wilson. Unlike the Irish-Americans, whose animosity toward Britain was matched by that they felt toward Wilson, Jewish-Americans did not match their hate of Russia with a hate of Wilson. Although they looked with disfavor at American aid and possible American participation in the war on the side of Russia and her allies, they could not but be grateful for Wilson's interest in the welfare of the peoples suffering in the conflict.

By 1916 any worries the American Jews might have had about Wilson's attitudes toward immigrants from Eastern and Southern Europe were disappearing. His humanitarian appeals to the nations at war in behalf of their minorities established him as the guardian of the persecuted and champion of the downtrodden.[28] Democratic strategists were, of course, aware of the Jewish concern for the plight of their overseas brethren and of the growing Jewish respect for Wilson; the temptation to trade upon both was too great to be resisted. During the campaign the party distributed a special State Department memorandum which described its good work among foreign Jews.

Although the memorandum had in all probability been politically inspired, its boast was grounded in fact. In Europe and Palestine the State Department had helped and, in many cases, had saved Jewish communities from total destruction. This was true especially of Palestinian settlements, for from the day Turkey entered the war against the Entente powers the United States was the chief protector of thousands of Jews—subjects of Russia, Great Britain, and France— in the absence of representatives of those nations. The burden on America of its role as protector became evident when the Turkish government began mass expulsions and arrests of Jews from Palestine. Under urging from prominent American Jews, the State Department lent its facilities to transmit messages to Jewish leaders in Turkey and Europe and to forward medical supplies to disease- ravaged areas. Brandeis, a Zionist leader and intimate of Wilson, persuaded Lansing to prevail upon the American ambassador to Turkey, Henry Morgenthau, Sr. (a Jewish-American who, because of his sensitivity, tended to minimize Turkish policies toward the Jews) to put pressure on the Porte. Although the State Department was surely aware of the implications and ramifications of Zionist activities, it took no official notice of them. "When Jewish leaders pled for a homeland at the Peace Conference in Paris," observed Frank E. Manuel, "they could represent a living if decimated settle- ment in Palestine. This is the ultimate significance of the American diplomatic defense of the Palestinian Jews during World War I."[29]

Food, relief, and politics have an inevitable and inescapable connection and interaction during wars. The war in Europe and the Holy Land which brought suffering to the Jews of East Central Europe and threatened Jewish settlements in Palestine made a pro- found impact on the American Jewish community from which the Zionists were able to profit. At the outbreak of the war, American Zionist membership was small—roughly twenty thousand out of an estimated Jewish population of three million. By 1918 the member- ship had grown to about 145,000. The dramatic increase in the num- ber of Zionists was principally due to the efforts of Brandeis and Dr. Shmarya Levin, popular and gifted orator sent by the World Zionist Executive Committee to "stimulate the moribund" American Zionist Federation. Levin was especially effective among Yiddish-speaking Jewish-Americans. The plight of the Jews in Europe and the Otto- man Empire furnished strong arguments for a Jewish state and for Zionism as the means to end ages-long persecution of Jews in Europe. It was in the Jewish middle class that Zionist ideology found its greatest support. The upper class, mainly German in origin, and its rabbis, too, were militantly anti-Zionist. The working class on the eastern seaboard, a great many of whom were under Socialist influence, remained hostile. Recent immigrants from Eastern Europe were indifferent. Notwithstanding these divergent attitudes toward the establishment of a national home, however, Jewish-Americans did share a determination to help their brethren abroad.

When the Zionists began to inject their political aspirations into the problem of relief, confusion resulted. Collaboration on giving relief was possible, but the range of positions on Palestine as a Jewish homeland continued to be very wide. While Brandeis awakened in Jews in America a responsibility for Jews abroad and then sought their help to secure Palestine for Zionism, the American Jewish Committee—controlled by wealthy Jews and led by Louis Marshall—preferred to help without organizing the Jewish masses, and "shied away from Jewish nationalism." The resultant confusion is well exemplified by a remark of anti-Zionist Jacob H. Schiff during a discussion of the problem, "I am divided into three parts; I am an American, I am a German, and I am a Jew."[30] Until the announcement of the Balfour Declaration, which came several months after the American entry into the war, Schiff remained adamant in his conviction that "separatism"—"the formation of a large separate Hebraic group with national aspirations," in the United States or elsewhere—was "reprehensible." After the Balfour Declaration, Schiff found himself "getting more and more in favor of an autonomous Palestine under British suzerainty" which, he believed, would become a Jewish country within the British Empire in due time.[31]

The imminent collapse of the Ottoman Empire and the abdication of the Russian Tsar in March, 1917, were two powerful factors which aided the cause of Zionism. With the entry of Turkey into the war, the balance of power among Germany, Austria-Hungary, France, and England, which had prevented the complete partition of Turkey, came to an end. Realizing that the disruption of the Turkish Empire was imminent, Great Britain, France, and Russia began to make plans to gratify their territorial ambitions at the expense of Turkey. Turkey's alignment with the Central Powers supplied the rationale, pretext, and convenience for such action. In the middle of March, 1916, the three powers entered into the secret Sykes-Picot agreement through which Russia reserved for herself Constantinople and the straits; France claimed Syria; and Britain, in order to secure an overland route to the East and prevent any other nation's dominion in proximity to the Suez Canal, bespoke a vast territory which would give her control over the Persian Gulf and ports in Palestine. Because of a clash of interests in regard to Palestine, the agreement specified its internationalization, in which Great Britain reluctantly concurred. Concerned over the future of French domination of Syria and its concomitant threat to the English position at Suez, Great Britain regarded internationalization as a temporary expedient. Her main aim was to make Palestine a British-controlled buffer area; the Balfour Declaration was to be a means to this end. By giving a pledge for a Jewish homeland, Britain would thus be able to govern Palestine and keep it in escrow for later fulfillment of that pledge.

Only subsequently to the Sykes-Picot agreement did the British government begin seriously to consider Zionist aspirations. Early in March, 1916, unaware of the negotiations preceding the agreement, Zionist leaders submitted to the British government a plan which, in anticipation of a joint British-French administration of Palestine, provided for equal political rights for Palestinian Jews and for the facilitation of immigration and colonization. When David Lloyd George became Prime Minister in December he was apprised of the plan, but as George Antonius pointed out, ". . . the Zionist programme, with its equal regard for British and French designs on Palestine, did not altogether suit Mr. Lloyd George's book."[32] On February 7, 1917, Sir Mark Sykes and Herbert Samuel, under authorization of Lloyd George, met with Zionist leaders at the London home of Dr. Moses Gaster, chief rabbi of the Sephardic community. Sykes and Samuel informed the Zionists of their opposition to the internationalization of Palestine. In turn, the Zionists promised without hesitation to support the establishment of an exclusively British protectorate of the Holy Land provided their aspirations had British support. This was an historic meeting—it set the stage, a few weeks before the United States entered the war, for the formulation of the Balfour Declaration nine months later.

Once its decision was made, it was not difficult for the British government, and particularly Lloyd George and Lord Balfour, to justify their championing of Zionism as benevolent and high idealism—a fulfillment of Biblical prophecies, a solution to the age-old problem of anti-Semitism, and an atonement as well, by Christians, for their persecution of Jews. Actually, at a time when the fortunes of the Allies seemed not very bright—economically and militarily theirs was a precarious position—the government of Great Britain also saw the pledge as a most effective propaganda device to win over to the Allied cause Jews in the United States, the Entente nations, and revolutionary, turbulent Russia.

From the very first day of the war, the British government had been certain of the importance of winning the support of the American Jews. Sir Cecil Spring Rice, British ambassador to the United States, believed their power to be considerable; equal, if not superior, to that of the Irish. The British were aware that the partnership with Russia, the land of pogroms, militated against Jewish pro-Allied attitudes and that so long as it continued, slogans of liberty would ring false. Their suasive efforts directed toward the American Jewish community were skillfully managed either directly through prominent Jews or indirectly through the British information agency, Wellington House. Nonetheless, German-Jews, who were the "upper crust" and leaders of the Jewish-American group, continued to stand with German-Americans in encouraging American aloofness from the war.

Then, too, the German government was not oblivious of the pro-German sentiment of Jews in the United States, undertaking to preserve and nourish it through the *Zentralstelle für Auslandsdienst* of the German Foreign Office. Dr. Isaac Straus of the German-Jewish *Komité für den Osten* was sent to the United States in 1914 to direct propaganda among the Jews. The ubiquitous and enterprising Louis Hammerling, owner and director of the American Association of Foreign Language Newspapers, supplied the Jewish press with copy from the German Information Bureau.[33] When the Germans took a strong stand against the persecution of Jews in Turkey in 1915, the German ambassador to the United States, Count Johann von Bernstorff, publicized the action. In a letter to the editor of a Jewish newspaper in Boston, he said that the "benevolent and understanding attitude of the German Government toward the Jewish problem" guaranteed that after the war everything would be done "to improve the condition of the Palestinian Jews."[34]

After the March revolution in Russia, the British persuaded themselves that the promise of a Jewish homeland would be effective also in overcoming defeatist propaganda against the war among the

Russian masses. More than that, they were of the opinion that it would inhibit Russian Jews from supporting the more extreme revolutionary parties in Russia and influence them to support the Kerensky government which had pledged itself to continue in the war on the side of the Allies. Interestingly enough, Colonel House had the same notion. He "wrote Wilson of his plans for organizing the American Jews in an attempt to stem the defeatist tide among the Jews in Russia."[35]

The British-Zionist gentlemen's agreement brought vigor and unity to Zionism. Through it Weizmann in England and Brandeis in the United States were able to lead from strength. Zionist leaders who had been hitherto either neutral or pro-German became pro-British.

3

It was not until November 2, 1917, that the Balfour Declaration was issued. There were three reasons for the delay. The first was unexpected opposition from prominent non-Zionist Jewish leaders in Great Britain for whom Zionism raised the problem of dual loyalty; their strong protests could not be ignored. The second reason was the long but eventually successful negotiation for French acceptance of the declaration which would give Britain exclusive control of Palestine. The third reason was the necessity for Wilson's approval of the terms, the precise wording of which exacted its own toll in time.

Two factors were responsible for Wilson's interest in the Jewish problem: his humanitarian impulse to help the Jews in Palestine and Europe and his friendship with Brandeis. Wilson saw no real contradiction between humanitarian interest in the plight of the Jews and the American national interest. As he told Morgenthau, whom he appointed ambassador to Constantinople, "Remember that anything you can do to improve the lot of your co-religionists is an act that will reflect credit upon America, and you may count on the full power of the Administration to back you up."[36]

Wilson's interest in Zionist aspirations was stimulated by Brandeis and later by Felix Frankfurter and Rabbi Stephen S. Wise. Brandeis, who had devoted much of his time to the study of Jewish problems, felt that Zionism was the means of bringing pride and dignity and a feeling of security to Jews everywhere. Unlike other prominent German Jews in the United States, he was not concerned with, and indeed thrust aside, all arguments that political Zionism would in any way undermine the position of Jewish citizens in America or in any other nation. Considering Brandeis the leader of the American Jews, appreciative of his friendship with Wilson, and intensely desirous of enlisting Jewish sympathies, the British found Brandeis a useful lever. This, in turn, strengthened Brandeis in getting the Western powers to accede to the wishes of the Zionists, as at the same time it increased his power and influence in Zionist circles.

The first dramatic instance which indicated the growing authority of Brandeis and which augmented the incipient Allied and American recognition of Palestine as the Jewish national home occurred in the spring of 1917.[37] On May 16, Morgenthau, former American ambassador to Turkey, called upon Lansing to advance a plan which, at first, Lansing thought "impossible." According to Morgenthau, Talaat, Enver, and Djemel held the "destiny of Turkey" in their hands. The first two "wished themselves out" of the German-Turkish alliance because of the rising discontent of the people. Believing that the "cordial and intimate terms" which had existed between himself and Talaat and Enver when he was ambassador would be valuable in opening negotiations, Morgenthau proposed that he be sent to Switzerland to arrange a secret meeting. There he would explain that it would be in the interest of Turkey to obtain then the "friendship of the Allies" and he would "persuade them to agree to conclude a separate peace." Later Lansing "went over the plan point by point" and decided that although its chance of success was one in fifty, the United States should not miss even that slight opportunity to gain "so tremendous advantage as would result from alienating Turkey from the Teutonic Alliance." Lansing received Wilson's permission to discuss the matter with Balfour. According to Lansing's account of May 22, Balfour "thought the plan well worth trying . . . he had real hope of its success." On the 28th, the British chargé, Colville Barclay, informed Lansing that Lord Robert Cecil of the British Foreign Office had approved Morgenthau's mission and suggested Egypt as preferable for the rendezvous. The purpose of the mission was disguised by making it appear to be "an attempt to alleviate the conditions of the Jews in Palestine"; to that end a Zionist, Felix Frankfurter, was to accompany Morgenthau and thus enhance its "Jewish" aspect. It was finally agreed, with Brandeis' knowledge, that they would sail for Gibraltar, there to meet secretly with the representatives of the French and British governments as well as the "dragoman" of the American embassy at Constantinople.[38]

Early in June Brandeis cabled Weizmann asking that he try to contact an American commission "traveling to the East." Although Brandeis' cable did not state the purpose, destination, or membership of the mission, Weizmann sensed that it might affect the cause of Zionism. From Sir Mark Sykes and Ormsby-Gore he learned that "attempts were being made to detach Turkey from the Central Powers," that the mission was headed by Morgenthau, and that the Foreign Office "did not attach much importance to the maneuver." When he found out two weeks later that Morgenthau was accompanied by "some Zionists," he became more concerned. According to Weizmann, Balfour "seemed to be almost as much in the dark" as Weizmann himself as to its "exact purposes and plans."[39] Weizmann claimed, "The British did not like the smell of it, and they wanted Mr. Morgenthau to be turned back before he reached Egypt." Fearing that official British opposition to the project would jeopardize American aid, Balfour suggested that Weizmann intercept Morgenthau "and keep on talking till I had talked him out of this mission." At Gibraltar Weizmann and Colonel Weyl, French Zionist, convinced Morgenthau, who revealed to them his purpose, that the effort would fail and very likely ruin his diplomatic career. "It was no job at all," boasted Weizmann, "to persuade Mr. Morgenthau to drop the subject. He simply persuaded himself, and before long announced his intention of going to Biarritz instead of Egypt."[40]

What Weizmann called the Opera Bouffe Intermezzo cleared the way for the British military campaign of 1917 in Palestine—which gave Britain actual possession of the Holy Land—and the Balfour Declaration, the promise of a Jewish national home there. It is also a clear example of an attempt by hyphenate-Americans and their friends abroad not only to influence the foreign policy of the United States but also to change the direction of a policy already determined.

There is little doubt that Wilson was aware that Zionists constituted a small minority of the American Jewish community. From 1914 on, he received letters from Jews which indicated their opposition to political Zionism: one among them expressed displeasure over Wilson's reference to a "Jewish nationality"; another pleaded, "My flag is the Red, White, and Blue, how then can I have any other National Homeland?"; and another warned against being misled by "Christian romanticism."[41] Yet, despite this and opposition from Lansing, Wilson decided in October, 1917, to endorse the preliminary draft of the Balfour Declaration—which he had been under pressure from the British government and American Zionists to do. On September 4, House had informed Wilson of a cable from Lord Cecil requesting that he "ascertain unofficially if the President favors such a declaration." Three days later House reminded Wilson of the matter, but added some misgivings: "Have you made up your mind regarding what answer you will make to Cecil concerning Zionist Movement? It seems to me that there are many dangers lurking in it, and if I were the British I would be chary about going too definitely into that question." His apprehension was not apparent earlier that year when he wrote Wise, "I hope the dream which we have will soon become a reality."[42] On October 6 Balfour cabled House that in view of reports that the German government was attempting to capture the Zionist movement, the cabinet had again considered a message of sympathy for the movement and asked that he forward Wilson's opinion of the message.[43] Three days later Weizmann told Brandeis of the "formidable offensive which had been launched" against the declaration by British non-Zionists, urged that the President be insistent on a specific text, and asked that Wilson's views be "buttressed by telegrams from important Zionists and other American leaders."[44] On October 13 Wilson replied to House's letter of September 4 by saying that he "concurred in the formula suggested" and would appreciate House's letting the British know.[45]

Wilson's agreeing to the declaration was, as Rappaport has stated, "prompted largely by a concern over the anti-war position of American Jewish radicals and the war weariness of their Russian brethren."[46] Preoccupied with the many facets of the war, he probably looked upon the declaration itself as a minor incident. But to Weizmann, Wilson's approval was crucially important in that it overcame non-Zionist opposition to the British government's course.[47]

With Wilson's concurrence, the way was cleared for a final draft of the message of sympathy. On November 2, 1917, the Balfour Declaration was published: "His Majesty's Government view with favour the establishment in Palestine of a national home for the Jewish people, and will use their best endeavours to facilitate the achievement of this object, it being clearly understood that nothing shall be done which may prejudice the civil and religious rights of existing non-Jewish communities in Palestine, or the rights and political status enjoyed by Jews in any other country."

It was not, however, until August 31, 1918, on the eve of the Congressional election, that Wilson made his first public statement in support of the Balfour Declaration. Ignoring Lansing's warnings that it was, in itself, a violation of the principle of self-determination, Wilson wrote, at Wise's request, a letter of greeting on the occasion of the Jewish New Year in which he, in effect, endorsed the declaration. After the publication of the letter Brandeis "declared that opposition to Zionism could henceforth be considered disloyalty to the United States."[48]

The Fourteen Points and the Balfour Declaration were primarily war measures—propaganda devices to arouse, strengthen, and win over the national sentiment of the submerged, persecuted, and dissatisfied peoples. To the Jews, and more particularly to the Zionists among them, the Balfour Declaration was a promise of political nationhood, lost twenty centuries ago, and a pledge that the age-old humiliation of the Jews was about to end. Although born of practical political and military considerations, the promise of a Jewish national homeland reinforced the idealistic and moral motivation of Zionism which was to survive long after the British and French policies which led to the Balfour Declaration were forgotten.[49]

In the spring of 1922, Henry Cabot Lodge, Republican of Massachusetts, having discovered and convinced himself of the voting power of ethnic groups, introduced a resolution in the Senate supporting the Balfour Declaration and its promise of a Jewish national home in Palestine. Anti-Zionist American Jews and the *New York Times* believed the resolution was prompted by Lodge's desire for the vote of his Jewish constituents.[50] The Senate resolution of April 12, 1922 (Senate Joint Resolution 191), gave Zionism bipartisan support. After that, every President and as many as thirty-three state legislatures reaffirmed that stand. In 1944 and 1948 both party platforms declared a determination to honor previous American pledges.

The aftermath of the Second World War brought the right opportunity to bring to fruition the Zionist dream. American sympathy, which grew out of the monstrous atrocities committed by the Nazis against millions of Jews,[51] and the weakening of British power in the Mediterranean and the concomitant American assumption of responsibilities there, merged with domestic political considerations

94

and thus led to President Harry Truman's decision to back the partition of Palestine and the creation of a Jewish state in 1948. The fact that Soviet Russia—then a non-atomic power but, as ever, ready to reap advantages from internal discontent in the West and in the Middle East—indicated its support for a Jewish nation, may have had an important bearing on the final decision of the American government. Nineteen forty-eight was a presidential election year in America, a year of decision for the Middle East. To postpone redemption of the promise of a Jewish state was then not politically feasible.[52] However, no matter which factor was most important in Truman's historic recognition of a Jewish state, the President was able to claim, as he did to the author, that he was governed not by Zionist pressures but by the promises and pledges of his predecessors in the White House and in Congress.[53]

Unquestionably, Truman was prompted also by human sympathy; he kept his "faith in the rightness" of the policy in spite of pressures from "extreme Zionists."[54] "As a student of the Bible," Truman told the writer in 1959, "I have been impressed by the remarkable achievements of the Jews in Palestine in making the land of the Holy Book blossom again." The Balfour Declaration, the Congressional resolution of 1922, and the platform planks of both parties, he recalled, were promises which had to be kept. And, as he wrote in his *Memoirs*, the decision to create a Jewish state was American ". . . because it was based on the desire to see promises kept and human misery relieved."[55]

Chapter VI

POSTSCRIPT TO SELF-DETERMINATION: THE HYPHENATE CHALLENGE TO INTERNATIONALISM

What we seek is the reign of law based on the consent of the governed and sustained by the organized opinion of mankind.

—Woodrow Wilson, July 4, 1918.

The war came to an end on November 11, 1918. An exhausted world awaited the fruition of the pledges and high resolves that had promised a just peace, national independence, and security to all its peoples. Americans began to try to convince themselves that the war they had fought had been indeed a war to end all wars. The battles were over, but passionate hatred and nationalistic fervor remained. The war to save and spread democracy gave way to chauvinism destined to lay the groundwork for another European upheaval—and another world war.

As Woodrow Wilson sailed for France in December at the head of the American Peace Delegation, he left behind a hostile Congress. Although his party had suffered defeat in the 1918 Congressional elections, he remained certain that people everywhere would endorse his lofty ideals, so well expressed and so well received. He went to Paris to bring justice, peace, and "open diplomacy." His mystic faith, despite his political setback and despite Theodore Roosevelt's warning that he had "no authority whatever to speak for the American people," continued strong and unabated. The tumultuous crowds which greeted him with unbounded and genuine enthusiasm in the European capitals proved amply to him that his confidence in the common man was justified. His principles had been successful during the war; they had strengthened the will of the people, they had given hope, they had rallied a multitude of nationalities behind the Allies, and they had brought final victory. Would the principles designed to win the war also win the peace? Would the people, in Europe and in America, support him, at this most crucial and important time, in securing an honorable peace?

Had Wilson, before he left for Europe, been aware of, and if aware had he understood, the confusions among nationality leaders in the United States, he probably would not have been so sure of the

96

success of his mission. Six weeks before the fateful Congressional election, George Creel, head of the Committee of Public Information, had organized a vast meeting of the "oppressed nationalities of Central Europe." On September 15 at Carnegie Hall, Thomas Masaryk, Ignace Paderewski, leaders of Yugoslavs, Rumanians, Ruthenians, irredentist Italians, and others were given the opportunity to express the gratitude of the nationalities which they represented in the United States and in their native lands. Their harmony was impressive and gave rise to the immediate establishment of the Mid-European Democratic Union. The unprecedented concord lasted only until a few days after the election, when, to the dismay of their many American sympathizers, bitterness engendered by rival territorial claims of the Poles, Ukrainians, Yugoslavs, Italians, and other groups broke up the union. The acrimony was a portent of things to come at the Peace Conference and after.

Selfish national interests in Europe, partisan politics in the United States, and the President's unwillingness to compromise militated against the realization of Wilsonian hopes and dreams. Wilson's own principle of self-determination strengthened nationalistic sentiment, stirred patriotic emotions, and whetted the territorial appetites of the leaders of nations which had won, regained, or saved their freedom on the basis of it. Once the war had been won and the dream of independence satisfied, victory increased demands for more territory and more security at the expense of others' national self-determination. No ethnic entity in Europe or elsewhere was too small to claim or demand the right of self-determination. Nationalistic aims triumphed over Wilsonian principles. At the summit of his career Wilson was rejected in Europe. Worst of all, he was repulsed by his own people.

2

Henry Cabot Lodge, an enthusiastic disciple of Captain Alfred Mahan, championed an American navy second to none and as a true exponent of the "New Manifest Destiny," advocated the spread of American power and prestige beyond continental limits. While the Massachusetts statesman sought to broaden American influence, he also advocated closing American gates to the peoples of the Old World and the Orient. Restricted immigration and unrestricted expansion were bound, so Lodge believed, to increase American strength and steer the United States to a position of world power and leadership.

In 1882 Lodge was concerned as he watched Chinese immigrants displacing American workingmen, and he applauded wholeheartedly the passage of the Chinese Exclusion Act. In December, 1888, Lodge said in his Forefathers' Day address to the New England Society of Brooklyn: "Let every man honor and love the land of his birth and the race from which he springs and keep their memory green. It is a pious and honorable duty. But let us have done with British-Americans and Irish-Americans and German-Americans, and so on, and all be Americans. . . . If a man is going to be an American at all let him be so without any qualifying adjectives; and if he is going to be something else, let him drop the word American from his personal description."[1]

Like Professor Wilson of Princeton, Lecturer Lodge of Harvard was alarmed by the arrival of Eastern and Southern Europeans—Italians, Czechs, Slovaks, Poles, Russians, and others—who were disembarking in ever increasing numbers at the ports of Boston and New York. Like Wilson before he became President, Lodge differentiated between the desirable immigrants from Western Europe and the undesirable ones from Italy and the Slavic heartland. Like Wilson, he nevertheless hoped that the hyphen, once exposed to the process of assimilation, would "drop of its own weight." But unlike Wilson's, Lodge's attitude toward Eastern and Southern Europeans continued after he entered politics, after he was elected Representative and later Senator. It was only at the summit of his political power, when animosity toward Wilson merged with fear for the future of the Republican party, that Lodge not only found good things to say about immigrants but also stimulated and championed their ethnocentrism and their interest in the lands of their origin.

In 1918, and more particularly during the 1920 presidential elections, Lodge's hatred for Wilson and partisan considerations produced a most remarkable metamorphosis in the dauntless advocate of restricted immigration and the enthusiastic proponent of American expansion. To defeat Wilson and bring victory to the party, Lodge cast aside his fears of the immigrant and his own admonition to do away with "British-Americans and Irish-Americans and German-Americans, and so on." He called upon hyphenated Americans to revenge themselves on Wilson, on the peace of Versailles, and on the Democratic party. Their response was most gratifying to the Republican strategists.

Almost a year before the final Treaty of Versailles was signed on June 28, 1919, Lodge and other Republicans prepared the groundwork for the hyphenated Americans' revolt against the Democrats. As chairman of the Senate Committee on Foreign Relations, Lodge invited representatives of nationality groups to air their criticisms of the forthcoming peace conference. At hearings during August and September, 1918, claims and counterclaims were presented by spokesmen of Slovak, Czech, Estonian, Latvian, Lithuanian, Greek, Hungarian, Irish, and Yugoslav (Slovene, Serb, and Croat) organizations.[2] The significance of these hearings, which produced a voluminous record, was not lost on Republican strategists. Good politics demanded that the interest of American hyphenates in the lands of their origin and their discontent with Wilson be cultivated and exploited to the full.

By 1920 millions of ethnic Americans saw the various promises and pledges made during the war neglected, refused, or compromised at the conference tables. With the notable exception of Polish-Americans, all were ready to vent their bitterness and disappointment on Wilson and the Democratic party. Wilson, once the champion of self-determination, spokesman for the oppressed and downtrodden, became the betrayer of the nationalistic hopes of those same peoples who, because of Wilson, had seen their native lands emerge from centuries of bondage. To German-Americans 1920 offered the opportunity to revenge themselves against the man who led America against the *Vaterland,* while to the Irish-Americans it gave the occasion to retaliate for Wilson's refusal to separate Ireland from British control. To both groups it furnished the rationale to vindicate their prewar admonition to stand aloof from the European War.

To overthrow Wilson and unseat the Democrats from national power was a paramount goal of the Republican party; what better means than by defaming the League Covenant, Wilson's justification for the unconditional and wholehearted entry into the war? Toward that end, Lodge enlisted, among other things, the aid of hyphenated Americans.[3] An American nationalist and a traditional isolationist, he became in 1920 a pleader for Irish, Italian, Armenian, Zionist, and other extra-American causes. While on one hand he warned of the consequences of Wilson's peace treaty, which would entangle the United States in European distresses, he himself did not hesitate

99

to embroil the United States in European entanglements—but only those which promised votes on election days.

Under the leadership of Lodge and the "Irreconcilables," a union was soon forged between hyphenated Americans, 100 per cent Americans, and isolationists. Ironically, the very emphasis on pure Americanism enticed many of the 50 per cent Americans to join the coalition. This was particularly true of those ethnic Americans who had found it difficult to support American entry into the war or whose loyalty had been held suspect during the heyday of American war enthusiasm. To them, the fervid appeals of Americanism were the opportunity to gain, regain, or strengthen their status as the best-of-all-possible Americans. Hatred of Wilson, hatred of Versailles, hatred of Britain, hatred of all things foreign coalesced into a formidable unholy alliance—an alliance that was to reëmerge on the eve of the Second World War. In its wake Anglophiles became Anglophobes. Historic anti-British prejudices were revived by those like William Randolph Hearst who equated patriotism with "twisting the lion's tail." Even progressives became members of the "Battalion of Death" which vowed to destroy Wilson's League. "Among other motives, it happened," writes Chester Bowles, "that many of them—including Johnson, Borah, Norris and LaFollette" represented large constitutencies of more than seven million German-Americans.[4] Wilson's hope for mankind and America's prestige was being perverted either to suit or abate the hatreds, fears, grievances, jealousies, and ambitions of vociferous and well-organized minorities.

3

The call to all nationality groups to air their disappointments during the presidential campaign of 1920 opened the floodgates for ethnic grievances. The war, which had united all Americans and silenced opposition among those who disapproved of American participation, was in the past. There was now no reason to repress anti-British and anti-Wilson feelings. To the German-Americans the campaign of 1920 furnished the opportunity to rebuild prewar influence, gratify deep-seated animosities, and condemn Wilson and all he stood for; the time to pass judgment had come. As German Day celebrations were revived, as sauerkraut replaced liberty cabbage on American tables, and as liberty measles reverted to those of the German strain, German-Americans welcomed the resurgence of isolationism. Isolationism was a vindication of their prewar defense of the traditionally American principle of non-entanglement. "In two days," exclaimed the editor of the *Akron Germania* on July 2, 1920, "we celebrate again our declaration of independence from England. How the times have changed!" The sentiment common in the German-American press was a wish to defeat Wilson and achieve revenge for the wartime anti-German provocations.[5]

In May, 1919, the Steuben Society of America was organized to replace the German-American Alliance. Its first publication, *Issues of To-day*, promised retaliation against those who had "gotten" German-Americans during the war.[6] George Sylvester Viereck, leading spokesman of United States Germandom, denounced the "League of Damnations" and guaranteed three million votes to any presidential candidate agreeing to oppose the peace treaty. The choice of German-American leadership for the presidency was Senator Hiram Johnson. His opposition to the treaty and to the League Covenant, his "unadulterated Americanism," and his progressive domestic record met with their approval. But when Warren G. Harding received the Republican nomination, German-American editors were consoled to learn that he had been opposed by the pro-British American press.

The German-American press described Wilson as a "despot" who violated the laws and the spirit of the Constitution, an Anglophile "of the worst variety" who, in order to save the British Empire, had contravened the injunctions of Washington and Jefferson against permanent alliances. The "100% American" editor of the *Cincinnati Freie Presse* warned that Wilson's League of Nations was a device to guarantee British control of the world and a promise that America would supply "cannon fodder" to retain it. As the campaign progressed, German-American leaders urged their followers to go "to the polls to teach the politicians that they must henceforth seriously reckon with the voters of German stock." The *Toledo Express* reminded German-Americans that they were "the index of the scale." A strong appeal signed by the editors of the *Cincinnati Freie Presse* and the *Wächter und Anzeiger,* distributed and published in many other papers, summoned all German-Americans to cast their votes against James M. Cox, the Democratic nominee: "Every vote for Harding is a protest against the persecution of Americans of German origin during the last years." To many German-American editors Cox was an "opportunist," a "cheap, American politician," a "nativist," one who had "double-crossed" Ohio Ger-

101

man-Americans, and a "fervent hater of Catholics." In contrast Warren Harding was praised for his belief in "America first," for his support of an immediate peace treaty with Germany, and for his demands that American troops be withdrawn immediately. Harding was the true embodiment of Washington, Jefferson, and Lincoln to the editor of the *Akron Columbia,* while the editor of the *Toledo Express* found it pleasing that Harding's father-in-law was of German origin, spoke German fluently, and "had never been ashamed of his descent." The Republican National Committee enlisted the anti-Wilson German-American press in the battle. To ensure a wider distribution of German-American opinion, its advertisements in major German-American publications contained quotations under the heading "What the German-language press has to say about the two candidates for president."[7]

The Democratic National Committee tried desperately to stem the pro-Republican tide among German-Americans. In the wet-or-dry issue of the campaign it saw hope that the anti-prohibitionist German-Americans might vote on the basis of social habit rather than on the basis of national origin. In an attempt to appeal to German-American concern with the prestige of Germany, Democrats promised that Cox would secure the admission of Germany to the League. Their efforts were of no avail.[8]

Of the disillusioned ethnic groups the Irish-Americans were the best-organized, the most vociferous, and the most effective. In the last months of the war and immediately after, Irish-American organizations—the Clan-na-Gael, the Friends of Irish Freedom, the Ancient Order of Hibernians, and others—formed Self-Determination Clubs, Roger Casement Councils, and Robert Emmett and Wolfe Tone Associations, and held numerous rallies. Until early 1919 Irish leaders still hoped that Wilson would respond to the united voice of Irish-America demanding, as did Boston's Cardinal O'Connell, that "Ireland, like every other country, must be free, one united Ireland, indivisible, unseparated, now and forever. . . . Let the test of sincerity be Ireland. Then we will be convinced that truth still lives."[9] By the end of March, Irish-Americans became convinced that Wilson did not stand "the test of sincerity" and that "truth" no longer lived.

Basing their attack on Article X of the League Covenant, which obligated each member to assist any other member in the case of external aggression, Irish-American leaders interpreted it as a design to protect the British Empire. Like the German-Americans they condemned, as a contradiction of Washington's Farewell Address, what Wilson considered the heart of the Covenant, and saw in it a pledge to send Irish-American men to help Britain retain its power—even to the extent of helping crush possible future Irish revolts.

In the spring of 1919, Eamon de Valera, Sinn Fein leader, came to the United States to raise funds and champion Irish independence. While de Valera was moderate, Judge Daniel F. Cohalan, the Irish-American leader, was extreme in his demands; the former shied away from bitter attacks on Wilson, the latter injected personal animus in his speeches for Irish independence. When Henry White, a Republican career diplomat, objected to the Senate Committee on Foreign Relations' granting de Valera a hearing, on the ground that Irish aspirations had "nothing to do with the making of peace," Lodge replied, "Neither did the Monroe Doctrine come within the jurisdiction of the Peace Conference." Though Lodge admitted that Irish independence was not within the province of the conference, he justified his interest by saying, "You know what the Irish vote is in this country. . . . They are bitterly opposed to the League, and the fate of the Democratic party . . . is in their hands."[10]

By the end of 1919 the political consequences of Irish dissatisfaction were ominously clear to the Democratic party. In October of that year, Senator David I. Walsh, Irish-American Democrat of Massachusetts, who had supported Wilson and urged patience upon Irish-Americans, broke with the President and came out against the League Covenant. So far as the Democratic party was concerned, its backbone, the hitherto faithful Irish vote, was gone.[11]

Another of the many major ethnic groups once enthusiastic toward Wilson and now disillusioned was the Italian-Americans. Wilson's principle of self-determination had conjured up a vision of a large, majestic, and glorious Italy. Nineteen-nineteen was to have been the year Italy would find its place in the sun.[12] At Paris these hopes and ambitions came into conflict with those of Italy's neighbors, particularly Yugoslavia. The port of Fiume became the focus of contention and bitterness. Italians regarded Fiume as Italian territory, while Wilson was persuaded that it should belong to Yugoslavia. When he spoke glowingly in Boston of Yugoslav aspirations without mentioning Italian claims, Italian-Americans naturally became suspicious and their admiration of Wilson diminished.

The *Gazzetta del Massachusetts* issued a ringing summons on March 1: "The Italians of Boston, of the United States, of the whole world, have now just one thing to do . . . to arouse themselves, to agitate, and to cry out in a loud voice: We are disappointed, Mr. President!" Fiorello LaGuardia, president of the New York City Board of Aldermen, responded by organizing nationwide opposition to Wilson and the treaty.

Lodge reacted with alacrity to Italian-American agitation; it was another fortuitous factor to be exploited in the interest of party victory. Without hesitation and without studying relevant facts, Lodge began to insist that Fiume was "as essential to the well-being of Italy as the mouth of the Mississippi was to the United States." When it was pointed out that its essentiality was Yugoslavian rather than Italian, Lodge refused to acknowledge the possibility that he might be wrong. As Thomas Bailey observed, "There were not enough Yugoslav voters in Massachusetts to make it politically profitable for the Senator to admit his error." The Republican state convention endorsed in October a resolution favoring Italian demands.[13]

To check their defections from the Democratic party, Walsh appealed to Italian-Americans to act as Americans. He "stressed the necessity for all who came to the United States to forget their country of origin and think strictly as Americans." Walsh's "insidious words" were immediately denounced; the audience was urged never to forget "Roma Alma Mater."[14] As in the case of his fellow Irish-Americans, Walsh's plea was condemned by Italian-American spokesmen, and resentment continued undiminished.

To nourish Italian-American discontent with Wilson, Republican strategists again exhumed from his 1902 *History of the American People* Wilson's injudicious remarks about Italians, which had stood unaltered in later editions. The harmful passage was reproduced in the Italian-American press, and Italian-Americans were admonished that they "would do well to clip out this extract and keep it as a remembrance from Professor Woodrow Wilson of Princeton University."[15] Similar and certainly more damaging passages from the writings of Lecturer Henry Cabot Lodge of Harvard were either forgotten or excused.

To defeat Wilson, Lodge was also able to draw upon the disaffection of a great many smaller nationality groups. Armenian- and Syrian-Americans, a great many of whom resided in Massachusetts, were bitter over the treaty. Their craving for the independence of their native lands, expected as a result of the collapse of the Ottoman Empire, was compromised in the mandate system and by the ambitions of the Western powers. When Syria became a French mandate in February, 1920, Dr. Abraham Rihbany, spokesman of Syrian-Americans, urged his followers to vote against the League. Greek-Americans, whose homeland gained territory at Paris, felt that Greece should have had much more; in March, the ever-obliging Lodge introduced a resolution to that effect in the Senate. Jewish-Americans, though pleased with the Balfour Declaration and its inclusion in the mandate system and with the various treaty provisions guaranteeing minority rights in the new or re-created states of East Central Europe, became concerned over the revival of anti-Semitism in Poland and Eastern Europe. To the American Jews such early disregard and violation of the treaty was proof that the treaty was "mere scraps of paper." And when the American minister to Poland, Hugh Gibson, and the specially appointed investigator Henry Morgenthau, Sr., anti-Zionist Jewish-American, denied the existence of Jewish pogroms in Poland, they were shocked that the administration accepted what they believed to be a prejudiced report.[16] Lithuanian-Americans, whose native land had achieved its independence through Wilson's principle of self-determination, urged in vain that Washington stop Polish encroachments on Lithuanian territory. Even some Polish-American leaders, concerned over Soviet designs on Poland, began to appeal to the Republicans for help. In 1920 Lodge was petitioned for assistance in getting military aid to the Polish government. Alert to the possibility of tempering the still unbounded Polish-American gratitude toward Wilson, Lodge suggested that the only way to help Poland was by the President's summoning a special session of Congress—an unlikely event.[17]

The restiveness of ethnic Americans within the Democratic traces brought on a flurry of remedial efforts. House's son-in-law, Gordon Auchincloss, asked the vacationing House "to get something favorable" for the Poles in Europe because he believed "it would be a big thing for the party."[18] In the White House, Joe Tumulty begged the President "to keep alive" the Division of Work with the Foreign-Born of the Committee on Public Information, but lack of funds forced its disbanding.[19] In the last month of the presidential campaign, Cox, convinced that any appeals for ethnic votes were useless, decided to condemn hyphenism as a threat to pure Americanism. In a speech at Columbus, Ohio, he bitterly attacked Italian, Greek, and other ethnic groups as a "motley array of questionable groups and influences . . . an array that to survey brings the crimson blush of humiliation to an American." At the same time he leveled charges against the "Afro-American party, whose hyphenated activity has attempted to stir up troubles among Negroes upon false claims that it can bring social equality."[20] Although Irish-Americans were not included in the indictment, Irish-American editors and leaders considered it as an insult to them also.

Cox's denunciation of hyphenism was matched by an equivalent from Harding. The Republican candidate, with victory in sight and perhaps realizing his future responsibilities, took a strong stand against ethnic agitations. The Irish issue, he stated, was an internal English problem, "not a question for official America"—an almost exact repetition of Wilson's policy. On September 18, Harding criticized "meddling abroad" because of its tendency to divide America into rival groups which are "led away" by leaders from " 'America first' " to " 'hyphen first.' " He dreaded an organized "hyphen" vote which would have the balance of power in American political life.[21] Harding's stand on hyphenism did not deter other Republican candidates or those who campaigned for him from continuing their appeals for the ethnic vote.

On the first Tuesday after the first Monday of November, 1920, the American people recorded their mandate. Cox was defeated, and so was Wilson. The day of reckoning so eagerly awaited by Irish, German, Italian, and other ethnic groups had come and gone. "Wilsonism is forever abolished," headlined the *Toledo Express*. "The People have spoken. Ours is the victory." The editor of the *Cincinnati Freie Presse* echoed, "The free people of America have crushed the snake of Wilsonism." The *Wächter und Anzeiger* boldly claimed that Harding had been elected by Americans of German and Irish blood, which fact would more than ever convince politicians of the voting power of the "German element." The paper reminded the Republican party that it was on trial and would be held to "strict accountability for the promises made during the campaign." The *Toledo Express* underlined the warning: "Let us make it clear to the newly-elected gentleman, at the very outset, that we constitute a real power, that we have a right to make ourselves heard, and that we will never again allow anyone to deprive us of that right with impunity."[22]

106

4

What, exactly, was the meaning of the "mandate" of 1920? What did Americans vote for or against? In electing Harding did they vote against the League of Nations, against the idea of peaceful settlement of disputes—in itself a proud American contribution to world diplomacy?

Of all the factors contributing to the confused "mandate" given the Republicans, the ethnic factor was, perhaps, one of the most important. In electing a Republican President, German-Americans voted for Germany, Irish-Americans voted against Britain and for Ireland, Italian-Americans voted against Yugoslavia, Greek-Americans voted for the inclusion of Northern Epirus in the kingdom of Greece, Lithuanian-Americans voted against Poland, Arab-Americans voted against Britain and France, and Chinese-Americans voted against Japan. All of them, and many more, voted against Wilson—or so, at least, was the conviction of their ethnic leaders and American politicians. While American nationalists voted "a plague on Europe," millions of hyphenates, many of whom had been stirred to action by Wilsonian idealism during the war, voted "a plague on Wilson." A babel of tongues, a confusion of hatreds, a coalition of 100 per cent Americans and 50 per cent Americans, an array of conservatives and uncompromising liberals, and a desire to return to isolationism all merged to defeat Wilson, weaken America's prestige, deny to the United States the fruits of victory, and give the incoming administration a befuddled mandate.

What of those ethnic Americans whose hostility toward Wilson had been softened? What did the campaign of 1920 prove to them? To be sure, it increased their self-consciousness and convinced them of their political power. This they were not to forget in the years to come. But what of the price they paid for allowing their leaders and the Republican opponents of Wilson to persuade them to revenge themselves against the Democrats? What was the cost of the proof of their political assertiveness? Their very agitations intensified some doubts in the minds of many here and abroad of American capability for participation in world affairs and led to concern over the ability of the United States to assimilate immigrants. They stimulated scholarly and polemical discussions on whether America was a "Nation or Confusion" and whether the melting pot was a myth or reality, and produced fears that hyphenism might displace pure Americanism. With the triumph of ethnic nationalism came xenophobia, anti-alien organizations, exclusionist movements, and suspicion toward immigrants. Within several months of the election Arizona, Arkansas, Delaware, Idaho, Kansas, Louisiana, Missouri, Montana, Nebraska, Nevada, New Mexico, Oregon, Texas, and Washington enacted alien land laws similar to that passed by California. In 1924 Congress passed the restrictive Immigration Act with its controversial national origins provisions.[23] In 1925, Frederick Jackson Turner, noted student of the influence of the frontier on American history, was persuaded that the national population had approached its saturation point.[24]

The Immigration Acts of 1921 and 1924 were to a great extent symptomatic of an eagerness to integrate a shaken social order. As Nathan Glazer put it, "America had decided to stop the kaleidoscope and find out what it had become."[25]

Chapter VII

THE SECOND WORLD WAR: THE HYPHENATE CHALLENGE TO ISOLATIONISM

We need the Italian and German vote for Roosevelt.
—Chairman, Italian Democratic Committee of Pittsburgh, November, 1940.

The borders of the Reich are to be drawn where the borders of German blood lie. —*Neues Tagebuch,* May 16, 1936.

My order is that an Italian citizen must remain an Italian citizen, no matter in what land he lives, even to the seventh generation.
—Benito Mussolini.

In March, 1933, Franklin Delano Roosevelt was inaugurated President of the United States. A month before, President von Hindenburg of Germany had surrendered the future of that country to Adolf Hitler and his frenzied dream of a Third Reich to last a thousand years. In Italy, Fascist Benito Mussolini expanded his plans to build a new Roman Empire. In the Far East, arrogant Japanese war lords, defying both the United States and the League of Nations, tightened their hold upon North China from their puppet state of Manchukuo. Woodrow Wilson's League, the hope of mankind, had been struck a mortal blow. In Europe and in Asia, democracies were retreating before dictatorships and brazen aggression.

As Roosevelt took the oath of office on that cold March day, much of what was left of Wilsonian idealism was being menaced by war threats from Berlin, Rome, and Tokyo. If Roosevelt was aware of the forebodings, he did not refer to them as he addressed the huge crowd before him on the grounds of the Capitol. His main concern was with measures to bring quick recovery from the collapse of the American economy. His message contained only one simple, unembellished statement on foreign policy: "In the field of world policy, I would dedicate this nation to the policy of the good neighbor."

But neither Germany nor Italy nor Japan wanted to be good neighbors. In the wake of a rapid and concentrated succession of

109

their unneighborly acts, the whole structure of world order and peace which had been proclaimed at Versailles began to collapse. In October, 1933, the Führer of the Germans withdrew his nation from the World Disarmament Conference and the League of Nations. Two years later he denounced the Versailles Treaty. In 1936 he boldly marched his troops into the demilitarized Rhineland. Meanwhile, Il Duce, convinced by his Ethiopian success that democracies were things of the past, bound his future with that of Hitler. These men of limitless ambitions forged the Rome-Berlin Axis, which was soon extended into a formidable Triple Alliance: Berlin-Rome-Tokyo. While England and France hesitated, temporized, and wondered whether Fascism or Communism was the greater threat, the Axis powers relentlessly pursued their aggressive plans. On August 23, 1939, Hitler and Stalin ended any indecision as to which ideology was the more evil by their startling announcement of the Nazi-Soviet Non-Aggression Pact. When, only a week later, the Nazis invaded Poland, and England and France challenged Nazi and Fascist ambition by force of arms, it was already much too late. This became ominously clear as the German armies conquered one European nation after another. Within a brief time, all of Continental Europe was under the Nazi heel. As Great Britain, isolated and alone, was readying itself for its "finest hour," only one power stood against Nazi, Fascist, and imperial Japanese designs to carve the whole world into the image of their dreams—the United States of America.

From the first overt act of aggression to the very "day of infamy," December 7, 1941, there was no clear consensus as to what course America should follow. The first impulse was to stay aloof from European troubles. A little more than a decade had elapsed from the end of the First World War—the war to end all wars—to the recrudescence of German imperialism under Hitler. Disillusionment resulting from America's previous intervention in Europe remained strong and unabated. But with each Nazi and Fascist thrust the American people became more aware of the deadly facts of Axis power. They watched the threat to democracy in mounting consternation and dread. As one crisis followed another, public opinion became unsure, divided, and confused. Instinctively a great majority turned to the historic principle of isolationism to immunize the nation from war. It had served well in the nineteenth century. Could it still be the basis for American foreign policy?

A great many thought that it could. Charles A. Beard, respected American historian, was their most articulate spokesman. This doctrine, wrote Beard, was "simple," "clear," and "definite."[1] But to others isolationism was a relic both negative and dangerous. To Robert E. Sherwood, noted playwright and Roosevelt's speech writer, it was unpatriotic. The ensuing debate, which became more acrimonious as one European state after another was either dismembered or extinguished, did not produce a clear division of views. Democrats turned against Democrats, Republicans against Republicans. Liberal and conservative views were crossed in this bewildering controversy. Ethnic loyalties became enmeshed with American loyalties, thereby losing for isolationism its simplicity, its very meaning, its good name. Indeed, "isolationist" became a "dirty word"—an opprobrious label shunned by the advocates of isolationism who, by 1940, chose to call themselves "nationalists," "continentalists," or "America Firsters."

By the time the Japanese ended the bitter debate with their attack on Pearl Harbor, isolationism already meant different things to different people. Gone was the original division between those who believed in collective security and those who rejected it as a violation of the American tradition against entangling alliances. The "hyphenated uproar" of the days of the First World War repeated itself during the Second World War. It involved the same groups, but they had become better organized and more experienced in the ways of American politics. With the re-emergence of ethnic nationalism, the historic maxim of isolationism was perverted to suit the hopes, desires, and hatreds of those Americans whose bonds with the lands of their origin were strengthened by the events in Europe. The ethnic version of isolationism was detrimental to the true meaning of traditional isolationism: "keeping Americanism unentangled with loyalties in Europe" and having a free hand and final word as to whenever or wherever America would be involved. Organizations like America First, which had been founded upon "chaste" isolationist principles and led by men of conservative and some liberal orientations, became a rallying point for pro-Nazi, pro-Fascist, and, particularly during the Nazi-Soviet "honeymoon" period, even Communist fanatics. America First afforded these groups the advantages of respectability, "American" arguments, protection, and opportunities to gain converts. Unable to rid itself of these elements, the America First movement lost stature in the eyes of the people and weakened its cause.[2] To many ethnic groups isolationism meant An-

111

glophobia and anti-communism. They were supported by pro-Nazi, pro-Franco, pro-Fascist, and anti-Semitic forces. Believing themselves to be defenders of the national interest, they called themselves American patriots—followers of Washington and Jefferson. Not so with some other ethnic groups which were fiercely anti-German; they were interventionists and internationalists. They too were vocal, but they could not compete with the former, who had little difficulty in identifying themselves as "true-blooded," "one hundred per cent" Americans. Both managed, though in different ways and with different goals, to implicate the national interest of the United States with that of the native lands.

The Axis declaration of war on the United States voided, in essence, all the neutrality laws with which the nation had hoped to fence out the conflict, but it did not end the emotional and sentimental allegiances of ethnic Americans to the sorrows or aspirations of their ancestral lands. "What to sophisticated ears only yesterday may have been an outworn phrase of I-Am-an-American-Day declamations," remarked *Fortune* in 1942, "has become again one of the fundamental facts of our national existence: we are a Nation of Nations."[3]

2

In November, 1934, the United German Societies of New York celebrated Annual German Day. This was their version of "I Am an American Day"—a tradition established during the First World War for the demonstration of loyalty and enthusiasm for their adopted country by ethnic Americans. In accordance with custom, Carl Nicolay, chairman of the day, asked President Roosevelt to send a message to be read at the festivities: ". . . We shall demonstrate to all the world, that first of all we are loyal, lawabiding and enthusiastic American Citizens, first and last, while at the same time proud of the heritage of our forefathers who have done so much to help in building up, in freeing, in keeping free and united this great Country of ours." The Western European Division of the State Department saw no reason not to honor the request and drafted a telegram for the President's signature. In reporting the reaction to the wire, Nicolay wrote: "The tremendous enthusiasm created thereby found a happy expression when the Chairman—upon concluding reading your Excellency's greetings and after the thunderous applause had somewhat subsided,—asked the assembly to rise while winding up his

112

address as follows: 'As racial unity to which we German Americans pledge ourselves anew with unshakeable faith, we reiterate our loyalty to the Flag and Constitution of America and its President, and here and now hail both Germany's peerless leader and America's great President.' "[4]

One year before, on October 2, 1933, the Steuben Society of America, having noted that the reaction to "certain features" of the new German regime was subjecting American-German relations to a "severe strain," informed President Roosevelt that it behooved the Society to take action conducive to their "protection and continuance." The Society's secretary, John Tjarks, explained that among its outstanding aims and purposes "is the promotion of friendly relations between the United States and the country of our forbears, Germany." He singled out the "propagation of a trade boycott" as "detrimental to the interests of the American people" and the Jews of Germany, "in whose interest the boycott is proclaimed." The German Jews, Tjarks informed the President, had repeatedly appealed to the world to refrain from actions unfriendly to Germany because they only inflamed "already highly wrought feelings." He added that during the 1919 revolution, when "thousands were killed in the German Civil War against Bolshevism," no country had felt constrained to intervene. The Society held firmly that "a return to normalcy in Germany" would be expedited when "threatened application of pressure and intervention" ceased to be voiced by official or unofficial spokesmen of public groups in America and elsewhere. Summing up his organization's position, Tjarks wrote:

We hold no brief for the "New Germany" . . . we are an American organization, interested in American institutions and American principles and . . . we do not consider it to be within the province of this or any other country to presume to prescribe to Germany what form of Government its people shall adopt. We do not deny to other groups in this country their right to express themselves, if they feel justified in doing so. But we emphatically deny their right to carry on a high pressure propaganda in this country for the purpose of stampeding it into actions which are contrary to the public welfare, and a menace to its peaceful relations between two friendly nations.[5]

Eight year later, on April 30, 1941, Theodore H. Hoffmann, national chairman of the Steuben Society, in a speech delivered over station

WHA in Milwaukee, claimed that the majority of thirty-two million German-Americans wanted to keep America out of the war. He defined the attitude of the society by saying, "Americans of Germanic extraction do not want Communism, Fascism or Nazism, and they do not want British imperialism. They want Americanism."[6]

The predilections of these two German-American organizations—one, pro-Nazi; the other, respectable and outwardly anti-Nazi—toward the vicissitudes in Germany illustrate not only the "tragedy" of German-Americans but of other ethnic groups also. Hitler and Mussolini used two distinct strategies in their attempts to subvert former nationals to their purposes. One was the exploitation of the emotional and cultural attachments of the assimilated majority of their emigrants and the descendants of the emigrants; the other was the utilization of a small minority of their emigrants who, unable to accommodate themselves to America, readily adopted the ideologies of Fascism and Nazism. The latter provided disciplined and well-organized "shock troops" to do the "dirty work"—to infiltrate the established and respected German- and Italian-American organizations and to enter into coalitions with subversive ethnic or nativist groups of similar orientation—and, if necessary, to distract attention from the former. While the first strategy took advantage of the natural sympathy for the welfare of *landsmen* and *paesani,* the other either overtly or covertly sought converts to Fascism and Nazism. According to Hermann Rauschning, Hitler said, in exposition: "It is a good idea to have at least two German societies in every country. One of them can always call attention to its loyalty to the country in question, and will have the function of fostering social and economic connections. The other may be radical and revolutionary."[7]

The strategies were successful. Beginning in 1922 and continuing well into the last days of the Second World War, Fascist and Nazi agents alienated large numbers of Americans of Italian and German heredity from their fellow Americans. Fascist activities in the United States followed soon after Mussolini's 1922 march on Rome. Nazi activities antedated Hitler's advent to power in 1933. Although the aims and operational methods were parallel, there were some significant differences. The first Fascist agents were prominent friends of Mussolini, whose propaganda was organized and financed by the Italian government. Their activities were coördinated with the proselytizing efforts of Italian consuls and diplomats who were ready to do everything, even to administer the Fascist oath to Italian-Americans.[8] An estimated task force of 25,000 specially trained followers of Mussolini pledged themselves to win to the cause of Fascism "five million" Italian-Americans, the bulk of whom had arrived at the turn of the century and were, Il Duce believed, not yet assimilated.

Where Fascist agents were bold and brazen, Nazi agents had to be discreet and timorous. Where Fascists sowed their seeds openly, Nazis had to sow secretly and sporadically. While Mussolini was convinced that the American melting pot had not had time to absorb the Italians, Hitler was "painfully" fearful that it was already too late for reclamation—the German-American, "cultural fertilizer" and old-timer in America, after "mating again and again with other races," had perhaps lost his "blood."[9] Mussolini chose his friend Count Ignazio Thaon di Revel, nephew of an Italian admiral, to head the Fascist League of America. When he arrived in the United States he neither changed his name nor hid his true purpose. Hitler dispatched Kurt Georg Wilhelm Lüdecke and Heinz Spanknöbel, obscure party members, to spread Nazi propaganda. Lüdecke posed as a traveling salesman, Spanknöbel as a clergyman. It was only after Hitler came into power that Nazi agents lost their timidity and shed their disguises. With the establishment of a Nazi government came efficient and consolidated operation: better men, more money, and central authority.

By the early 1930's the seeds of Nazism and Fascism were bearing fruit in America. The melting pot began to steam and crystallize anew. A "replica of explosive Europe" was built on American soil. Axis agents infiltrated respectable German- and Italian-American organizations, took over control of many well-established journals and newspapers, and exploited foreign-language radio broadcasts. Their campaign sought to inspire fanaticism and support for their regimes among the unassimilated minority of German- and Italian-Americans, and to decoy the assimilated but sentimental majority from Nazi and Fascist brutality by making it self-conscious, ethnocentric, apathetic toward national defense, and suspicious of European democracies. Which of these two groups was more detrimental to the American national interest? The first, despite sanctimonious espousals of loyalty to the United States, was overtly subversive. What of the second, whose loyalty seemed unfeigned? While political ties bound the unassimilated to Fascism and Nazism, social and cultural ties bound the assimilated to Italy and Germany. Both groups were useful to the two dictators. Both groups saw what American involvement in Europe would mean to the parent countries. The single word *isolationism* was the bond uniting many of the second group with the first in common enthusiasm and determination.

Neither Hitler nor Mussolini was satisfied with simply fostering American disunity through German- and Italian-American communities. Attempting to effect complete disunity, they encouraged and supported the anti-British feelings of the Irish-Americans and the isolationist tradition of the Swedish- and Norwegian-Americans. They affiliated their movements with those of other subversive groups, some of which they themselves had created. By late 1938 there were at least eight hundred organizations in the United States which "could be called pro-fascist or pro-Nazi."[10] To set capital against labor, white against Negro, Catholic against Protestant, Christian against Jew, they utilized the services of the Ku Klux Klan, the Coughlinites, the Knights of the White Camellia, the Crusader White Shirts, the Silvershirts, the Russian National Fascist Revolutionary Party, the Canadian Union of Fascists, the German-American Bund, the German-American Business League, the Italian-American Black Shirts, Latin American Falangists and Sinarquists, the Japanese-American Chamber of Commerce, the Ukrainian United Hetmans Organizations, and many others. By the time Mussolini invaded Ethiopia and Hitler marched into the Rhineland, their concerted effort to divide and conquer the American people had already engendered Fascist movements in the United States, had affected and complicated American neutrality policies, and most of all, had made many Americans of German and Italian origin think and vote as Germans and Italians. They had succeeded in dividing the American people, but not in conquering them.[11]

3

On the eve of the American Revolution an English emigrant, Thomas Paine, told the colonists that by separating themselves from Great Britain they would also separate themselves from its wars. "The conclusion was immediately irresistible," writes Samuel Flagg Bemis, and "laid the foundation" for the policy of isolationism.[12] More than a century and a half later, a leading Nazi lecturer, after extensive trips throughout the United States, prophesied the emergence of a "German Thomas Paine" who would separate the German-American from American wars—wars in which "the German element in America has always marched in the second rank." "One man will arise and gather them together—a German Thomas Paine. He will not found a new party or club or association but he will bring together all those who are of German blood into a natural community. They will all come to it as soon as they have become conscious of the simple truth that they are not 'Americans' but *'Amerikaner,'* people of German blood on American soil. They will drop the hyphen which has been hung upon them and will no longer call themselves 'German-Americans' but simply *'Amerikaner,'* which is an untranslatable word. . . ."[13] A "German Thomas Paine" did not materialize, but many German-Americans did become conscious of being *"Amerikaner"* and voted as such.

In 1933 a leaflet written by a German-American, "When Will Germany Receive a German-blooded Ambassador from America?" was widely distributed in Germany and among German-Americans. The author expressed dissatisfaction with President Roosevelt, who, "in spite of the fact that his overwhelming victory in the election could be ascribed to a great extent to German votes," gave "no important political appointments to German-Americans." He concluded: "It is Germany's task in the struggle for the recognition of the German-American in American political life to give the German who has emigrated to America a definite position in constitutional law which will strengthen his prestige in America. He should no longer be regarded by Germany as the cast-off scum of the nation, but he who has been born in Germany should remain a German citizen his whole life long regardless of the acquisition of foreign citizenship. . . ."[14]

The Nazi government did not regard German-Americans or any other Germans living abroad as "cast-off scum," but rather as objects of an all-out effort to "unite the German colonies abroad on a National Socialist basis." This was the task of three major organizations: the specially created *Auslands-Organisation der NSDAP* (AO) and two previously private institutions which were reorganized and used by the Nazis although ostensibly functioning independently, the *Volksbund für das Deutschtum im Ausland* (VDA) and the *Deutsches Ausland-Institut* (DAI). The aim of the AO was to have abroad trained agents who had "mastered" Nazi ideology and who would be able to "communicate it to other Germans." The aim of the VDA, *"in its broadest sense,"* as described by a district leader, was "the fulfilment of the meaning of German racial unity, the permeation of all

117

Germans with the racial idea; *the aim in the more restricted sense* is
. . . maintaining and protecting Germandom in all countries of the
earth, and especially by the cultivation of German cultural forms of
activity and expression." The DAI was probably the most important
instrument in the execution of the Nazi plan for the unification of
Germandom. Subsequent to its establishment in 1917, it had as-
sembled a comprehensive record of emigrants and their activities.
With a thoroughness typically Germanic, the institute maintained "a
card index file of the family history of Germans who have left the
Fatherland." It also disseminated propaganda abroad through various
kinds of publications and "periodical broadcasts transmitted to foreign Germans by the powerful short-wave stations of the Reich radio
system." In short, the institute was a "seismograph" which registered
"everything relating to the cause of 'Germanism.' "[15]

In *Mein Kampf* Hitler professed his disturbance over the effects
of emigration on Germany. He was distressed that in the future the
German people "would remain merely cultural fertilizer . . . despite
all our knowledge and ability, our blood nevertheless is destined to
decline." It was to be expected that once in a position to do so, he
would attempt to alter that course. Discussing the official program of
the NSDAP, which he wrote in 1927 on Hitler's order and which
was reviewed by Hitler, Gottfried Feder said: "The best, most capable, Vikinglike Germans are often those who went out into the wide
world as bearers of culture. . . . They belong to the great German
racial family *(Volksfamilie)*, which ought not to and dares not let
them be lost. These Germans ought no longer to be cultural *ferti-
lizers* but rather conscious outposts, champions of Germandom in
the world; they ought not to be 'apostles of humanity' but rather
bearers of the Nordic idea."[16] Was it too late to bring former German citizens and their descendants back into the fold? Was it too
late to change the "apostles of humanity" to apostles of the "Nordic
idea"?

The *Auslands-Organisation* and the *Volksbund für das Deutschtum im Ausland* thought not. Otto Schäfer, a VDA district leader,
wrote in a 1933 report on German-American immigrants that they
"would have possessed greater powers of resistance against America's
Anglo-Saxonism, if a strong German Government had . . . supported
them in their . . . maintenance and cultivation of Germanism. . . ."
The result was a loss of "20 million persons in the United States, to

the great detriment of Germany later." Gauleiter Ernst Wilhelm Bohle, head of the Nazi party's Foreign Organization, echoed Schäfer in believing that a strong German government would stay the acculturation of emigrants and also bring about their rejoining Germandom. He acknowledged in the 1934 *Almanach der natio-nalsozialistischen Revolution* "that Germans abroad are still in part cool to the movement because they do not know what they want," and added that their education in understanding Hitler's will had been made the "task of the group leaders abroad." Colin Ross showed concern over whether or not millions of German-Americans would recognize their decisive moment as *Amerikaner:* "I believe in 'America's German Hour'. I have no proof for it and I freely admit that the development of the German element in the United States would seem to indicate the opposite." He felt, nevertheless, that two circumstances supported his conviction that "German blood in the United States will once again play a creative and determinant role": "the German rebirth and the collapse of the old American idea."[17]

4

Early in 1941 a report entitled "Research Project on the Influence of Nationality Groups on Election Returns" was submitted to the President.[18] "Two preliminary investigations," wrote Louis Bean, statistical analyst in the Department of Agriculture and director of the project, "one a statistical analysis of the nationality factor in the 1940 election, the other an investigation of nationality propaganda carried on by the Nazi government in this country reveal that this country now faces the danger of nationality groups as factors in American politics." Anticipating Samuel Lubell's theory that the ethnic element was largely responsible for the foundation of mid-western isolationism,[19] Bean, after analyzing the election returns, was convinced that the "different reactions to political developments" constituted a "phenomenon which cannot be explained by . . . economic or historic factors." His study of the growth and development of the Democratic vote since 1932 showed "that while in 1936 the Democratic vote increased considerably throughout the Nation, it decreased in certain Middle Western States, in parts of Texas, and in certain districts of New York, New Jersey, and Pennsylvania." According to Bean, the tendency continued in the 1938 and 1940 elections "where in those same districts the Democratic vote decreased

119

even more than in the national average. A comparative statistical study . . . brought out a clear connection between the nationality groups in certain sections of the country and the vote in those sections."[20] In such states as Wisconsin, Minnesota, North Dakota, and in certain districts in New York, New Jersey, Connecticut, Texas, and Nebraska the "variation of the regional vote from the national average was proportionate to the strength" of German- and Italian-Americans there resident. Comparing the presidential election of 1940 with that of 1916, both of which occurred during European wars, Bean noted "similar regional variations from the national average."[21]

In addressing himself to the question of "how these German elements of the Nation were brought to vote as German groups rather than as individual American citizens," Bean came to the conclusion that the German government was "exceedingly successful" in in-

NEW JERSEY

	Change in Democratic percentage of two-party presidential vote between 1936 and 1940	German percent of total population
Salem	— .1	2.7
Burlington	— 2.6	4.8
Gloucester	— 3.1	6.2
Sussex	— 4.3	3.2
Cumberland	— 4.5	4.1
Camden	— 4.5	6.9
Mercer	— 4.6	6.1
Cape May	— 4.9	4.5
Morris	— 5.3	6.2
Somerset	— 5.3	6.7
Warren	— 6.1	4.6
Monmouth	— 6.2	5.6
Ocean	— 7.2	6.2
Atlantic	— 7.4	5.9
Union	— 7.4	9.3
Passaic	— 7.7	6.9
Essex	— 9.5	9.4
Hudson	—12.2	11.8
Bergen	—13.6	12.4
STATE	— 8.3	8.5

NORTH DAKOTA

Central and South Central Counties	Change in Democratic percentage of two-party presidential vote between 1936 and 1940	German and Russian-German percent of total population
Ward	—18	11
Foster	—17	13
Adams	—23	16
Burleigh	—30	21
Dickey	—22	24
Stutsman	—25	28
LaMoure	—21	29
McLean	—31	30
Sioux	—27	31
Wells	—35	31
McHenry	—31	32
Hettinger	—27	33
Kidder	—36	35
Pierce	—32	38
Dunn	—36	42
Stark	—39	43
Morton	—41	48
Grant	—48	52
Oliver	—50	53
Emmons	—46	56
Mercer	—48	58
Logan	—41	60
Sheridan	—40	61
McIntosh	—48	72

fluencing German-Americans to use "their vote in the interest of their former homeland without regard to the interests of the United States." Bean assessed the German-American press as "90 percent pro-Nazi, the Italian press 80 percent fascist." He also called attention to the various studies of German-Americans made for the Nazi government.[22]

In his memorandum Bean cautioned that should the political behavior of the German-Americans who voted not as Americans but as Germans "develop and spread to other nationality groups, this Nation cannot maintain its unity and will be split up into innumerable national or racial minority groups each feuding with the other

Influence of the German Population Factor
On the Presidential Elections, 1932-40

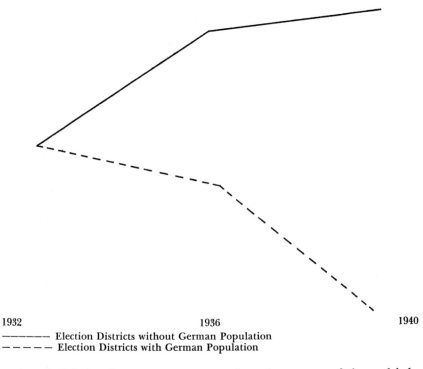

1932   1936   1940

——————— Election Districts without German Population
— — — — — Election Districts with German Population

and each fighting for supremacy over the other—none of them thinking of the American Nation as a unified whole and of the supreme
loyalty owed to it."[23]

Bean's warning was sound. It would have been equally or perhaps even more relevant had he pointed out to the President that
both Democrats and Republicans had been following the same practice—dividing and splitting the American electorate into numerous
nationality blocs. To be sure, Nazi and Fascist agents made German-
and Italian-Americans conscious of their origins. But that was true
also of the parties; each carried out extensive research to determine
ethnic electoral strength. Of course, there was an important difference. Hitler and Mussolini hoped to use the voting power of their
former nationals in the interest of their own national ambitions;
the American party strategists hoped to use it for victory on election
days. Nonetheless, the ethnic American was made aware not of his
Americanism, but his hyphenism and his foreign status. During
campaigns, whether in times of peace or war, American politicians

were after the German vote, the Italian vote, the Jewish vote, the Polish vote, and the many other ethnic votes. Nor were they fastidious about getting support from Fascist or Nazi elements, so long as the leaders could convince them of their ability to deliver the vote.

President Roosevelt knew, of course, about party activities in the ethnic arena. If he had any misgivings, he did not mention them. On the eve of the 1936 election, Representative A. J. Sabath, chairman of the Western Division, Nationalistic Groups, Democratic National Committee, told him, "The chairmen, directors, organizers, and executive committees of the twenty one nationalistic groups . . . have efficiently and loyally conducted a most strenuous campaign through the press, mail, pamphlets, and meetings covering nine and in some instances eleven states penetrating not only political organizations, but social and benevolent organizations."[24] During the campaign period Roosevelt was barraged with ethnic communications. Ernest L. Klein, president of the American Foreign Language Press Bureau, sent to the White House a copy of a letter to readers of German-language newspapers and members of German-American fraternal and social organizations and societies in Illinois which urged "support of Roosevelt on the basis of his recognition of German-Americans through his appointment" of George H. Dern as Secretary of War. Frank K. Waldherr, of the German American Voters League, advised the President that his organization had "organized a strong German Austrian Hungarian group of key men and are opening headquarters . . . to campaign for the German-Austrian-Hungarian vote." Erhard Mueller of Michigan told Roosevelt that he could "carry Pennsylvania if strong propaganda" in the German language were put out by the National Committee. James A. Farley informed the President of a request from Robert L. Soergel, editor of the *Akron Germania,* that Roosevelt send a "greeting message" for his paper's German Day edition, an "opportunity to make early propaganda for the reëlection." Perhaps the most calculating letter of all came from Jack Ingegnieros, president of the Federation of Italian American Democratic Organizations of the State of New York, who explained the necessity for United States recognition of Italy's annexation of Ethiopia in order to secure for the party the entire Italian-American vote.[25]

In preparation for the 1938 campaign the Foreign Language Citizens Committee of the Democratic National Committee set up twenty-six nationality divisions to work toward securing the ethnic vote. Among them were the Armenian, Chinese, Danish, Finnish, French, German, Greek, Italian, Polish, Puerto Rican, Jewish, Swedish, Scandinavian, Norwegian, and Yugoslavic. No ethnic group of any importance was overlooked. On February 15, 1937, the chairmen of the divisions visited with the President. The "delegate" of the Italian-Americans was Generoso Pope, owner of *Il Progresso Italo-Americano,* "the greatest Italian daily in the land," an admirer of Mussolini, "a power in Tammany Hall," and the successful pretender to deliver the Italian vote. The representative of the Croatian-American community was John D. Butkovich, who was to become a prime mover behind the American Slav Congress, a Communist-inspired front organization.[26]

By 1940 the attempts of foreign governments and the American parties to isolate immigrant Americans reached their peak. Indeed, many ethnic Americans became so conscious of their hyphenism that they felt slighted when important government officials omitted references to them in speeches. "Would appreciate your suggesting immediately to President Roosevelt," cabled the chairman of the Italian Democratic Committee of Pittsburgh to the Democratic National Committee, "that he make some favorable comment about the Italians and Germans in America in one of his radio broadcasts because mention of other nationalities . . . was received here as an intentional omission. We need the Italian and German vote for Roosevelt."[27] With the increased competition for the ethnic vote came heightened sensitivity on the part of ethnic Americans. Perhaps the most tragic example of this occurred on June 10, 1940, when President Roosevelt, at Charlottesville, Virginia, referred to the Italian attack on France as a "stab in the back." Italian-American reaction was so strong that it overshadowed the import of the address: the United States proposed to support Great Britain to the utmost short of war. One Italian-American wrote to Roosevelt that his address had brought sorrow to many. "In the United States where all nationalities are presented the public looks upon the President to lead them. It does not matter that we are born citizens of the new land, but if the name is German or Italian we are insulted. . . . We are part now of a divided nation: We know only one country and pledge allienge [*sic*] to one flag but the population does not believe us." In her remarks the writer captured the tragedy, shame, and confusion that befall those Americans whose hyphenism is reinforced by American politicians or by foreign governments, particularly when their native lands are pitted against the United States. She pleaded, ". . . think of us when you speak over the air. We are citizens, we salute only one flag and are peaceful. Nationalities have a strong tie on all the people, but sincerely know every man women and child born of Italian parantage will fight to defend our shores from any invader, but what are these people to do if the English and French are taking upon themselves to insult us." Her concluding sentences expressed a conception common among many Americans of foreign origin: "There is a strange problem here, other nations do not face; in Europe regardless on what side one lives the government is united and all the people are one by birth. In the United States all the people are citizens and the division only comes according to what side the President takes, for to the ignorant this gives strength to insult the other nationalities."[28]

While Italian-Americans worried over the effect the President's address might have on their rights and status, the politicians were primarily concerned with the effect on the Italian-American vote. "As you know," wrote a Congressional candidate to Democratic Chairman Edward J. Flynn, "the Italian-Americans are 'off the reservation' this year because of a feeling against the President because of his 'stab in the back' reference to Mussolini. This is a serious matter. . . . It is my understanding that Republican speakers are planning to use the . . . statement as a slogan in the Italian wards. . . . Democratic speakers seem to be at a loss. . . ."[29] Mark Bogart underlined the situation. "I believe," he informed the White House, "there is grave danger of his losing the State of New York. This conclusion is based upon the fact that most of the 'Italian' vote, and a good portion of the 'Irish' vote, for divers reasons, having swung over to Mr. Willkie. . . . It is almost impossible to convert the Italian people to support President Roosevelt." Luigi Antonini, general secretary of the Italian Dress and Waist Makers' Union of New York City, told the President's secretary, ". . . since June 10, 1940, a whispering campaign was conducted by fascist agents in the Italian communities of our Nation, with the evident intention to bismearch [sic] our President." Representative James Shanley of Connecticut thought the President "might be interested" in reactions to the Charlottesville speech. One Italian-American had told the Congressman that his people had been trying for years to live down an association with a stiletto or knife and felt they had been succeeding; though Roosevelt's anger was probably justified, his failure to state

125

emphatically that the words were not directed against Italian-Americans was deeply resented. Shanley added that a wave of sentiment in New England against Italians seemed "unjustified and inimical to the best interests of our nation." Roosevelt replied that none would regret more than he a public utterance of his that wounded the sensibilities of any loyal citizen or alien.[30]

Of particular interest was the reaction of Generoso Pope. Immediately following Roosevelt's Charlottesville appearance, according to an Italian News Service release, Pope "began to work on his Italian-American readers by making capital out of a deliberately fostered misunderstanding and a false line of reasoning with considerable appeal to the masses." He expounded the theory that the President and Italian-Americans in agreement with him "condemned not the present government of Italy but the entire Italian people." The real purpose of this and similar material in *Il Progresso Italo-Americano*, the Italian News Service held, was Pope's "desire to become known as the champion and defender of the Italian-American community with an eye to greater profit . . . and the acquisition of further honors from the government at Rome." In the 1940 campaign Pope played an ingenious dual role. Through his newspapers he, in the words of the Italian News Service, "assured the Italian-American vote to Willkie while cannily safeguarding his own personal and local Tammany interests by declaring himself a regular Democrat. . . ." Pope's apparent purpose was to make his readers look upon his party allegiance as "purely strategical and intended to allay the suspicions and play on the blind confidence of the party leaders."[31]

Pope's political agility did not escape the attention of Democratic national headquarters or the presidential staff. His conferences with the Republican candidate were duly noted. By overplaying his hand he became *persona non grata* in the White House. But not for long. Almost immediately after Pearl Harbor, Pope began seeking to "reestablish himself . . . and to gain recognition for himself and for his newspapers." His persistence led Presidential Aide William Hassett to ask the Office of War Information for a "summary of Pope's activities." In March, 1943, the O.W.I. supplied Hassett with not only a report on Pope's career but also background information on his staff, a photograph of Pope giving the Fascist salute, a photostatic copy of a letter from Il Duce to Pope, and a letter from the president of the Mazzini Society charging that "the Pope newspapers are among

126

the main channels through which Fascist propaganda is spread in the United States. . . ." The evidence was conclusive that Pope was the "self-appointed spokesman Number One for Italian Fascism."[32]

The White House continued to shun Pope until the 1944 campaign. In October, party Chairman Flynn began to press for his "reinstatement." Flynn, who had seen nothing wrong in Pope's being appointed a member of New York's Draft Appeal Board Number Six shortly after the 1940 election, wanted the President to shake hands with Pope in the interest of party victory. On October 9, Flynn phoned twice "to urge that the President let Generoso Pope come in just for a handshake and to be seen coming out of the White House. . . . This would have most beneficial effect on attitude of the Italians." Evidently believing in Pope's ability to deliver the Italian-American vote, Roosevelt consented. On October 12 (Columbus Day), Edwin Watson, secretary to the President, wired Pope, "The President hopes you can come down and see him for brief talk one day next week." The next day Pope replied, "Will be very happy to see the President. . . ."[33]

5

During the 1940 campaign both parties made overt appeals to Americans of foreign origin. The Democratic party, doubtful of its ability to stop the shift of the Italian- and German-American vote to Willkie, concentrated on other ethnic groups to counterbalance the anticipated loss. The Republican party, elated over the prospect of gaining strength from Italian- and German-Americans, openly welcomed them and other nationality groups as well in its ranks. Nor did the Nazi government remain inactive. Despairing over the failure to reap "great advantages from politically organizing a so-called German-American element," because of the ineptness and bungling of Nazi agents, particularly the German-American Bund leader Fritz Kuhn, the Nazis decided "to exert direct political influence" on the parties' national conventions.[34]

In the fall of 1939 the German Embassy in the United States had begun to formulate plans and procedures in regard to the Republican platform. The isolationist wing of the party was viewed as a key tool in the effort to keep the Americans out of the war. On the eve of the convention, Hans Thomsen, the German chargé d'affaires in the United States, informed his government:

There will . . . be violent discussions at the Republican Convention in Philadelphia on June 24 concerning the wording of the Republican foreign policy electoral platform. The rapidly thinning ranks of the isolationists among the Republicans, as seen for instance in the change of course in foreign policy by the presidential candidate Senator Vandenberg . . . must be supported in their struggle in Philadelphia. To this end a well-camouflaged lightning propaganda campaign might well prove useful, for which there are the following possibilities where German influence would in no case be visible to the outside:

1) A well-known Republican Congressman who works in close collaboration with the special official for press affairs will invite some 50 isolationist Republican Congressmen on a 3-day visit to the party convention, so that they may work on the delegates of the Republican party in favor of an isolationist foreign policy. 3,000 (three thousand) dollars are required.

2) In addition the Republican in question is prepared to form a small ad hoc Republican Committee which, as a counterblast to the full-page advertisement by the White Committee [The Committee to Defend America by Aiding the Allies, under the chairmanship of William Allen White], "Stop Hitler Now[,]" would, during the party convention, publish in all the leading American newspapers a full-page advertisement with the impressive appeal "Keep America out of War."

The cost of this would be about 60,000 to 80,000 (sixty to eighty thousand) dollars, of which half will, in all probability, be borne by his Republican friends.[35]

On June 19, Thomsen wired further details to his government:

An effective and particularly favorable opportunity . . . presents itself in connection with the Republican Party Convention . . . and the election organizers [*Wahlleitung*] with whom I am in constant touch. . . . Some 50 Congressmen will be going to Philadelphia to explain our views to the delegates. . . .

. . . It will be particularly effective if American politicians themselves provide enlightenment regarding our political aims and the mistakes of Roosevelt's foreign policy. The special representative for press matters is therefore keeping in close touch with several Senators and Congressmen in order that their speeches may receive the widest publicity. . . . These speeches, whose aim is to prevent America's entry into the war . . . will be printed each time in . . . the *Congressional Record* by these Senators and Congressmen, and then an edition of 50,000 to 1 million copies will be sent by them to specially chosen persons. In this manner German influence is not visible to the outside, and thanks to the privilege of free

128

postage enjoyed by American Congressmen, the cost of this large-scale propaganda can be kept disproportionately low. . . . Up to the present nearly a dozen such operations have been or will be carried out during the Republican party convention.[36]

After it had become evident during the convention that Willkie, who was "ready and determined to extend to the English every possible aid short of active military assistance," would be nominated, the isolationist wing of the Republican party succeeded in "anchoring" the platform's foreign-policy plank to two "most important" principles, according to Thomsen:

"1. The Republican party is firmly opposed to involving this nation in a foreign war.

"2. The Republican party stands for Americanism, preparedness, and peace."[37]

The German chargé d'affaires took credit for the maneuver:

"This success of the isolationist Republicans in the field of foreign policy was made possible in part by the promotion campaign authorized by telegraphic instruction No. 666, of June 17. This fact is reflected, for instance, by the circumstance that the above-quoted principles of the Republican platform on foreign policy were taken almost verbatim from the conspicuous full-page advertisements in the American press (e.g., the *New York Times,* June 25, p. 19), which were published upon our instigation."[38]

In September, 1939, Thomsen had cautioned his government that Nazi agents should "avoid anything that could be interpreted . . . as a backing of the isolationists and German interference in America's day-to-day politics," advising further,

. . . we should operate only with the following historical arguments in this contest of opinions over the ways of preventing America's entry into the war: The senseless and useless sacrifice of lives and national wealth in the World War; the vast burden of public debt due to participation in the war; the economic disintegration in the post-war period; the munitions industry as a war profiteer; Britain's cynical role as a debtor; Britain's outrageous chicanery with regard to American trade and shipping; Britain's double-dealing in 1916 (concealment of secret treaties); the results of the lying slogan "make the world safe for democracy"; America's refusal to ratify the Versailles Treaty.[39]

Perhaps by coincidence the platform of the following year listed many of the same arguments in the "contest of opinions over the ways of preventing America's entry into the war." It read, in part:

"The Republican Party is firmly opposed to involving this Nation in foreign war.

"We are still suffering from the ill effects of the last World War: a war which cost us a twenty-four billion dollar increase in our national debt, billions of uncollectible foreign debts, and the complete upset of our economic system, in addition to the loss of human life and irreparable damage to the health of thousands of our boys. . . .

"The Republican Party stands for Americanism, preparedness and peace."[40]

Certain that he had influenced the Republican platform, Thomsen set his sights on the Democratic Convention. On July 19, he reported to his superiors:

> . . . isolationist Republican Congressmen at the Republican Convention succeeded in affixing firmly to the party platform the language of an isolationist foreign policy. . . . Nothing has leaked out about the assistance we rendered in this.
>
> It seemed advisable therefore to undertake similar action during the Democratic Convention in Chicago. The special officer for press relations has seen to it that several reliable isolationist Congressmen went to Chicago in order to exert influence on the delegates with the purpose of including, at least formally, in the Democratic platform as well, a pledge of nonparticipation in a European war. . . .
>
> In addition to other means, the Congressmen used for the purpose the tried and proved promotion aid [*Propeller-Hilfsmittel*] on a sensational advertisement in the leading Chicago newspaper. Accordingly, there appeared in the *Chicago Tribune* on the 15th, the opening day of the Convention, an effective full-page advertisement similar to that in the *New York Times* of June 25. . . . For travel assistance and cost of the advertisements $4,350 have been disbursed. . . .[41]

Although Thomsen described the manner in which this was accomplished in a separate despatch which was not found, several other documents provide, perhaps, a clue. On May 4, Under Secretary of State Sumner Welles refused to comment on a report that W. R. Davis, who had "made a number of oil arrangements for the Mexican Government," had given "$250,000 to the Democratic party, divided between the National Committee and an organization in Pennsylvania." On July 5, the German Legation in Mexico was asked by the Foreign Ministry to supply an explanation. The Legation replied on July 8:

"In February 1940, D[avis] acting through Walter A. Jones paid about 160,000 dollars to the representative of the Pennsylvania Democratic organization for the purpose of

1. promoting the candidature of [group garbled] in opposition to the anti-German Senator Guffey;

2. buying the approximately 40 Pennsylvania delegates to vote against Roosevelt at the party convention. . . .

Welles' reserve is to be explained on the grounds that D[avis] now is representing a power that must be reckoned with even by the Government."[42]

Nazi and Fascist attempts to interfere in American politics did not end with conventions. During the 1940 campaign, thousands of copies of books and other pieces of propaganda literature attacking Roosevelt and preparedness policies were distributed. Efforts to divide and confuse the Americans continued until the Japanese attack on Pearl Harbor. After December 7, 1941, though overt Axis machinations ceased, the political parties continued to roil the ethnic waters in the interest of party victories.

Chapter VIII

THE SECOND WORLD WAR:
THE HYPHENATE CHALLENGE TO
AMERICAN UNITY

War came to the American people on December 7, 1941. The undeclared war on the United States by Japan was soon followed by declarations of war by Germany, Italy, Slovakia, Hungary, Bulgaria, Croatia, and Rumania. The war united Americans in a common determination to defeat their enemies in the Far East, Asia, Africa, and Europe. In no way, however, did this solidarity of purpose resolve the deep perplexities, torn emotions, shaken morale, and almost instinctive fears of the foreign-born citizens of the United States. For too many years before the war they had listened to ancestral voices and allowed misguided or unscrupulous American politicians, ethnic leaders, and foreign governments to accentuate their hyphenism. For this surrender to a mistaken conception of American citizenship, they now paid a heavy price.

"There is dynamite on our shores," warned *Fortune* in 1942, "and we should explode it in the right direction." The editors of *Fortune* recognized three basic patterns of behavior among American ethnic groups: "unqualified support of the war" by such nationalities as Norwegians and Czechs; "support, but with elements of confused reluctance" by Poles and Slovaks; "submission, with traces of subversive defiance" by Germans and Italians. The overwhelming majorities of immigrant groups, according to this national magazine, were "motivated partly by sincere allegiance to the U.S., partly by their petrified nationalisms from over there." Noting the presence of a "replica of explosive Europe" on American soil, *Fortune* asked whether the United States could "transform it into a working model of political warfare."[1]

Several months before the attack on Pearl Harbor, the government had initiated various programs to avert a unity-destroying explosion of the ethnic "dynamite." At least a dozen departments or agencies had been given special assignments on aspects of the problem. The Office of Strategic Services and the Department of Justice—through the Alien Registration Section—scrutinized, compiled data on, and prepared analyses of nationality organizations, the foreign-language press, and the ethnic population. The studies of political orientations within nationality groups, editorial policies of their major newspapers, and their relative numerical strength were made available to other departments and agencies. The National Youth Administration, in its defense training programs, attempted to alleviate discrimination in the training or employment of the foreign-born. The Office of Education prepared radio scripts, entitled "Americans All—Immigrants All," which were widely broadcast. Similar efforts were made by the Immigration and Naturalization Section of the Department of Justice and the adult education units of the Works Progress Administration—they furnished scripts of "I'm an American" in both English and foreign languages, produced movies, and wrote special textbooks for the foreign-born. The Departments of Agriculture, Commerce, Interior, and Labor, the Federal Works Agency, the Library of Congress, and other federal units worked in other troublesome ethnic areas. The Department of State, within a few days after the beginning of the war, supplied lists which classified the American ethnic population as loyal or disloyal, while the Army prepared to evacuate Japanese-American communities from the West Coast to camps in the interior.[2] But, as Harold Hoskins pointed out in March, 1942, ". . . no one governmental agency has been given the responsibility of heading up a constructive, nationwide program" for immigrant groups. Because of the importance of the problem, he believed this incredible.[3] The very fact that the government doubted the loyalty of some ethnic groups and felt it imperative to keep a watchful eye on all Americans of foreign origin gave ample proof of the tragedy of the immigrant American and his descendants—an inability to withstand the guile of foreign and native politicians who strove continuously to enslave him to his hyphen.

On December 10, 1941, the Department of State, recognizing a complication to the ethnic problem in attempts by exiled leaders to set up "free movements" among their former countrymen in America, was obliged "to make clear the attitude" of the government. In carefully chosen words, it pointed out that "in general the Government of the United States does not favor 'free movements' " and "disapproves of any attempt to enlist the support of American citizens of like racial background on the theory that they are 'fellow nationals. . . .' " Nevertheless, in "cognizance of the existence of a number of committees representing free movements," they would be allowed to organize so long as they abided by the laws of the United States. Permission to organize, however, the Department of State added, was not to be construed as endorsement by the government of aims, boundary claims, or specific leaders. The statement read, in part: "The United States in composed of citizens from many national backgrounds. Despite a natural interest in their country of origin, all American citizens of whatever background owe, and have, an undivided allegiance to the United States. . . . The Government of the United States does not look with favor on any activities designed to divide the allegiance of any group of American residents between the United States and any foreign government, in existence or in prospect. The first concern of the United States must always be the unity of the country. . . ."[4]

By 1943, according to the Office of Strategic Services, there were 215 leading organizations of foreign political import in the United States, not including many small local or state societies: Albanian, 2; Arab, 7; Armenian, 4; Austrian, 8; Basque, 3; Belgian, 2; Bulgarian, 5; Carpatho-Russian, 14; Czechoslovakian, 18; Danish, 4; Estonian, 3; Finnish, 12; French, 3; German, 20; Greek, 17; Hungarian, 10; Italian, 20; Latvian, 3; Lithuanian, 10; Norwegian, 4; Polish, 13; Portuguese, 4; Rumanian, 4; Russian, 7; Spanish, 6; Swedish, 2; Ukrainian, 10; and Yugoslav (Slovene, Croat, and Serb), 13.

These ethnic organizations mirrored ideological differences brought over by leaders in exile from the parent countries and also differences within the American leadership. Some examples illustrative of these intra-group varieties are these obtaining in 1943. In the Albanian-American community there was one "Republican" organization (Free Albania) which strongly opposed the restoration of King Zog's regime and one monarchist (Vatra—Pan-Albanian Federation of America) which acknowledged his claim. Armenian-Americans were asked to support the liberal Armenian Democratic Liberal Union, or the violently nationalistic anti-Soviet Armenian Revolutionary Federation of America, which was a branch of the Armenian Tashnag party, or the pro-Communist Armenian Progressive League of America, as well as the supposedly non-political Armenian General Benevolent Union, which the Armenian Democratic Liberal Union attempted to control. Austrian-Americans were split between the supporters of socialism (Assembly for a Democratic Austrian Republic), the advocates of restoration of the monarchy (Free Austria Movement and Austrian National Committee), and those favoring *Anschluss* with Germany (Austrian Labor Com-

134

mittee). In the Bulgarian-American community there were socialist organizations (Bulgarian Socialist Labor Federation of America), Communist roof organizations (Federation of Bulgarian-Macedonian Educational Clubs), nationalistic organizations (Macedonian Political Organization of the United States and Canada) which advocated the "liberation" of Macedonia from Bulgaria and approved of King Boris' collaboration with the Axis. Among the many Carpatho-Russian organizations there were Communists (American Carpatho-Russian Congress and the Carpatho-Russian National Committee) and anti-Communists (League for the Liberation of all Russians in Galicia and Carpatho-Russia). Czech-Americans were divided between the Czech-American National Alliance which supported Eduard Beneš' exile Czechoslovak government, the all-inclusive Czechoslovak National Council of America, and the Slovak League of America which opposed the Beneš government. German-Americans were asked to choose from twenty organizations: some of these were pro-Nazi (German American National Alliance, German Day Association, and German-American Citizens League);[5] some were anti-Nazi (German-American Anti-Nazi League); some were pro-Communist (German-American League for Culture); some were created specifically to unify German-Americans behind the American war effort (Loyal Americans of German Descent); and some were critical of America's prosecution of the war (the isolationist and traditionally pro-German roof organization, the Steuben Society of America).[6]

Soon after hostilities began, the government became concerned over the disruptive effect of the foreign-language press which closely paralleled that of the ethnic organizations. In 1943 the Office of Strategic Services listed 250 "leading publications of foreign political import." Several months before America's entry into the war, President Roosevelt had been urged to authorize the Department of Justice to devote "real attention to the foreign language press in a definite, organized way and as soon as possible."[7] Before Pearl Harbor, the German- and Italian-American press, which had over six and one-half million readers, exhibited various degrees of partisanship ranging from a violent pro-Nazism and pro-Fascism to a well-calculated detachment. Although openly pro-Axis and anti-Axis papers were few—about two dozen, according to *Fortune*—a real problem was presented by the established and influential publications. The great majority of these was pro-German and pro-Italian; some were more cautious, some more diplomatic, some avoided overt Nazi and Fascist

135

propaganda, but all were definitely partial to the interests of their fatherlands. With the advent of war, many of the publications which had previously favored the New Order became noncommittal, perhaps in expectation of government censure. Indeed, after Roosevelt's "stab in the back" speech of June 10, 1940, the entire Italian-American press broke out in a rash of statements of loyalty to the United States. As weeks passed with no government interference or molestation, the editors regained their confidence. The German-American press took advantage of isolationist sentiment and attacked Roosevelt as a "second Wilson," blasted interventionists as traitors to the "beloved memory of George Washington," and heaped scorn on the "anglophile capitalists" who wished to bring America into the war on England's side. The Italian press was less cautious. Generoso Pope, publisher of *Il Progresso Italo-Americano,* the biggest Italian daily, and the other Italian papers, thought that it was "ridiculous for Italo-Americans to give 'special pledges of loyalty.' " Pope had his staff write editorials in English praising Americanism and editorials in Italian praising the glory of Mussolini.

After Pearl Harbor many of the pro-German and pro-Nazi papers became more circumspect. German-American publications such as the Chicago *Abendpost,* Winona (Minnesota) *America-Herold und Lincoln Freie Presse, Rochester Daily Abendpost,* and *Detroiter Abend-Post und Familienblätter* were "cautiously pro-German" and "critical of the Administration and of America's chief Allies." The pro-Fascist Italian-American press, which until America's entry into the war had praised Mussolini, began to promote "devotion to the cause of liberty." This sudden change in editorial policy, observed *Fortune,* may have weakened rather than strengthened the average Italian-American's support for the American way of life. "Long infected by a completely cynical interpretation of democratic processes, he may easily take our toleration, and even support, of such quick-change artist tricks for an admission that his disregard was justified."[8]

Among the ethnic communities whose homelands were either conquered or threatened by Hitler and Mussolini, the foreign-language press was also active. Here the publications mirrored ideological, social, and religious differences within each ethnic group. To cite some examples, the Hungarian-American press included the pro-Fascist weekly *Otthon (American Home);* the clerical, ultra-nationalist, anti-Communist, and pro-Naxi *A Jo Pasztor (The Good Shepherd); A Mi Lapunk (Our Paper);* the pro-Horthy, pro-Habsburg, and anti-Semitic *Magyar Jovo (Hungarian Future)*; the anti-Fascist, anti-Horthy, and anti-Nazi *Amerikai Magyar Nepszava (American-Hungarian People's Voice)*. Similarly, the Russian-American press offered a varied fare: anti-Soviet and pro-Nazi papers like *Rossiya (Russia)*; the traditionally anti-Soviet *Novoye Russkoye Slovo (New Russian World)* and *Russkaya Zhizn (Russian Life)*, which after the Nazi attack on Russia began to endorse the Soviet prosecution of the war and modified its anti-Soviet slant; the openly pro-Communist *Russky Golos (Russian Voice)*; and many more. Nazi and Fascist sheets also turned up among the Bulgarian Croats, Slovaks, Ukrainians, and some others. The Polish-American press was divided between the pro-exiled Sikorski government *Dziennik Chicagoski (Chicago Daily)* and *Dziennik Dla Wszystkich (Everybody's Daily)*; the anti-Sikorski *Dziennik Polski (Polish Daily)* and *Nowy Swiat (New World)*; the pro-Communist *Glos Ludowy (People's Voice)*; the conservative *Narod Polski (Polish People)* and a more liberal *Nowiny Polskie (Polish News)*; the militantly anti-Pilsudski, pro-Sikorski *Przewodnik Katolicki (Catholic Leader)*; the socialist-oriented *Robotnik Polski (Polish Worker)*; and numerous others.[9]

2

The American government was deeply concerned over the effect of ethnic loyalties on the country's unity and morale. This anxiety led to unfortunate and, often unjustified, suspicions and restrictions of aliens and naturalized citizens. The continuous surveillance made ethnic Americans aware of their inferior status and second-class citizenship. While the government was distressed and worried, the American parties remained aloof and detached. While the government imposed alien registration laws and enemy alien laws and inaugurated plans to adjust, accommodate, and reconcile the ancestral emotions of the immigrant to the land of his adoption, the parties, in their never-ending hunt for the ethnic vote, continued to excite, stimulate, provoke, and estrange him from his fellow-Americans.

Within a few days after the 1940 election, the Democratic National Committee was heartened by analyses of "activities" among the non-German and non-Italian ethnic groups. On the basis of election results in wards populated by a majority of Polish-Americans, the committee was certain that the concentrated campaign to win the Polish-American vote had been successful.[10] Preparing for the 1942 Congressional campaigns, the Democratic party became apprehensive over the Polish vote. A "Memorandum on Poles in Chicago" told White House staff members that Polish-Americans were growing cooler toward the President and the New Deal, some of the reasons being these: Roosevelt's failure to encourage the Red Cross to send relief to "several hundred thousand Poles" in Siberia; his failure to acknowledge two letters from a prominent Polish-American, a "Republican who voted for the President"; and his failure to include the Poles, "who therefore felt slighted," in a speech urging American pilots to join with the British and Chinese. The result of these "sins of omission," according to the memorandum, was increased isolationism and sympathy with many of the policies of the *Chicago Tribune*—"an entirely new situation among the 700,000 Poles of the Chicago area."[11]

"Isolationism is not dead," reported the secretary of the Democratic National Committee to Roosevelt in December, 1942. From answers to letters sent after the 1942 election to each Democratic Congressional candidate, Democratic strategists learned that in the Midwest, with the exception of districts dominated by the "Polish-Slav vote," isolationism was "as strong as ever." A substantial number of the replies revealed the "presence of Isolationists who were afraid to speak openly but who voted their convictions." The secretary reëmphasized that "the principal alien-tie-isolationist group" was located in the central states, particularly Illinois, adding that "every letter complained" of large opposition votes from German- and Swedish-American groups.[12]

It was not, however, until the 1944 presidential campaign that the fear of losing the Polish and other ethnic votes became really strong to the Democrats. From early 1943 until Election Day in 1944, reports indicating dissatisfaction and possible revolt among Polish-Americans and other nationality groups arrived in ever-increasing numbers at the White House and party headquarters. In February, 1943, George Zator, president of the Pulaski League of Queens County, wrote the President that "politically eighty (80%)" of Polish-Americans who "literally" worshipped his name had been and still were members of the Democratic party even though the administration treated them as though they were "political undesirables." Zator wanted to know why no Polish-Americans were appointed to government positions. In August an irate Polish-American doctor asked the President to answer twenty-five questions of great interest to Polish-Americans. These ranged from a request for names of "men of Polish extraction" in the Cabinet, foreign service, and officer ranks of the Navy and Army to how many men and women of Polish descent died in the war; and on to what he or Churchill had done "to prevent the invasion and rape of Poland" and what, if anything, they were doing currently for Poland. The defiant conclusion asked of Roosevelt if he knew the "strength of the Polish vote" which "can elect or defeat any candidate for any office," and warned that the Polish-Americans would not "waste their vote." Another Polish-American, writing "as an individual," asked the President "to offset this trend and to choke off" charges against him by making "one brief statement about Poland and clear up this tremendous web of uncertainty that hangs like a pall of smoke over Polish-Americans"; this, he felt, "would be a big factor in deciding Polish votes this fall."[13]

The Democratic party became particularly apprehensive when Charles Rozmarek, president of the Polish American Congress (organized in May, 1944, which claimed to represent "six million Americans of Polish descent"), showed an interest in Thomas E. Dewey, the Republican presidential candidate. The interest was evinced at the same time the Republican party decided to make a determined bid for the support of ethnic groups. The Republican challenge had to be met. "It is imperative," the White House was informed, "that the President's address to the Foreign Affairs Assn. answer Dewey's 'straddling' on appeal to hyphenated American voters. Polish, Italian, and others place their homelands above America and the situation must be explained to them."[14] The Foreign Language Division of the National Citizens Political Action Committee asked Stephen Early to supply it with "as many as possible past statements, addresses, speeches, and writings of the President" in which reference was made to Polish-Americans and to Poland. The use of such material, wrote Celia Heller of the Polish Group, "would increase our effectiveness in the campaign among Polish Americans. . . ."[15] From the publicity director of the Democratic National Committee and from individual Polish-Americans, Roosevelt received letters, copies of campaign material, and tear sheets from Polish-American newspapers which indicated "the type of vicious and scurrilous campaign that the Republicans are indulging in to swing the Polish vote. . . ."[16] In October three lengthy documents concerning enemy radio broadcasts endorsing Dewey were sent to the White House. In an obvious attempt to confuse the hyphenates in America, enemy announcers, according to these documents, stressed themes derived from Dewey's speeches—

139

"the betrayal of Poland, the Romanian Armistice, the Morgenthau Plan, etc."[17]

By the middle of October, Democratic strategists were able to persuade the President to take positive action to win what they believed to be the wavering ethnic vote. On October 11 (Pulaski Day), Roosevelt received a "Memorial of the Polish American Congress" from Rozmarek and other prominent Polish-American leaders;[18] on October 12, Roosevelt overcame his distaste for Generoso Pope and shook hands with him[19]—all in the interest of party victory.

Future historians may find that attempts to use the Polish-American vote in the interest of Poland may have harmed more than helped the President in the deliberations over Poland's future status. The very threat to withhold or deliver the Polish-American vote may have modified the question of Poland itself to that of the appeasement of Polish-American leaders, whose main interest, as far as American politicians were concerned, was either to increase their power and hold over Polish-Americans or to obtain prominent positions in government. It is doubtful that Roosevelt read carefully the memorandum of the Polish American Congress which recommended various policies to insure the freedom and independence of Poland at the end of the war. Ethnic leaders like Rozmarek and others were too closely identified with ethnic politics. Their interest in Poland, rightly or wrongly, was suspect. None had bona fide access to the White House. It might have been far otherwise had these ethnic leaders been willing or able to allow recognized Polish intellectuals, untainted by ethnic politics, to present their views to the President or the Department of State. By drawing on their prestige as artists, scholars, or scientists and not on their ostensible ability to deliver the Polish vote, they would have been more effective in influencing American policies.

The publicized interest of the President in the Polish question aroused the sensitivities of other ethnic groups. "It is also important that Roosevelt speak about the smaller nations and minority groups," advised E. Klein. He told the President that the Republicans had "carried on a very vicious and effective campaign" among all foreign-born citizens, adding, "I have never seen such well organized and effective campaign in the foreign language field." From a correspondent in Minnesota Roosevelt learned that Finnish-Americans were showing signs of disappointment. The president of the Ukrainian Congress of America warned him that the Memorial Committee of the Polish American Congress which had met with him on October 11 had failed to inform him that the "preponderant majority of the population involved in the Soviet-Polish border dispute is neither Polish nor Russian, but purely Ukrainian." The president of Free Albania censured Roosevelt for not mentioning Albania in his speeches. The chairman of the Lithuanian Committee to Re-elect Roosevelt warned him of a small group of Lithuanian-Americans who call "themselves 100% Americans, but whose main objective is to undermine unity of the democratic way of life" and asserted that Dewey was being "made a Catholic in the eyes of the Lithuanian Roman Catholics." A German-born citizen, having noted a "strong tendency" of German-Americans to vote Republican, asked Roosevelt to address German-Americans, drawing a distinction "between doctrine of national-socialism and the true German."[20]

Thus, throughout the war, while the government of the United States attempted to unite ethnic Americans behind the war effort, the American parties in their appeals for the ethnic vote encouraged a large segment of the electorate to divide itself into competing units, each concerned with the future of its native land—concerns which may or may not have been in the true interest of the United States.

Part III

THE COLD WAR AND THE HYPHENATE CONSENSUS

Chapter IX

THE ELECTION OF 1948

The year 1948 was a presidential election year. Only three years had passed since the United States and its allies had defeated their enemies—Nazi Germany, Fascist Italy, and the empire of Japan. The war had been won. The victory was total. But there was no return to normalcy.

Unlike the aftermath of the First World War, the American people were united in their support of the war-born world organization. In San Francisco on the eve of victory, the Allies, with majestic solemnity, had dedicated themselves to the idea of collective security. The League of Nations, which had died in the 1930's, was resurrected and re-formed into the more potent, more energetic, and more salutary United Nations. Soon after this high resolve to bring peace to the war-torn and war-weary people of the world, Soviet Russia, which had poured its armies into the vacuum created by the collapse of Germany and Japan, began to threaten the peripheral areas of the free world. The sustained challenge of Russia and Communism reinforced and confirmed the revolution in American foreign policy which had begun with the many commitments made by the government during the war years. The traditional American principle of non-involvement in European affairs was pronounced dead. In its place was the principle of world-coöperation and involvement in the affairs of all nations—old, new, and yet to be born. The reversal was overwhelming. The energy of the American people, which throughout most of their history had been directed toward keeping the New World distinct and separate from the Old, was now unleashed with more prodigious zeal to bind America's destiny and its future with the hopes and fears of the peoples of Europe, Asia, and Africa.

Before the election year the Cold War was already deeply rooted. The Democratic party could take credit for winning the Second World War, but what of the peace that did not ensue? To be sure, the American people supported their new President, who had assumed the guidance of the mourning nation after Franklin D. Roosevelt's death. Most applauded the Truman Doctrine, the Marshall Plan, the policy of containment of Russia, and the bipartisan Vandenberg Resolution which had laid the foundation for a system of defensive alliances within the United Nations and was soon to give birth to its most celebrated offspring—NATO (North Atlantic Treaty Organization). Their unity of purpose against Soviet ambition augured well for taking the Cold War out of the presidential campaign of 1948. This aim was not to be achieved.

From the time of Harry S. Truman's nomination in Philadelphia to the counting of the last ballots in the early morning of the day following election, few believed the Democratic party would rewin the Presidency. The Democratic administration which had come into being in 1933 seemed about to end in 1948. Pollsters, political prognosticators and commentators, and many Democratic party chieftains were sure that Truman would lose. Governor Thomas E. Dewey, the Republican nominee, was confident. Only Truman, apparently, retained unbounded faith in himself and in his party.

The Democratic party entered the contest with both right and left wings severed from the main body. Large segments of liberals announced their support of former Vice President Henry A. Wallace, presidential candidate of the new Progressive party, who believed that Truman's "tough policy" toward Soviet Russia would lead to war. The "solid South," discontented with Truman's stand on civil rights, banded into the "true Democratic party"—the Dixiecrats— under the leadership of J. Strom Thurmond.[1] Within the main body of the party there were also many dissatisfied and restive elements. Of these, and most important, in the opinion of the Democratic National Committee, were the foreign-language groups. German-Americans and, to a lesser extent, Italian-Americans had been "alienated as a result of two world wars," and were ready to avenge themselves against the party. Scandinavian-Americans remained strongly Republican. Jewish-Americans, Democratic strategists believed, were upset over the Roosevelt-Ibn Saud talks which had followed the Yalta conference and were generally unhappy over the "lack of forcefulness" by the Democratic leadership regarding Israel. Polish and other Slavic-Americans were bitter over the Yalta and Potsdam decisions which they thought had set the stage for Communist control of Eastern and Central Europe. The gloom in the Democratic party was understandable; the enthusiasm and jubilation in the Republican party equally so.

The Cold War produced a consensus among the majority of hyphenated and non-hyphenated Americans. Leaders of both parties dedicated themselves to a policy of coöperation with and aid for all nations threatened by Communist expansion; isolationism was not going to be an issue weakening American unity. The trend toward bipartisanship in foreign policy which had begun even before the San Francisco Conference and culminated in the Vandenberg Resolution was not welcomed by all ethnic leaders. True bipartisanship would make bargaining with one or the other party difficult, if not impossible. More than that, it promised to take issues which affected the fate of East Central Europe and Asia, such as the Yalta and Potsdam Agreements, out of the political campaigns.

One of the first foreshadowings of the effect of bipartisanship on the aims and objectives of nationality groups appeared in a letter of March 7, 1945, from Senator Arthur H. Vandenberg, who had been a critic of Roosevelt but had become a champion of bipartisanship, to Frank Januszewski, owner of the Detroit *Polish Daily News*, with whom Vandenberg often conferred on Polish matters:

I have not altered my view respecting Poland—both for her own precious sake and as a "symbol." I could get no greater personal satisfaction out of anything more than from joining—aye, in leading—a public denunciation of Yalta and all its works as respects Poland. But we *must* ask ourselves whether this is the best service I can render in recapturing some elements of justice for Poland—not merely for Poland's sake but also and particularly for a permanent World Peace which can never survive injustice. . . . we must deal with the realities. . . . The Yalta decisions enjoy . . . President Roosevelt's stamp of approval. . . . Also [they] bear Churchill's stamp of approval. . . .

A year later, in July, 1946, Januszewski sent Vandenberg an article published in his paper, which attacked Vandenberg's "role in the postwar negotiation regarding Poland," and asked him to comment on the "attitude of 350,000 voters of Polish descent who were angry about the postwar fate of Poland." The Senator replied:

I dislike to pursue this discussion, lest it might seem that I am pleading for votes. I do not care to be further misunderstood or misrepresented. The votes are of no personal consequence to me because the outcome of my personal campaign is a matter of substantial indifference to me. . . . playing politics with our foreign policy. But by splitting our country wide open, I would have crucified the American unity which is indis- . . . Yes: I'll admit that I could have split this country wide open by pensable to "stopping Moscow" and I would have invited Stalin to "divide and conquer." I would also have robbed a new, free Poland of any hope. I would have served the Soviets, not the United States and

147

certainly not a new, free Poland. The price of this unity was a complete reversal of the Administration's appeasement and surrender attitudes at Yalta....[3]

To many an ethnic leader this was a discouraging omen. Bipartisan solidarity in the face of a common enemy did not, however, deter politicians from introducing foreign-policy problems in their continuing quest for the ethnic vote. In 1948 this was done somewhat subtly—not so in 1952.[4]

"In 1948," wrote Jack Redding, Director of Public Relations of the Democratic National Committee, "there was a combination of events which doubled, perhaps trebled, the importance of the votes of United States citizens of foreign extraction." In his unusually candid book on the strategy of the National Committee, *Inside the Democratic Party,* Redding devoted a considerable part to the tactics the Democrats used to capture and hold the ethnic vote—one of the important factors in Truman's return to the White House, in Redding's belief. Senator J. Howard McGrath, chairman of the Democratic National Committee, who had had extensive experience with foreign-language groups in his home state Rhode Island, decided in January to devote considerable attention to the Americans of foreign origin who were eligible to vote. This turned "what had seemed certain defeat into victory," according to Redding.[5]

McGrath asked Antoine Gazda, the Austrian inventor of the Oerlikon anti-aircraft gun, to help him "analyze the situation in the nationality groups." Gazda, in turn, called on Michael (Mieczyslaw) Cieplinski, whom he had helped to flee from German-occupied Poland. Their report brought out that approximately 25 per cent of the total white population of the United States was of foreign or mixed origin and that the 1940 Census listed twenty-one million with a mother tongue other than English.[6] The report suggested a "clear-cut pattern for working out the solution," and pointed to "the possibility that increasing the Democratic vote among these peoples would bear political advantage disproportionate to the effort involved," recalled Redding. McGrath appointed Redding to carry out this objective and to outline campaign strategy.[7]

Early in February Redding began a series of discussions with Cieplinski, whose abilities and qualifications soon impressed him. Cieplinski, within a few months after his arrival in the United States in 1940, had become general manager of a Polish-American paper in New York; during the war he and Victor Ridder, publisher of a

German-language newspaper, had formed the Foreign Language Newspaper Association "to aid the United States government in the war effort"; during the 1944 presidential campaign he had advised Senator Claude Pepper on problems affecting Polish-Americans; and he had maintained "professional contact with all foreign language groups." Upon Redding's recommendation, McGrath appointed Cieplinski executive director of the Nationalities Division.[8]

The Nationalities Division thought there was a need for a special approach to each nationality group because it felt that some—like the Italian-, Polish-, Spanish-, Slovak-, and Russian-Americans—were "basically emotional," and that appeals to them, therefore, had to be made "on an emotional plane"; other groups—like the German and Scandinavian—were felt to be "more impressed by cold logic, figures and concrete plans." The Nationalities Division first consulted influential editors, publishers, business leaders, and clergy. Next were organized "language subdivisions" through which the National Committee was given access to the foreign-language press. Each subdivision, in consultation with Democratic state committees, appointed local representatives—936 in all—wherever there were large ethnic groupings. Volunteers translated party publicity and news releases into the "style and language demanded by the various foreign language newspapers" and most of the material was "printed substantially" as submitted.[9]

Long before the Democratic Convention, the Nationalities Division planned for party participation "in the more important events in the life of the racial groups, such as national conventions or meetings." Arrangements called for the reading of a message from Truman, "an outstanding speaker" to extol the virtues of the administration, and publicity in the foreign-language press. Such activities, in the opinion of the Nationalities Division, "impressed the Administraton's helpful record" and "created a very favorable response" from nationality publications—especially in the absence of similar Republican efforts.[10]

Just prior to the convention, the Nationalities Division saw to it that representatives of nationality groups were granted hearings "to build up prestige in their respective groups." It also classified convention delegates according to country of origin; "out of the 1,018 delegates . . . 264 were of foreign extraction." Receptions held for these delegates in McGrath's office were then intensively reported in the ethnic press. All of this, claimed the Nationalities Division, accounted for "a great amount of pubilicity in the 780 foreign language newspapers."[11]

President Truman was informed of the Nationalities Division's activities and, said Redding, listened "enthusiastically" to the unfolding of plans to win and hold the nationality vote. He was told of the need for a platform plank which, by promising legislation to admit thousands of refugees, would assuredly win for him the gratitude of all minority groups. The President agreed it was "vital." Because Truman had already manifested a deep humanitarian interest in the plight of distressed peoples in Europe and elsewhere, all that was needed was to transform the "esteem [this sympathy engendered] for the President into votes for the Democratic party," wrote Redding. With the support of Truman and the national chairman, the Nationalities Division was able to influence prominent Democrats "to provide in their campaign plans for work among these foreign-speaking groups."[12]

The Polish-Americans, one of the large nationality groups, presented a difficult problem to the Nationalities Division. Hitherto, without great effort on its part, the Democratic party could count on the support of Polish-American leadership. However, in 1948 Charles Rozmarek, president of both the Polish National Alliance and the Polish American Congress—a roof association of almost all Polish-American organizations—who had supported Roosevelt in 1940 and 1944, was wavering "in his allegiance." In March Truman saw Rozmarek, but the meeting, according to Matthew J. Connelly, the President's secretary, "was not successful."[13] There was great concern that this prominent Polish-American leader might succumb to pressures from the Nationalities Division of the Republican party, as he had almost done in 1944, and announce his support of Dewey. Cieplinski, himself a Polish-American, was particularly apprehensive. Despairing of his ability to persuade Rozmarek to remain with the Democratic party, he chose Edward Pluzdrak, a vice president of the two Polish-American organizations headed by Rozmarek, to serve as the national chairman of the Polish-American committee within the Nationalities Division. But Pluzdrak seemed unable to overcome Rozmarek's strong influence either.

At this critical point Cieplinski may have been reminded of a period in Polish-American history during the First World War when the Polish pianist Ignace Jan Paderewski, by the sheer weight of his world prestige, dramatically "captured" the united allegiance of Polish-Americans. Cieplinski saw Paderewski's counterpart in the "tremendously popular" Tadé Styka, who could become the instrument for weakening Rozmarek's influence. There was, however, one difficulty—Styka was an "avowed Republican." Undaunted, Cieplinski dwelt upon his friendship with Paderewski in order to "continue to press Styka on the subject of President Truman, despite Styka's political preference."

In March Cieplinski finally persuaded Styka to meet Truman. Before agreeing, Styka insisted that he wanted first to see the President and "observe him close up; then he would make up his mind." Until then he did not wish to commit himself, nor did he wish any publicity that might indicate "he was talking politics" with President Truman. "That was a tough one!" recalled Redding. How could a meeting with the President of the United States be arranged "on such terms" and "in such a way that Styka would not be committed, but also without offense to the President?"

This delicate situation was finally resolved by Redding and Cieplinski through asking a group of prominent Polish-American editors to meet with the President in the White House. Truman was not told of the "Styka situation." So far as the President was concerned, wrote Redding, "Styka went incognito." The editors, of course, immediately noticed the presence of the famous painter and, as Redding put it, were "agog." During the meeting Truman "was at his best." With a large prewar map of Poland near him, he lectured on world problems as they affected Poland and the United States. He also outlined his plans for refugee legislation which would relieve the sufferings of the victims of German and Soviet aggression, but "made no promises of an easy solution." Styka, seated in a rear row, listened attentively and soon became convinced that Truman was his man. After leaving the White House, Styka "immediately began what for him was the ultimate compliment: a full-length portrait of the President."

Throughout the campaign Styka was an "articulate advocate of the Democratic Party" and worked diligently "to advance the cause of Truman's election." In an October ceremony "performed in the White House before the President and the entire Cabinet," Styka presented the completed portrait to Truman. All seventy-two Polish-

151

American newspapers printed a reproduction of the portrait, as well as Styka's personal eulogy of the President. "Thus," Redding exulted, "we had the President's candidacy wrapped in the folds of Polish national patriotism as represented by one of the great Polish heroes—Styka." The ceremony and the accompanying publicity were so effective that when Rozmarek announced his support of Dewey a few days later, it was Redding's opinion that "he delivered to the Republicans one vote, his own. With Styka, we had taken the bulk of the Polish voters."[14]

Styka's conversion to the Democratic party was interpreted by the strategists in charge of the ethnic vote as a "political triumph." The favorable publicity among Polish-Americans following the dramatic "Styka affair" was soon augmented by a practical political act—the insertion of a "displaced-persons" plank in the Democratic platform which singled out Poland for special consideration. The combination of these two factors—one emotional and the other concrete—was certain, Redding was convinced, to bear ample fruit.

It "took some doing" for the officers of the Nationalities Division to persuade the Platform Committee to include such a plank. The chairman of the Platform Committee, Senator Myers of Pennsylvania, who had previously approved the recommendation of the Nationalities Division to insert a statement on Israel, refused to mention Poland in the plank concerning displaced persons. "There is no precedent," said Myers, "for mentioning Poland in the platform of the party. If we mention Poland, logically we might have to mention every other country in the world." Senator Theodore Green of Rhode Island, a member of the Platform Committee and a recently appointed vice-chairman of the Democratic National Committee in charge of the Nationalities Division, did not agree with Myers. "While the party platform was being typed into what was presumed to be its final form," recalled Redding, Green made a personal appeal to McGrath. The party chairman immediately responded. Writing to Myers on July 13, McGrath asked that he do his "level best to get the attached language into the platform"; without it the platform "is worthless as far as millions of people are concerned."[15] Evidently McGrath thought the problem was of great importance, for on the same day he also conferred with Attorney General Tom Clark—under whose jurisdiction laws concerning displaced persons would be administered—and President Truman. At the conclusion of the conference Truman requested the Attorney General to "tell Senator Myers in the name of the President that Harry S. Truman wanted the recommended language in the platform." This was done and the final plank in the Democratic platform read: "The United States has traditionally been in sympathy with the efforts of subjugated countries to attain their independence, and to establish a democratic form of government. Poland is an outstanding example. After a century and half of subjugation, it was resurrected after the first World War by our great Democratic President, Woodrow Wilson. We look forward to development of these countries as prosperous, free, and democratic fellow members of the United Nations."[16]

The plank was "headline news" in the Polish-American press. The Nationalities Division of the Democratic party was proud of its accomplishment. The platform of the Republican party did not mention Poland, nor did it say anything about displaced persons; its silence delighted and encouraged the strategists of the Democratic party. "The inside story of McGrath's and the President's personal intervention," wrote Redding, "was electric in its effect on Styka and other Polish leaders."[17]

In the early spring of 1948 the Democratic National Committee became worried over reports that Jewish-Americans had become critical of the party's "lack of forcefulness regarding the problem of Israel."[18] Fearful that "this weakness" would be exploited by both the Republicans and Wallace's Progressive Citizens of America, the committee decided to solicit the support of President Truman. "We have the Zionist Jews in the office every day," Redding told Truman, "and the pressure is building up a terrific head of steam." According to Redding, the President replied, "It's no use putting pressure on the committee. The Palestine issue will be handled here. And there'll be no politics involved."[19] As President of the United States Truman was "explicit" in emphasizing and demanding and hoping that the Palestine issue be taken out of politics, but as head of his party he could not overcome partisan pressures from the party, as well as from the opposition, to bring it into the campaign.

Nineteen forty-eight was the first presidential election after the end of the Second World War. Events in Europe, in the Middle East, and in the United States made it a propitious time for the Zionists to demand that previous pledges for a Jewish National Home be honored. The promise, embodied in presidential declarations beginning with that of Wilson and Congressional resolutions beginning with that of the Republicans in 1922, was now impossible of postponement. By 1948 Zionist organizations which claimed to speak for the Jewish population in the United States were well organized; the threat, whether real or merely ostensible, to withhold the Jewish vote could not be ignored by party strategists. At that time Zionist pressure for American support was virtually unopposed and unchallenged by any other pressure group.[20] Equally important was the fact that many Christian American organizations as well as individuals approved Zionist aspirations. Their motives were mixed: many were deeply moved by the plight of Jewish survivors of Nazi concentration camps; others, like Dorothy Thompson, felt that "the salvation of the Jews must . . . come in part as an act of repentance from the Christian world";[21] and there were some who preferred that the remnants of European Jewry go to Palestine rather than come to the United States. Then, too, the American public was neither fully cognizant of nor responsive to the heightening Arab hostility to Zionism or the importance of the Middle East to the security of the West. In 1948 the United States was the unchallenged world power which still held a monopoly in atomic weapons. Moreover, Soviet Russia's favorable attitude toward Zionist aspirations lessened the likelihood that Arab opposition would find a strong patron and thus jeopardize American national interest.

In the light of these circumstances party strategists were convinced that they had nothing to lose and everything to gain by competing for and catering to the Jewish vote. Both the Republican and Democratic 1944 platforms contained planks on Palestine. The Republican plank called for the opening of Palestine to "unrestricted immigration and land ownership" as a preliminary step to fulfill the "intent and purpose of the Balfour Declaration of 1917 and the Resolution of a Republican Congress in 1922" and thus make possible Palestine's becoming a "free and democratic Commonwealth." It condemned Roosevelt for failure "to insist" that Great Britain "carry out the provisions of the Balfour Declaration and of the mandate. . . ." The Democratic plank simply stated that it favored "the opening of Palestine to unrestricted Jewish immigration and colonization, and such a policy as to result in the establishment there of a free and democratic Jewish commonwealth."[22] In their 1948 platforms both parties, as well as the Progressives, again inserted planks on the Palestine issue. The Democrats took pride in Truman's "granting immediate recognition to Israel," pledged "full recognition to the State of Israel," supported the admission of Israel into the United Nations, and favored "revision of the arms embargo to accord to the State of Israel the right of self-defense."[23] The Republican party, as Senator Arthur Vandenberg explained to Secretary of Defense James Forrestal, who urged that the question of Palestine be taken out of politics, felt that because the "Democratic Party had used the Palestine question politically," it was "entitled to make similar use of the issue."[24] Its plank read: "We welcome Israel into the family of nations and take pride in the fact that the Republican Party was the first to call for the establishment of a free and independent Jewish Commonwealth. The vacillation of the Democrat Administration on this question has undermined the prestige of the United Nations. Subject to the letter and spirit of the United Nations Charter, we pledge to Israel full recognition, with its boundaries as sanctioned by the United Nations and aid in developing its economy."[25]

Within a few weeks before the election both presidential candidates were pressed by Zionists to repudiate the peace plan of Count Bernadotte, the United Nations mediator in the Israeli-Arab war, which, in return for western Galilee, proposed Israel's relinquishing its claim to the Negeb, assigned to it by the partition resolution of 1947. Israel wanted both regions. Dewey responded first. On October 22, ten days before the election, the Republican candidate stated that he had always felt that the Jewish people were entitled "to a homeland in Palestine which would be politically and economically stable," and that he had approved "the majority report of the United Nations Special Committee which recommended a partition of Palestine." He also called attention to his "whole-hearted support" of the Republican plank on Palestine. Although Dewey did not make any direct reference to the question of boundaries, Truman immediately retaliated by accusing Dewey of injecting the Palestine issue into the campaign—which, he said, made it "necessary" for him to restate his position. Six days later, in Madison Square Garden, Truman again attacked Dewey for playing politics with Israel. Omitting mention of boundaries, he traced at great length his pro-Israel policies. Dewey did not again address himself publicly to the problem, but instead permitted Senator Irving Ives, New York

Republican, to denounce Truman in the final campaign rally for "running out on every commitment he had made to the Jewish people" and "undermining" the United Nations by his constant vacillations.[26]

The presidential election of 1948 offered Jewish-Americans, and more particularly the Zionists among them, an auspicious and unique occasion to vote for any of three candidates—Dewey, Truman, or Wallace—with the expectation that whoever won would be bound by his pledges to support and shelter the young nation in the midst of a hostile Arab world.

Although the Republican platform, with the exception of a plank concerning Israel, contained no references to nationality groups, the party did not overlook the ethnic vote. The Nationalities Division of the Republican National Committee was as busy in the pursuit of the hyphenated vote as the corresponding Democratic unit.[27] One of the men who helped Dewey with the "foreign language group activity" was Bernard Yarrow, an ethnic expert since 1937.[28]

The first indication the Democrats had of the entry of the Republicans into the competition came on August 18, 1948, when the *New York Times* reported on its front page that Dewey had "told a delegation of Americans of Italian extraction" that he favored giving Italy control of its former African colonies—Libya, Somaliland, and Eritrea. The delegation, headed by Edward Corsi, included Judge Eugene V. Alessandroni of Philadelphia, the Very Reverend Bonaventure J. Filitti of St. Patrick's Old Cathedral of New York, Judge Felix Forte of Boston, Leo Nunes of New York, president of the American Chamber of Commerce for Trade with Italy, and Ercole Sozzi of New York, its former president. "The Communist menace," Dewey was reported to have told the delegation, "will receive another setback, if the Italian people are now given an ample opportunity to take part in the future development of the resources of these African areas." Corsi was to leave for Italy the next day with a letter of introduction from Dewey to Alcide de Gasperi, Prime Minister of Italy.[29]

Upon reading Dewey's statement, the officers of the Nationalities Division of the Democratic party became incensed. To them, the pronouncement "was a well-conceived blow designed to sway the Italian vote in the United States," "an appeal to the imperial pride and ambition of the Italian people"—a "pride and ambition [which] had been basic to Mussolini's fascist power." Democratic strategists expected the Italian-American press to display prominently Dewey's statement, with a consequent lessening of Truman's appeal for many Italian-Americans. Anticipating this, Redding called Charles Ross, presidential press secretary, to request that Dewey's speech be answered by the White House. Ross refused; Truman did not wish to violate the bipartisan approach to foreign policy. Redding countered Ross's arguments by averring that Dewey's statement had already affected the promise to keep foreign policy out of internal politics and, therefore, the Democratic party "had the right" to defend its position. Ross, however, was "obdurate."

Redding could not accept Ross's decision. "Cieplinski," he recalled, "was all over me." He had messages too from centers of "Italian voting strength." He was particularly concerned over reports from New York which stated that the party "stood in danger" of losing the support of *Il Progresso Italo-Americano,* one of the most influential Italian-American papers, and its publisher Generoso Pope.[30] He appealed Ross's decision directly to the President through McGrath, getting "nothing but sympathy." This did not stop Redding. He turned to the State Department, where he talked to a "spokesman" of Secretary of State George Marshall. There too he found little solace. In the State Department "I found 'politics' to be a dirty word," wrote Redding, "and was promptly brushed off." Redding then went to the office of Senator Theodore Green, senior Democrat on the Foreign Relations Committee, but found that Green, who might have been sympathetic, was out of town and unavailable. "In desperation" he returned to the State Department and got in touch with Under Secretary of State Robert Lovett. Redding described Lovett, a Republican, as "incensed" at Dewey's "invasion of the nonpolitical foreign policy sphere" and as "willing to talk." Lovett outlined the damage done by Dewey's statement. He pointed out that former Italian colonies were not self-sustaining and could therefore constitute an "insupportable drain on the economy of Italy." The Italian government itself, he further explained, in order to prevent the Italian Communist party from taking over control, "wanted no part of these ex-colonies." Supported with these facts, Redding called on Clayton Knowles, political correspondent of the *New York Times,* and gave him the "complete answer to the issue raised by Dewey" as it had been outlined to him by Lovett. He cautioned Knowles not to indicate the source of the information.

The next morning the *New York Times* "had an even bigger spread on page one which, in effect, blew Governor Dewey out of the water." The headline ran: "Democrats Roiled by Dewey Proposal on Italian Colonies; Making of Political Hay out of Bipartisan Foreign Policy Is Laid to Governor; Marshall Won't Talk; State Department Is Called Concerned Because of the Delicacy of Negotiations." Knowles wrote that concern had been aroused that the bipartisan foreign policy which had been "born in the war years" might fall "in the heat of the Presidential election campaign." Democratic strategists, he wrote, who were seeking to return President Truman to the White House were outraged. In Dewey's statement they saw an "outright bid for the Italian-American vote" at a time when he "was neither in a position to deliver on his proposal nor responsible if American negotiators were unable to obtain something comparable."[31]

The blast from the Democrats attacking Dewey's appeal for the Italian-American vote was augmented by support from an unexpected source—the Negro press, which, as has been pointed out, attacked Dewey for his pro-Italian stand.[32]

The Nationalities Division was not content to be on the defensive on the Italian question. Long before Dewey's "bid for the Italian-American vote," both Redding and Cieplinski had worked diligently to secure it for the Democrats. "There was an added fillip," recalled Redding, "to our effort to win Italian-American votes" which also helped in winning the support of Americans of Spanish descent. On "I Am an American Day" and again on Columbus Day, President Truman delivered a message in which he "not only recognized that Columbus was an Italian, from Genoa, but also commented on the fact that crews of his three tiny discovery ships were Spaniards." The presidential message was "enormously" popular among Spanish-speaking citizens in New Mexico and California. The chairman of the Spanish committee of the Democratic Nationalities Division, Dr. José Cesteros, spent his own money to broadcast this message over all radio stations reaching the Spanish-language group and to have it printed in Spanish-language newspapers. Redding was convinced that the President's "recognition of the role of Spaniards in the discovery of America" was bound to draw Spanish-Americans to the Democratic side. He concluded, "A little thing, but it produced votes."[33]

During the last months of the 1948 campaign, the Democratic Nationalities Division revived the issue of isolationism by reminding ethnic Americans of the previous Republican isolationist record and warning them of a residue, small but powerful, of isolationist "die-hards." They pointed out the "bickering" of Republican lawmakers over "terms of support to Greece and Turkey" and the Republican "quibbling" over Marshall Plan funds. The Nationalities Division believed that voters of foreign origin wanted the United States to take an active part in world affairs. All that was needed to win their full support "was to carry out an aggressive program of driving those issues home."

A good example of this "aggressive program" was the strategy used with Greek-Americans. Because the Truman Doctrine was extremely popular among Greek-Americans, there was no need of "battling" for their support. The only thing necessary was to "channel their efforts," and to this end Stephen Scopas, president of the Greek-American fraternal organization AHEPA, was urged to become chairman of the Greek committee of the Nationalities Division. Scopas proved to be a tirelessly energetic organizer and fund-raiser. He initiated registration drives among not only Greek-Americans but among other nationality groups also, and chartered buses to carry "Greeks by the hundreds to county courthouses or ward offices." In some places, Redding reminisced, Greeks "marched to the local office of registration with flags flying and to the music of a Greek band."

In the planning of the "aggressive program" Cieplinski was "in-valuable," as Redding thought. The director of the Nationalities Division believed "ardently" in Truman's program and since he "idolized" the President, "there was no chore too arduous, no meeting too small for Cieplinski's attention." Under his direction the publicity office prepared releases for the foreign-language press, and messages to nationality groups on White House stationery were submitted to the President for his signature. Through this latter device "each nationality group was assured of the President's knowl-edge and interest in its individual organizations."

German- and Scandinavian-Americans were the "hardest to sway" to the Democratic side. To win their vote the Nationalities Division decided to follow two separate strategies. On the Scandinavian-American front it "fought nothing more than a containing opera-tion." Not so with the German-Americans, a more substantial group of voters. Here more energy was exerted to capture and hold them against Republican efforts, which were under the leadership of Gov-ernor Harold Stassen, "the biggest ace the Republicans had," and his lieutenant, Victor Ridder, German-American publisher. Having reasoned that German-Americans were "easily impressed by cold logic, by facts and figures," Redding and Cieplinski determinedly publicized Truman's record in regard to Germany: the Berlin airlift, the resumption of postal relations between the United States and Germany, and the economic aid to West Germany which had "endeared" the President to German-Americans. The Nationalities Division wanted to make Truman a hero of German-Americans, particularly so because neither Wilson nor Roosevelt had been. To help bring this about, Cieplinski asked his close friend Dr. Gerhart Seger, editor and publisher of the *Deutsche Volk-Zeitung,* to bring to the attention of the German-American public the President's record in regard to West Germany. Seger, already an admirer and supporter of Truman, fell to with fervor. In the late summer and fall he gave, by Redding's figures, seventy-two lectures in the "main centers" of German-American population. It was felt that the impression Seger made was particularly strong because "he had no direct connection with the political fortunes of any candidate."[34]

"Who *Really* Elected Truman?" Immediately after the election the *Saturday Evening Post* commissioned Samuel Lubell to find the answer. Four months later, having completed a study of fifteen key states and cities which had been "decisive in the November voting," Lubell published his findings.[35] Among the many "crosscurrents" influencing the election, Lubell singled out the ethnic vote as significant. Of particular importance, in his judgment, were the German-, Italian-, and Polish-American voting records. "Truman," he wrote, "hit just the right pitch in the matter of issues. He had fighting, folksy tones to appeal to the Roosevelt elements—labor, unorganized as well as organized; the foreign-born and their first and second generation offspring. . . ."

Throughout the nation, observed Lubell, Italian-American precincts which had gone "two or three to one for Roosevelt plumped for Truman six to one." Evidently the campaign leaflets telling how Truman had " 'saved Italy from communism,' " with which Italian-American wards had been "saturated," had brought the desired results. Democratic strategy among Italian-Americans, suggested Lubell, was effective in overcoming the resentment of some Italian-Americans occasioned by Roosevelt's "stab-in-the-back" speech following Mussolini's attack on France.

Polish-American wards in Cleveland, Detroit, Milwaukee, Pittsburgh, and Chicago voted for Truman "three to one." The Polish-

American community in Buffalo gave Truman "a fourth of his total city vote." The Republican party, wrote Lubell, expected Polish-Americans to "swing to them in resentment against Roosevelt's alleged 'betrayal' of Poland," particularly since the heads of two of the "strongest Polish-American societies"[36] had endorsed Governor Dewey. Apparently the failure of the Republican strategists to incite, abet, and accentuate Polish-American dissatisfaction with Roosevelt's policy toward Poland took the issue of Poland out of the campaign.[37] In Buffalo, out of twenty-two linotype operators, many of whom "had set type for stories accusing Roosevelt of 'selling out' Poland," only one voted for Dewey. ". . . what really rankled them," explained Lubell, "was the Taft-Hartley Act." John Kryzinski, a Democratic ward leader, told Lubell, "The Poles voted for their pocketbooks, not for Poland." A "Polish Republican" gave another explanation for the Polish vote in favor of the Democratic party. According to him, Republicans lost in Buffalo because "not one Pole was named a commissioner," while the Democratic party ran a Polish-American and an Italian-American for Congress "for the first time, electing both."

In his analysis of the factors responsible for Truman's victory in the Midwest, Lubell thought it most significant that the swing toward Truman in this area was "most pronounced" among voters of German descent. "In my opinion," reported Lubell, "it will rank as one of the greatest ironies of American history that Roosevelt, in his very act of dying, removed the roadblock to a successful assault upon the stanchest Republican citadels." It was this "sensational"—but scarcely noted, according to Lubell—"movement of voters of German descent out of the Republican fold" which "snowballed" into the "Truman miracle"—the "greatest upset in American history." With Roosevelt the "German hater" dead, German-Americans in Missouri, Ohio, Minnesota, Wisconsin, and Iowa were able to vote on the basis of economic interests. Truman's foreign policies, the Marshall Plan, the Truman Doctrine, and the Berlin airlift stirred "no conflicts" among German-Americans. On the contrary, observed Lubell, these policies became popular "even among former isolationists."

The Nationalities Division of the Democratic party was, of course, delighted with Lubell's post-mortem analysis. Its hard work during the campaign apparently had paid off. The phenomenal success of the Nationalities Division, its directors were convinced, "was a classic example of great political returns rewarding competent leadership and strenuous effort, at a small financial expense." They and Lubell may have been right.[38]

Chapter X

SOVIET RUSSIA AND THE SLAVIC-AMERICAN

Long live the unity of Slavs under the leadership of the U.S.S.R.!
—George Petkov, Third American Slav Congress, September, 1946.

"Three years after the end of the second world war, the drums are beating for a third." So began the preamble of the Progressive party platform of 1948. "The American people want peace. But the old parties, obedient to the dictates of monopoly and the military, prepare for war in the name of peace," read the first plank. Having declared its members "the present-day descendants" and political heirs of "Jefferson, Jackson and Lincoln—of Frederick Douglass, Altgeld and Debs—of 'Fighting Bob' LaFollette, George Norris, and Franklin Roosevelt," the Progressive party charged the Democratic and Republican parties with the betrayal of the American people. In the long bill of particulars it condemned both parties for refusing "to negotiate a settlement of differences with the Soviet Union"; for rejecting the United Nations as an instrument for peace and reconstruction of the war-torn world; for the promulgation of the Marshall Plan—a plot "to rebuild Nazi Germany as a war base and to subjugate the economies" of European countries to "American Big Business"; and for the inauguration of the Truman Doctrine—a military and financial scheme to promote "corrupt, fascist governments in China, Greece, Turkey, and elsewhere." These foreign policies, avowed the party of Henry A. Wallace, profaned "the name of peace."

It was no accident that the unrestrained condemnation of the bipartisan foreign policies was immediately followed by a series of planks aimed at American minority groups. That platform accused both parties of having denied "the Negro people the rights of citizenship"; of having passed legislation "to admit displaced persons, discriminating against Catholics, Jews, and other victims of Hitler"; of having aimed "to reduce nationality groups to a position of social, economic, and political inferiority"; and of having moved "to outlaw the Communist Party as a decisive step in their assault on the democratic rights of labor, of national, racial, and political minorities, and all those who oppose their drive to war." To restore the "traditional American freedoms" which it said both parties, "acting for the forces of special privilege, conspire to destroy," the Progres-

162

sive party pledged itself, among other things, to demand "the immediate de jure recognition of the State of Israel," the admission of Israel to the United Nations, and the lifting of the "arms embargo in favor of the State of Israel." So far as the Arabs were concerned, this plank appealed to the "Arab workers, farmers and small merchants" to accept the state of Israel "as being in their best interest" and not to allow themselves to be "used as tools in a war against Israel on behalf of British and American monopolies. . . ." The platform called for the repeal of the "anti-Catholic, anti-semitic Displaced Persons Act of 1948" which permitted the entry of "fascists and collaborators." In a separate plank entitled "Nationality Groups" the "Progressives" proclaimed themselves the party which recognized the "varied contributions of all nationality groups to American cultural, economic, and social life," and considered them a "source of strength for the democratic development of our country"; advocated "the right of the foreign born to obtain citizenship without discrimination"; asked for an immediate repeal of "discriminatory immigration laws based upon race, national origin, religion, or political belief"; asked that Japanese-Americans be reimbursed for the "losses suffered during their wartime internment"; and proposed legislation to facilitate the naturalization of "Filipinos, Koreans, Japanese, Chinese, and other national groups now discriminated against by law."[1]

Unwittingly, perhaps, the Progressive party became a rallying point for Soviet efforts to frustrate American decisions to contain and defeat Communist attempts to subjugate the world. The platform of the American Communist party openly endorsed the Progressive party—"an inescapable historic necessity for millions who want a real choice now between peace and war, democracy and fascism, security and poverty."[2] To the Soviet government the party of Henry A. Wallace and Glen H. Taylor, its presidential and vice-presidential candidates, was the means by which to essay control of Slavic and other nationality organizations in the United States.

2

Several years before the outbreak of the Second World War, Soviet Russia, in sinister symmetry with the determined efforts of the Axis powers to direct and influence the organizations of their former nationals, set out to infiltrate and capture the leadership of Slavic-American and other groups. The Soviet task was more difficult to accomplish than were the similar efforts of Germany, Italy, and Japan. Many Slavic-Americans—the Poles, Ukrainians, Serbs, Croats, Slovenes, Slovaks, and others—were hostile to the Soviet government. In almost all cases this animus was deeply rooted in the historical past and continued to be nourished not only by grievances antedating the Soviet period but also by religious and political considerations. Nor could the Soviet Union expect any sympathy from its own former citizens and their descendants.

On the eve of the Second World War Slavic-Americans were divided into antagonistic groups mirroring European events. It was the dissension and antipathy within the Slavic-American community which attracted the attention of the Communist party. The first opportunity to fish in the troubled waters of ethnic politics came with the partition of Czechoslovakia and its final conquest by Nazi Germany following the appeasement at Munich in 1938. The Nazi absorption of the Sudetenland, the concomitant Polish and Hungarian demands for Czech territory, and the establishment of the Nazi puppet regime of Slovakia under Tiso accentuated the already-present mutual suspicions of Slavic-Americans.[3] Czech-Americans turned against Polish-Americans, Slovak-Americans against Czech-Americans, and Hungarian-Americans against Czech-Americans. Carpatho-Russian-Americans were bitter and resentful toward Slovak-Americans for the traitorous action of Tiso. Among the remaining Slavic-American groups hostile feelings which had existed before 1938 were aggravated by the rapidly moving ominous events in Europe. Bulgarian-Americans opposed the Serb-Americans, while Macedonian-Americans transferred from Europe to America their enmity toward Bulgarians and Serbs. Among the Yugoslav-Americans, the Slovenians seemed passive; Catholic Croats scorned the Orthodox Serbs. Ukrainian-Americans, whose native land was divided between Poland and Soviet Russia, were both anti-Polish and anti-Communist.

Disillusionment with the Western powers, who had allowed Nazi Germany to extinguish the independence of Czechoslovakia, spurred many Slavic-Americans to unite in a common effort against the scourge of Hitlerism flooding their native lands. In the fall of 1938 a meeting to protest the Munich agreement and the establishment of Slovakia was called in Pittsburgh by several of the non-Catholic Slavic-American organizations; among the most prominent were the Slovak Evangelical Society of America, the United Russian Orthodox

Brotherhood, and the Serb National Federation. The All-Slav Congress selected as chairman Ivan (John) Butkovich, president of the Croatian Fraternal Union. The meeting was not large, but it adopted many resolutions and appeals which received considerable publicity through the publications of the participating organizations.

Hitler's invasion of Poland with its implied threat to the other Slavic nations in Europe led to the calling of another All-Slav Congress in Pittsburgh.[4] Because of the participation of some Polish organizations the second meeting was considerably larger than the first. There was unanimity in its resolution directed against Nazism and Fascism. No sooner had this second conference of the All-Slav Congress begun than news arrived of the Nazi-Soviet non-aggression pact and the Soviet invasion of Poland that followed.

The Nazi-Soviet honeymoon period produced an understandable shock within the ranks of Slavic-Americans. The Communist organizers of the All-Slav Congress, like the American Communists generally, immediately rebounded with a "new line." Those leaders of Slavic nationality organizations who openly attacked the Soviet participation in the fourth partition of Poland were denounced as "warmongers," "agents of capitalism," or "tools of Wall Street." As one Slav state after another lost its independence, Slavic-American Communists justified the destruction of Poland as a means which would lead to "the salvation of the Polish proletariat" and the end of the "rotten ruling clique of Josef Beck." During the presidential elections of 1940 they joined the American Communist party in an open attack on President Roosevelt, charging him with the violation of the traditional principle of isolationism. "The Yanks are not coming" was their most favored slogan.

The ending of the Nazi-Soviet honeymoon by the German invasion of Russia produced a dramatic reversal. Now the slogan changed abruptly to "The Yanks are coming." In typical Communist fashion, Roosevelt, who had been denounced as a traitor to American traditions, suddenly became the "hero of the masses." In the wake of growing sympathy for Russia, soon to become an ally of the United States, American Slav Communists encouraged plans to bring "unity" among Americans of Slavic descent. The first attempt to unite the "fifteen million" Slavic Americans came within a month of the Nazi invasion of Russia. The initial call for a "National Congress of American Slavs," to be held in Pittsburgh, November 21-23, 1941, read in part:

TO ALL AMERICAN SLAVS:

This call is addressed to all American Slavs, loyal to the American ideals of freedom and democracy. It is addressed to all descendants of the heroic, peaceful and liberty loving Slavs. It is addressed to all Slavs, because as Americans, and also as Slavs, one danger and one duty confronts all of us.

In Europe, the Slavs are in the forefront of the fight against Hitler. The Nazi armies have overrun and destroyed every Slav state. They are now trying to destroy the greatest Slav state—Russia, which is an ally of the United States and Great Britain. . . .

. . . As freedom loving Americans of Slav descent, we declare our full support for the effort of our government, and President Roosevelt, to bring about the full destruction of Hitlerism, by increasing production for national defense and giving all aid to Great Britain, the Soviet Union. . . .

We American Slavs must also do our duty, to our country and to our heroic Slav people. In order to achieve this, we must take the example from our patriotic brothers and sisters in Europe, and unite our forces in a great CONGRESS OF AMERICAN SLAVS.

The congress was postponed "to permit the inclusion of all the main organizations of Slav Americans." The real reason for the postponement, however, was the lack of support from many Slavic organizations which suspected its leadership and purpose. The Serb National Federation, the Polish National Alliance, the Polish Roman Catholic Union, and the Czecho-Slovak Society of America, and several others withdrew their support, believing the congress to be a "fifth column 'whitewash' movement predominated by Communists." Time was needed to overcome these depletions as well as for "further mobilization."

It was not until April, 1942, that the American Slav Congress was duly constituted. By that time Communist organizers had succeeded in removing any doubts from the minds of many loyal Slavic-Americans and many Slavic-American leaders by obtaining seemingly official "sanction" from unsuspecting government officers who had been solicited for their support and interest. During December, 1941, a small group of Slavic-Americans had decided to notify the State Department of its aim to hold a congress for the purpose of mobilizing "American Slavs for aid to the war effort of the United States." The committee (which included some anti-Communists, notably Blair F. Gunther, then a member of the Educational Committee of the Polish National Alliance) asked Congressman James A. Wright to send a letter in their behalf to the Secretary of State inquiring whether a congress of American Slavs would be "contrary to the State Department's policy concerning 'free movements.' " On January 19, 1942, Secretary of State Cordell Hull acknowledged receipt of the inquiry. "The courtesy of the sponsors in inquiring as to the attitude of this Department," he wrote Representative Wright, "is appreciated, although you of course realize that the final decision as to whether or not such a congress should be held does not lie with the State Department." The concluding paragraph contained the following remarks:

"The full support of our war efforts of American citizens of Slavic descent, who are such a large factor in our production programs in heavy industry, is particularly important. All efforts, however, should aim at minimizing differences in racial background and at stressing the fundamental unity of the country. Provided therefore that the purpose and program of such a congress aims at stimulating American unity and is concentrated on this subject and not on controversial problems relating to the future of Eastern Europe, it could be of constructive assistance."

Armed with what was interpreted to be the "approval" of the American government, the Congress of American Slavs became "legal and desirable." It was also possible to obtain endorsements from other prominent American officeholders. Mayor Edward J. Kelly expressed his "great pleasure" on learning "of the details of the American Slav Congress" and congratulated the leaders of the congress for accomplishing "a salutary effect upon those who are unmindfully careless in their actions, in their speech and in their associations with fellow men."

In the stirring "Call for the American Slav Congress," Gunther and Zeman—president and secretary of the board of directors of the American Slav Congress—asked "all American Slavs, loyal to the American ideals of freedom and democracy, to unite in a great Congress of American Slavs." The call, which pledged, among other things, the "labor and strength" of the "over fifty (50%) percent of the workers in industries vital to national defense" who were Americans of Slavic descent concluded:

"This Congress of American Slavs will be held with the full approval of the government of the United States of America, in Detroit, Michigan on April 25 and 26, 1942.

"We ask every American Slav Fraternal, Cultural, Religious, Sport, Veteran and Labor Organization to elect delegates. We especially call upon our young people, Americans of Slav descent, to elect delegates. . . .

"We ask you to see that conferences and mass meetings are held in your localities on an 'American Slav Sunday' to be designated by the Congress."
The congress received the endorsement of many of the Slav leaders and organizations.

By perhaps pure coincidence the convening of the American Slav Congress was preceded earlier in the month by the Second All-Slav Congress in Moscow. At that meeting Lieutenant General Alexander Gundorov, president of the Soviet All-Slav Committee, greeted the delegates—Russians, Ukrainians, White Russians, Poles, Slovaks, Serbs, Croats, Slovenes, and Bulgars—with a plea to unite the Slav family of nations into "one united anti-Fascist front." One significant outcome of this conference was the establishment of an All-Slav newspaper, *Slavanie,* which was to be distributed also in the United States. Some Slavic-American papers, like the *Russky Golos,* told their readers of the purposes and aims of the Second All-Slav Congress.

The Soviet government was also aware of the forthcoming American Slav Congress. On April 7, *Pravda* took cognizance of the fact that "in far away America, on the other side of the Atlantic, the Slavs who live there have raised their voices. They are preparing for a Slav Congress. At many gatherings and conferences in New York, Chicago and Detroit our brothers are calling for unity of the Slavs, for harmony, and for struggle and victory against Hitler Germany."

On April 25, the American Slav Congress held its first session in Detroit, Michigan. Delegates from ten nationality groups represented religious, cultural, fraternal, athletic, social, and trade union organizations of Americans of Polish, Czech, Slovak, Serb, Croat, Carpatho-Russian, Ukrainian, Slovenian, Macedonian, and Bulgarian backgrounds. The rostrum was decorated with flags of all Slavic nations, including Soviet Russia. Large posters were inscribed with such slogans as "Put the Fifth Columnists behind the Bars," "Smash Fascist Japan," and "Open the second front and crush Hitler now." The session opened with a welcoming address from Gunther, who was still not aware of the presence of Communists among the sponsors of the congress. Congratulatory messages were received from Governor Van Wagoner of Michigan, Mayor Jeffries of Detroit, and Mayor Kelly of Chicago. The keynote address was delivered by Leo

Krzycki, vice president of the Amalgamated Clothing Workers of America, C. I. O., and soon to be president of the congress. "They said it cannot be done," he remarked, and continued, "Witnessing the glorious march of the Slavs marching onward, do you realize what we have started today? We have started an arsenal of democracy. . . . Our enemies know and fear the mighty wrath of the American Slavs. . . ."

During the morning session Gunther announced that a telegram had been sent to the Federal Bureau of Investigation requesting that the American Slav Congress be permitted to coöperate with the bureau in rooting out fifth columnists. He said the offer had been accepted by the bureau, and a list of all its offices in the United States had been sent to the congress. A message from the war-time capital of Soviet Russia, Kuibyshev, was read and "wildly acclaimed." The credentials committee reported that 2155 delegates, 47 national organizations, and 35 newspapers were officially represented at the first session of the congress.

At the closing session of the congress reports and resolutions from various committees and panels were read and approved. Among them was one urging the opening of a second front, another proclaiming Sunday, June 21, as Slav Sunday, and another which paid tribute "to the mothers, wives, and sweethearts of this war . . . our gallant, deathless, heroic women." Another resolution urged the formation of a National Committee of American Slavs to uncover pro-Fascist groups. Paul V. McNutt, head of the newly created War Man Power Commission, addressed the victory rally gathering of approximately 10,000 persons.

The publicity release issued by the congress at the end of the conference hailed its success and achievements:

The response to the first American Slav Congress ever held exceeded all anticipations of the organizers. . . .

The delegates were mostly brawny men from coal mines, steel mills, machine shops—the men on whom the nation is counting for much of its war essential goods production and wholesome-looking women whose faces showed hardening lines of determination beneath war smiles. Present among the delegates were men . . . of distinction in many fields of activity—scholars, writers, clergymen. . . .

One of the wires greeting it was from a Czech group in Teheran, Persia, there were many from Slavic groups in Chile, Argentina, Canada and throughout America. Soviet writers and scientists and members of

169

the Yugoslav government in Kuibyshev wired the congress messages of greetings and good wishes.

The Congress was not only an event significant in the history of America's 15 million Slav-descended citizens but fraught with meaning for the destiny of the more than 200 millions of Slav peoples across the seas engaged in a life-and-death struggle against Nazi enslavers.

For the first time in recorded history the peoples of the diverse Slavic groups were reaching a common understanding on a world-wide issue—a matter that gave delegates a feeling of considerable satisfaction. . . .

The American Slav Congress was a success. But unknown to many participants, some leaders of Slavic nationality organizations, and to officials of the United States government, the congress, which had originated as an assembly of Slavic-Americans, developed into an organization dominated by Communists or Communist sympathizers.

Most delegates attending the American Slav Congress, as well as some committee chairmen, were not Communists. Many representatives of Slavic-American organizations who had withdrawn their support from the abortive All-Slav Congress of November, 1941, joined and actively supported the American Slav Congress. Important government officials, ignorant of its true purposes, gave this Slavic roof organization "official" status through their favorable endorsements, congratulatory telegrams, and actual presence. This sanction by American leaders, always eager to associate themselves with ethnic politics, undoubtedly accounted for the large number of delegates present.[5] Patriotic Americans of Slavic descent, convinced thus of the "legality" of the American Slav Congress, were reluctant to offer any opposition. Many Slavic-American leaders who continued to suspect the aims of the congress were intimidated lest their criticism or non-participation be interpreted as "interference with the war effort." Those leaders of organizations like the Polish National Alliance, the Polish Roman Catholic Union, and the Czecho-Slovak Society of America who remained critical of the congress were pressured into submission or inactivity through intimations or accusations branding them as Fascists, Nazis, or fifth-columnists. Many of those who attended the congress did so in order to avoid being called "anti-patriots or anti-Slavs."

Thus an opportunity was given to the American Slav Congress, under the leadership of its president, Leo Krzycki, to infiltrate many Slavic-American groups; this infiltration in turn made available the pages of the foreign-language press.

From the day of its inception the American Slav Congress was an important instrument for Communist efforts to subvert Americans of Slavic descent to Soviet purposes. In this attempt Soviet Russia was aided by its being an ally of the United States and by the growing prestige resulting from the Red Army's success in turning earlier defeats to victories—a prestige which many Slavic peoples outside of Russia were more and more inclined to share. As Soviet armies poured into Poland, Russian plans for the future of the Slavic states became clear. Yet the American Slav Congress continued to support Soviet policies. Many leaders of Slavic organizations, convinced of Communist infiltration of the congress, began to secede from it until, by the beginning of the Cold War, it was thoroughly dominated by Communist or radical left-wing pro-Soviet elements. And, as such, it became an "important weapon of Moscow's political warfare against the United States."[6]

The American Slav Congress offered Soviet Russia not only the opportunity to defend its plans concerning the future of many Slavic states, but also to beguile the Western leaders during the fateful war conferences. On December 22, 1943, the *Soviet Monitor,* No. 4015, in its *Evening Bulletin* "American Poles Welcome the Teheran Decision," stated in part:

> Over 1,500 Americans of Polish descent, at a meeting organized by the National Council of American-Soviet Friendship in New York, unanimously approved the declarations of the Moscow, Cairo, and Teheran Conferences. . . .
>
> The resolution adopted by the meeting urged Americans of Polish descent to give President Roosevelt their full support and welcomed the formation of a Polish Army in the U.S.S.R. as the basis of a lasting Soviet-Polish friendship. . . .
>
> The meeting was addressed by the well-known Polish Professor Lange, of the University of Chicago; by the Catholic Priest and Honorary President of the "Kosciuszko" League, Orlemanski; by the President of the American-Slav Congress, Kazicki [*sic*]; by the Democratic Senator Tunnell of the State of Delaware; and by Mr. Corliss Lamont, President of the Council of American-Soviet Friendship.[7]

The Soviet effort to confuse Poles here and abroad, as well as the governments of the Western powers, was evidently synchronized with the determined efforts of pro-Soviet American Poles to influence President Roosevelt's decisions regarding Poland. It is impossible at the present time to assess the effect of these activities on

American decisions at Yalta. In March, 1945, Krzycki, as president of the American-Polish Labor Council which was founded in January, 1944[8] (Krzycki was also president of the American Slav Congress), informed Roosevelt of the support of the council for the Yalta Agreement. In his letter he asked that the President send a greeting to the forthcoming conference of the council. "A greeting from you, Mr. President, . . . would assist us to clarify the issues in support of the Yalta agreement, and your wise and capable leadership." Krzycki assured Roosevelt that the 600,000 members of the American-Polish Labor Council were loyal trade-unionists of Polish descent who vigorously rejected the "divisive and vicious utterances of certain Polish misleaders" who had "no right to speak for all of us Americans of Polish origin or descent."[9] When no answer was received, Eugene Jasinski, executive director of the American-Polish Labor Council, wrote to James Barnes at the White House informing him that at the suggestion of Joe Berger of the Democratic National Committee he was enclosing a statement for the President's signature which would be read to the delegates. The statement read in part:

America has long been proud of the manifold contributions of its citizens of Polish extraction. . . .

I have been personally gratified, by the consistent understanding and support which they have displayed towards the efforts of our government, to maintain and consolidate our fighting partnership with our great allies for destroying the evil power of Nazism and Fascism, for creating the foundation of enduring peace, and for securing the economic well being of our respective peoples. . . .

By its perservering [sic] and patriotic efforts, the American-Polish Labor Council is contributing to the all-important task of welding and maintaining the unity of our great nation.

Jasinski included also a copy of the call to the members of the council. It pointed out that groups headed by the National Committee of Americans of Polish Descent (KNAPP) and leaders of the Polish American Congress were "spreading the poison of hate against our gallant British and Russian Allies" and "campaigning against our own government and especially President Roosevelt. They propose that our Congress *reject* the Yalta agreements, and thereby wreck the very foundation of American-Soviet-British coalition. . . ."[10] On April 4 Krzycki telephoned the White House to declare that Charles Rozmarek, president of the Polish American Congress, was a member of a "disruptive minority among loyal American Poles" sabotaging the Yalta and San Francisco conferences. William D. Hassett, secretary to the President, referred this "intelligence" to the officials of the Department of State "for attention."[11]

In late February, 1945, L. Mlekowski, secretary of "Polonia" Society—I.W.O. District No. 1, Chicago, informed President Roosevelt that "we, attending the celebration of the birthdays of these great democrats: Lincoln and Kosciuszko, held under the auspices of Polonia Society, express our great enthusiasm because of the decisions of the historic conference at Jalta." He then assured the President of the society's immense satisfaction at seeing Poland, "country of our forefathers arising to a new and better life with the help of the splendid American-Anglo-Soviet coalition" and confidently stated that the "new Democratic Poland will live as a good friendly neighbor with our allies, Soviet Union and Czechoslovakia." Mlekowski closed by mentioning the society's "deep conviction" that President Roosevelt's "labors during the Crimean conferences are worthy of the ideals left by the great Lincoln."[12]

The Second American Slav Congress was held in Pittsburgh on September 23, 1944, "as a sequel" to the eighth plenary session of the All-Slav Committee held in Moscow on August 13.[13] According to the Credentials Committee more than 2,500 delegates representing American Slavic organizations were present. The congress adopted resolutions of support for President Roosevelt and "his win-the-war-and-peace policies" and pledged support of the work of the Office of War Information, the Fifth War Loan Drive, and Russian war relief.

The Third American Slav Congress was held a year after the end of the war. The meeting, in New York City, was heralded by the *Russky Golos* with the following statement: "The voice of the American Slavs will be heard on September 22 in Madison Square Garden. It will be heard in Paris where meetings of the United Nations are taking place. The louder the voice of the Slavs, the more influential it will be in those places where statesmen meet to make decisions on which depend fates of all the people.

"The Russian Americans, loyal to the United States and loving the great, heroic people of their own, must send their delegates in as great numbers as possible to the Third Meeting of the Congress of American Slavs. . . ."[14]

By 1946 the American Slav Congress had been well infiltrated with Communist leadership. According to the roll call of delegates

173

published in the *Slavic American* there were 1,998 delegates, 1,734 representatives of Slavic organizations, 264 visitors, 45 delegates from Canada, 2 from Mexico, 12 "guests from Europe" (Soviet Russia, 6; Poland, 2; Czechoslovakia, 1; and Bulgaria, 3).[15] The Russian delegation was headed by Lieutenant General Gundorov, then head of the All-Slav Committee in Moscow.

The keynote speech was given by George Pirinsky, executive secretary of the American Slav Congress and former editor of the Bulgarian-Macedonian *Communist Weekly*.[16] In his address Pirinsky attacked the United States for abandoning the foreign policies of President Roosevelt. "What has transpired since Roosevelt died and since the war's end has convinced all of us, . . ." he said, "that the struggle for peace will be a very hard one. . . ." Pirinsky singled out President Truman as most responsible for "departing fast from the path of Roosevelt." He concluded: "Some of our policy makers in Washington and most of our commercial press would like to convince the American people that this discord stems from what they call Soviet expansion in eastern Europe. . . . But we, who come from those Slav countries . . . know that what actually is happening there is not 'Soviet expansion' but a mighty upsurge of the people's forces toward a militant political and economic democracy. . . ."

Krzycki, president of the congress, repeated Pirinsky's theme. "The policies of Roosevelt, which guided our nation to victory together with our allies," he thundered, "are being abandoned and replaced by a suicidal policy of atomic diplomacy which can only lead to atomic war." Neither Krzycki nor Pirinsky had a kind word for American foreign policies—or a harsh word for the Soviet Union. George Petkov, chairman of the All-Slav Committee of Bulgaria, expressed the consensus when he cried, "Long live the unity of Slavs under the leadership of the U.S.S.R.!"

At the closing session of the congress, messages from Joseph Stalin, Marshal Tito, and George Dimitrov of Bulgaria were greeted with cheers from the crowd of 15,000. References to Henry Wallace met with enthusiastic approval, while the name of Secretary of State James Byrnes, whom the meeting chairman, Louis Adamic, charged with being "hell bent on getting Joseph Goebbels' dreams to come true," was booed.[17] To the "marked delight of the Soviet delegates, Paul Robeson sang their 'Song of the Fatherland,' " the political significance of which, according to the House Committee on Un-American Activities, "was manifest to all." The members of the Soviet

174

delegation had planned to tour the United States and hold speaking engagements. They decided to cancel these after the Department of Justice requested them to register as agents of a foreign power.

The congress sent "observers" to an International Conference of Slavs in Belgrade in December, 1946.[18] After their return these individuals lectured throughout the United States urging Slavic-Americans to unite for peace—which meant, in the Communist lexicon, opposing American foreign policies. One of the returning observers was Krzycki. In his pamphlet *My Peace Mission to Europe,* issued by the congress September, 1949, he accused the "American war lords" of initiating the Cold War.[19] "The American Slav Congress," he wrote, "has insisted from the beginning that friendship and understanding between the United States and Eastern Europe, particularly with the Soviet Union, is essential to durable peace." He attacked Truman for "shamelessly" repudiating the policies of Roosevelt and cautioned that the Cold War made the task of the American Slav Congress "formidable."

In another pamphlet, *What I Saw in the Slavic Countries,* published by the congress in 1946, Krzycki described his experiences during his 1945 tour of the capitals of Russia and the satellites. The president of the congress disclosed that he had been awarded the Polonia Restituta by Boleslaw Bierut, Communist president of Poland, and that he had been given a four-hour interview—"the longest interview that the president has had with any American." At the end of his discussion with the Polish leader, Krzycki was more convinced than ever that "nothing is more erroneous than to label the Polish Government a 'stooge of Moscow.' " Krzycki's Moscow reception delighted him. "As I alighted from the plane," he proudly recounted, "I suddenly stopped in my tracks, speechless, for before me was an array of important people. . . . There was Lt. Gen. Alexander Gundorov, president of the All-Slav Committee in Moscow. . . ." But even greater honor was to come. "On January 3," wrote Krzycki, "was the most memorable day of my whole stay in the Soviet Union for it was then that I spent 90 minutes with the man who has been the great architect of the present Soviet state—Joseph Stalin." This, as the Committee on Un-American Activities observed, "was more time than had been allotted to American Secretary of State James F. Byrnes."

In a later report on his interview with Stalin, whom he likened to Abraham Lincoln,[20] he declared that "Stalin wants American work-

175

ers of Slav extraction. He wants to help them out if they are unemployed in the United States—wants to know if Slavs over here who are good mechanics will help Russia out for a couple of years by going there to work for Russia."[21]

3

The First American Slav Congress was held for the purpose of mobilizing "American Slavs for aid to the war effort." The Second American Slav Congress had as one of its purposes "to reelect President Roosevelt" and to speed victory. The Third American Slav Congress was called to "establish world peace," which had been endangered by the "reactionary forces," and "to be on the watch at coming elections." The Fourth American Slav Congress was held in September, 1948, "to roll up the largest possible Slavic American vote for the peace program of Wallace."[22]

During the presidential elections of 1948 the congress, now thorougly infiltrated with Communist sympathizers, became an active supporter of Wallace's Progressive party. In a thoroughgoing effort to win over Slavic and other nationality groups to the Progressive party, Krzycki became the chairman of the Nationalities Division and a member of the Platform Committee.

By 1948 almost all of the major Slavic-American organizations had withdrawn their support from the American Slav Congress. This, however, did not seem to be of great concern to the leaders of the congress, although their claim of representing 15,000,000 Slavic-Americans was changed to a claim of representing 10,000,000. With the decision of the congress to support Wallace for the presidency, a "sinister aspect," in the words of Truman, was added to the Wallace movement. "It provided," wrote Truman, "a front for the Communists to infiltrate the political life of the nation and spread confusion. Without the conscious knowledge of many members of the new Progressive party, the Reds were working swiftly and skillfully to gain control of the nominating convention and to dominate party committees and the platform." Wallace, who, according to Truman, "seemed to have been transformed into a mystic with a zeal that verged on fanaticism, was apparently unaware of the purposes to which the Communists were putting his 'progressive' movement. . . . He simply did not understand what was happening."[23]

With Krzycki's appointment came a concentrated and renewed

drive to infiltrate nationality groups through their fraternal, cultural, and political organizations and also through the Communist and pro-Soviet foreign-language press.[24] On November 2, Election Day, the Progressive party polled over one million votes.

Chapter XI

LIBERATION OR CONTAINMENT

". . . I wonder what Latitude or Longitude I've got to?" (Alice had not the slightest idea what Latitude was, or Longitude either, but she thought they were nice grand words to say.)
—Lewis Carroll, *Alice's Adventures in Wonderland.*

Their defeat in the 1948 presidential election was a bitter blow to the Republicans. It was totally unexpected. It shook the foundation of the party, shattered confidence in Republican leadership, and reopened deep wounds which the campaign had been unable to heal. Could the party recover from this devastating defeat? Was it forever doomed to stay in the wilderness?

Some Republicans felt that a major fault of Governor Thomas E. Dewey's strategy lay in his not forcefully attacking Democratic performance in the field of foreign affairs. Allen Dulles, who had been the foreign-affairs specialist on Dewey's campaign train, was, according to James Forrestal, sure that the bipartisan restraint which had prevented Dewey's using the "sequence of diplomatic decisions at Teheran, Cairo and Yalta" for political purposes had been responsible, in large part, for his defeat. Republican advisers, Dulles told Forrestal, had failed to realize "that they were the challenger and not the challenged." In Dulles' opinion, they had been wrong in believing "that injecting these issues into the campaign would have been destructive of the effort toward bipartisan foreign policy."[1]

By 1951 the Republican National Committee seemed to have decided to act in the light of criticisms such as those which had been voiced by Dulles. Many factors appeared to favor the ascendancy of the party: the Korean War; "corruption in high places"; Communism, Alger Hiss, and McCarthyism; the China "sell-out" and the "Yalta betrayal"; and then, too, there was Liberation—the freeing of captive nations in East Central Europe—versus Containment—the abandonment of "countless human beings to a despotism and godless terrorism."[2]

The hard fate of East European peoples offered an irresistible opportunity to appeal to special groups of Americans whose roots were behind the Iron Curtain. The Republican National Committee knew of Dewey's earlier efforts to win the ethnic groups and was aware of

178

his campaign organization toward that end. But the committee was more impressed with the successful tactics of the Democratic National Committee, which it believed to be the probable reason many Americans of foreign origin did not desert to the Dewey camp. Accordingly, early in 1951, in a determined bid for twenty-eight million nationality votes in seventeen key industrial states, the Republican National Committee set up an Ethnic Origins Division on both national and state levels under the direction of the committee's former executive director A. B. Hermann.[3] To head the Foreign Language Group Activities section of the Ethnic Origins Division, Party Chairman Arthur E. Summerfield chose Arthur Bliss Lane.

Lane seemed well suited to the position. He was an independently wealthy retired career diplomat and "a person of completely American origin."[4] As a former minister to the Baltic States and Yugoslavia and former ambassador to Poland, he was a familiar figure to recent émigrés and political exiles in the United States. He was a member of the board of the National Committee for a Free Europe. As a board member of the Polish Institute of Arts and Sciences, he had access to many prominent Polish scholars and intellectuals. His book, *I Saw Poland Betrayed*,[5] had been favorably received by critics and widely read. Lane had been one of the first to urge an investigation of the massacre of Katyn Forest, where the bodies of more than 10,000 Polish army officers and intellectuals had been found. (A Congressional committee subsequently corroborated the growing suspicion of Russian, rather than German, guilt in the mass murder.) Lane had other qualifications. His opposition to Communism was well known to the American public. He had been one of the first supporters of Senator Joseph R. McCarthy.[6] In 1948, before he was identified with the Republican party, he had openly urged the Polish American Congress to use its influence on both parties to repudiate the Yalta Agreement, thus to give notice that the United States was "through with the policy of appeasement." The refusal of the Democratic party to yield to the subsequent request of the Polish American Congress did not surprise Lane. What did shock him was the refusal of the Republican party, "largely through the influence of Cabot Lodge," he thought, to insert such a plank in its platform.[7] The rejection of his advice made him all the more anxious to apprise his fellow-citizens of his views. Soon his stand against Alger Hiss as one of the architects of the "Yalta betrayal" was noted in many newspapers, including the editorial pages of the *Washing-*

ton Times-Herald.[8] The controversy emanating from Lane's activities did not escape notice.

"I have decided to become a professional politician," Lane informed a friend soon after he had agreed to work for the Republicans as an expert on foreign-language groups. "I intend to pound on Yalta until it is included in the platform, even though I may break the timber in so doing."[9] And pound he did. But Lane was not a professional politician, as he was to discover.

Sincerely convinced that the United States had betrayed Poland and the other Iron Curtain nations in East Europe, Lane saw in his new assignment a chance to rectify his country's mistakes. He felt nothing amiss in the possibility that his activities among foreign-language groups might affect the formulation of American foreign policy. On the contrary, he welcomed pressures from these groups which would "intimately" entwine with foreign policy, "especially in the realm of psychological warfare," their hopes for their ancestral lands. At the same time, however, Lane was definite in stating that religious organizations and institutions should keep out of foreign affairs. "Foreign policy," he recorded after his attention had been called to the National Council of Churches' study conference report on United States responsibility in international affairs, "should be left primarily to persons who have devoted their lives to this study."[10]

To Lane, repudiation of the Yalta Agreement meant replacing the Democratic policy of containment with a Republican policy of liberation. The change, he believed, would bring hope to the oppressed peoples in East Europe and aid their underground movements. "If we want to have those people on our side," he later pleaded, "we have got to show them that we are really planning for their eventual independence just as many foreigners planned and died for ours." He foresaw unrest in the captive nations, but did not anticipate that the Russians would use military force to crush uprisings. Quite the opposite; he was convinced that mounting resistance would deter the Soviet government from aggressive designs not only in Europe but elsewhere as well.[11]

Lane did not realize that the National Committee was more interested in his potential ability to "liberate" Americans of East European descent from Democratic "containment" than in his advice and opinions on foreign policy. Nor was Lane conscious of the complicated and intricate politics within the very ethnic groups he sought to influence. Most of his friends from East Europe were either exiled leaders or recent immigrants who had little understanding of the attitudes and voting behavior current among their former fellow-citizens. Nor was Lane aware that though leaders of those ethnic groups were strongly anti-Communist, their primary aim was liberation of the satellite states, their countries of origin; ethnic nationalism and, even more important, personal-power considerations would prove to be more potent than avowed anti-Communism. In spite of these weaknesses Lane completed his assignment with some success. Only belatedly did he come to recognize that by allying himself with ethnic politics and the Republican National Committee he had weakened his ability to influence and affect foreign-policy decisions. Had he remained aloof from politicking, it is more than probable that he would have had the ear of the President directly, or indirectly through reappointment to the Department of State.

The first task that Lane set for himself was to assume responsibility for a plank in the forthcoming Republican platform which would repudiate the Yalta Agreement—this plank to be his principal argument in swinging foreign-language groups to the G. O. P. candidate. In June, 1951, he asked Governor John Lodge of Connecticut, a member of the Platform Committee, to help. Cognizant of the Governor's respect for the nationality vote, Lane reminded him that repudiation of the agreement was "essential not only from the viewpoint of international morality but also because of its practical effect on the foreign language voters."[12] As far as Lane was concerned, the Republicans could not miss.

It was not until January, 1952, that Lane made an all-out effort to insert planks in the platform promising repudiation not only of the Yalta Agreement but the Teheran and Potsdam Agreements as well. At his request the National Committee wrote to the men who then seemed most likely to become the Republican presidential candidate—Earl Warren, Harold Stassen, Robert Taft, and Henry Cabot Lodge (who represented General Eisenhower)—urging them to approve a foreign-policy plank which would "in effect repudiate Yalta." The committee also informed them that Lane had been appointed "to help us in connection with foreign language groups in the forthcoming campaign," and that, in his opinion, it was of importance, "in order to win the support of those voters who have relatives in countries behind the Iron Curtain," for the Republican party to repudiate the Teheran, Yalta, and Potsdam Agreements. To these letters was attached a draft of Lane's proposed plank.[13]

Two days later Lane himself wrote to Senator Taft stressing his conviction that "politically" the foreign-language groups would support and rally behind a policy having "as one of its eventual aims the liberation of the mother lands of American citizens of Albanian, Bielorussian, Bulgarian, Croatian, Czech, Estonian, Hungarian, Latvian, Lithuanian, Polish, Rumanian, Russian, Serbian, Slovak, Slovene and Ukrainian descent." He was most sure of a favorable reaction from the Polish-Americans—one of the largest groups—to a Republican denunciation of the wartime agreements with Soviet Russia which, in Lane's view, were responsible for the dismemberment of Poland.[14]

Of the replies received from the potential standard-bearers, only Taft's was satisfactory. Accordingly, Lane decided to support the Ohioan in the primaries.[15] At the same time, however, he renewed his efforts to convince the other three. "I would gladly come up to Philadelphia for a talk," he wrote to Stassen, "to give you some of the background . . . especially the relationship of the foreign language vote."[16] He emphasized to Governor Warren the importance of support from foreign-language elements: "Nothing . . . can appeal more fervently to the mind of a person whose heritage comes from what is now behind the Iron Curtain, than the unqualified statement of repudiation of Yalta." Lane pointed out that the party had not only a great opportunity to indicate its adherence to the principles of the Atlantic Charter, but a chance at the same time to "gain the votes of those American citizens who deeply resent the fact that the United States Government sold their respective motherlands down the river to Communism."[17] In April he wrote directly to Eisenhower informing him of his position with the National Committee as an adviser on foreign affairs, "especially with regard to the so-called ethnic groups," and asked him to support a plank in the platform which would repudiate the Yalta Agreement. "This would have a tremendous effect," he added, "not only on the voters of Polish descent but on many other groups of foreign descent. . . ."[18] On the day he wrote to Eisenhower, he complained about his inability to draw positive responses from those who managed the General's political affairs. "Is this the policy," he asked a member of the National Committee for Eisenhower for President, "of these same Republicans [Dewey men] in 1952? If so, millions of votes of American citizens of Polish origin may be lost, and the election to boot."[19]

In the end, Lane's platform efforts were successful. By the time delegates began to gather at Chicago convention headquarters in June, the idea of liberation was already fixed in the minds of influential Republicans. Earlier in the month, the Ethnic Origins Division and Research Division of the National Committee had circulated a pamphlet, *Republican Policy of Liberation or Democrat Policy of Containment,* which called attention to the growing support for the liberation policy as a "Republican policy in the making. . . . especially well received by American citizens of Polish, Hungarian, Czech, Slovak, Lithuanian, Latvian, Estonian, Bulgarian, Rumanian, Ukrainian, Byelo-Russian and Russian descent."[20] The pamphlet carried quotations from such prominent party men as John Foster Dulles, Robert Taft, Charles Kersten, H. Alexander Smith, and Styles Bridges. In effect, it endorsed Representative Kersten's resolution on liberation, House Concurrent Resolution 119, introduced on June 7, 1951, which he urged the platform committee to adopt. The resolution, purportedly favored by 82 Republican Congressmen and 75 well-known citizens, mostly ethnic leaders, stated in part: "We believe that all the people who have been subjugated by the Communist tyranny are entitled to their earliest possible liberation. . . . To assist in bringing about this liberation from Communist slavery, we shall offer positive aid and moral support to active fighters now struggling for such liberation."[21]

Meanwhile, the Republican National Committee had facilitated Lane's access to eminent Republican figures whom he urged repeatedly to support his stand on the Yalta Agreement. Because the key person in the drafting of the foreign-policy plank was John Foster Dulles, Lane labored to win him to his viewpoint. "I had numerous talks with Foster Dulles in Chicago," recalled Lane, "urging him, not only because of the international importance but for political purposes also, to make this plank as strong as possible."[22]

In 1950, when Dulles was an adviser to the State Department, he had analyzed astutely the dangers of subjecting foreign policy to the vicissitudes inherent in domestic political campaigns. "If, at a time of national peril," he wrote, "two Presidential candidates should compete in making novel and unseasoned proposals, designed primarily to win votes, the end of that campaign would leave our foreign relations in a shambles."[23] In 1952, Dulles' sense of discernment was less keen; he seemed ready to throw caution aside in order to try for a windfall of votes. The future Secretary of State did not need much prodding from Lane. In a magazine article, he promised a new dynamic policy based on moral principles—a policy which would move beyond containment. The only way American policy could achieve its objectives, he wrote, was by making *"it publicly known that it wants and expects liberation to occur."*[24] With the support of Dulles the planks were adopted.

The 1952 Republican platform charged the Truman administration with losing the peace "so dearly earned by World War II." It condemned Teheran, Yalta, and Potsdam as "tragic blunders" which left friendly nations such as Latvia, Lithuania, Estonia, Poland, and Czechoslovakia "to fend for themselves against the Communist aggression which soon swallowed them." It promised to "repudiate all commitments contained in secret understandings such as those of Yalta which aid Communist enslavements," and anticipated "genuine independence of those captive peoples," adding:

We shall again make liberty into a beacon light of hope that will penetrate the dark places. That program will give the Voice of America a real function. It will mark the end of the negative, futile and immoral policy of "containment" which abandons countless human beings to a despotism and godless terrorism, which in turn enables the rulers to forge the captives into a weapon for our destruction. . . .

The policies we espouse will revive the contagious, liberating influences which are inherent in freedom. They will inevitably set up strains and stresses within the captive world which will make the rulers impotent to continue in their monstrous ways and mark the beginning of their end.[25]

Thus, the successful candidate, Dwight D. Eisenhower, was bound to a program for which he had hitherto shown little enthusiasm.

2

The Republican National Committee was prepared to use the foreign-policy planks in the pending campaign. The task of mobilizing the effort to secure the nationality vote fell to the willing hands of Arthur Bliss Lane, head of the Foreign Language Group Activities section of the Ethnic Origins Division. Lane was ready. Long before the final adoption of the platform he had openly solicited help and advice from, primarily, Americans of foreign origin. Many were delighted to hear that he was to be in charge of the nationality groups for the Republican party—"That's the best news I've had in a long, long while," wrote one of his correspondents. Some were certain that with the help of Lane the party would break the Democratic hold over ethnic groups. One characterized foreign-language groups as "a most important field, which is ripe for plucking."[26] Soon leaders of various nationality groups sent drafts and proposals concerning their native lands to Lane's office for his consideration as adviser on American foreign policy for the Republicans.[27] The Ethnic Origins Division rerouted to Lane the plans and suggestions "for corralling" the nationality votes which it received from many individuals throughout the country. He was asked to go over a large number of letters from those professing to have the right answers for the party and to "consider the possibility of utilizing" their services.[28]

One of the first persons whom Lane was asked to encourage was Waclaw M. Wusza, who was typical of the ethnic advisers he collected. Wusza, according to the autobiographical sketch he submitted, seemed, at first, ideal for Lane's purposes. A professional newspaperman, he came to the United States in 1913. During the First World War he was editor-in-chief of two Polish-American newspapers—the *Polish Daily News* and, later, the *Polish Daily Record,* both Republican-oriented. Wusza went back to Poland in 1930, intending to return to the United States in 1939, but the war prevented his doing so. During the German occupation, he claimed, he was in the underground. When the Soviets subsequently occupied Poland, he worked for the Communist government in the province of Posen as an economic adviser. "My aim," explained Wusza, "was to notify the English and American Embassy about everything what's is going on [*sic*] Poland." It was in this endeavor, apparently, that he had met Lane, then United States ambassador to Poland. Wusza returned to the United States in 1947.[29]

Lane received many ideas, plans, and insights as to the voting behavior of American ethnic groups, primarily Polish-Americans, from Wusza. His first suggestions stressed the importance of Yalta, the Democratic appeasement of Russia, and Truman's weakness before Stalin. He saw in the investigation of the Katyn Forest massacre potential campaign material. In July Wusza urged the National Committee to expand its activities to "every county, especially in the States where Polish votes can have a serious importance," and to organize special committees of men who knew local conditions.

He explained thoroughly how to go about capturing the allegiance of nationality groups. From Wusza, Lane learned in detail of the politically divided loyalties of the Polish-Americans—that some organizations were traditionally Republican, some Democratic. Wusza offered to prepare propaganda material for the foreign-language press and promised to get in touch with representatives of different nationality groups for help in this. He studied and analyzed the Polish-American press and reported that some prominent editors and leaders were "flirting" with Democrats. He was, for example, disturbed that one editor of an important paper repeated an opinion of Representative Antoni Sadlak of Connecticut that Eisenhower would not receive the Polish-American vote. This "tactic" of the editor, Wusza charged, gave the readers the impression that the Polish National Alliance was against the Republican party. Wusza volunteered to go to the convention of the alliance to find out "what Poles and other foreign speaking groups think."[30] The National Committee and Lane were impressed; they would have offered Wusza a position with the committee had he been an American citizen. Instead, he was recommended to Radio Free Europe, where Lane believed he could be of "considerable help in reaching the Polish-speaking community in this country," and because of his many contacts, "political acumen," and knowledge of conditions behind the Iron Curtain, he "could be a valuable adjunct" to the National Committee for a Free Europe.[31]

3

Meanwhile the All-American Origins Division and the Ethnic Origins Division of the Republican National Committee were busy compiling statistical information on ethnic groups. By June, 1952, they made available detailed analyses of the distribution of Americans of foreign origin by politically strategic states, cities, and, in some cases, Congressional districts. Their figures were based either on church and organization membership or on the census and immigration reports. No nationality group, however small, escaped attention. More than thirty groups were listed, among them the Carpatho-Ruthenians, Croatians, Czechs, Germans, Greeks, Lithuanians, Poles, Armenians, French, Portuguese, Spaniards, Swedes, Jews, Russians, Chinese, and even Filipinos, only 30,000 of whom lived in the United States. Whenever possible, the Ethnic Origins Division relied more on information from churches and organizations than government sources. To cite an instance of the discrepancies, the division gave 4,157,000 as the number of Polish-Americans; the census figure (which included the Polish-born, the native-born of Polish or mixed parentage, and Polish Jews) was 2,786,199. (In the directives given to Republican candidates for political offices the number given for Polish-Americans was 6,000,000.) The Ethnic Origins Division also made available lists of foreign-language publications in the United States, presumedly based on data from the Common Council of American Unity. The lists gave the name, place, publication date, and type of each publication, as well as the names of the editors and publishers. Rosters of all ethnic churches and organizations, by states and cities, were supplied. The importance of the clergy was not overlooked. The division furnished lists of names and addresses of the churchmen, suggesting that the candidates arrange visits. It felt that parishioners, particularly women, vote the way their spiritual advisers do.[32]

In addition, plans were made to place in the hands "of the electorate of foreign linguistic origin or background" phonograph records with political messages. To give these records "retention value," it was proposed that the reverse side of the "political talking-tract" carry the "Star Spangled Banner" and the national anthem of the "old country." Lane endorsed this idea for its intended psychological effect. By August the project was ready.[33]

4

The first reactions to Eisenhower's nomination from spokesmen of nationality groups had not been encouraging. Eisenhower was considered by many Slavic-Americans to be a friend of Stalin. It was charged that, by agreeing to Stalin's demands, he had been responsible for sending to Siberia six hundred thousand prisoners of the Russians who had been liberated by the American army in Germany. He was also blamed for facilitating the Russian invasion of East Europe by his refusal, so the story went, to follow British advice to invade Europe from the Balkans. *Human Events,* a weekly Washington newsletter, reported that many Polish-Americans were indignant over Eisenhower's acceptance of the Soviet Order of Suvarov and his later acceptance, when he was president of Columbia University, of a grant from the Communist government of Poland to establish a chair of Polish literature.[34]

From the Middle West came stories of growing anti-Eisenhower sentiment among German-American voters. Some stressed that Taft, by his appeals during the primaries to the German-American vote there, left a residue of ill-will toward the General. Voters of German stock, the accounts claimed, associated Eisenhower with the Carthaginian peace imposed on Germany, with the abortive Morgenthau plan which aimed at the reduction of the industrial potential of the *Vaterland,* and with the "heartless exiling of some 200,000 Germans to Russia for slave labor." From a correspondent in Milwaukee, Lane learned that "it was hard to convince many . . . German friends to vote for the *General,*" but that if a "National Organization of German Americans could be formed . . . there would be a million or more votes which could be swayed to the Republican Party."[35] Lane also discovered that on the very eve of the convention, some of his advisers, concerned over the anti-Eisenhower sentiment among the various nationality groups, had been ready to put pressure on the delegates to vote for Taft. This, as one report stated, was not done because it was "risky"; "there wasn't any money to do it," and there was "no courage."[36]

Other memoranda repeated conversations overheard in Republican clubs frequented by ethnic leaders. One indicated that Eisenhower had been described as one of the "founders (creators) of the Yalta agreement" and that during the ensuing discussion a participant had said, " 'We shouldn't be foolish! Don't you realize that Eisenhower's people don't care for the Polish votes like Dewey's in 1948. Up to now we didn't hear a word from them what to do. They are too busy. But Eisenhower had a time to spend a few days among the Indians. They are more important, than we are.' "[37] The General, in the opinion of ethnic leaders, had to be taken off the Indian reservations and put into the field—the reservations of non-Indian Americans. This became even more imperative as adverse news from strategic ethnic areas poured into National Committee headquarters. From these reports the committee learned that the Nationalities Division of the Democratic National Committee was working "feverishly" to hold on to the wavering ethnic vote; that the "highly able Democratic propaganda machine" was ready to "play up" the anti-Eisenhower grievances among the foreign-language groups; that the Democrats too had chosen prominent representatives of nationality groups as advisers; and that some foreign-language newspapers, influenced by Democratic Congressmen of ethnic extraction, were attacking the Republicans.

What especially irked Lane and his co-workers was the part of the Democratic platform which took credit for exposing "the shocking revelations of Soviet guilt" in the Katyn Forest massacre. They were also concerned about the other parts of the platform which mirrored the Republican promises to restore "the liberties of Poland and the other oppressed Soviet satellites, including Czechoslovakia, Hungary, Rumania, Bulgaria, Albania, Lithuania, Estonia and Latvia and other nations in Asia under Soviet domination. . . ." Of special interest was the Democratic plank which reasserted and reaffirmed the "Wilsonian principle of the right of national self-determination," thus making it a part of Democratic policy "to encourage and assist small nations and all peoples in the peaceful and orderly achievement of their legitimate aspirations toward political, geographical and ethnic integrity. . . ."[38]

With some misgiving and reluctance, Eisenhower, at the prodding of the National Committee, accepted the liberation policy. But even so he did not, at first, go as far as was expected of him. On August 13, after a conference with Representative Kersten, Eisenhower declared that the Truman Administration's policy of " 'mere containment' " did not "go far enough in bringing freedom to peoples now ruled by Communist masters." His official statement as issued by his press secretary, James C. Hagerty, read: "A true program for peace for the United States must include as one of its peaceful aims the restoration of the captive nations of Europe and the right freely and honestly to determine their own fate and their own form of government. Similarly, the same right must be achieved by the captive nations of Asia." The Eisenhower release was not synonymous with Kersten's interpretation of their conversation. According to the *New York Times,* the Wisconsin lawmaker had made the "big news of the day" with his statement to the press that "American foreign policy must be aimed at the ultimate freedom for captive nations." Kersten added that he had urged support of "an amendment to the Mutual Security Act providing $100,000,000 to encourage resistance among the captive peoples. . . ." Evidently Eisenhower was concerned over a possible misunderstanding of his views, for Hagerty announced that Eisenhower's statement was " 'in no way an endorsement' " of Kersten's plans. " 'The general,' " said Hagerty, " 'was merely referring to a stand which the United States must take in letting the captive people behind the Iron Curtain realize that we are for the restoration of the form of government that they

189

themselves would vote.' " Nevertheless, the view of W. H. Lawrence of the *New York Times* was that "political observers thought that General Eisenhower's statement of plans to restore eventual liberty to nations such as Poland, Czechoslovakia and China might have a major effect on the not insubstantial nationality vote in the United States."[39]

There was to be no turning back. On August 25, in a speech before the American Legion in New York, the Republican presidential candidate outlined a "new" and vigorous foreign policy. The address embodied the hopes of the Ethnic Origins Division; it was filled with appeals to the ethnic vote: "All these people [behind the Iron Curtain] are blood kin to us. How many people today live in a great fear that never again shall they hear from a mother, grandfather, a brother or a cousin? Dare we rest while these millions of our kinsmen remain in slavery? . . .

"The American conscience can never know peace until these people are restored again to being masters of their own fate. . . .

"We must tell the Kremlin that never shall we desist in our aid to every man and woman of those shackled lands who seeks refuge with us, any man who keeps burning among his own people the flame of freedom or who is dedicated to the liberation of his fellows."[40] Almost concurrently, on August 27, John Foster Dulles chose Buffalo, New York, one of the largest centers of Polish-Americans, to announce Eisenhower's support for the policy of liberation.

On October 5—Martyrs' Day, commemorating the end of the Hungarian War of Independence—Eisenhower reaffirmed that the party was committed to a foreign policy aimed at liberating "enslaved peoples through peaceful means."[41] The next day, Senator Richard M. Nixon, the Republican candidate for the vice-presidency, in an address from the steps of the New York Public Library, where he reviewed the General Pulaski Day celebration, blamed the Yalta Agreement for the enslavement of Poland and asked for its repudiation.[42]

Eisenhower, however, was reluctant openly to advocate repudiating wartime agreements with Soviet Russia. His closest advisers did everything in their power to prevent the mounting pressures from the National Committee from influencing him in favor of such a statement. In the end, the committee won out. Lane believed that it was he who had finally convinced the General. "I personally boarded

190

the Eisenhower Special in California," he wrote, "and told General [W. B.] Persons that if a statement were not made we would stand to lose the Polish-American vote."[43] Somewhere between California and Colorado word got out that the Republican candidate was going to endorse repudiation. When Eisenhower reached Denver he was greeted by former Senator John A. Danaher, director of the Division of Special Activities of the National Committee, and a group of Polish-Americans who had come to receive personally the long-awaited statement from the future President. At the Brown Palace Hotel, Eisenhower, after conferring with the Polish-Americans, issued a General Pulaski Day message which noted the presence in the Republican platform of a pledge to repudiate the Yalta Agreement:

> It is my great privilege to send fervent greetings to American citizens of Polish descent, on this anniversary of the death of their great Polish patriot, Gen. Casimir Pulaski.
>
> Pulaski, a Pole, realized that the independence of the United States was closely linked with his most earnest desire, the independence of his beloved Poland. He was therefore glad and proud to fight and die for the freedom of the United States. . . .
>
> On this memorable day we pray for the independence of Poland, now captive under Communist domination. The platform of the Republican party pledged repudiation of the Yalta Agreement which, through the violation of the principles of the Atlantic Charter and through its unilateral violation by the Soviet government, has resulted in the enslavement of Poland.
>
> Thus we will give hope to the people of Poland and to all the American friends of Poland, whether or not of Polish origin, and the assurance that their liberty is forever in our minds.[44]

Thus the All-American Origins Division and the Ethnic Origins Division of the National Committee were certain of securing many crucial votes among those nationalities whose native lands were overrun by Soviet Russia.

Eisenhower's acquiescence in the pledge of repudiation of the Yalta Agreement by no means ended the campaign to influence the ethnic vote. To be sure, some Pulaski Democratic clubs changed their names to Pulaski Citizen clubs; other Slavic-American Democratic societies decided to work for Eisenhower; and some politicians of Slavic descent left the Democratic party to support the Republican candidate.[45] But it was also found that some groups, for example, the National Committee of Americans of Polish Descent, opposed American encouragement of "revolution behind the Iron Curtain unless such encouragement was backed with material aid." The *New York Times* reported a statement of Henry Kogut, vice president of that organization, that said, ". . . United States encouragement of a revolution in Poland—without a United States commitment to help the Poles revolt—would harm, rather than help the cause." Mrs. Sophie Schoen, another vice president, said, " 'These nations are in no position to resist. They would be crushed, their people slaughtered.' "[46] The prophetic words were to haunt many an American, hyphenated or not. Had Eisenhower anticipated the 1956 Hungarian revolt, he would, perhaps, have been more restrained in his promises to liberate the homelands of those Americans of foreign origin.

The political strategists in charge of the ethnic vote certainly realized that each nationality group was not homogeneous, that each was divided into organized rival "publics." They were aware of differences in political attitudes between those who were foreign-born and those of succeeding generations. Nor were they unmindful of the presence among nationality groups of deep antagonisms which led to divergent aims. Reports from the field repeatedly pointed out that in some areas environment seemed to be stronger than heredity. One of Lane's correspondents was astonished that in "Texas Poles declare themselves . . . as Americans." Others showed concern over political pressures from labor organizations to vote, supposedly, for the Democratic party. To many an ethnic leader, political reasoning from other than ethnic premises was invalid and not to be tolerated. The most ominous implications were drawn from reports indicating that second- and third-generation descendants of immigrants, who thought like average Americans and had forgotten the mother tongue, could not be easily influenced through the foreign-language press or nationality organizations. Even the issue of Communism "as a basis of propaganda" did not seem to make much headway. After all, read one report, "Democrats are prepared to fight Communism too," and "Stevenson is now a deadly enemy of Communism." Lane recognized this latter weakness and began to take steps to reduce the difficulty foreign-language groups had in taking "an over-all point of view with respect to Communism" without thinking "in terms of nationalism and of party interests in their respective countries."[47] Political strategy and appeals had to be formulated which would make the immigrant and his descendants more aware of their national origins, subordinate the issue of Com-

192

munism to nationalistic aspirations, and mitigate mutual hostility among them. Success in this enterprise would mean bringing a multitude of Americans of foreign origin closer to the Republican party.

In September, 1952, the Office of Coördinator of Foreign Language Groups was moved to the Washington Hotel, seat of the Republican Campaign Headquarters. There, in the nation's capital, the final phase of the presidential campaign was organized. Danaher and Lane appointed directors for seventeen foreign-language groups.[48] Each was requested to organize, coördinate, and integrate political activities within his group. It was hoped that through these director-representatives conflicting interests within and among the groups would be discussed and eventually resolved. The seventeen nationality leaders and their numerous assistants had no difficulty in deciding on liberation and the "Yalta betrayal" as overriding issues which would bring desired results. Under their aegis various foreign-language pamphlets and leaflets were written and distributed. "These thirteen nationalities in Eastern Europe," read one brochure, "were betrayed by the Democratic Administration during the past decade— Estonians, Latvians, Lithuanians, Poles, Ukrainians, Byelorussians, Czech, Slovaks, Hungarians, Bulgars, Rumanians, Carpatho-Russians, and East Germans."[49] In addition, articles and speeches were planted in foreign-language newspapers and radio programs. Speaking tours for prominent ethnic and non-ethnic individuals were arranged. Committees of Crusades to Lift the Iron Curtain were organized as aids "for securing the vote of various Slavic groups." Under the auspices of the committees, "Liberation Centers," "Liberation Rallies," and "Liberation Weeks" were held in states with large concentrations of nationality groups. Republican governors of New York, Connecticut, Pennsylvania, Maryland, and New Jersey gave full coöperation to this effort by signing appropriate proclamations hailing "Liberation Weeks." The momentum of the activities carried them into Democratically-controlled states. When apprehension that a policy of liberation might lead to war was expressed, speakers from the National Committee countered by stating that a firm policy toward Soviet Russia based on American disapproval of its enslavement of free nations would lead, on the contrary, to peace; the containment policy had "in fact already led to war in Korea," and the loss of Manchuria and North Korea.

The newly appointed directors were grateful and dedicated men. They exuded confidence; their excitement was contagious. No problem, however difficult, was considered unsolvable. When, to cite an instance, reports kept indicating that Eisenhower was still being identified with the wartime policies of Roosevelt, one director suggested a novel way which he believed certain to end the persistent "myth." He proposed drafting for Eisenhower's signature a statement which would blame Roosevelt for halting the American armies at the Elbe River in 1945; which would claim that had Eisenhower's military opinions not been overruled by the Democratic administration, East Europe would not have been taken over by Communists; and, lastly, which would warn Polish- and Czech-Americans that they deserved "little compassion" should they vote for Stevenson, who approved the policies which had "betrayed" their "Fatherland and relatives." The director's plan and money for its implementation in twelve or fourteen foreign-language papers were approved. There was some discussion of having it printed on yellow throw-sheets for air-dropping "over such places as Hamtramck." The reason for yellow was to emphasize dramatically the conclusion of the statement: "If you men and women of Polish and Czech descent can, after reading the above, vote for the Democratic candidate . . . you are as yellow as this paper." Eisenhower's sanction was needed to put the plan in operation "within 48 hours." It did not materialize.[50]

Efforts to isolate Americans of foreign origin from their fellow-citizens continued. No state was overlooked, no group spared. On the West Coast, Americans of Polish, Czech, Croatian, Slovene, Slovak, Russian, Serbian, Hungarian, Lithuanian, and Bulgarian descent were subjected to a concentrated barrage of propaganda. Soon the chairmen of the foreign-language group activities there were able to exult that the effectiveness and thoroughness of their organizations in California, Oregon, and Washington were "unprecedented in the annals of California political campaigns" and that the effort to capture the ethnic vote had progressed beyond the "most optimistic expectations." From Chicago, Lane learned that the *Sun-Times* straw poll had shown "that purely democratic wards . . . inhabited by Poles and Bohemians for the first time are for the Republicans." An observer of the "Russian circles" in New York reported that "out of three Russian dailies in New York, one (circ. 12,000) is safely Communist, one (circ. 2,000) safely Republican, and one (circ. 33,000) is now Republican too." This same person, who took credit for the above switch "though the editor would not admit" the truth of this, estimated that in the New York area alone the Republicans could "count on at least 70,000 Republican votes among the Russians and Russian Jews, as against some 15,000 for Stevenson —the Russian Jews only" and calculated that the Orthodox Church with a membership of 400,000 and the overwhelming majority of Russian-Americans in the United States were Republican. He also informed Lane that he had published some two hundred articles in the Russian-language papers, reminding him that a Republican editorial policy in the foreign-language press is more important, and "means much more" than the editorial orientations of the "too 'objective' " papers like the *New York Times* and others. Similar enthusiastic and optimistic reports were received from chairmen in New York, Connecticut, New Jersey, Pennsylvania, Ohio, Michigan, Wisconsin, Illinois, Arizona, Nevada, and Utah. No worker in the ethnic field toiled more zealously than Lane. Within one month, October 2 to November 2, he gave "hundreds" of speeches from California to Connecticut.[51]

5

With the increased activities to capture the ethnic vote, the policy of liberation became hopelessly entangled in domestic politics. Irony lay in that the more the issue of liberation became associated with the nationality vote, the less likely was its realization. The Democratic party, apprehensive over its apparent inability to control the ethnic vote, defended itself by charging the Republicans with foul play. Its presidential candidate, Adlai E. Stevenson, termed the liberation policy a "cynical and transparent attempt, drenched in crocodile tears, to play upon the anxieties of foreign nationality groups in this country."[52] President Truman bitterly commented that the Republicans, by stirring up "our citizens who have ties of blood" with the peoples of East Europe, "are playing a cruel, gutter politic game with the lives of countless good men and women behind the iron curtain." He charged the Republican party with talking "loosely" about liberation. "Nothing could be worse," he said, "than to raise false hopes. . . . Nothing could be worse than to incite uprisings that can only end by giving a new crop of victims to the Soviet executioners." Without mentioning Dulles' name, Truman accused the future Secretary of State of willingness, despite knowledge of the "precarious situation the world is in . . . to have the Republican Party, and the Republican candidate, say things that increase the risk of war, simply in order to get votes."[53] But at the same time, Stevenson, Truman, and the Democratic Nationalities Division offered another—milder—brand of liberation.

The Democratic party could not compete with the Republican over the issue of liberation. The Republicans went so far with their promises that the Democrats could not go further without pledging outright immediate use of force to free the captive nations. On September 13, after analyzing the effect on Slavic groups of Lane's and Kersten's appeals, the Research Division of the Democratic National Committee concluded that as a "most useful procedure" the Democrats should emphasize the constructive and positive steps which the administration had undertaken against Communism: "The stand for a more liberal Displaced Persons program and immigration policy, the protests against mass deportation and genocide, etc." The division's recommendation was adopted.[54]

The Republican charge that the Democratic policy of containment was responsible for the abandonment of "countless human beings to a despotism and godless terrorism" behind the Iron Curtain, was now answered with a countercharge that the "snobbish" Republicans, by the establishment of a "paper Curtain," had kept many of these unfortunate people from coming to America, and thus were responsible for "the human tragedy of mortgaging quotas." During the campaign Democratic candidates were supplied by the National Committee with appropriate directives stressing the platform:

"Solution of the problem of refugees from communism and over-population has become a *permanent part of the foreign policy program of the Democratic Party* . . . [italics added].

". . . The gates must be left open. . . .

"We pledge continuing revision of our immigration and naturalization laws to do away with any unjust and unfair practices against national groups which have contributed some of our best citizens. . . ."[55]

The foregoing plank was compared to the Republican platform which "was absolutely silent on the need for fair, just, and decent immigration and naturalization." Americans of ethnic origin were reminded that in its 1932 platform the Republican party had claimed as Republican policy the "restriction of immigration"; that it had been the first to enact "into law the quota system"; and that in 1952 the Republicans had kept "silent on immigration or boast of their snobbishness."

President Truman's October address in Buffalo clearly showed the influence of the Research Division of the National Committee. He said, in part:

But we must not encourage rash adventures. We are not going to ask the unarmed people of the Iron Curtain countries to rise up against their aggressors, and sacrifice themselves before firing squads of the Kremlin. That may be what the Republican candidate for President and his foreign policy advisers are urging—in order to get votes in this country. But we are not going to do it. . . .

There is, however, one more thing we want to do, and we find it very hard to do, because of Republican opposition. That is to find new homes and new opportunities, particularly in our own country, for some of the people of those lands. . . .

This National Origin Quota System is a Republican invention. It was conceived and written into law under a Republican President and a Republican Congress in the 1920's. . . .

Now the Republicans took full credit for this discriminatory policy. They boasted of it, as one of their achievements, in their 1932 platform. . . .

But the Republican party platform doesn't even have the word immigration in it. . . .

The National Origins Quota System isn't the only bad feature of this new immigration law. The whole statute breathes prejudice against the foreign born—alien and naturalized citizen alike. It establishes a cruel and restrictive procedure against aliens, and a second class status, before the law, for naturalized citizens.[56]

As the political campaign entered its last stage, Democratic candidates told Americans of Central and South European descent that the Republican vice-presidential candidate, Nixon, stood for "Republican snobbery"; that he was "certainly" not interested in people who came from those areas; that he had voted to override Truman's veto of the 1952 Immigration Act "to continue the snobbish national quota principle"; and that as a Representative in the House he had supported a feature of the "Displaced Persons legislation which had the effect of excluding thousands of Poles—largely Catholics and Jews. . . ."

Italian-Americans, who, as one directive described them, "do not forget their former home," heard that the Republicans represented a "policy of exclusionism," while the Democrats represented a "policy of inclusion." They were then subjected to an interesting version of American immigration history:

In the early days of the Republic, under the leadership of Presidents like Thomas Jefferson and Andrew Jackson, the nation went *far* towards giving freedom and opportunity to everyone who *came here*—then:

But *after 1850* came a great new wave of people, *including many from Italy* and *Eastern Europe*.

And *groups sprang* up which said: "Let's keep everything for those who've been here a long time. First come get all the *gravy*."

For a *while* these people who hated "foreigners" and immigrants even organized a political party called the Know-Nothings or *Nativists* and this party was one of the *groups* which entered into the Republican party.

So it's not surprising to find that on the whole the Republican party has stood for the principle: "Let's keep the large end of the loaf for the people whose ancestors came here before *1850*."

Polish-Americans were told that the Democratic Congress had provided for admission of 18,000 Polish veterans; Czech-Americans and Slovak-Americans were reminded that the Democrats had made possible the admission of Czechoslovaks who had fled their homeland after the Communist *coup d'état;* German-Americans were asked to recall the "new program for German Ethnic expellees" which permitted 54,744 Europeans of German ethnic origin to enter the United States; and Greek-Americans were told that it had been the Democratic Congress which asked for the admission of 10,000 Greek refugees.[57] Thus, immigration, one of the greatest privileges America has offered to the world, was dragged into the battles for the hyphenated vote.

6

On November 4, 1952, General Dwight D. Eisenhower was elected President with a spectacular plurality of 6,616,232 popular votes. Naturally, the All-American Origins Division and the Ethnic Origins Division of the Republican National Committee were jubilant. Within a few days after the election state chairmen, newly elected legislators, and the directors of the seventeen nationality groups sent their appreciations to the National Committee and Lane. Most were convinced that foreign-language groups had played an important part in the outcome. Some emphasized the contribution of individual nationality groups, claiming credit for it, and some stressed the Polish-American vote, more than any other, as the "single factor which was responsible for the victory."[58] Lane, while admitting that the victory resulted from no single factor, nevertheless held that the campaign activities among the ethnic population accounted for more than three million normally Democratic votes in politically strategic areas.[59] No one seemed to challenge his claim, which was particularly astounding when analyses of election figures in ethnic wards showed that Polish- and Czech-Americans had not voted as solidly for Eisenhower as had been expected. One research organization reported, for example, that in German-American wards and precincts in Baltimore, the actual vote for Stevenson was 55 percent and for Eisenhower 44.1 percent; in some Czech-American wards and precincts in Chicago, Stevenson polled 67.3 percent to Eisenhower's 32.7 percent; in Polish-American wards (which also included Negroes) in Akron, Boston, and Cleveland, the vote for Stevenson was much higher than that for Eisenhower.[60] Confronted with these percentages from, to be sure, scattered areas, the Ethnic Origins Division interpreted them as evidence of ineffective propaganda techniques and took credit for cutting into the hitherto solidly Democratic immigrant districts. Both Republican and Democratic political strategists in charge of the ethnic vote refused to believe that Americans of foreign origin are either capable of voting or willing to vote as Americans. "Exceptions" to this thesis were noted for special attention in subsequent campaigns. The belief that ethnic Americans of second, third, fourth, and even fifth generations vote on the basis of heredity was thus perpetuated.

Exploitation of the emotions of nationality groups might have brought immediate political gains, but it was certain to impede the incoming administration's freedom of action in the pursuit of realistic foreign policies. Here was a good example of the incompatibility of international morality with misguided realism in domestic politics.

Chapter XII

POSTSCRIPT TO LIBERATION

"It seems very pretty," she said when she had finished it, "but it's *rather* hard to understand! . . . Somehow it seems to fill my head with ideas—only I don't exactly know what they are!"

—Lewis Carroll, *Through the Looking Glass.*

What, then, of the promise to liberate East Europe? What of the initiation of Republican positive policies as opposed to the negative Democratic policy of containment?

Liberation of the satellites meant different things to different people. To the Republican National Committee it meant a way to win and hold the ethnic vote. To the Democratic National Committee it meant a threat to its hold over Slavic nationality groups. To men like Arthur Bliss Lane, Charles J. Kersten, many Republicans, and some nationality leaders it meant a "grand new strategy" which would destroy Russian control in East Europe and Asia through economic pressures, subversion of Communist regimes, encouragement and subsidization of resistance movements, and propaganda offensives (psychological warfare). To James Burnham, author of *Containment or Liberation,* who supplied a rationale for the policy of liberation, it meant American recognition of the "right to self-determination and therefore to independence of all the nations of the Soviet Empire, including the nations located within the pre-1939 Soviet boundaries."[1] To others liberation meant reducing the cost of national defense, an end to national anxiety, the ultimate victory without economic strain or danger of war. To the nationality leaders of Ukrainian and Byelorussian organizations it meant rolling the frontier back to the very walls of the Kremlin. To the Republican directors of the foreign-language groups within the Nationalities Division and some nationality leaders, it also meant patronage for a job well done. To a great many Americans of Slavic descent it meant apprehension and fear that it might lead to war and the murder of their relatives behind the Iron Curtain. But nobody seemed to consider that before the United States could think of liberation it must liberate its ethnic groups from the politicians who had enslaved them to the hyphen.

To John Foster Dulles it meant the initiation of positive foreign

200

policies. It did not mean a "war of liberation" led by the United States, nor did it imply that it was necessary or desirable that the United States "try to foment violent revolution." That, according to Dulles, "would mean only the exposure and massacre of those who most cherish freedom. Nonviolent methods can be more efficacious." Nevertheless, after the Hungarian Revolution of October, 1956, the government of the United States found it necessary to proclaim to the world that it had not been responsible for the abortive uprising and introduced resolutions at the United Nations clarifying liberation as a policy which did not mean United States incitement to violent change. In April, 1957, Dulles again redefined liberation: an "evolution toward independence that the United States would welcome and aid."[2]

What has been the effect of this ambiguous term on American foreign policy? What effect did it have on the European peoples, at a time when overwhelming military control and nuclear stalemate made impossible the type of liberation that they had known during the nineteenth century?

The pursuit of and reliance on the ethnic vote militated against positive foreign policies. By advocating liberation the party gave the American people the illusion that the United States had limitless power and that all previous failures, if such they were, had been the results of betrayal. It produced fears in Allied capitals. It gave the Russians the opportunity to brand the United States a "power-mad" aggressor; and later, when liberation did not occur, it gave them the chance to taunt that liberation had been only a campaign gambit to gain votes and was not to be taken seriously.[3] More than that, the unredeemed pledge of liberation was destined, especially after the failure of the Hungarian Revolution, to shatter confidence in America's promises and to weaken the spirit of rebellion in East Europe.

2

"The primaries for the Congressional elections of 1954," wrote Arthur Bliss Lane in January, 1953, in a memorandum to be submitted to the Republican National Committee, "are only fifteen months away. Preparations will shortly be made, if they are not already being made, for those primaries." Because of the impending elections, if for no other reason, it was important that the incoming administration fulfill pledges to American voters of Slavic descent.[4]

201

Lane was convinced that a policy of liberation was going to be substituted for that of containment, but was not certain when and how it would be done. On January 7 he suggested to Secretary of State Dulles that as a step preliminary to the change all State Department officials who had been involved in the formulation of the policy of containment and the Yalta and Potsdam Agreements be immediately transferred to "the field" where, presumably, they would have no power to make important decisions.[5] Lane hoped that the announcement of the repudiation of the Yalta Agreement would come directly from the President in the form of a unilateral declaration, but he felt that the British government should be notified in advance as "a matter of courtesy." Such swift action on the part of the new administration would clearly indicate, Lane felt, that the State Department had completely reversed former policies; he felt, too, that such action would be clearly understood by Soviet Russia, that it would "enhearten those who are still enslaved," and that it would have the right effect on foreign-language groups in the United States.[6]

Many events during the first weeks of January, 1953, seemed to substantiate and strengthen the hope that the campaign pledges were going to be realized. Within a matter of hours after the 83rd Congress convened, a number of resolutions from various nationality groups asking that the Yalta Agreement be declared null and void were presented.[7] At the same time Representatives Robert Hale, Thaddeus M. Machrowicz, and Charles J. Kersten introduced three House Joint Resolutions (36, 111, and 162) and Representatives Lawrence H. Smith and Albert H. Bosch introduced two House Concurrent Resolutions (13 and 22) demanding that the Congress of the United States should "forthwith" repudiate the "private agreements concluded at Yalta and Potsdam."[8]

Influential Republican members of the House Committee on Foreign Affairs were in favor of taking some immediate action with respect to the Yalta Agreement. There were some, however, who felt that the large number of resolutions on the agreement pending before Congress might produce a "tendency to let the whole matter go to sleep." Representative John Vorys, a member of the Foreign Affairs Committee, and Lane agreed that such a development would be worse than no action at all. Both preferred executive rather than Congressional initiative, but saw no reason for not having Congressional hearings on the agreement. They believed that such public

202

hearings, at which persons who had full knowledge of the background that had led to the "Yalta betrayal" would be asked to testify, would strengthen the new foreign policy.

In the Senate prominent Republicans were ready to recommend and urge that the President repudiate the Yalta Agreement. On February 4, the *New York Times* reported Senator Robert Taft as saying that he was sure that Congress would quickly support the President in the action. According to Lane, Taft envisioned no difficulty in getting the desired Congressional approval, especially since the Democrats, "with their minds on the 1954 elections, would wish to woo the foreign language voters by endorsing Eisenhower's proposal." Lane, differing from this view, told Taft that the Democrats had endorsed the agreement during the campaign and that a switch "would seem to be purely political." Nevertheless, Lane believed that if the Democrats had a change of heart it would be fine "from the point of view of impressing the Soviet Union" that Congress should take the same position as the President.[9]

From Senators Alexander Wiley, Karl Mundt, Homer Ferguson, Representative Walter Judd, and Vice President Nixon, Lane got the impression that they were in favor of immediate repudiation of the agreement. He was particularly "enheartened" when Wiley asked him to prepare a bill of particulars on Yalta which would point out the damage the agreement had done to American foreign policy and which would also delineate the steps the government would have to take to accomplish repudiation. All these Republicans, according to Lane, were of the opinion that it would be best accomplished through a presidential order. Ferguson suggested that because it was an executive agreement rather than a treaty, it should "die with the administration which adopted it." Others suggested that should effective opposition from the "President's entourage" develop, the Senate should pass appropriate resolutions calling upon the President to take action. There was reluctance on the part of some Senators to adopt the latter course. These Republicans indicated that it would be necessary to "count noses beforehand," and even then there would always be the danger of some Senators "going to sleep over the proposition." They agreed that should such an eventuality occur, it would be worse than no action at all, "as it would convince not only the Communists but many supporters of Roosevelt and Truman that the representatives of the American people are in favor of Yalta and its provisions." Lane remained hopeful that Taft, the majority leader, would be able to convince the President.[10]

Dulles, during the hearing on his nomination for Secretary of State, further increased the belief that a policy of liberation would soon be inaugurated. On January 15 he told the Senate Committee on Foreign Relations that the enslaved people deserved to be free, and that "from our own selfish standpoint, [they] ought to be free because if they are the servile instruments of aggressive despotism, they will eventually be welded into a force which will be highly dangerous to ourselves and all of the free world. Therefore, we must always have in mind the liberation of these captive peoples."[11]

On January 14 Kersten, convinced that a "positive" foreign policy was about to be announced, introduced House Concurrent Resolution 21 which asked that a "Joint Committee on Extraordinary Methods of Protecting the National Security" be established. The resolution would put into effect recommendations from Representative O. K. Armstrong's study on psychological strategy in the Cold War which Kersten had brought to the attention of Congress the day before. One of the significant features of the resolution was a provision, Section 2 (4), which called for the " 'cooperation with and encouragement of private individuals and private organizations desirous of combating communism, including *nationality organizations and groups whose members have an origin or particular interest in Communist dominated countries*' "[12] (italics added). This, of course, meant that the committee would coöperate with such organizations as the Polish National Alliance, the Polish American Congress, the Serbian Defense Council, and other such groups, thus binding together Americans of various foreign origins "in an anti-Communist movement." In addition the resolution supported Armstrong's recommendation that the Psychological Strategy Board be integrated within the National Security Council. Both Kersten and Armstrong were of the opinion that with "proper and vigorous use of psychological strategy," the United States would be able to offer hope of liberation, to increase resistance to Communist control, and to help "break the grip of the Red rulers." Lane hoped that Armstrong would be appointed director of the proposed board and that James Burnham, Isaac Don Levine, Eugene Lyons, and William Henry Chamberlain would become some of the members.

The introduction of the resolution coincided with the announcement of the establishment of a presidential committee under the direction of William H. Jackson for the study of psychological warfare. The purpose of the presidential committee, according to Anthony Leviero of the *New York Times,* was to bring about a "dynamic thrust in the 'cold war,'" and to carry out the campaign pledges by kindling "a nonviolent liberation movement in Soviet satellite countries." Lane and some others felt concern that there was to be a five-month wait for the committee's first report—it would give Stalin "so much longer to make his plans."[13]

Although President Eisenhower's inaugural address did not in any way specifically promise the repudiation of the Yalta Agreement or the establishment of a policy of liberation, it was, nonetheless, interpreted by some members of the American press to mean that "containment is out." When George F. Kennan spoke out against liberation that same week, Lane took the opportunity not only to answer Kennan but to encourage those who were disappointed with the inaugural address. At the same time, he reminded the Republican party of its obligation to the voters of foreign origin. On January 21 Lane wrote to the *New York Times* that it was a pity, "from the point of view of our international standing," for Kennan to have criticized the policy of liberation of the new Secretary of State—particularly since it had been "one of the most telling arguments in the recent Presidential campaign which appealed to American voters whose origin stemmed from nations now behind the Curtain." The policy, he continued, was a part of the Republican platform and had not been rejected "but endorsed by the voters on Nov. 4"; the "enunciation of such a policy is the first step in repudiating the policies of appeasement and containment, policies which have led to the war in Korea." Lane boldly concluded that the policy of liberation "is consistent with the principles which President Eisenhower announced in his inaugural speech of Jan. 20. The new Administration is obligated not only to American voters, but also to the peoples behind the Iron Curtain, to carry out this policy."[14]

There were some who did not share in the optimism that prevailed during the first weeks of the new administration. Republican directors of the nationality groups and many nationality leaders who had been intimately connected with the campaign became increasingly distressed as weeks passed and no word of patronage was received from the National Committee. Lane and members of the committee became worried over complaints that the directors would be unable to keep their organizations together unless promises, "explicit or implicit," were carried out. Lane reacted to these reports by writing to leading Republicans that these valuable workers might be lost to the party if, immediately after victory, indifference was their reward. Party neglect in 1952 might make it difficult or impossible to obtain their services and coöperation in the 1954 Congressional campaign. Lane attached a list of nationality leaders to his letters, expressing his hope that the stalwarts might be rewarded with appropriate positions.[15]

There were some ethnic directors who were afraid that the National Committee would replace them with professional politicians or with other ethnic leaders in order, principally, to satisfy patronage demands. One, a former president of the Slavic Federation of California, warned Lane that such a step was "out of the question." "Only the Slavic peoples themselves," he wrote, "are capable of forming their own organizations, without aspirations of any group of professional politicians or any other individuals." He cautioned that "the American-Slavic voter has been exploited to an extreme. Those days are gone forever. We can only work with them but we cannot exert any superiority by telling them what to do."[16]

Other ethnic directors, apprehensive over their future status especially because their groups had not delivered as many votes as they had promised, blamed the Democrats or each other, charging that some had sold themselves or their newspapers to the opposition, or that they had been the victims of intra-group strife. One correspondent, for example, pointed out that during the campaign the Democrats had concentrated on getting "as many senators and congressmen as possible, losing hope that they will get their President." Thus, in Fall River, Massachusetts, "inhabited by many Poles, Democratic Congressman won by . . . one vote." He mentioned, in addition, that the Polish-American newspaper *Kuryer Polski* had called attention on November 24 to the fact that although "thousands of positions" would be available to the Republicans, Polish-Americans could not expect to benefit because the great majority had voted Democratic. He was sure that the Democrats would use this statement in the elections of 1954, and offered various plans to nullify its effect.[17]

There were, of course, many ethnic directors who were optimistic and looked forward to immediate rewards for a job well done. In the wake of victory they recommended the establishment of a permanent organizational apparatus for the various ethnic groups "so that it would not be necessary to organize . . . every four years." Others felt that the nationality organizations which during the campaign had been linked with the All-American Origins Division and the Ethnic Origins Division should be "kept in permanent touch with headquarters . . . and . . . should be maintained on the highest cooperative level." One reason for the success of the Democratic party during the preceding twenty years, Lane was told, was "that they have built up permanent organizations among the Polish Americans and other foreign language groups." Another director suggested that the National Committee extend its ethnic activities into Rhode Island, where the Democrats had prevented large numbers of such nationalities as the Italian, Irish, French Canadian, Portuguese, and many others from going over to the Republican column. Lane wholeheartedly agreed with most of these suggestions and recommended them to the National Committee's chairman.[18]

3

Most pessimism that the new administration would not honor its campaign pledges to repudiate the Yalta and Potsdam Agreements was dispelled on February 2. On that day President Eisenhower in his State of the Union Message said: "We shall never acquiesce in the enslavement of any people in order to purchase fancied gain for ourselves. I shall ask the Congress at a later date to join in an appropriate resolution making clear that this Government recognizes no kind of commitment contained in secret understandings of the past with foreign governments which permit this kind of enslavement."[19]

There was no doubt. On the same day, on the floor of the House, Kersten hailed the address as one which denounced "the secret Yalta agreement which was never ratified by Congress or the American people and which gave Stalin a seemingly legal strangle hold on his criminal gains." He read his resolution (House Joint Resolution 162) declaring the Yalta Agreement null and void and not binding on the United States.[20] Several days later Democratic Representative Thaddeus Machrowicz, evidently expecting some action by the government to liberate East Europe, inserted in the *Congressional Record* an article by Peter Chambers, "General without an Army Awaits D-Day." It concerned General Wladyslaw Anders, hero of the Second World War who had led the Polish armies in the Middle

East, Italy, and North Africa, Inspector General of the free Polish army in exile. According to Chambers: "Now, though the Polish Government in London is not recognized by any of the great powers, General Anders has the ear of the President of the United States. What better ear can you have if you want to alter the map of Europe? And he is relying on 75,000 Poles in Britain to follow him if D-day comes."[21]

No one was more pleased than Lane. His unselfish and diligent work in behalf of the Republican party was bearing fruit. He was cheered by the "bold and unequivocal" manner with which the President charted a new foreign and domestic policy. He applauded the State of the Union Message, which had torn down "what was wrong and contrary" to the traditional principles, and he looked forward to a foreign policy "based on international morality." Lane felt the United States could once more "unashamedly" assume world leadership. He believed nothing "could have more vitally re-kindled" the hope of the enslaved peoples of Europe for eventual liberty than the presidential pronouncement, "We shall never ac-quiesce in the enslavement of any people in order to purchase fan-cied gain for ourselves." To his co-workers in the Ethnic Origins Division he wrote that the President's message had made clear that Eisenhower favored the repudiation of the Yalta Agreement and that repudiation would have an immense effect on voters of foreign origin. He was particularly pleased that, with the approach of the 1954 primaries, the foreign-language groups would be able to ap-preciate the real difference between the policies of Eisenhower and those of the preceding administrations.[22]

Lane's jubilation was short-lived. Three weeks later, on February 20, 1953, Eisenhower sent the promised draft resolution to Congress. It asked that both houses join with the President in a declaration that the United States rejected Soviet perversion of the international agreements made during the war which had led to the subjugation of free peoples. It did not ask a declaration that the Yalta and Pots-dam Agreements be null and void, nor did it promise American ac-tion to liberate East Europe. The resolution read:

Resolved, That the Senate and House concurring,

Join with the President in declaring that the United States rejects any interpretations or applications of any international agreements or understandings, made during the course of World War II, which have

208

been perverted to bring about the subjugation of free peoples, and further

Join in proclaiming the hope that the peoples who have been subjected to the captivity of Soviet despotism shall again enjoy the right of self-determination within a framework which will sustain the peace; that they shall again have the right to choose the form of government under which they will live; and that sovereign rights of self-government shall be restored to them all in accordance with the pledge of the Atlantic Charter.[23]

Those who advocated repudiation of the Yalta Agreement concurred with the lead editorial in the *Chicago Tribune* of February 22—that Eisenhower had asked "the Republican Congress to absolve Mr. Roosevelt and Mr. Truman of all blame." To many, this was too bitter a pill to swallow. The draft resolution was, nevertheless, introduced as House Joint Resolution 200. Together with the other resolutions which demanded immediate repudiation of the agreement (House Joint Resolutions 36, 111, and 162, and House Concurrent Resolutions 13, 22, and 68), it was referred to the House Committee on Foreign Affairs. In spite of Dulles' testimony in behalf of the Eisenhower Resolution, none of these measures was reported out of committee. The Senate itself dropped the whole matter.[24]

Lane, although distressed by Eisenhower's "innocuous resolution" which suddenly reversed "the Administration's point of view," was still hopeful that last-minute pressure would force the President to address a note to the Soviet government which would make clear that the United States condemned and repudiated the Yalta Agreement. "Unless some action of this sort is taken," he wrote, "the psychological effect will be completely lost on people behind the Iron Curtain," and, at the same time, the administration would "lose the support next year of the very groups which came to the Republican side in 1952 because of the promises which have not as yet been fulfilled." Lane was certain that if nothing were done the situation would be grave for the administration both domestically and internationally.[25]

If there was any hope left, it was completely gone with the announcement several days later that President Eisenhower had nominated Charles E. Bohlen to the post of ambassador to the Soviet Union. To the "liberators" and "repudiators," the nomination of Bohlen, a Foreign Service career officer who had been identified with the formulation of the policies of Roosevelt and Truman, was outright treason. *Human Events* reported that *"L'affaire* Bohlen" had stirred up "intense atmospheric disturbances in the political situation," and went on to say that political observers in Washington believed "that the thunder and lightning presage a storm which will have profound effects on the stability of the new regime." Some Republicans began to show real concern over the possibility of losing the 1954 Congressional elections. Lane read in *Human Events* that this anxiety was accentuated by the "revolt among the Polish-Americans" and by signs that the German-Americans were "to say the least disgruntled." Republican ethnic experts began to send warnings to the National Committee and the White House that some of the nationality groups were " 'up in arms.' "[26]

Lane was "completely disheartened" over the Bohlen appointment. He blamed "the smart boys around Eisenhower" who, having "taken hold," did not welcome advice from persons who had spent their lifetimes in foreign service. He wrote the chairman of the National Committee that in 1952 "approximately three million voters of foreign language origin, who usually voted Democratic, came to the support of the Republican candidates"; that the Eisenhower Resolution, which "was based on the feeling that it would be unwise to criticize the Yalta agreement itself, but instead to criticize its violations," had already produced bitter disappointments in several foreign-language groups; and that the subsequent nomination of Bohlen intensified this feeling of disappointment. It was most important, he advised, "from the point of view of keeping our ethnic groups . . . on our side," that an aggressive foreign policy be adopted.[27]

Lane's concern seemed to be substantiated from reading a report in *Human Events* that the Polish-American press, led by seven dailies, had expressed bitter indignation over the Eisenhower Resolution—the " 'betrayal of the century' " in view of his having "categorically" pledged repudiation—and Dulles' insistence that Bohlen, "one of the architects of Yalta," be approved as ambassador to the Soviet Union. According to the newsletter's account the New York daily *Nowy Swiat,* the Detroit *Dziennik Dla Wszystkich,* the Chicago *Alliance News,* and other Polish-American papers described Bohlen as " 'the grave digger of Poland' " and labeled "Dulles' effort in alliance with the Democrats to put over the endorsement of Yalta" as " 'the worst double-cross since Roosevelt.' "[28] There were also indications that the German-American press was deeply disturbed.

The *Steuben News* ran a front-page editorial accusing the administration of " 'not keeping faith with the German people who voted Eisenhower into the White House.' " Many German-Americans evidently were convinced that they had played an important role in the Republican victory.[29]

The Bohlen nomination split Republican ranks in the Senate. Bohlen's testimony upholding the Yalta Agreement during hearings on his nomination further aggravated the bitterness.[30] It was only because of Eisenhower's personal intervention and the "ardent support" of Taft that the final vote was favorable. "The ghost of Yalta," said George E. Sokolsky, "still rides. . . . It is impossible to tell a Pole that he must forget his enslavement because Roosevelt made a mistake. . . ."[31]

The only thing left was to try to soothe the feelings of many nationality groups by inserting in the *Congressional Record* the usual plethora of platitudes recognizing the various holidays, constitution days, successful and unsuccessful revolutions, and heroes of their native lands.

4

The East Berlin uprising of June 17, 1953, revived the idea of liberation. ". . . one of the President's major campaign promises," wrote Joseph and Stewart Alsop, "is getting its acid test." The insurrection would prove whether or not the policy of liberating Russia's satellites meant anything. According to the Alsop brothers, the East German revolt divided the "highest policy makers in the administration" into two factions: "the Liberators," said to include Dulles and the "President's expert" on psychological warfare, C. D. Jackson, who were willing to take considerable risk in giving full support and encouragement to the revolutionaries; and those who, remembering the ill-fated Bor revolt in Warsaw in 1944, believed that it "would be both short-sighted and cold-blooded" to offer encouragement unless the United States were prepared to risk war. The Alsops thought that Stalin's death and the resulting unrest offered an "opportunity that will not come again," and bemoaned the "feebleness and indecision" of the government. *Life* saw in the Berlin uprising a vindication for the policy of liberation and a defeat for "those apostles of containment who have refused to bet on (let alone foment) the forces of revolt within the Soviet Empire."[32]

211

Lane, while agreeing that the Alsop article was "on the whole very good," believed their analogy ill-chosen. The "premature" wartime Bor revolt had been instigated by the Russians, who allowed it to be subsequently "snuffed out" while Soviet armies waited across the Vistula. He hoped, and so advised the State Department, that the United States would issue a dramatic statement on liberation, which, he was certain, would have a tremendous impact on the people behind the Iron Curtain, especially in East Germany, Czechoslovakia, and Poland.[33]

Secretary of State Dulles hailed the revolution in Berlin as proof of his long-held belief "that the Soviet was overextended having under its control some 600 million non-Russians representing what had been 15 or more independent nations." During his press conference of June 30, Dulles reminded the newsmen that in his book, *War or Peace,* written three years earlier, he had said, " '. . . the Communist structure is over-extended, over-rigid and ill-founded. It could be shaken if the difficulties that were latent were activated.' " This, he went on, did not mean "an armed revolt which would precipitate a massacre, but that short of this the people could demonstrate an independence such that the Soviet Communist leaders would come to recognize the futility of trying to hold captive so many peoples. . . ."[34]

In the House of Representatives Kersten reacted to the Berlin revolt by introducing fourteen House Concurrent Resolutions (101-107, 114-120) which asked for the withdrawal of recognition of the governments of the Soviet Union, Poland, Rumania, Czechoslovakia, Hungary, Bulgaria, and Albania, and for an expression of hope by Congress for the early liberation of the people of China, Bulgaria, Albania, Czechoslovakia, Hungary, Rumania, and Poland.[35]

David Lawrence, editor of *U.S. News and World Report,* called the East German Revolt "a propitious moment in history," and asked the United States and its allies to inform the peoples behind the Iron Curtain that the West was "with them in the heartfelt hope that they can soon rise up en masse to recover their rights." Lawrence advocated immediate economic and moral help. He was sure that military help from the outside would be unnecessary "when revolution from within is astir."[36]

As days and then weeks passed with no effective action taken to "meet the faltering Soviet Policy" Lane became deeply discouraged and looked forward to a trip to Italy in order to escape the constant recriminations from leaders of nationality groups.[37]

5

During the remaining months of 1953 the Republican National Committee's primary concern was not the ethnic vote but replenishment of its treasury. When Lane was asked to contribute to the 1954 Congressional campaign, he voiced his disappointment over the broken promises. In his letter to the finance chairman he pointed out that he had spent over five thousand dollars from personal funds to bring over to the Republican side the Polish-American vote and that he was convinced that the emphasis on the repudiation of the Yalta Agreement had brought "at least two million normally Democratic voters" to the party. It was unfortunate, he wrote, that the foreign-policy planks had not been implemented and that, because of inaction, many Americans of foreign origin had lost faith in the administration. What was perhaps worse, he reminded the chairman, the Communists had very effectively "pointed out that we do not intend to assist in the liberation of countries behind the Curtain, this having been a campaign pledge to gain votes." Unless these promises were to be fulfilled, Lane refused to make a contribution.[38]

In the fall of that year Lane decided to dissociate himself from the National Committee and left for Europe with the intention of not returning until after the elections. He was disturbed over reports that the party probably would not use the issue of Communism in the campaign and feared that the failure of the administration to repudiate the Yalta Agreement would "cause the Administration a lot of headaches next year in the Congressional elections."[39]

In December an advisory committee of Republican ethnic leaders was called to Washington to meet with the National Committee for discussions about the impending campaign. The meeting was not a happy one. The nationality leaders had scarcely had the opportunity to express indignation over Yalta, liberation, absence of patronage, and indifference from the party, when they were told that the White House was opposed to "any effective organization of Nationality Groups." When Lane heard of this development, he showed no surprise, although he hoped that despite their resentment the nationality leaders would not work against the party. It was his opinion that White House opposition came from Max Rabb, Eisenhower's adviser on minority matters.[40]

Lane did not give up completely. A few months before the election, while he was still in Europe, he wrote to Leonard Hall, the Republican chairman, that it was not too late for the ethnic groups to play an important role in the campaign, especially in such industrial states as Illinois, Indiana, Ohio, Pennsylvania, New Jersey, Connecticut, Michigan, and Wisconsin. He suggested that the President issue a statement reaffirming his support of the platform with regard to the Yalta Agreement. Lane was sure that the question could still be used to gain the support of ethnic groups. This assumption was based, in all probability, on the information and suggestions he had received from various advisers on ethnic political behavior. According to one, the Republicans could point out that Eisenhower's failure to repudiate the agreement was due to lack of full support for the party in 1952 from ethnic Americans. He illustrated his point by saying that of the eleven Polish-American Congressional candidates, Polish-Americans had elected eight Democrats and only three Republicans. This disparity made it impossible for Eisenhower and Dulles to repudiate the agreement. Interviews with Polish-Americans and other nationalities, he hastened to add, proved that had they been properly informed, they would have voted overwhelmingly Republican. This student of nationality voting behavior was convinced that with "these arguments" the party would be able to receive the help of the post-Second World War "New Immigration," which, according to him, was "gaining a big influence among the Poles." Lane was certain this information regarding conditions within the foreign-language communities was accurate.[41]

The White House, however, continued in its decision against differentiating between groups within the electorate—"all voters being 'American.'" To Lane, who believed that in 1952 three million normally Democratic voters of ethnic origin had supported Eisenhower, this was "fantastically stupid" and "illogical." Of course every voter is an American, Lane wrote to a prominent Republican, hoping that he would use his influence to reverse the decision, but that should not mean that all voting groups have the same interests. For the good of the party, Lane believed, it was necessary to feel "the pulse" of each nationality group in order to find out "wherein lay the fundamental interests of each."[42]

6

In the 1954 Congressional elections the Republican party failed to win control of either house. It seemed that Lane may have been right and the White House wrong in believing that ethnic Americans were "Americans." Soon after the election Lane was invited to National Committee headquarters for consultation. During the meeting he analyzed the defeat as the result of Republican failure to pay attention to marginal districts inhabited by foreign-language groups. In December Lane wrote a series of letters to the leaders of Polish, Czechoslovak, Hungarian, Yugoslav, and Armenian groups asking them to submit a list of persons of foreign origin who "might be considered" for important government positions, and asked for their advice, suggestions, and 1956 campaign plans.[43]

The nationality leaders were prompt in answering Lane's letters. Many indicated that patronage alone was not enough; that patronage must be accompanied by a promise to honor the pledges of 1952 which had been responsible "for bringing over to the Republican side the traditionally Democrat vote." Some wrote that much work had to be done "between now and 1956" in many states where there were "foreign language elements," but they were pessimistic about New York, Michigan, Illinois, and Pennsylvania. Others reported that in New York, Polish-Americans who had voted for Eisenhower had reverted to the Democrats in 1954; "undoubtedly this vote made the difference between victory and defeat." One suggested that it was not the time to "cry about spilled milk" and hoped that the "adversity in the recent elections" would make the party "beware of the possibilities in 1956." It is significant that none blamed Eisenhower for the failure to honor the campaign pledges. They were convinced that a "Closed Circle" of men around him were the real culprits. "We think he is the greatest president in our times," wrote one, ". . . yet it was only natural that something would be forthcoming in a way of patronage. . . ." The replies of some vented their bitterness. One wrote that the Republican party "will be finished in 1956 . . . unless a miracle happens." He characterized Republicans as "extremely" partisan, prejudiced, untrustworthy, with foresight "centered around their immediate circle." He commended to them the Democratic art of politics. Recalling the decision against ethnic appeals, he charged the party with "deliberately repudiating the right of equality" of Americans of foreign descent to serve the United States. That privilege, he felt was reserved for Americans of German and English descent and the Jews and Negroes. He wrote that "the rest" do not count, even though had it not been for "the rest," there would have been no 1952 victory. In addition to the forty million Americans of Slavic descent, he claimed, there are millions of other origins; were they "not worth considering"? It was the view of this embittered ethnic leader that Jews and Negroes were recognized by the party because they were organized as pressure groups; this selective recognition was "forcing" the others to become pressure groups which "would really demand and command." He had refused to try to influence Slavic groups to vote Republican during the 1954 campaign, not wishing to insult their intelligence. As to patronage, he was convinced that he could not have obtained even a janitorial position in the State Department because his name was not "Brown, Smith, or Jones." The Democratic party had been after him with "unbelievable assurances," but he had decided to await "what's behind the horizon." At the same time, however, he expressed fear "for the very existence" of the party, which even "last minute somersolts [sic] of the Administration" would not be able to save. In concluding, he gave Lane permission to "read this letter to Dick Nixon and others, even to the President," and warned that the foreign-language vote meant "either to be or not to be" for the party.[44]

Spurred and supported by these reports, Lane wrote to Hall offering his services without salary. He was ready to extend foreign-language activities to Americans of Spanish, Mexican, Puerto Rican, and Portuguese descent living in Texas, Arizona, New Mexico, California, New York, and Rhode Island. He was certain that these Americans would be interested in knowing that the Republican party stood for friendship with Latin America "in good as well as in bad times."[45]

Months went by; no specific ethnic campaign plans were made. In July, 1955, the National Committee abolished its Nationalities Division, transferring the "foreign language situation" to Rabb in the White House. By this time Lane had had too extensive an experience in politics to allow him to be "heartbroken." He was convinced that certain persons in the White House were responsible for the unrealistic and "illogical" behavior. He believed these persons did not consider "the relationship of those people to the lands of their origin" and did not realize that questions such as the Yalta Agreement which did not seem to concern the White House politicians did ". . . directly affect our foreign policy and were . . . basic policies in the 1952 Campaign" which must be carried out. Lane, depressed and seeing no hope of any action from the President, began to think that he "liked the prospect" of having Governor Frank J. Lausche of Ohio as the Democratic candidate for the presidency. Lausche, he thought, had the right attitude toward Communism and foreign-language groups, and his Slovenian descent "would make him particularly acceptable to these groups."[46]

As election time neared, the National Committee began to consider the feasibility of reactivating the Ethnic Origins Division. In February, Lane was told that reactivation of his division was imminent. Despite previous disappointments, Lane was again ready to offer his services. This time, however, he insisted on definite assurances that Eisenhower's campaign pledges on the Yalta Agreement would be put into effect; that a policy of liberation would be announced; and that ethnic groups would be organized on a national level. The latter, he believed, was important because of "the psychological significance of the relationship between ethnic groups and the formulation of foreign policy, which would not be evident if the ethnic groups were organized only on a state level." Lane justified his demand for assurances on the ground that some people did not understand that "spiritual or sentimental values sway—and rightly so—the votes of people whose kin live in slavery."[47]

Perhaps because of Lane's requirements and White House sentiment the idea of reëstablishing the Ethnic Origins Division was again dropped. In a last effort Lane solicited help from Dulles and other Republicans to overcome those who "did not appreciate the importance" of foreign-language elements "in controlling an election." He was convinced that the President had not been given the right advice and that Presidential Assistant Sherman Adams, having come from the "non-ethnic"(sic) state of New Hampshire, did not understand the ethnic vote. Lane could not fathom why Adams did not wish to distinguish between the various nationality groups, while he was perfectly willing "to play up to" the farmers, Negroes, labor unions, and other such groups. Unsuccessful in his attempts to win party support for his views, Lane wrote to Lausche that after having read his speeches on liberation and the Yalta Agreement, he was sure that their thoughts coincided. He asked for an interview to discuss means of restoring the prestige of the United States.[48]

7

In July, 1956, four months before the elections, the National Committee apparently having overcome White House opposition, decided to appeal for the nationality vote. A. B. Hermann was reappointed director of the Nationalities Advisory Group consisting of eighteen nationality leaders. At the first meeting of this group, the party chairman told them, "Time after time the people you represent have proven the margin of victory for us in marginal districts. Your committee played a vital part in 1952. We must fight even harder this year. . . ." Hermann followed the chairman, telling the group that their "people came over to the Republican party in great numbers in 1952. They were fed up with 20 years of Democrat misrule climaxed by the Yalta agreement which resulted in the loss of many of their homelands to the Communists." The group's feelings were expressed by one of the members: "This is the land of my adoption. I've done well here. I love this country and I want to contribute by working for the political party I believe is best for this country—the Republican Party." The absence of one man was conspicuous—Arthur Bliss Lane.[49]

Lane was asked to head the reactivated Nationalities Division, but he refused to do so. He was discouraged by "giveaway" summit conferences at Geneva and by those members of the administration who had "little conception of the role" that the United States should play. He felt that he had no right to "entrust foreign policy to novices who are primarily only political men." Lane was disappointed over the stand the State Department took when the Polish people of Poznan rose against their oppressors in June. Moreover, he was perturbed by the absence of strong criticism by the Polish-American leadership toward official American policy. In a letter to the editor of the *New York Times,* he chided Polish-Americans for being too lenient in appraising American foreign policy, reminding them that America has reason to thank Poles such as Kosciuszko and Pulaski for contributions to American independence. Believing that the Poznan riots were the start of an independence movement throughout Soviet-controlled Europe, Lane urged the United States to reiterate its stand for a policy of liberation and warned, "If we are to convince foreign peoples of our own sincerity in preaching the doctrine of freedom and democracy we must first convince ourselves that we are honest. And we cannot do this if we preach platitudes only in election years." Lane could not "honestly support" Eisenhower unless the campaign promises were kept. But the Republican party had no desire to revive the "ghosts" of Yalta and liberation.[50] A month later, on August 12, 1956, at the age of sixty-two, Arthur Bliss Lane died.

If Yalta and liberation were not going to be the Republican issues of the campaign, how would the party appeal to the ethnic groups? On July 31, the *New York Herald-Tribune* supplied the answer. According to Staff Reporter Earl Mazo, the Republican party, in its attempt to get the nationality vote, would have a platform plank promising an easing of immigration restrictions. "The foreign policy plank," wrote Mazo, "is expected to appeal to those whose native lands are now dominated by Russia." The *Herald-Tribune* also reported that Senator Prescott Bush of Connecticut, in a conference at the party offices with twelve representatives of nationality groups, promised to include in the platform a "strong endorsement of President Eisenhower's position on immigration."[51] Thus, the Republicans, who in the 1932 and 1940 platforms had urged the continuance of immigration restrictions, and who had failed to include an immigration plank in the 1952 platform, adopted the 1952 Democratic strategy and thrust immigration into the never-ending contest for the elusive ethnic vote. The platform plank on immigration read in part:

"The Republican Party supports an immigration policy which is in keeping with the traditions of America in providing a haven for oppressed peoples, and which is based on equality of treatment, freedom from implications of discrimination between racial, nationality and religious groups, and flexible enough to conform to changing needs and conditions.

"We believe that such a policy serves our self-interest, reflects our responsibility for world leadership and develops maximum cooperation with other nations in resolving problems in this area."[52]

The Democrats, of course, did not allow this strategy to go unnoticed. In their plank, *"Freedom for Captive Nations,"* they condemned the Republican party "for its heartless record of broken promises to the unfortunate victims of Communism. Candidate Eisenhower's 1952 pledges to 'liberate' the captive peoples have been disavowed and dishonored." The Democrats once again declared their ". . . deepest concern for the plight of the freedom-loving peoples of Central and Eastern Europe and of Asia, now under the yoke of Soviet dictatorship. The United States, under Democratic leaders, has never recognized the forcible annexation of Lithuania, Latvia, and Estonia, or condoned the extension of the Kremlin's tyranny over Poland, Bulgaria, Rumania, Czechoslovakia, Hungary, Albania and other countries." On self-determination the platform read: "We rededicate ourselves to the high principle of national self-determination, as enunciated by Woodrow Wilson, whose leadership brought freedom and independence to uncounted millions."[53]

8

The mood of the citizens of the United States was shattered on the eve of the 1956 presidential election by two nearly simultaneous events: the Hungarian Revolution and the British-French-Israeli invasion of Egypt. Particular consternation was produced among many Americans of East European origin and many Americans of Jewish faith. The sudden uprising and initial success of the Hungarian people against their Soviet oppressors held out hope that even in the atomic age, liberation can occur. When the Soviet Army "reconquered" Budapest on November 4, the day of Dwight D. Eisenhower's reëlection, that hope was extinguished. Similarly, the rapid success of the Israeli Army as it knifed through Egyptian territory toward Suez, was briefly inspiring to those whose dreams it embodied. Soviet and American pressures brought frustration and humiliating defeat.

The suddenness and very complexity of these two events, beginning and ending as they did, on the eve and day of the election, gave little time to ethnic and Democratic leaders to mobilize, give direction to, and influence the electorate against the administration. This is not to say, of course, that had the two events occurred earlier in the campaign the outcome might have been different. Most certainly, however, they would have made it difficult for the Republican party, in view of its stand on "liberation," to defend, justify, and rationalize its failure to help the Hungarian Freedom Fighters or its alignment with Soviet Russia in the Suez Canal crisis.

Part IV

CONCLUSION: THE FUTURE OF THE
HYPHENATE IN AMERICAN POLITICS

Chapter XIII

THE HYPHEN AND AMERICA'S NATIONAL INTEREST

Are ethnic-group sentiment and political activity justifiable in domestic affairs, but unjustifiable and unpatriotic in foreign affairs? What have been the effects of ethnic-group pressure on foreign policy, on Americans of foreign descent, and on the national interest?

Most, if not all, ethnic leaders refute the allegation that a valid distinction exists between their involvement in those domestic issues which relate to the status of their group in America and those foreign-policy issues which bear on their native lands. Thus, to most Irish-Americans, particularly during the second half of the nineteenth century and the first decades of the twentieth, concern about fair employment practices and political recognition on all governmental levels, plus the desire to liberate Ireland, was good Americanism. Thus, too, to many American Jews, concern over the welfare of Israel, anti-Semitism, the liberalization of immigration, and the safeguarding of civil rights and liberties is good democratic practice and good Americanism. To many Catholics, their stands on aid to church schools, censorship, marriage and divorce, Communism, birth control, and liberalization of immigration, as well as on an American ambassador to the Vatican, are also good Americanism. So, too, the attitudes of, for example, Hungarian-, Polish-, and Lithuanian-Americans toward the Soviet Union as an enemy not only of their homelands but of Christianity and the American way of life are good Americanism.

Indeed, there are some ethnic leaders who say that today, in the period of the Cold War, nationality groups should be encouraged to play a more vital role "in effectuating the success of American objectives." One such leader held, at the 1960 Republican platform hearings, that the parties should recognize this "vital task" of ethnic groups and encourage them "to exert their tremendous influence on behalf of America's interest abroad." Another leader at the same hearings said that nationality groups whose native lands have been absorbed by Soviet Russia should be encouraged, "nay URGED" by the parties to support actively their "antecedental nations abroad"; French-Americans should help French citizens "to withstand the wiles, deceits and threats of the Soviet," Italian-Americans should

223

reassure relatives in Italy that "freedom is of precious concern to America," and German-Americans must continue to inform "kin abroad that America remains dedicated to the vital necessity of a free Germany, united under a free and democratic government. . . ."[1]

Rationalization of the immigrant's sentiment toward his native land in terms of the American national interest has been a source both of strength and of weakness of ethnic leadership and the politicians who have encouraged it. The misconceptions that often arise out of the attempt to equate diverse national or ideological interests have frustrated the immigrant's desire to become an "American," and misled him, his leader, and the politician who woos him, as to the real meaning of foreign-policy actions and motives of the United States and the country of his origin. Caught between these two groups which tend to confuse his loyalty, the immigrant and his descendants have had great difficulty in rooting themselves deeply in the soil of the adopted land. The immigrant has been frequently told by his leaders that the American government and Presidents believe it to be "un-American" for the immigrant to forget the land of his origin, and he naturally assumes this to be true. It is indeed difficult for a recent arrival to resist the admonition of one ethnic leader which was reproduced in the *Congressional Record:* "Let us not forget the immortal words spoken by a great President of the United States. In his speech President Coolidge said: 'I have no use for those who came here from other countries and forget the countries of their origin. He who forgets the country of his birth and looks down upon his parents will never be a good American; he will change his loyalty as quickly and as easily as he forgets his ancestors.' "[2]

In the 1860's the Irish-American Fenian Brotherhood, which aimed to liberate Ireland, mistook the anti-British feeling in America as pro-Irish sentiment. American politicians, who found the Irish vote useful on Election Day, and the administration, which wished to impress the British with the vulnerability of Canada, made it possible for the Fenian leaders to convince themselves and the Irish-Americans that their activities and the ensuing Fenian raids into Canada were in the American national interest. John Mitchell, who, on his arrival in the United States in 1853, announced his determination to "make use of the freedom guaranteed . . . a citizen or inchoate citizen of America to help and stimulate the movement of European Democracy and especially of Irish independence," was soon disillusioned with Irish-American leaders' dealings with American politicians.[3] In

1867 he said of the majority of Irish-Americans, "Our people are credulous, enthusiastic, impatient,—a tempting material for the charlatan."[4] The Fenian movement collapsed without having accomplished its objective. Significantly, the death of the brotherhood coincided with the improvement of British-American relations. After refusing to take over the leadership of the rapidly disintegrating movement, Mitchell wrote an incisive epitaph for it, one that could be read with profit by ethnic leaders:

The Fenian *Imperium in Imperio* was an anomaly; and though the Americans very well knew that it was powerless to effect its avowed object, and though they were fully resolved not to allow it to complicate their relations with England, yet they felt it as an affront and laughed at it as a farce. The American government has its hands firmly fixed on the whole movement, and has made use of it to hold up *in terrorem* before the eyes of England, by way of inducing her to be more compliant in the diplomatic discussions which are going on between London and Washington; just as a man holds a bull-dog by the collar, sure that he can let him slip against his enemy, or else drive him back to his kennel. Neither has the government by any means done with the Fenians in that capacity; it expects more of the same kind of service; and so it deals very gently with them—(for in fact these Irish have votes, and your politicians must deal with them "as though he loved them)."[5]

During the First World War the Polish-, Czech-, and other Slavic-Americans were enticed to believe that their desire to free their home lands was in the American interest. Unlike the Fenians they were more successful in helping their compatriots to liberate their native lands from the Germans, Austrians, and Russians. But they, too, misconstrued American motives. To be sure, there was real sympathy for the oppressed nationalities in Eastern Europe. And what if Wilson profited from it on election days? To champion the births of small nations in the heart of the rapidly disintegrating Austro-Hungarian and Tsarist empires seemed to carry no risks. Americans and their leaders were sure that ethnic support would neither positively nor negatively affect vital American interests.

It was different during the Second World War. The *inter bella* period had given the new nations the opportunity to prove their right to be independent. Many of these were unable to hold the sympathy of the United States because of their undemocratic and authoritarian governments. Indeed, a great majority of Slavic-Americans who had worked and prayed for the independence of their native lands became disillusioned with them. And thousands who had returned to their homelands with the hope of contributing their political and technical skill and knowledge acquired in America were forced to come back to the United States. But these were not the real reasons for the supposed "betrayal" of Eastern Europe at Yalta by the American government. At the end of the Second World War, consideration had to be given to America's national interest, especially since the United States was globally involved and could no longer return to the isolationism of pre-war years. During the Yalta Conference, where the fate of many Eastern European countries was finally decided, Roosevelt was certainly aware of the six to seven million Polish-Americans; he even obliquely referred to their voting power, but this made no impression on the Soviet dictator.[6] The war with Japan was still far from being ended; the atomic bomb was yet to prove its effectiveness; and there was a need, Roosevelt was convinced, for Russian coöperation in a final thrust against the Japanese Empire.

The Cold War, with its main objective containment of Russia, has appeared to give common ground to the national interest of the United States, the aspirations of exiled leaders, and the yearnings of many ethnic Americans for the liberation of their homelands. (To be sure, there is seldom a well-defined American national interest to which any citizen, hyphenated or not, can adhere.) This period also coincides with the strong desire of various ethnic groups who had difficulty supporting wartime American foreign policies "to appear as loyal Americans" and "demonstrate their patriotism by their vocal opposition to communism." For them, Norman Graebner observed, "hostility to Russia was more than the normal reaction to a troublesome and aggressive antagonist; it was the very essence of Americanism."[7] At best, this recognition of a common enemy indicates but a negative and transitional unity. What if a thaw in the Cold War should occur?[8]

It should also be acknowledged that while leaders of East European nationality groups in the United States enthusiastically support and advocate foreign policies which aim to contain, weaken, or destroy Soviet influence and power, it does not necessarily follow that these leaders endorse such policies in other areas. Though rightful anxiety over Soviet successes and imperialistic designs places these people within the American consensus, their primary concern—the fate of their native lands—may not. The former outwardly extends and supports the American policy of internationalism; the latter may and, at times does, confine and oppose it.[9]

Then, too, it should be noted that intense participation of ethnic Americans in the affairs of ancestral lands is not always welcomed therein. Resentment has been noticeable, for example, in the relationships between Israeli officials and American Zionists, between the leaders of the emerging African states and those American Negroes who have "rediscovered" Africa, as in other cases.

Has it been in the national interest of the United States actively to support foreign groups hoping or fighting for liberation of their homelands? Has it been in the national interest to give moral encouragement to such revolutions or uprisings? It was relatively safe for the American people to indulge themselves in quixotically championing the idea of self-determination in the nineteenth century—the century of peace—when the United States was weak, but also secure within its borders. It has been far otherwise in the turbulent twentieth century, and it is even more perilous now, in the era of the ultimate weapon.

The advice of Secretary of State John Quincy Adams in the first decades of the nineteenth century has, perhaps, a more prophetic meaning for today than it did for that time. The Greek revolution against the Turks in the early 1820's, which stirred American emotions, offered the first necessity for expression of official policy toward liberal uprisings against foreign domination. Significantly, the need for such an expression came at the very time when the government of the United States was about to formulate the historic Monroe Doctrine. Adams, who was soon to embody the principle of isolationism within the Monroe Doctrine, gave the answer in a public address on July 4, 1821. While the United States, he exclaimed, would always respond with sympathy for any foreign group fighting tyranny, "she goes not abroad in search of monsters to destroy. She is the well-wisher to the freedom and independence of all. She is the champion and vindicator only of her own." Such active intervention, he warned, would change "the fundamental maxim of her policy from liberty to force."[10]

In the Cabinet deliberations preceding his December 2, 1823, message to Congress, in which the dicta of the Monroe Doctrine were discussed, President James Monroe was ready to include a vigorous statement expressing American sympathy for the Greeks. Adams objected to its inclusion, on the grounds that the United States should "disclaim all interference on our part in Europe; to make an American cause, and adhere inflexibly to that." To Adams, as Samuel Flagg Bemis said, such a statement meant "a sudden departure from the policy of George Washington."[11]

One hundred thirty-five years later another Secretary of State gave similar advice. Cordell Hull, after reading a draft of an address to be delivered by Secretary of the Interior Harold Ickes before the United Palestine Appeal on May 24, 1936, advised him to change "have championed the cause of oppressed minorities in other lands" to "have expressed our sympathy in behalf of oppressed minorities in other lands."[12]

On March 7, 1954, Joseph Martinek, addressing the Czechoslovak Society of America's jubilee banquet in St. Louis, Missouri, employed a typical defense for the participation of ethnic organizations in movements for the liberation of the lands of their origin "from foreign tyranny and the establishment of them as free and independent countries." Charging that ethnic organizations have been "unjustly suspected" of *"foreign nationalism"* and divided loyalty, Martinek said, "What the critics fail to see and perceive is the outstanding fact that in almost every case such participation in the liberation movements meant, and in fact was,—*export and extension of American political ideas and ideals of freedom and democracy to respective old homelands of immigrants."*[13]

Americans have been quick to support revolutionary movements even though they may have been distant from the action and often ignorant of the problems involved. They have felt a righteous impulse to interfere in struggles for national liberation. Memory of their own self-liberation has remained fresh; any cry for independence or the right of self-government has been almost certain to arouse strong sympathy. These attitudes have been held particularly by those leaders who have professed to be followers of Washington and Jefferson. How could Americans, who like to believe the shot that was fired at Concord is still heard around the world, avoid being moved by the Greek Revolution of 1821, by the European revolutionary movements of 1848? How could they not have sympathized with Thaddeus Kosciuszko,[14] who had first fought for American freedom and then later had tried to lift the Tsarist yoke from Poland, or with Hungarian Revolutionist Louis Kossuth, or with the many others who were apparently re-enacting Bunker Hill and Valley Forge on European soil? Secretary of State Daniel Webster, at a banquet honoring Kossuth in 1852, looked forward expectantly to a government after an American model on the Danube, and endorsed Hungarian independence, Hungarian self-government, and "Hungarian control of Hungarian destinies."[15] Even the Brahmins of Boston espoused movements for national liberation. Although they resented the Irish intrusion in their city, they sympathized with the Irish victims of British imperialism, received the Irish leader Charles Parnell in their homes, and contributed generously to the Irish cause.

The warm responsiveness of Americans to revolutionary causes has seldom gone beyond the emotional stage. So long as support for liberation movements in no way involved or threatened to involve the United States in active interventions inimical to its national interests, Americans have given free rein to their enthusiasms. When it became evident, however, as it did in the cases of Kossuth, Parnell, and others, that intervention was the goal of those leaders, enthusiasms have waned as readily as they had waxed. The very solid Bostonians who had supported the Irish revolutionary movement from the late 1840's turned against it in the early 1880's, when the British-Irish conflict began to threaten the growing friendship between Britain and the United States. When James Russell Lowell became minister to Great Britain in 1881, he declared—despite his long sympathy for the Irish cause—that because of their "shoe citizenship," which they "put off and on as may be most convenient," the Irish-Americans were harming America and could "never be true patriots of their adopted land."[16]

These characteristics in American behavior have continued to affect, color, and influence attitudes and policies toward those peoples in Europe, Asia, Latin America, and Africa who have either lost their freedom or been unable to gain or regain it from foreign rule.

The fact that the citizens of the United States are from many lands has made available to its leaders a knowledge and understanding of the aspirations of peoples everywhere. This has contributed to American strength, and, at times, to American weakness. As was true in the past, it is good that nations yearning to be free have a champion in the United States.

Those who encourage ethnic groups to believe that their aspirations are congruous with American interests have seldom taken into consideration the attitudes of the immigrant population toward their native lands. "As a whole, the foreign stock in the U.S.," as *Fortune*

229

put it, "has an oddly undiscriminating attitude toward the regimes in the countries of their descent."[17] Many of them have great difficulty in differentiating between Fascist, Communist, or democratic regimes; this inability to distinguish readily among kinds of government is aggravated by their attitudes toward the lands of their birth. When the average Italian- or German-American identified himself with Italy or Germany before and during the Second World War, he was not a Fascist or Nazi. The Italian-American basked in the glory of Mussolini's achievements reflected upon Italy, while the German-American could not help being pleased with the early successes of Hitler's attempts to establish a thousand-year *Reich*. "Mention Italy to him [the Italian-American]," *Fortune* observed, "and he thinks of meadows, mountains, colors, dishes, songs—not of concentration camps, castor oil, executions, and the Axis."[18] Naturally, the interest of these two ethnic groups in their fatherlands was suspected by the United States government. Conversely, it was assumed that the aspirations and activities of the Slavic- and Chinese-Americans, whose native lands were overtaken by Communism, an enemy shared with the United States, supported and aided American foreign-policy objectives. But there is always the possibility that as some of the Communist governments come into increasing prestige and power, the immigrant population's hostile attitudes might soften under the influence of exported propaganda, and they would thus become less dependable supporters of American policies aimed at the defeat of Soviet expansionism.

In October, 1956, Wladyslaw Gomulka, the Communist chief of Poland, electrified the world by his dramatic and apparently courageous stand against the military pressure of Nikita S. Khrushchev, who had arrived in Poland with the intent to bind that country closer to Soviet Russia. Gomulka's victory was soon followed by a request from his government for American economic assistance. The plea produced a delicate problem in United States foreign policy. Although there existed a precedent for giving aid to a Communist government (Yugoslavia), there was some anxiety in the administration, according to a *New York Times* writer, Harry Schwartz, over the reaction of the large numbers of American voters of Polish ancestry. It was concerned lest its decision to help the Polish Communist government might "have adverse political consequences in the United States among voters who demand the complete end of Communist rule in Poland." The Administration was also undoubtedly aware that the chairman of the Foreign Affairs Committee, Thomas S. Gordon, a Polish-American, was strongly opposed to United States aid to Poland.

The fears proved to be unjustified. On January 27, 1957, Schwartz wrote, "The bravery of Wladyslaw Gomulka . . . apparently captured the admiration of most Polish-Americans," and "The potent political forces of the organized Americans of Polish ancestry has been thrown behind the Communist Government of Poland in the latter's effort to obtain United States economic aid." According to Schwartz, some observers felt this attitude of the estimated six million Americans of Polish origin constituted "the most dramatic change in political thinking of the last decade." The strongly anti-Communist Polish-American community began to exert its influence on the American government to give "such aid even though it might tend to strengthen the present Polish government." This was reflected in the major Polish-language newspapers as well as in nationality organizations. The force of the pro-Gomulka feeling became clearly manifest when Gordon relaxed his previous position and indicated that he favored aid to Poland if it would not consolidate the Communist regime.

The State Department was aware of the metamorphosis in Polish-American thinking. Having decided to aid Gomulka, it nevertheless was reluctant to lay bare the Congressional opposition to the loan which had been made known to it. The Deputy Secretary of State for Economic Affairs, Clarence Douglas Dillon, was convinced, according to Sidney Hyman, that there was a "good chance to overcome it if the State Department . . . were to come armed with political reinforcements quietly drawn from two sources. One was the farm-state representatives, who could see . . . a means of reducing some of the huge agricultural surpluses. . . . The other was the Polish community in America, and Catholic sentiment in general—both of which favored helping the distressed Poles despite their Communist government."[19]

In pressing for, and later supporting, the decision to give aid to Poland, the Polish-American community—by no means completely united in admiration for Gomulka—laid itself open to a degree of unfortunate and doubtless unjustified suspicion. "Some observers fear," wrote Schwartz, "that the wave of pro-Gomulka sentiment is so great that it raises serious danger of Communist infiltration and subversion of a nationality group that has been one of the stanchest foes of communism in this country."[20]

Another case in point is the Communist infiltration of the Chinese-American community and its "change of heart" which became noticeable in some Chinese-American organizations during the Cold War. The same trend was also observed in editorial policies of some Chinese-American newspapers.[21]

The voting power of Chinese-Americans has not been sufficient, in the words of Professor Rose Hum Lee, to "constitute a threat to any political candidate," nor has it been influential in "shaping" American foreign policies toward the "Two Chinas." In consequence, Americans of Chinese ancestry "have not been subjected to any untoward pressures to show which China they support," although some leaders, under the influence of agents or propaganda from Communist China, have been "obtaining recognition and prestige . . . for which they yearned but never received in the U.S.A." Should the United States recognize Communist China, "these people," she warned, "will step forth and be leaders of the Chinese with few loyalties to American society." Even some present leaders "identified" with Nationalist China may, according to Rose Hum Lee, decamp to the "opposite side." "Ample evidence of such possibilities," concluded the author of *The Chinese in the United States of America*, "has already occurred in countries of South East Asia. The citizens of the U.S.A. need to be forewarned."[22]

It should be recalled that the very first group of immigrants and the successive waves and trickles that followed were not representative of the societies they left. From the seventeenth-century Pilgrims to the twentieth-century refugees, they were dissident peoples who were dissatisfied with religious, economic, or political conditions of their homelands. To view Europe, the Middle East, or Asia through reflections of the ideas and activities of these groups is bound to produce distortions and misconceptions. Illustratively, in Yugoslavia, there are more Serbs than Croats and more Croats than Slovenes; in the United States the reverse is true. In Czechoslovakia, Czechs outnumber Slovaks; in America, the proportion is not so disparate. Nevertheless, the Slovaks, the Slovenes, or the Croats have often been able to convince American politicians and the government that they alone are truly representative of their native lands. With the recent involvement of the United States in the Middle East, it is important to know that the Arabic-speaking peoples in the United States are

232

Christians, while their native lands are overwhelmingly Moslem in religion; and that the American Zionist leaders, who by no means represent all of American Jewry, do not mirror the hopes and aims of the Israeli government or the Israeli population.[23] George Kennan in his recent work *Russia Leaves the War* credits the "newly immigrated Jews" from Tsarist Russia, who had "an intense desire that Tsarist absolutism should be swept away," as one of two groups (the other being "native-born American liberals") which "pretty well dominated the formation of American opinion with respect to Russian matters."[24]

The American electorate is a macrocosm of many peoples from many lands. Seldom, however, does it reflect the "true weight" of the nations which these people represent. An ethnic group's electoral power—be it real, potential, or merely ostensible—seldom corresponds either to the political importance of its country of origin or to the emphasis given it by American policy-makers. In the United States, as Arnold Toynbee recently told the Italian people, Ukrainian-Americans are more powerful than Russian-Americans, Slovaks are more powerful than Czechs, the Irish than the English, the Greeks than the Turks, the Jews than the Arabs. And all of these, singly or jointly, one might add, are more powerful than Americans of Asian origin. This domestic political power, unrelated as it is to world realities, has, because of the undue importance given to it by American politicians, "gravely complicated" the conduct of foreign policy. While ethnic groups tend, often unwittingly, to distort the true meaning of the national interest to suit their emotional attachments to ancestral lands, the American parties, as Toynbee rightly observed, subordinate the national interest to the competition for the votes of the ethnic groups. "America was so successful in isolating itself politically for such a long period of time that still today," commented Toynbee, "although America knows well that its competition with the Soviet Union is a matter of life or death, it still nourishes the deep feeling that internal politics is supreme."[25]

Seldom have those who look upon the political activities of immigrant groups as representative of the wishes and desires of the peoples in the oppressed native lands considered the political time lag. With the passage of years and events, facts and attitudes become outdated and romanticized. This is not unlike the case of those simple men who in mature and responsible years yearn for the carefree days of childhood, when in reality those days were never carefree. The unwillingness to weigh this in the balance has led the United States to pay disproportionate attention to the ideas of recent émigrés. Indeed, one of the weaknesses of Radio Free Europe, a privately sponsored propaganda agency, but as far as the Soviet satellites are concerned a companion to the official Voice of America, is that recent immigrants compose a large proportion of its staff. As Harrison Salisbury correctly observed, "The most persistent criticism . . . is, that the media place too much emphasis on petty internal squabbles and émigré policies. There are very few Eastern European émigrés who retain any political standing in their home communities." The *New York Times* analyst further cautioned, "Antagonism engendered by the 'private' broadcasts of Radio Free Europe is directed not against a committee of private citizens whose very existence is unknown to the satellite listener but against the United States and Americans in general."[26] The alleged request of the American ambassador to Poland, Jacob D. Beam, that Radio Free Europe's broadcasts to Poland be terminated because of their "misinformation and a too-blatant propaganda line" may have stirred the State Department into taking appropriate remedial steps.[27]

5

Ethnic groups in the United States have complete liberty to urge the government to formulate and execute foreign policies in favor of their ancestral nations. This has been acknowledged and recognized as their birthright and prerogative in the American political system. Indeed, it has been encouraged by the most important political instrument: the parties. Ethnic leaders have taken advantage of this right both in times of peace and times of war. It has seldom been questioned during peacetime, but it has become of grave concern during wartime. Today when questions of peace and war have become as interdependent and indistinguishable as domestic and foreign issues, the attempts of ethnic leaders to influence American foreign policies favorable to lands of their origin has to be viewed in the interests of both the United States and the Americans of foreign stock.

Many ethnic leaders have been increasingly successful in making many Americans believe that they and their children and their children's children are duty-bound to act in the interest of their ancestral lands—that the emotional umbilical cord can never be severed. A belief is thus being perpetuated that the United States is a multinational state which cannot and should not be fully united. The doctrine, "once hyphenated, always hyphenated," is a threat to American unity, but it is more than a threat to the majority of immigrants and their descendants, whose loyalty and devotion to America—a sanctuary from the ills of their homelands—is unbounded. While ethnic leaders emphasize the contribution of the immigrant to America and try to bargain with that contribution for policies favorable to their aims, the immigrant himself would stress America's contribution to him and ask only that he be allowed to share in the fruits of America's great past and be given the opportunity to plant strong roots to guarantee America's and his future. As proof of immigrant contributions to America, ethnic leaders are quick to compile long rosters of prominent immigrants who have made illustrious names for themselves. Seldom do they acknowledge the fact that these people in whose glory they bask would have had little if any chance to discover their potential, their worth, and their genius in the country of their origin. It was in America that they were able to cultivate and achieve their greatness—and when they did so, they did so as Americans.

One of the consequences of the close identification of ethnic interests with American policy toward lands of origin is often a distortion of the real meaning and purpose of foreign policy, a distortion which may or may not be to the advantage of the ethnic groups and the parent lands. American foreign-policy decisions are based, with rare exceptions, on national rather than "ethnic" reasoning. However, because of ethnic agitations and claims, it is frequently assumed at home and abroad that they are based on domestic ethnic political considerations. Another consequence is continuing accentuation of the hyphen. Still another is the almost necessarily concomitant pledge of the ethnic leader during times of crisis that his group will wholeheartedly coöperate with announced policy. When self-appointed Slavic-American spokesmen informed Secretary of State Hull during the Second World War that "fifteen million" Slavic-Americans had pledged support of the war effort, harm was done to loyal Americans of Slavic descent.[28] Similar unfairness occurred when the president of a Slovak-American organization, in an appeal to President Roosevelt to aid in securing the nomination of a prominent Slovak-American for Congress, stressed that such a nomination would encourage American Slavs in the fight "against our common enemy."[29]

No American, hyphenated or not, need emphasize his patriotism nor need he be enticed or rewarded to fulfill his obligations.

Ethnic leaders are in constant fear of losing their grip on hyphenated Americans. Their consternation becomes particularly acute when they are confronted with unmistakable portents of ethnic acculturation or accommodation to the American environment. Political assimilation means an end to their claims of leadership and their opportunities for personal political success, an end to political demands, an end to "riding the ethnic horse" on Election Day.[30]

It is quite common among ethnic leaders to exaggerate their power to speak for minority groups and to overrate their influence among them. This is particularly true of leaders of non-English-speaking groups. "It is apparent," observed Rose Hum Lee in her study of the Chinese in the United States, "that the leaders who control all-Chinese associations located in most Chinatowns do not represent the three subgroups of the Chinese population." Many insist on maintaining separation and on the promotion of sectionalism, "while they declare the opposite to the American public." They are a "dividing rather than a constructive force." The present leadership, claimed Professor Lee, tends to "berate the American-born and the better educated for not being concerned with the welfare of the Chinese as a whole." This, she concluded, is nothing but a device to "earn favourable public reaction, whereas in truth they fear the loss of their leadership to the better-informed Chinese."[31] The latter observation is applicable to many other ethnic leaders in America.

"The United States is one nation," editorialized the *Saturday Evening Post,* "not a bundle of nationalities."[32] It should be stressed that disloyalty is not implicit when special policy suggestions of immigrant groups run counter to the broad interests of their adopted country. It is not wrong for American citizens, who because of blood ties are affected by conditions in their native lands, to urge the United States to do whatever possible in behalf of those lands or former compatriots. But what of those Americans who are motivated, not by a sense of shared anguish, but by the ambitions of leaders such as Adolf Hitler, Benito Mussolini, and Fidel Castro?

The American people have always responded materially and spiritually to sorrow and injustice beyond their shores. They will continue to do so in the belief that no nation has hope in any but a democratic world. Indeed, in the current struggle between freedom and totalitarianism, the future of the United States may depend not only on safeguarding freedom at home, but also on preserving, winning, and reëstablishing freedom elsewhere. In this struggle *all* of the American people have a great stake. To win, they and, more particularly, their party leaders, must demand the responsibility and discipline necessary to withstand unremitting pressures from abroad. Aims and hopes of ethnic groups, stimulated and reinforced as they often are by internal politics, have reflected and no doubt will continue to reflect upon American foreign policies. Nonetheless, ethnic leaders should be made cognizant of the priority of the general interest over particular interests of any given group. It is precisely this which led Senator William Fulbright to discuss on the floor of the Senate his growing concern over "the development in the United States of special pressure groups for purposes of pushing U.S. foreign policies in special interest directions." While representative government is designed to blend conflicting interests in such a way that the national interest is served, he warned, there are limits "beyond which special interests cannot go without undermining the conduct of our foreign policies. . . . There is a shadowland between the legitimate activity involved in the organization of special interest groups to influence foreign policy and the illegitimate activity proscribed by the Logan Act."[33] Not to be ignored is the culpability of politicians and ethnic leaders in deliberately encouraging credulous ethnic Americans to believe that foreign-policy actions will be taken to fulfill campaign pledges, when they know that in effect nothing will be done. This is becoming particularly important at the present time when there is evidence that friends and foes of the United States are becoming increasingly aware that campaign planks and promises to American ethnic organizations are designed only to serve internal politics and not to serve as objectives of foreign policies.

What of the future? Is the *Saturday Evening Post*'s conclusion correct: "Although citizens are free to speak for ancestral countries the expectation must be that the special ties of overseas emotions will gradually weaken and fade away"?

237

Chapter XIV

THE FUTURE OF THE HYPHEN

Do ethnic Americans vote along lines of their national origins? How effective has their influence been on American foreign policies? And what of the future: will hyphenism wane and with it the pressures of ethnic groups in behalf of their native lands?

The student of immigrant political behavior must submit himself to a large variety of divergent and often contradictory opinions and interpretations held by sociologists, historians, political scientists, political strategists, ethnic leaders, and journalists. He is told that Americans of foreign origin vote *en bloc;* that they can be "swung" to either of the major parties by the proper "baits"; and that while both statements may have been true in the past, neither is true today. There are some who qualify these conclusions by distinguishing between the voting predilections of the urban and rural foreign-born; of the "new" immigrants from Eastern and Southern Europe and the "old" immigrants from Northern and Western Europe; of the immigrants of Catholic or Jewish faith and those of Protestant religions; of the unassimilated foreign-born, the more assimilated first and second generations, and the supposedly completely assimilated third generation.

There are some, armed with statistical tables, who want the student to believe that ethnic groups, like the general population, vote in accord with the predisposing factors of sex, age, economic status, and education and therefore cannot be considered as special factors in politics. Others, equipped with different or sometimes even with similar statistical tables, conclude that foreign birth does have an effect, particularly on such issues as foreign policy, immigration, and civil rights, questions touching on ancient loyalties and social status in America. The latter group is supported by Thomas A. Bailey, who, in his *A Diplomatic History of the American People,* lists "hyphenated Americans" as the fourth "most significant" factor which has "profoundly influenced" American attitudes toward foreign policy.[1]

Those who believe in the effect of immigrant groups on American foreign policies are by no means unanimous in their interpretations. Some, although they may or may not "sympathize with the solicitude of the hyphenate for the fate of his native land," cannot

238

condone his activities which "tend to embroil the land of his adoption" in non-American affairs; others defend and applaud ethnic participation in the formation of foreign policy, on the ground that "America recognizes diverse loyalties," or that it "makes a positive contribution" to a better understanding of world problems, or that it is an "export and extension of American political ideas and ideals of freedom and democracy." Those holding views between these opposites say that while it is true that some nationality groups have "periodically organized their efforts in the foreign policy field with excessive zeal," this fact should not cause fear or alarm. After all, "we *are* a nation of immigrants" and therefore the political activities of immigrant groups should be viewed in the same way as other native pressure groups, such as the American "cattle growers in their feelings about foreign beef." And then there are those who, having reviewed and digested the disparate opinions, inform the student of immigrant political behavior that "at any rate" the controversy is bound to end with the waning of hyphenism "in the foreseeable future."[2]

What of the ethnic leaders themselves? What is their answer to the question about the existence, influence, and effectiveness of ethnic-group loyalty and group voting? Most of them seldom hesitate to indicate the numerical strength and voting power they represent whenever they appear before party-platform committees, and Congressional hearings, or when making demands upon party leaders. Yet, at the same time, they openly resent the accusation that ethnic or religious minorities vote as groups. This accusation, they counter, implies that Americans belonging to these minorities do not vote as individual citizens but as disciplined units of organized groups and, worst of all, questions their loyalty to the United States. The accusers, they say further, are motivated by malice, bad intent, and at best, by confusion. Though their reaction is understandable, many ethnic leaders can nevertheless recognize that except for a rejection of the implication of disloyalty, denial of the existence of group voting and their ability to affect it jeopardizes their political power to influence policy decisions.

When ethnic leaders deny the existence of group voting, they deny what is true and what is false. To extricate themselves from this dilemma, some qualify denial by distinguishing between bloc and group voting, rejecting the presence of the former and justifying the existence of the latter. Others neither justify nor deny. Still others, while reluctantly admitting that voting on the basis of foreign origin may in some limited cases and at certain times exist, the fault—if it is a fault—lies not with them or with ethnic Americans but with the parties. Those who deny the existence of bloc voting point out that ethnic leaders, like labor leaders, cannot get their members to vote as they want them to vote. They can only recommend and exhort; they cannot give orders or expect orders, if given, to be followed. Thus, they conclude, the allegation of bloc voting, which implies something sinister like "invisible government" and foreign loyalties, is mistaken and ill-informed. As far as group voting is concerned, some ethnic leaders readily call attention to studies which report or indicate that the average American does not vote in a "completely individualistic way." That is, voting is influenced by an assessment of his own interests and outlook, which are in turn influenced by membership in groups. No American votes simply as an American. He votes as a laborer, farmer, or businessman; as yellow-, black-, or white-skinned; as Protestant, Catholic, or Jew. Such behavior and reactions, they claim, are natural in a democracy. Only under totalitarianism do people vote as citizens in general. Voting behavior, they believe, reflects not only economic status, but also religion, ethnic origin, or racial composition. It is no less legitimate for a man to vote from ethnic, racial, or religious considerations than, let us say, to vote from social or economic considerations.

There are spokesmen of ethnic groups which because of small size or other reasons have not exerted political pressures who ask that party attention be accorded on bases other than numerical strength. At the 1960 hearings of the Republican platform committee, James H. Tashjian, of the American Committee for the Independence of Armenia, pleaded from such a premise. Both parties, he said, are duty-bound to recognize "the great historical truth about America," i.e., the citizenry is wholly composed of nationality stocks or ethnic groups. "It is erroneous and abortive to the scheme of things to refer" to ethnic Americans as minority, language, cultural, or religious groups. Speaking in behalf of relatively few persons, Tashjian urged that no ethnic group be credited with a greater contribution to the nation than another because of its size, but "rather in ratio to the inherent qualities of the peoples from which these nationality groups have sprung. . . . The ethnic concept of America must not only be undenied but must be accepted and encouraged."[3]

Some ethnic leaders hold that the nature of American politics is

240

such that groups within American society, as well as politicians, will always continue to work with each other and take chances with each other; the American system allows such activity. Because there is such tremendous freedom, the possibility of excesses is great. However, these leaders feel that the system eventually punishes those who go too far. Some feel that even if certain ideas are pushed to extremes—as in instances like Irish-American pressure on foreign policy in the nineteenth and early twentieth centuries, the liberation policy in 1952, the recognition of Israel—their advocates harm neither themselves nor the United States.

An increasing number of responsible ethnic representatives, confronted with allegations, charges, and countercharges about the issue of real or apparent cohesiveness of ethnic-group voting and loyalty, are anxious about the problem. They note that in every election season, ethnic and religious leaders are confronted with political leaders' appeals for support. They also point out that journalists, political observers, and public-opinion pollsters continually talk and write of the Jewish vote, the Polish vote, the Irish vote, the minority vote, the immigrant vote, etc. While they welcome the interest of the parties in their organizations, at the same time they nevertheless are concerned over the charges that they can be manipulated. What is of most concern to them is the realization that party promises which are seldom kept accentuate the uniqueness of particular groups and thereby hinder the process of political assimilation. Once having agreed that there is group voting and that Americans, under pressure and influence from political leaders and/or ethnic leaders, may react on the basis of their foreign origin, they admit that some basic problems still remain unanswered. The real issue is not whether an ethnic vote exists, but what it is used for and what the effect of this use is on American politics and on the political assimilation of the groups themselves. More and more ethnic and religious leaders have shown concern over the growth of the balanced ticket, the pressures to separate the electorate into specific blocs or groups, the incitement to prejudice, and the general interest versus special interests, be it in the field of domestic policies or the field of foreign policies.

While the scholarly fraternity is rent by these conflicting hypotheses concerning the ethnic American, the politician, the one most immediately concerned, has remained remarkably consistent in his beliefs. The politician, who has learned to think in terms of the farm

vote, the labor vote, the veteran vote, or the business vote, has convinced himself of the presence of the ethnic vote. No study, dispas-
sionate and objective though it may be, has been able to shake or
weaken his persistent credence in the unassimilability of foreign
stock. Confronted with data which negate the immigrant vote, he
dismisses them on the basis that the wrong appeals for ethnic support were used. Instead of discouraging him from involvement in
immigrant politics, these data only spur him to find the right issues
to bewitch the hyphenates.

"How can you say," asked one Senator, "that immigrants do not
vote on the basis of their nationality? Whenever I speak before a
nationality group I have only to mention a Garibaldi, Pilsudski,
Kosciuszko, or a Kossuth to receive a tumultuous ovation."[4] The
experience of James MacGregor Burns, a professor in the Department of Political Science at Williams College, who was a Congressional candidate in 1958, attests to this kind of reflex action: "One
night I attended a rally of Slovak-Americans. Speaker after speaker
extolled the Slovaks, sometimes in their own language; I felt at times
as though we were living in Bratislava. When my turn came I asked,
'May I do you the honor of addressing you not as Slovaks but as
Americans?' They looked at me blankly. They applauded me politely,
too, but when the next speaker hailed the Slovaks as the repositories
of virtue and the carriers of culture, they burst into enthusiastic
applause."[5] It is doubtful that these reactions are indicative of the
beliefs and feelings of the majority of these particular ethnic groups
or show that those who listen to the politician in the halls of the
Sons of Italy, Kosciuszko Clubs, or the Magyar National Homes represent a preponderance of opinion. The pat references to their
national heroes are bound to evoke applause, but in no way should
these conditioned responses to the limning of past glories be construed to mean that their votes are safe in the politician's pocket.

The late Senator Herbert H. Lehman, a distinguished political
leader and former Governor of New York, believed that Americans
vote on the basis of national origin. Indeed, according to the *New
York Times,* Lehman held that the nationality of the voter has a
greater influence than his religious affiliation.[6] So long as the politician continues convinced of the ethnic vote, so long as he believes
that it is not politically wise to disregard pressures from ethnic leaders, so long will the persistent belief of the voting power of nation-

ality groups affect American political life and the ethnic leader. So long as political strategists remain convinced they can predict as well as influence the direction of voting among ethnic groups, so long will the belief that ethnic groups have not been assimilated in the political life of the United States continue. It is the politician, not the immigrant, who has created and nurtured this belief, a belief which he cannot easily destroy.[7]

The student of ethnic political behavior is perhaps on much safer ground when he concerns himself not only with the judgments and ideas of the objective scholars but also with the opinions of political strategists. Myth or not, it is the politician, the Congressman, the Senator, the President, who influences, formulates, and, at times, executes foreign and domestic policies, often on the basis of his belief in the existence of an ethnic vote. In the continual catering to the ethnic vote by the political parties there is much that is primitive, irrational, and increasingly foreboding.

2

In this era of compulsory American involvement in world affairs the influence of ethnic groups on foreign policy is growing rather than diminishing. In 1951 Johan Smertenko, an active participant in politics and an observer of the ethnic American in that field, wrote: "Today, when immigration has been reduced to a trickle of the former flood and when the percentage of foreign-born is the lowest in our nation's history, the hyphen of the new immigrant is no longer contracting. On the contrary, it is emerging into public view more prominently than at any time in our generation."[8] Many of those observers of American politics who, since the turn of the nineteenth century, have been perennially predicting the speedy death of the hyphen, may also find it disconcerting to be told by Charles P. Taft, recent chairman of the Fair Campaign Practices Committee, that the self-consciousness of ethnic and religious minority groups in the United States is increasing rather than declining. While it is true that ethnic groups no longer appear to vote as cohesive units, some examples of bloc voting can still be found. Foreign-language groups residing in politically strategic areas continue to wield "decisive . . . political power within their communities," according to Taft. At times these groups have voted, and still do vote, as blocs. "In the political world," Taft wrote, "when blocs develop, they are courted for their bloc vote. And when a bloc is large enough

243

so its vote may elect or defeat, it not only is courted as a bloc but in some quarters is feared."[9]

In place of the anachronistic method of swelling party ranks with pliant immigrant groups, strategists today have substituted modern propaganda methods which attempt first to stir and then to solidify the group consciousness of Americans of foreign origin. In the past, before the advent of modern communication media and before many of the ethnic organizations merged into national bodies, a politician had to work hard to win isolated communities. Today, a Congressional candidate seeking the support of ethnic voters throughout the constituency can turn voters, so he believes—with the right appeal— not only in his own state but throughout the nation.

The continued prominence of foreign-policy issues enables these political strategists to exploit the hopes and fears of nationality groups. The breakdown of party loyalties, combined with the use of the "balanced ticket," encourages the current stress on ethnic-group responses in American politics. The raising of issues that appeal to deeply ingrained cultural traditions, attitudes, and experiences predisposes ethnic groups to vote as virtual blocs. Such foreign-policy planks as "liberation of captive peoples," "softness toward Communism," the "Yalta betrayal," and "self-determination" reach and bring to the surface the emotional and cultural attachments of ethnic Americans to their native lands. In almost all cases these issues are depicted as being in the national interest in order to take advantage of the strong desire of ethnic groups to be accepted as Americans.

The practice of the balanced ticket is perhaps the best example of the recognition granted to the ethnic vote by American politicians. The concomitant accentuation of the hyphen is fast becoming an unshakable tradition in state and national politics. Political candidates must, it seems, qualify for office not on the basis of ability but on the basis of national origin.[10] Indeed, there are some prominent politicians who would extend the concept of the balanced ticket to include the religious affiliation of presidential candidates.

The balanced ticket is a direct result of the strong belief held by political strategists that Americans vote on the basis of their backgrounds, national origins, or religious ties. Party leaders have always been convinced that members of groups, especially members of immigrant groups eager for status and recognition, are more likely to be zealous in supporting candidates who are of their own group.

Thus in many states where citizens of foreign origin reside, candidates are nominated and selected according to ethnic background with the expectation of thereby producing a winning ticket. A candidate so identified is presented as a compatriot who, if elected, will, in theory at least, signify that the group is the equal of other Americans and that its needs and sensibilities will not be overlooked.

The balanced ticket appeals on one hand to ethnic pride and on the other affirms loyalty to America. By appealing to the voter through his foreign origin, the balanced ticket recalls, accentuates, and identifies him with it and at the same time attempts to confirm his status and acceptance into American life. There is no question that in itself the balanced ticket has supplied opportunity to new citizens to increase their self-respect, prestige, and political power. This has been particularly true of Irish-Americans, who by means of it have gained great prominence in local, state, and eventually national politics. Indeed, Irish-American leaders were the first practitioners of this device. Once established at local and state levels, such leaders—particularly the Democratic—had no desire at the turn of the century to bestow political opportunity upon newcomers. Thus, the lone representative of the new immigrants in Congress from 1906 until the end of the First World War was Bohemian-born, and of Jewish faith, Adolph J. Sabath of Chicago.

To unseat Irish-American power, newer immigrant groups, as they became more and more politically sophisticated, were the natural wards and allies of the Republicans. In Rhode Island and New York French-Canadians and Italian-Americans were sent to Congress; in New Mexico a Spanish-American—each the first of his ethnic group to attain high political position. All ran on the Republican ticket. In the aftermath of the First World War, the rise of nativism, reaction to Prohibition, and Republican endorsements of the quota system alienated many of the newer immigrants from the Republican party. During the depression the economic factor began to predominate in the voting behavior of ethnic Americans. It was in the 1930's that the newer immigrant groups moved toward the Democratic camp, eventually forming a strong coalition behind Roosevelt. Ethnic organizations began to function politically at state levels. From then on, more and more representatives of the more recent immigrant groups—Poles, Ukrainians, Italians, Yugoslavs, Jews, Slovenians—reached Congress. The balanced ticket which had been so important to Irish-Americans was turning against them. The last decades have witnessed the critical emergence of the newer, non–English-speaking ethnic groups who increasingly have been threatening Irish-American control. These groups, numerically larger, who in the past could only resent Irish-American political power, are now demanding their share of the balanced ticket and equal opportunities for increasing their prestige. It is therefore not surprising that many prominent Irish-American leaders who have hitherto championed the balanced ticket as a perfect democratic device now show consternation over the practice, a practice which demands distribution of political offices to various groups. While Irish-Americans continue to hold important government positions, particularly in appointive areas such as the Cabinet and the federal judiciaries, at the local and state levels they are yielding to the newer groups. At the same time, students of voting behavior have discerned an Irish-American movement to the Republican party, particularly in the 1952 and 1956 elections.

Nineteen fifty-six, and also 1960, saw the acceleration of the balanced ticket in the religious field. For the Democratic Convention of 1956 supporters of Senator John F. Kennedy, a Catholic, prepared a statistical analysis which argued that key industrial states with their high "Catholic vote" and high electoral vote could be won by the nomination of a Catholic. Only such a move would return to the Democratic fold those who were "Ike" Republicans. On July 4 John M. Bailey of Connecticut, a Catholic and a shrewd political strategist, released a memorandum intended to influence the Democratic presidential nominee, Adlai Stevenson, to choose Kennedy as his running mate. Its concluding paragraph stated:

"Has the Democratic era ended? Has the party permanently lost its political base among the Catholics and immigrants of the large Northern cities that made a Democratic victory possible in 1940, 1944, and 1948? . . . A Catholic Vice-Presidential nominee could refashion this base as Al Smith did, and begin a new era of Democratic victories, without costing even the few electoral votes Smith did."[11]

Many students of politics and spokesmen for good government have raised objections to the reasoning behind the balanced ticket, and behind the appeals, often quite crude, with the argument that government should be staffed by the best-qualified people and that

246

group membership is an irrelevant qualification. To this, balanced-ticket partisans say, "Is not group representation itself a desirable quality?" Recently, however, many leaders of ethnic, racial, or religious groups have become concerned over the growth and expansion of the idea of a balanced ticket. They feel that too much concentration on representing groups fosters prejudice. If politicians engender enthusiasm within a group by nominating or presenting a candidate of that group, there is, of course, danger of encouraging undemocratic responses to candidates from another group. There is also the fear that in the interest of having a member succeed to elective office a group may let itself be manipulated by politicians who may have no scruples about injecting into the campaign scurrility and appeals to prejudice, usually unpublished.

At a time when America's best leadership must be enlisted in the global struggle for survival, political tacticians dissipate energy on the election of candidates who, they believe, will attract the ethnic or religious vote. To be sure, there are many students in the field, as well as a sprinkling of politicians, who point out that the emphasis on the balanced ticket in such states as New York, Connecticut, Illinois, and Michigan saps a real and potential reservoir of political talent; that neither the nation, the state, nor the nationality groups themselves benefit from this practice; that seldom does the quality of public servants emerging from this formula reflect the best a nationality group has to offer—the very system of selection is such that it rarely allows the best-qualified person from any nationality group to be nominated at a state convention;[12] that it is a matter of doubt whether a leader of a minority can, or actually does, represent the wishes of the group after his election; that political aspirations of each nationality group are limited to certain offices because of the "quota system" which haphazardly allots offices to a handful of ethnic leaders; that the real evil in the exploitation of the hyphen lies in the denial of an identification with America to the great majority of immigrants—they are forced to conceive of themselves as outsiders, inferiors, and second-class citizens; and that statistical studies refute the notion that ethnic groups "flock" in support of candidates of their own faith or race.[13]

But the political strategists remain deaf to these arguments, protestations, and remonstrances. When James A. Farley, a realistic politician and one of the early practitioners of the balanced ticket, stated with deep "resentment" his "inflexible position" that "the time has passed when any political party can or should piece out a political ticket based on proportional representation of creeds or races," and warned that "to follow this course is not to unite all as Americans, but to Balkanize our beloved country," he made little or no impression. Farley's "conversion" was interpreted by political bosses as only a "well-disguised" maneuver to obtain the nomination for the United States Senate, which would add to the slate another person of Irish origin and Catholic faith and thus unbalance the state ticket.[14]

The balanced ticket has become so strongly entrenched that in many states non-ethnic Americans have had to consider themselves as a minority group. When Tammany boss Carmine DeSapio—who, among other things, considers the balanced ticket a means of checking "the dangerous trend" of some ethnic Americans toward Republicanism or "political respectability in the suburbs"—was queried about his refusal to back "non-ethnic" Thomas Finletter for the United States Senate on the same slate as another "non-ethnic," gubernatorial candidate, Averell Harriman, his lieutenant said, "For five state-wide offices, you don't need more than one 'Wasp.' "[15] The term "Wasp" signals the emergence of another ethnic group—White Anglo-Saxon Protestants. The balanced ticket has become "such an obsession with New York politicians," wrote Robert Bendiner, "that it would be refreshing to vote for a slate made up of five Cherokees, all from Staten Island."[16]

3

In these circumstances it is not surprising that ethnic groups should seek to exercise their influence by soliciting support for policies which affect their homelands. Emphasis on the ethnic vote to the point where it is openly sought by politicians has given the leaders of nationality organizations a renewed opportunity to enhance their position, strengthen their ostensible hold over their members, and claim an ability to deliver the vote.[17] Many nationality organizations which in the past had converted ethnic resentment of native prejudices into a revival of interest in the mother country have now, through the attempts of the parties to exploit the ethnic vote, found respectability and a new way to tighten Old World political ties. Spurred to renewed activity, these organizations have become a vigorous force which is not only retarding the political assimilation of ethnic Americans but also extending the feeling of a common identity among third-generation descendants who had previously been unwilling to be so classified.

Some hitherto politically weak ethnic groups are approaching political potency. "The voting blocs of Poles, Italians, and Jews," wrote Nathan Glazer, "were never so important as in the 1940's and 1950's, twenty and thirty years after the end of mass immigration."[18] The success of some nationality groups in achieving their aims within the political structure has stimulated and excited others to emulation. During a convention of Lebanese-Americans in Springfield, Massachusetts, "the very middle of the greatest concentration of Lebanese in the United States," on the "heels of the crisis in Lebanon," the *Lebanese American Journal* complained:

Is this the way a nationality group in the United States should act? Decidedly not. Nationality groups in the United States are extremely conscious of the country of their origin. They promote it, they teach their young about it, they teach their adopted country about it, they seek to perpetuate the ideals, the customs of the land of their birth. . . .

A good contrast is that of the other federations, southern, western and mid-western. Why do they still continue to have better attendance than the Eastern? It's because they have a better spirit. They are true Lebanese and do not deny it nor hide it. We hope that their spirit will dominate more. Theirs is the good American, the honest, sincere spirit that eventually comes through, for the good of this country, their fellow Lebanese, fellow Americans and for Lebanon and the Lebanese there.[19]

In its prospectus the National Confederation of American Ethnic Groups appealed to nationality organizations to affiliate themselves with it, summing up the importance of "building a strong and effective NATIONAL CONFEDERATION" in these words:

"The Irish and Jewish groups—and now the Negroes, have learned the effectiveness and prestige that can be achieved through collective, unified action—and they are forging ahead. The many benefits these groups have derived from such action are self-evident. *Have you ever stopped to think where this leaves the nationality groups?* . . .

The NATIONAL CONFEDERATION OF AMERICAN ETHNIC GROUPS offers you the opportunity to help correct these great evils and to do for you and your people what the Irish, the Jews—and now the Negroes, are doing for their people."[20]

The inciting by some nationality groups of other nationality groups—which have been either indifferent or inactive—to organize themselves for the purpose of putting pressure on the American government to help their native lands, "may not," as Harold Hoskins observed, "always be in the best interest of the United States, but rather in the interest of a limited number of actively partisan and vocal individuals or groups."[21]

The political parties, through constant appeals for the ethnic vote and the encouragement of nationality groups toward organization, are forcing many Americans to vote as hyphenates. The "myth of the foreign-born vote" may very well be transmuted into reality.

4

The ethnic diversity of the population has been an important factor in the formulation and execution of American diplomacy. There is, of course, nothing unusual or objectionable in the politicians' use of foreign-policy issues as a means to gain domestic political power. But it is wrong to make to ethnic groups campaign promises which are impossible of fulfillment. All too often the officeholder finds himself subsequently hamstrung by those promises, which prevent his making decisions based on world realities. America is a land of pressure groups, and "among the more powerful and militant organizations," in Bailey's opinion, "are those formed by hyphenates to promote some foreign cause." Pressures from nationality groups have complicated, swayed, and, at times, undermined American foreign policy. "It is not unusual for the Washington government . . . to make decisions that are more conducive to the interest of foreigners than of Americans," Bailey commented.[22]

From the 1860's until the end of the First World War American policies toward Great Britain were substantially influenced by the real or imagined power attributed to the Irish-American vote. By the time of the Second World War Irish-American animosity toward the British had lost much of its former fervor. Nevertheless, it was still strong enough to add significant weight to the simulated isolationism of German- and Italian-Americans, the isolationist sentiment of Swedish-Americans and—before the invasion of Norway—Norwegian-Americans,[23] and the sincere isolationist attitudes of other groups as well, thus affecting American aid to the British. Today, despite the perennial and ritualistic introduction of a resolution for a united Ireland by some Congressman or Senator, Irish-American pressure in behalf of Erin has diminished. Polish-American and other Slavic-American groups which had worked toward independence for their native lands during the First World War became active again at the time of the Second World War when that independence was lost. They labor unremittingly for restoration of the status quo ante bellum. There is little doubt that recent American foreign policy toward the captive nations, the Middle East, the Trieste problem, the inclusion of Italy in NATO, and Germany was affected by regard for the sentiment or political power of Slavic, non-Slavic, Jewish, Italian, and German ethnic Americans.[24]

Pressure of ethnic groups on American foreign policies is directed toward the fruition of national hopes: retaining or seeking the return of national territories; winning and preserving national independence; and cessation of persecution and oppression of minority ethnic or religious groups in other nations. Since the end of the Second World War the attention of ethnic groups has centered in those areas where American foreign policy has assumed or is about to assume an active role. The question of Israel, the problem of captive peoples, the immigration issue, matters dealing with foreign aid, and the expansion and threat of Communism are areas where ethnic groups are playing a vigorous part.

5

It is not surprising that ethnic leaders in this hospitable and congenial "nation of nations" should seek to influence American foreign policy in the interest of their fatherlands. What is astonishing is that despite the tolerance and indifference of the American people, despite the absence of any significant attempts to assimilate or Americanize the immigrant, despite the babel of tongues, and despite a political system which encourages ethnic pressures, nationality groups have not been more effective, more active, and more decisive in their attempts to involve or implicate the United States in non-American affairs.

Several factors limit the influence of nationality groups on American foreign policy. Some stem from immigrant political behavior, so often affected by the inability to discard political attitudes and prepossessions of earlier experience in the native lands; others proceed from the vicissitudes of American politics. During the "hyphenate

251

uproar" for recognition following the outbreak of the First World War, Lady Novar wrote to the British ambassador in Washington from Government House in Adelaide, Australia, "If anything has been proved by the war, it is that America is no nation, just a collection of peoples who neutralize one another. . . ."[25]

Undoubtedly the various and often conflicting aims of nationality groups have at times counterbalanced each other to a degree which prevented the realization of their objectives. During the First World War some nationality groups such as the Polish, which saw in the American entry into the war an opportunity to achieve or regain independence for their native lands, supported preparedness and intervention; some, like the Irish-American, which discerned in the defeat of Great Britain a timely circumstance to free Ireland, were against American aid to the British and American participation; while others, like the German-American, which foresaw defeat for Germany's ambitions, assailed American involvement. Some Jewish-Americans, because of their hatred of Tsarist Russia, supported the German attack on Russia.

During and, more particularly, following the First World War many traditional isolationists found it expedient to ally themselves with the cause of Irish independence even though it involved interference in the affairs of Great Britain. The purpose, among other things, was to enlist Irish-American support for the defeat of Wilson's Peace Settlement and "Britain's League." It was not too difficult to convince Irish-Americans of the compatibility of isolationism and intervention in British affairs and, also, that throughout most of American history isolationism and animosity toward Britain were synonymous.

During the Second World War many immigrant groups again aligned themselves either for or against entry into the European conflict, depending on their particular interests—seldom, one may say, on the basis of American interests.

The "neutralization" of interests resulting from countervailing ethnic activities whenever the United States becomes deeply concerned with foreign affairs is not, however, so decisive an influence-limiting factor in policy as it appears on the surface. Communist expansion and threats to the independence of European nations and to Western civilization's major religions since the Second World War have overcome, at least for the time being, the interminable differences among a majority of nationality groups. Indeed, many of those which had championed isolationism in the 1930's and early 1940's became interventionists during the Cold War. These changed attitudes undoubtedly had some effect on the ease with which the United States turned from its traditional policy of non-intervention in world affairs to one of abrupt and headlong participation. As Representative Stuyvesant Wainwright of New York observed during the Congressional debate on giving aid to Communist governments: "The gentlewoman from New York is a very courageous person. She is defending international morality by refusing to aid a country which is clearly Communist and within the Communist orbit. It is a strange thing that many of the Members who are opposing her amendment—who are normally very isolationist—are doing so on the grounds that the Polish people in their districts are in favor of aid to Poland. We do strange things for politics in this House."[26]

While conflicting aspirations of various ethnic organizations may tend to negate their labors, they also, as it has been pointed out, tend to neutralize the actions of politicians who, fearing the rancor of ethnic leaders, have been reluctant to take any positive stands on foreign-policy matters. The Cold War produced a consensus among the European immigrant population and has also brought about a similar consensus among politicians of both parties. But it is not in the nature of American politics to allow such unanimity to persist. Some politicians, hoping to tighten their hold and influence on those whose native lands were overrun by Communism, promised to "go beyond containment" and "liberate" the Soviet satellites. An alliance was thus forged in 1952 between those who favored vigorous American leadership in world affairs and those nationality groups who saw in it the consummation of their hopes—liberation of their homelands. The alliance was a precarious one, at best—a ruse to capture the ethnic vote, at worst. To the politician this alliance promised to secure an alternative domestic regime; to the ethnic leader it promised a drastic foreign-policy change. It succeeded in bringing about the former, but not the latter. The "liberation" plank of the 1952 Republican platform, pledging that the captive nations would be freed, was inserted and approved with the tacit knowledge that, in fact, little if anything could be done. The change in administrations that followed the election brought no fundamental foreign-policy shift, despite the expectations quickened in the hearts of many ethnic groups by the Republican campaign. President Eisenhower's initiation in 1959 of an exchange of visits with Premier Nikita Khrushchev, which, it should be remembered, followed the proclamation of Captive Nations Week, produced further consternation and bewilderment among the ethnic leadership. Characteristically, those Congressmen who were concerned about voters of Eastern European background claimed "absorption with labor legislation or civil rights or mutual security," neglected to express any opinion, and as Richard Rovere observed, showed "an unaccustomed briskness at their work." Only a few members of Congress protested loudly.[27]

Nationality groups have been unable to unite internally in a common sustained and well-timed effort to compel the government of the United States to satisfy their demands. Political, social, or religious divisions, entanglements, and mutual distrusts present in the land of origin have often been transplanted into American soil with each successive wave or ripple of immigrants, exile leaders, or refugees. This was true of the Irish-Americans in the late nineteenth and early twentieth centuries; this has been true of Slavic-Americans during both of the world wars and to some extent during the Cold War. At times a core of ethnic leaders has been able to gain control over all the members—active or inactive—of a given nationality, through the establishment of roof organizations or the "rigging" of a convention. Armed with the ostensible power to speak for the whole group, this small but articulate elite has been able to induce political leaders to attend its wants.

There has been a notable absence of qualified, intelligent, and dedicated ethnic leaders. Leadership among immigrant groups varies as to ability, comprehension of issues, and knowledge of the workings of the American government. Many ethnic leaders in the very process of attempting to "sell" the votes of their groups to one or the other of the political parties have succeeded only in debasing their prestige and in weakening their power to influence decision-makers. Some who have coupled their demands for a favorable foreign-policy statement with a request for political patronage may or may not have received the latter, but rarely the former; some who have been primarily interested in the material advantage accruing from their position may have been able to persuade an understanding legislator to insert in the *Congressional Record* a generally ineffective but per-

254

sonally rewarding resolution or address; others because of excessive zeal and lack of tact have been responsible for changing presidential sympathy to antipathy. Few ethnic leaders have had bona fide access to the White House. Those who did have direct contact with the President were famous in fields other than ethnic politics. Men like Ignace Jan Paderewski, Thomas Masaryk, or Chaim Weizmann were able to draw on their prestige as artists, scholars, or scientists as a means to influence presidential decisions.[28]

To foreign-born, first-generation, and, to some extent, second-generation citizens, the President of the United States is omnipotent. They have the feeling that he can do anything he wants to do. In a lecture on the nature of American government beamed to Poland by Radio Free Europe on December 14, 1957, a Radio Free Europe official—a recent émigré—summed up the powers of the Presidency: "Louis XIV is said to declare that the State is I. How incorrectly by the way. However, if any U. S. President said 'The State is I' he would be fully justified to say so."[29] To many an immigrant the President has only to say the word and Ireland would be freed; Poland would be reborn; Israel would be preserved; the American might would be unleashed or checked; and the Soviets would withdraw from Eastern Europe. There is little realization that the President's powers are not so sweeping. This explains the differing attitudes of ethnic groups toward Presidents—from violent hostility, as was the case of the Irish-Americans toward Wilson, to unbounded reverence for him by the Polish-Americans. Until the end of the Second World War, President Franklin D. Roosevelt was the hero of the majority of Slavic- and Jewish-Americans. The Yalta Agreement and the subsequent meeting of Roosevelt and King Ibn Saud turned admiration into distrust.

These predilections are, of course, well known to American politicians. Indeed, they openly encourage them. Under pressure from the National Committees of both parties, many Presidents or presidential candidates have, with various degrees of reluctance, made promises aimed at winning ethnic support—promises which they knew to be either morally wrong or incapable of realization. To win the election was paramount. Should a President fail to honor a promise, vindication could always be found in exposing the culpability of the other party. If that was not possible, then there was the expedient of blaming a "group of willful men" in the White House who keep the President "in ignorance." The awe which many immigrants have for the President is, at times, sufficient to turn the support of ethnic leaders from a rival presidential candidate to the incumbent. President Roosevelt was a master at turning what is actually a regard for the office into personal veneration. By singling out for his special attention a recalcitrant ethnic leader during electioneering stopovers, he frequently obtained the backing of the man he had honored.[30]

It was only to be expected that ethnic Americans and some of the more perceptive leaders would come eventually to realize some of the causes limiting their influence as well as to be fully cognizant of the frequent post-election faithlessness of the politicians and parties. On April 27 and 28, 1956, a group of leaders representing twenty-three nationality groups met in Washington, D.C., to overcome these difficulties. It was observed that "after years of trying separately and reaping only indifference or unkept promises, it has become crystal-clear, at last, that the only way the nationality groups can achieve recognition and acquire enough weight and prestige to be listened to in Washington . . ." is to unite in a confederation. According to the published announcement of this newly created National Confederation of American Ethnic Groups, "The tragic events in Hungary and failure of our policymakers in both parties to heed the sound and timely advice of able and patriotic nationality group leaders have convinced even the most skeptical that *IMMEDIATE UNIFICATION* of all nationality groups into one big, powerful, overall national confederation is *IMPERATIVE*." Among the issues which were "stirring the Nationality Groups to unity and action" were:

Repudiation of 1952 campaign pledges for a policy of liberation of nations enslaved by Communism, and adoption instead of a policy of "unprincipled expediency" which includes betrayal of our friends and lesser allies, and immoral "deals" with the Soviets—admission to the U.N. of the USSR's European satellites.

Exploitation of the Nationality Groups by both political parties: Praise, flattery before elections; neglect, scorn, broken promises after elections.

TAXATION WITHOUT REPRESENTATION: The Nationality Groups have practically no representation in the policymaking bodies of government and the higher courts. Paying taxes to keep the government in business and serving in the armed forces to protect our country is not enough. GOOD CITIZENSHIP also means sharing the responsibility of running the government by helping to formulate its policies and to interpret its laws.[31]

It remains to be seen whether this specially created "big, powerful, overall national confederation" will succeed in overcoming the many difficulties that have plagued nationality leaders in their attempts to influence American policies. Evidently the call to arms did not produce any fear in the politicians despite its statement of distrust and its avowed purpose of direct representation of the views of ethnic groups. According to the confederation's first-year progress report: "Many Members of Congress, Democrats and Republicans alike, have been contacted and informed of our aims and objectives. So far 152 have expressed approval and willingness to support our program." Nor did the parties overlook the possibilities latent in this roof organization. In July, 1958, two years after its creation, A. B. Hermann of the Republican National Committee and John Redding of the Democratic National Committee addressed its Congressional Conference, and Michael Cieplinski, director of the Nationalities Division of the Democratic party, told the delegates that the federal government had had insufficient information concerning the opinion of ethnic groups and spoke of "the need of uniting in common action so that their voice could be heard by the administration."[32] The day following the appearance of Hermann and Redding, Slobodan M. Draskovich, a member of the confederation's policy-planning committee, said:

These two gentlemen seem to have thoroughly misunderstood us and the purpose which brought us here.

Our silence all these years apparently induced them and their associates in the major parties to assume we—the ethnic groups of America—are just awakening to the political realities around us, and that we are quite willing to discharge our patriotic and civic duties by joining and supporting 1 or the other of the 2 parties and thus enable our policy-makers to pursue further the weak, immoral, bankrupt and alarmingly defeatest [sic] policies they have practiced in the last 15 years.

Nothing can be further from the truth. I feel sure I am speaking for all of you here when I say that one of our aims is to bring about a reversal of that out-dated policy.[33]

The National Confederation of American Ethnic Groups displays, in essence, the difficulty the immigrant faces in his desire to be an American. The confederation's list of aims and purposes begins with a call to "unite its collective and individual members for a greater American unity and a militant democracy" and to "develop pride in and love for our system of government and its institutions." It then states opposition to Communist and totalitarian conspiracies; says it seeks to work for freedom, liberation, and self-determination for all people; and promises to "initiate plans for a more rapid assimilation of foreign-born citizens into American society." These and some others of the aims are admirable in the abstract; carefully pursued, they could greatly benefit the immigrant and his adopted nation. However, while the confederation speaks in favor of "rapid assimilation," it also promises to "create incentives to bring back into the fold large numbers of second and third generation youngsters who are drifting about . . . with no grounds in which to sink their young and ambitious roots" and hopes to "revive interest of large business concerns in foreign-language press and radio program advertising." Assimilation is not reached through policies which serve to perpetuate a fragmented society. "Full and fair representation in the higher courts, in Congress, and on all policymaking bodies of government" would "enable the ethnic groups to share fully in the rights and privileges, as well as responsibilities, of citizenship . . . ," according to the confederation.[34] While it is true that equality of opportunity must be a factor in achieving an integrated society, it is extremely doubtful that equality of opportunity is consonant with distribution of positions and authority on a nationality-quota basis.

6

While there is little doubt that ethnic assimilation has occurred in major areas of American life, there are indications that it has not fully taken place in the political field. Perhaps the best index of assimilation and differentiation is the voting behavior of ethnic groups. Only when it becomes impossible to identify, direct, influence, and predict the voting behavior of any given ethnic group can it be said that political assimilation has come about. As far as politicians and many ethnic leaders are concerned, this stage has not been reached. They remain convinced that Americans of foreign birth or descent vote on the basis of their origin and that the ethnic factor is a dominant force in politics, second—if that—only to the economic factor. From the point of view of party leaders the efficacy of the balanced ticket and the readiness of ethnic-group leaders to pledge or withhold support of either party in an election prove that ethnic solidarity exists and that ethnic groups have not been completely assimilated within the American political milieu.

It must be recognized, as has been previously suggested, that party and ethnic leaders may be wrong, or at least overconfident, in their beliefs and too sanguine about their ability to influence or deliver any given ethnic vote. No bona fide statistical studies have yet been made which either categorically refute or support generalizations that an ethnic group votes overwhelmingly for a candidate of its own background or that ethnic-group solidarity persists into third and fourth generations—or, for that matter, exists within the first and second generations. Appropriate studies to ascertain the degree of political assimilation at each governmental level—local, state, and national—might yield information of value. Many questions remain which such research could answer.

Despite the absence of statistical evidence, there is little doubt that group voting exists in the United States and that such political behavior manifests itself among nationality groups, generally in times of world crisis and more particularly when the fortunes of their native lands are threatened by political and economic events. Nor is there any doubt that political strategists take advantage of old-country hopes, fears, sentiments, and loyalties by their attempts to channel these for their own political purposes. At times ethnic groups fortuitously or otherwise benefit from the parties' intercession; more often they do not.

While some ethnic leaders remain untroubled by either the presence or effects of ethnic-group voting, while some welcome, advocate, and, indeed, urge political differentiation and vigorous ethnic activity, an increasing number of responsible ethnic leaders are worrying over the consequences of unremitting pressures by party strategists to hypenize the American people for political purposes. This concern is shared by many political leaders and students of politics. Recognizing and accepting the realities of American politics they ask only how to mitigate the excesses and irresponsibilities. One possibility is a gentlemen's agreement between parties not to go beyond propriety or certain limits and to abstain from making promises which cannot and will not be fulfilled. Another possibility is that the Nationalities Divisions of both parties, organized as they are to cater to the ethnic vote, be abolished in order to accelerate ethnic political assimilation. Still another possibility is a code of fair practices which would govern appeals to group voting and define the uses of foreign-language advertisements. Perhaps reform of the electoral system which encourages efforts to affect voting in industrial and highly urban states would abate some of the intemperate practices. Inauguration of any of these measures would be of great benefit to Americans of foreign origin, to the parties, and certainly to the United States as a political community.

APPENDIX

TABLE I.—Nativity and Parentage of Foreign White Stock by Country of Origin.

County of origin	Foreign-born	Native-born of foreign or mixed parentage	Total	Percent
England and Wales	584,615	1,443,230	2,027,845	6.0
Scotland	244,200	463,230	707,525	2.1
Northern Ireland	15,398	29,890	45,288	.1
Ireland (Eire)	504,961	1,891,495	2,396,456	7.1
Norway	202,294	652,380	854,674	2.5
Sweden	324,944	864,695	1,189,639	3.5
Denmark	107,897	318,710	426,607	1.3
Netherlands	102,133	272,535	374,668	1.1
Belgium	52,891	85,500	138,391	.4
Switzerland	71,515	215,660	287,175	.9
France	107,924	253,665	361,589	1.1
Germany	984,331	3,742,615	4,726,946	14.0
Poland	861,184	1,925,015	2,786,199	8.3
Czechoslovakia	278,268	705,890	984,158	2.9
Austria	408,785	816,465	1,225,250	3.6
Hungary	268,022	437,080	705,102	2.1
Yugoslavia	143,956	239,920	383,876	1.1
U.S.S.R.	894,844	1,647,420	2,542,264	7.5
Lithuania	147,765	249,825	397,590	1.2
Finland	95,506	172,370	267,876	.8
Rumania	84,952	130,100	215,052	.6
Greece	169,083	195,235	364,318	1.1
Italy	1,427,145	3,143,405	4,570,550	13.5
Spain	45,565	69,490	115,055	.3
Portugal	54,337	117,675	172,012	.5
Other Europe	86,375	128,030	214,405	.6
Asia	180,024	239,525	419,549	1.2
Canada-French	238,409	519,495	757,904	2.2
Canada-Other	756,153	1,468,325	2,224,478	6.6
Mexico	450,562	891,980	1,342,542	4.0
Other America	120,297	101,240	221,537	.7
All other and not reported	146,833	157,300	304,133	.9
Total	10,161,168	23,589,485	33,750,653	

Sources: 1950 Census, Nativity and Parentage, Special Report P-E No. 3A, Table 13, p. 75.

TABLE II.—Foreign-Language Media: Numbers, Circulation, Audience-Reader Potential.

Group	Radio stations	Total	Number reporting	Circulation reported	Mother tongue[b]	Church, organization membership[c]
		Communication media[a]			Ethnic statistics	
		Publications				
Albanian	3	3	2	2,015		
Arabic	10	15	7	14,500	107,420	
Armenian	7	22	10	28,000	68,320	
Bulgarian	1	6	4	12,048		
Byelorussian		5	1	910		
Carpatho-Russian	3	11	4	16,018		440,000
Chinese[d]	3	14	10	72,368		
Czechoslovak:						
Czech	30	33	20	298,572	520,440	1,099,000
Slovak	27	29	13	107,838	484,360	1,426,000
Danish	5	13	4	22,550	226,740	
Dutch		8	3	18,300	267,140	
Esperanto		1				
Estonian	1	4	2	4,012		
Finnish	20	19	12	60,784	230,420	
Flemish		1			54,340	
French	66	33	27	473,320	1,412,060	
Georgian		4				
German	72	92	68	404,341	4,949,780	4,771,000
Greek	54	25	16	143,240	273,520	746,000
Hebrew		17	2	25,725		
Yiddish	39	44	15	449,589	1,751,100	5,160,700
Hungarian	35	43	26	132,379	453,000	796,000
Italian	162	68	38	458,625	3,766,820	5,102,000
Japanese[d]	8	10	9	49,955		
Korean		2	2	709		
Latvian	2	3	1	12,014	31,590	
Lithuanian	27	41	20	237,298	272,680	642,000
Norwegian	10	24	7	41,654	658,220	
Polish	158	53	39	727,218	2,416,320	4,157,000
Portuguese	37	14	10	65,514	215,860	
Rumanian		7	4	11,207	65,520	100,000
Russian	10	44	10	71,600	585,080	
Spanish	269	104	88	2,402,949	1,861,000	
Swedish	18	23	8	81,001	830,900	
Ukrainian	29	47	12	69,131	83,600	653,000

TABLE II.—Foreign-Language Media: Numbers, Circulation, Audience-Reader Potential (concluded).

		Communication media[a]			Ethnic statistics	
			Publications			Church,
Group	Radio stations	Total	Number reporting	Circulation reported	Mother tongue[b]	organization membership[c]
Yugoslav:						
Serb	22[e]	6	3	33,712	37,640	
Croat		9	3	26,248	115,440	335,000
Slovene	10	10	8	80,000	178,640	182,000

[a] Based on N. W. Ayer and Sons, *Directory of Newspapers and Periodicals, 1958,* and Common Council for American Unity, *Foreign Language Publications in the United States, 1956.*

[b] Based on 1940 Census. U.S., Bureau of the Census, *Population: Nativity and Parentage of the White Population, Mother Tongue* (1943), Table 1.

[c] Based on data of Republican National Committee, 1952.

[d] Not including Hawaiian.

[e] Includes Croat.

NOTES

CHAPTER I

1. U.S., Congress, Senate, Committee on the Judiciary, *The Immigration and Naturalization Systems of the United States,* 81st Cong., 2d Sess., 1950, Report 1515, p. 23. See also Frances L. Reinhold, "Exiles and Refugees in American History," *The Annals,* CCIII (May, 1939).

2. Because a general census was not undertaken until 1820, it is not possible to obtain a verifiable total of immigrants or an exact distribution by countries of origin. The *Annual Report* of the Immigration and Naturalization Service of the Department of Justice for the year ending June 30, 1956, indicates that the grand total of immigration, 1820-1956, was 40,734,745. The absence of census tabulations of third-, fourth-, and fifth-generation Americans has not deterred nationality groups from staking out numerical claims in the ethnic mother lode. To cite a few instances, nationality leaders have asserted that there are 38 million Americans of German origin, 7 million of Polish, 150 thousand of Japanese. In an address before the Congressional Conference of the National Confederation of American Ethnic Groups, held June 30-July 1, 1958, Slobodan M. Draskovich, member of the policy-planning committee of that organization, said that members of ethnic groups number "86 million, or about half of our country's population." U.S., *Congressional Record,* 85th Cong., 2d Sess., 1958, CIV, A7659.

3. U.S., Bureau of the Census, *1950 Census, Characteristics of the Population,* II, Part 1, U.S. Summary Table 35, and *Special Reports,* IV, Part 4, chap. A, Nativity and Parentage Table 1; U.S., Immigration and Naturalization Service, *Monthly Review,* II (December, 1944), 77; and *Annual Report* (1950), Table 4. See also Edward P. Hutchinson, *Immigrants and Their Children, 1850-1950* (New York, 1956), p. 3; Robert A. Divine, *American Immigration Policy, 1924-1952* (New Haven, 1957), p. 192; Edward P. Hutchinson, "Immigration Policy since World War I," in Benjamin Munn Ziegler (ed.), *Immigration: An American Dilemma* (Boston, 1953), p. 17.

4. Quoted by Barbara Miller Solomon, *Ancestors and Immigrants* (Cambridge, 1956), p. 23, from *The Letters of Henry Adams,* ed. Worthington C. Ford (Boston, 1938), II, 575-76. This apprehension is well described and documented in Solomon. See also John Higham, *Strangers in the Land: Pattern of American Nativism, 1860-1925* (New Brunswick, 1955).

5. Woodrow Wilson, *A History of the American People* (New York, 1902), V, 212-13.

6. See Edward McNall Burns, *The American Idea of Mission: Concepts of National Purpose and Destiny* (New Brunswick, 1957), pp. 193-206. See also Solomon (note 4), pp. 59-81.

7. William I. Thomas and Florian Znaniecki, *The Polish Peasant in Europe and America* (New York, 1927), II, 1485.

8. William D'Arcy, *The Fenian Movement in the United States: 1858-1886* (Washington, 1947), p. 1.

9. Thomas and Znaniecki (see note 7), II, 1485.

10. See Will Herberg's excellent study, *Protestant—Catholic—Jew: An Essay in American Religious Sociology* (New York, 1955), pp. 18-35. For an exposition of events and circumstances leading to the establishment of the Polish-National Catholic Church, see Joseph A. Wytrwal, *America's Polish Heritage: A Social History of the Poles in America* (Detroit, 1961).

11. Emily Greene Balch, *Our Slavic Fellow Citizens* (New York: Charities Publication Committee, 1910), pp. 34-36 and 379. See also Melford E. Spiro, "The Acculturation of American Ethnic Groups," *American Anthropologist,* LVII (December, 1955), 1240-52.

12. Max Ascoli, "On the Italian Americans," *Common Ground*, III (autumn, 1942), 45-49.

13. James Bryce, *The American Commonwealth* (1914 ed.; New York, 1941), II, 103.

14. Thomas Jefferson foresaw the danger of immigrants' settling in compact groups, advocating their dispersion among older settlers so as to effect their "quick amalgamation."

15. The first newspaper printed in the Lithuanian language was published not in Lithuania but in the United States, beginning in 1874. *Lietuvos Istorija*, ed. A. Sapoka (3d ed.; Fellbach/Württemberg: Leidyklos Patria Leidinys, 1950), No. 52, p. 649.

16. See David Rodnick, "Group Frustrations in Connecticut," *American Journal of Sociology*, XLVII (1941-1942), 157-66; and Donald R. Taft and Richard Robbins, *International Migrations* (New York, 1955), pp. 527-28.

17. Louis Wirth, "Morale and Minority Groups," *American Journal of Sociology*, XLVII (November, 1941), 420-21.

18. Quoted by Thomas N. Brown, "The Origins and Character of Irish-American Nationalism," *Review of Politics*, XVIII (July, 1956), 334.

19. The importance of the immigrant vote was recognized by American politicians in the early 1800's. While Jefferson "labored hard and successfully to capture the loyalty of the newcomers," Hamilton and many Federalists underestimated "the political impotence of the policy of exclusion responsible for the Alien and Sedition Acts." Lawrence H. Fuchs, "Some Political Aspects of Immigration," *Law and Contemporary Problems*, XXI (spring, 1956).

20. Bryce (see note 13), II, 103.

21. Edward J. Flynn, *You're the Boss* (New York, 1947), pp. 10-11.

22. In his sociological study of an Italian-American slum area, William Whyte touches on this sense of the transferral of intangible desiderata. Expressing a sentiment prevalent in many nationality groups, Chick Morelli said in an address to the Italian Community Club: "Whatever you fellows may think of Mussolini, you've got to admit one thing. He has done more to get respect for the Italian people than anybody else. The Italians get a lot more respect now than when I started going to school. And you can thank Mussolini for that." William Foote Whyte, *Street Corner Society* (2d. ed.; Chicago, 1955), p. 274.

23. See, for example, Frank C. Hanighen, "Foreign Political Movements in the United States," *Foreign Affairs*, XVI (October, 1937). For Soviet attempts to influence Americans of Slavic descent, see U.S., Congress, House, *Report on the American Slav Congress and Associated Organizations*, 81st Cong., 2d Sess., 1950, House Report 1951.

24. See Oscar Handlin, "The Immigrant and American Politics," *Foreign Influences in American Life*, ed. David F. Bowers (Princeton, 1944), pp. 87-89.

25. See Alfred McClung Lee, "Subversive Individuals of Minority Status," *The Annals*, CCXXIII (September, 1942), 169.

26. See *New York World-Telegram*, May 18, 1948; *New York Post*, May 4, 1948; *New York Times*, May 7 and 27, 1948; and *New York Herald Tribune*, May 27, 1948. The Public Liaison Section of the Arab States Delegations Office has continually paid attention to the American nationality organizations of Arabic or Middle Eastern descent. "The primary function of the Public Liaison Section," wrote its chief, Sami Hadawi, to the editor of the *Lebanese American Journal*, ". . . is to be in continuous contact with organizations, institutions, societies, clubs, and groups interested in the Arab World . . ." (*Lebanese American Journal*, September 5, 1959). See also *ibid.*, December 17, 1957.

27. *New York Times*, May 15, 1936.

28. For a brief review of exile political activities in the United States and their effect on American diplomacy, see Henry M. Wriston, "Myths Feed American Frustration over Cuba," *Washington Post,* September 23, 1962.

29. See Harold B. Hoskins, "American Unity and Our Foreign Born Citizen," *The Annals,* CCXX (March, 1942), 153-59. See also Wirth (above, note 17).

30. U.S., Congress, Senate, *Brewing and Liquor Interests and German and Bolshevik Propaganda,* 66th Cong., 1st Sess., 1919, Senate Doc. 62, II, 2831. Similar criticism has been voiced by Hermann Hagedorn. His attempt to organize the National Patriotic Council of Loyal Americans of German Origin, whose purpose was to "testify to the American people the single-minded loyalty of the Americans of German origin to the United States and her free institutions," was thwarted by The Friends of German Democracy, a creation of the Office of Public Information. The latter's effort "to develop among German-Americans an interest in German democracy," observed Hagedorn, "was beside the point. Let the Germans have any form of government they wanted. Our aim was simply to make German-Americans into straight Americans, looking forward, not back." Hermann Hagedorn, *The Hyphenated Family: An American Saga* (New York, 1960), pp. 245-46.

31. See Harold D. Lasswell, *National Security and Individual Freedom* (New York, 1950), particularly pp. 150 ff.

32. See Bogdan Raditsa, "Clash of Two Immigrant Generations," *Commentary,* XXV (January, 1958).

33. Wirth (see note 17), p. 432.

34. See Louis L. Gerson, *Woodrow Wilson and the Rebirth of Poland* (New Haven, 1953).

35. Raditsa, *Commentary* (see note 32).

36. In 1939 an Hungarian-American organization being investigated by the Post Office Department endeavored to extricate itself by presenting facsimiles of letters from the White House and persons in official positions. When this came to the attention of Bernard G. Richards, a staff member of the Democratic National Committee, which had undoubtedly helped the organization to receive White House "recognition," he wondered if "some of these muddles could not be avoided by more frequent checkups with their office." Abstract of letter from Bernard G. Richards to Marvin McIntyre, February 3, 1939, in Franklin D. Roosevelt Papers (Franklin D. Roosevelt Library, Hyde Park, New York), OF 705. Cited hereafter as Roosevelt Papers.

37. Copies in the author's possession.

38. See chapter X, below. See also series of articles by Robert Taylor, *Pittsburgh Press,* November 16-24, 26, 28, 29, 30, and December 1, 1947.

39. An analysis of a 1952 poll made for the author by the Roper Public Opinion Research Center at Williams College, Williamstown, Massachusetts, shows overwhelmingly negative responses to the questions, "Are you a member of any social club or fraternal organization which is made up of members descended from some nationality group—like Irish-American, Germania-Mannerchor, the Franco-Americans, the Sons of Italy, etc.? Or does any member of your immediate family belong to any social or fraternal organization like this?"

40. Quoted by Thomas A. Bailey, *The Man in the Street: The Impact of American Public Opinion on Foreign Policy* (New York, 1948), pp. 15-16.

41. Quoted by Howard K. Beale, *Theodore Roosevelt and the Rise of America to World Power* (Baltimore, 1956), p. 93.

42. "Steam from the Melting Pot," *Fortune,* XXVI (September, 1942), 75.

43. Walter Lippmann, *Isolation and Alliances: An American Speaks to the British* (Boston, 1952), p. 16.

Chapter II

1. See Table I, Appendix.

2. Roy V. Peel, *The Political Clubs of New York City* (New York, 1935), pp. 251 and 260 ff.

3. Similar unofficial exile organizations are found in the United Kingdom. There is a difference, however, in that exile organizations in the United States are more closely allied with official American policy. Prominent officials, Senators, Congressmen, retired diplomats, and military men have played conspicuous roles in such bodies as the National Committee for a Free Europe, which operates its own broadcasting service, Radio Free Europe. Radio Free Europe has taken, as the 1956 Hungarian Revolution revealed, a more positive line than the State Department or the Voice of America. Frequently, leading politicians have appeared before the Assembly of Captive European Nations, and other exile organizations, and strongly stressed the principle of liberation and argued for active resistance to the Soviet yoke. While this does not mean official approval, it nevertheless suggests to Western Europeans and the Soviets that agreement exists between the aims of these bodies and the policy of the United States. In supporting exile movements there is always the danger of raising false hopes which in the end may do more harm than good. See also Henry L. Roberts and Paul A. Wilson, *Britain and the United States: Problems in Co-operation* (London: Royal Institute of International Affairs, 1953).

4. Confederation material in the author's possession. See also U.S., *Congressional Record*, 85th Cong., 2d Sess., August 22, 1958, CIV, A7658.

5. Approximately one-fifth of the white population of the United States speaks in a tongue other than, or in addition to, English. Lowry Nelson, "Speaking of Tongues," *American Journal of Sociology*, LIV (July, 1948-May, 1949), 202.

6. The outstanding work on the foreign-language press is Robert E. Park, *The Immigrant Press and Its Control* (New York, 1922). There is a current need for a follow-up study.

7. Albert Parry, "Good-Bye to the Immigrant Press," *American Mercury*, XXVIII (January, 1933).

8. "The Foreign Language Press," *Fortune*, XXII (1940).

9. The 1940 Census lists twenty-two million persons reporting some language other than English as a mother tongue; no similar data for earlier or later periods are available. See Nelson (note 5). See also Joseph S. Roucek, "The Foreign-Language and Negro Press," in Francis J. Brown and Joseph S. Roucek (eds.), *One America* (New York, 1945), p. 369; Roucek, "Foreign-Language Press in World War II," *Sociology and Social Research*, XXVII (July-August, 1943), 462-71, which estimated the total wartime foreign-language press at 1,600 publications; Yaroslav M. Chyz and Reed Lewis, "Agencies Organized by Nationality Groups in the United States," *The Annals*, CCLXII (March, 1949), 148-49; Chyz, "Number, Distribution and Circulation of the Foreign Language Press in the United States," *Interpreter Releases*, XX, No. 37; Philip Rubin, "The Yiddish Press," *American Mercury*, XXVIII (March, 1927), 344-53; Donald R. Taft and Richard Robbins, *International Migrations* (New York, 1955), pp. 532-35; *Foreign Language Publications in the United States: A Report by the Common Council for American Unity* (New York: The Council, 1956), Appendix; and *Directory of Newspapers and Periodicals* (New York, 1958). See also Appendix, Table II.

10. U.S., Congress, Senate, Committee on the Judiciary, *The Immigration and Naturalization Systems of the United States*, 81st Cong., 2d Sess., 1950, Report 1515, pp. 213-14. See also Appendix, Table II.

11. *Radio Stations in the United States Broadcasting Foreign Language Programs,* a report by the Common Council for American Unity (New York, 1956). See also Chyz and Lewis (above, note 9), p. 157; and Appendix, Table II.

12. Rudolph Arnheim and Martha Colling Bayne, "Foreign-Language Broadcasts over Local American Stations," Paul F. Lazarsfield and Frank N. Stanton (eds.), *Radio Research* (1941), pp. 3-64, cited by Senate Committee on the Judiciary, *The Immigration and Naturalization Systems* (1950), p. 213.

13. Carl J. Friedrich, "Foreign-Language Radio and the War," *Common Ground,* III (autumn, 1942), 65-72, cited by Senate Committee on the Judiciary, *The Immigration and Naturalization Systems* (1950), p. 214.

Louis Wirth, "Morale and Minority Groups," *American Journal of Sociology,* XLVII (November, 1941), 422 n., said in connection with Nazi and Fascist propagandizing in America:

"The foreign-language radio broadcasts may be presumed to have been a factor in and to have compensated in some degree for the reduced influence of the immigrant newspaper. However, because of the nature [of] and control over radio in this country, it is less susceptible than the press to direction from abroad and lends itself less readily to exploitation in behalf of causes contrary to public policy."

14. Senate Committee on the Judiciary, *The Immigration and Naturalization Systems* (1950), p. 214.

15. Adlai E. Stevenson, "This Time We Might Get Licked," *New York Times,* March 1, 1959.

16. The resolution, according to Representative Daniel J. Flood of Pennsylvania, "was originated and authored by Dr. Lev E. Dobriansky, a professor in Soviet economics at Georgetown University" and "national chairman of the Ukrainian Congress Committee of America." U.S., *Congressional Record,* CV, No. 164 (September 15, 1959), A8253. In testimony before the House Committee on Un-American Activities, September 9, 1959, Dobriansky said he was "responsible for the Captive Nations Week Resolution." Replying to Richard Arens, staff director of the committee, who asked what part he had played in promoting the resolution, Dobriansky answered, "It was my privilege to originate and author the original resolution of Captive Nations Week. Actually, I started on it a year ago with Congressman [Albert W.] Cretella in the House; and this year pursued it further, and successfully, on a bi-partisan basis with Senator [Paul H.] Douglas, of Illinois and Senator [Jacob K.] Javits, of New York; and on the House side, Congressman [Michael A.] Feighan, of Ohio, and Congressman [Alvin M.] Bentley, of Michigan." U.S., Congress, House, Committee on Un-American Activities, *The Crimes of Khrushchev,* 86th Cong., 1st Sess., 1959, the second part, September 9-11, pp. 11-12.

17. Henry P. Taylor, "We Preach; Do Nothing—United States Gives Lip Service," in Scripps-Howard newspapers of July 27, 1959, reproduced in U.S., *Congressional Record,* CV, No. 130 (August 3, 1959), A6641.

18. Marguerite Higgins quoting a Department of State summary of the conversation, *New York Herald Tribune,* October 17, 1960.

19. See U.S., *Congressional Record,* CV, No. 124 (July 23, 1959), 12929-31; No. 130 (August 3, 1959), 13612-13, A6641; and No. 131 (August 4, 1959), 13805. In contrast to Vanik's criticism, a "Special Edition, Captive Nations Week" issue of *ACEN News,* a monthly publication of the Assembly of Captive European Nations, described the resolution and proclamation as "acts of historic significance on several counts. First, because they emanate from the only authorized spokesmen of the leading nation of the free world, the President and Congress of the United States. Secondly, because they clearly emphasize the truth that as a result of the imperialistic and aggressive

policies of Soviet Communism the peoples of the Soviet-dominated nations have been deprived of their national independence and their individual liberties. Thirdly, because they recognize that the desire for liberty and independence of the people of the captive nations constitutes a powerful deterrent to war and one of the best hopes for a just and lasting peace. Fourth, because they not only give solemn expression to the serious concern of the American people and their government, so often and so consistently voiced in the past, for the fate of the captive peoples, but also officially pledge support for the just aspirations of these peoples to freedom and independence. Fifth, because they were accomplished at the very time when, in preparation of further expansionist moves, the Soviet rulers are more intent than ever upon consolidating their tyrannical rule over their eastern European springboard by securing the sanction of the United States and her allies for their ill-gotten conquests." *ACEN News,* Nos. 52-54 (July-September, 1959), p. 1.

20. William J. Petrus to Franklin D. Roosevelt, August 13, 1942, in Roosevelt Papers, OF 300, NY "V."

21. *New York Times,* January 7, 1957.

22. U.S., Bureau of the Census, *1950 Census, Characteristics of the Population,* II.

23. Paul Scott Mowrer, *Our Foreign Affairs: A Study in National Interest and the New Diplomacy* (New York, 1924), p. 119.

24. Cited in William Henry Harbaugh, *Power and Responsibility: The Life and Times of Theodore Roosevelt* (New York, 1961), p. 492.

25. This is an early example of the American Negro leadership's connecting American and African Negro interests. Reporting on the American Negro Leadership Conference on Africa held at Arden House, M. S. Handler said: "The mutual relationship and interaction between the many Jewish groups in the United States and Israel seem to have riveted the attention of Negro leaders, who decided at this conference to establish an intimate link between the American Negro community and the sub-Saharan African peoples. They feel that such a link would be of help not only to the sub-Saharans in attaining international status or freedom, but also to American Negroes by giving them a new impetus in their fight for civil rights." *New York Times,* November 26, 1962. See also above, pp. 156-58.

In April, 1963, the committee which had organized the Arden House conference on Africa decided to set up a "permanent national organization with the mission of identifying the American Negro's consciousness with Black Africa." African United Nations delegates sent S. O. Adefo, permanent representative of Nigeria, as a participant to the session. In December, 1962, President Kennedy had told the committee, during a White House meeting, that "he felt the 20,000,000 Negroes in this country had a responsibility for the role of the United States in Africa. . ." (*New York Times,* April 4, 1963).

26. See Paul E. Fitzpatrick to Matthew J. Connelly, September 10, 1948; Fitzpatrick to John M. Redding, September 10, 1948; and news release of the Democratic State Committee of New York, September 10, 1948, in Harry S. Truman Papers (Harry S. Truman Library, Independence, Missouri). Cited hereafter as Truman Papers.

27. Peel (see note 2), p. 266.

28. See also Hugh A. Bone, *Party Committees and National Politics* (Seattle, 1958), p. 90.

29. In November, 1949, the Ukrainian Congress Committee of America met in Washington, D.C. Eight hundred delegates from all the states participated in "this biggest gathering of Americans of Ukrainian descent." A few weeks before the meeting, Cieplinski informed John Redding, director of publicity of the Democratic Na-

tional Committee, that the chairman of the Ukrainian section of the Nationalities Division, Stephen J. Jarema, had an excellent chance of becoming president of the Congress, then controlled by Republicans, if helped by the committee. Cieplinski recommended an audience with the President for Jarema in order to strengthen the Democratic "position among Americans of Ukranian descent." Similar requests were also made in behalf of the Lithuanian group, "in the past strongly Republican." In order to encourage the "movement" of these two groups "in the direction of the Democratic Party," the President was asked to send greetings to both conventions, as he did. John M. Redding to William Hassett, November 2, 1949; Michael Cieplinski to Redding, October 26, 1949; Stephen J. Jarema to Cieplinski, October 24, 1949; and draft of proposed letter from Harry S. Truman to Fourth Congress of Americans of Ukrainian Descent, no date, attached to Redding to Hassett, Truman Papers.

30. See Bernard G. Richards to Marvin H. McIntyre, August 19 and September 24, 1936, Roosevelt Papers, 144 C; and Richards to Franklin D. Roosevelt, February 3, 1939, *ibid.*, OF 705.

31. Copies in Roosevelt Papers. Ethnic leaders evidently consider these translations of presidential statements a matter of prestige—recognition of their existence and importance. When the Democratic National Committee failed to translate a statement into Arabic, Saleem A Al-Hatem, an executive member of the National Organization of Arabic Speaking American Citizens, sent a telegram to the White House suggesting that "the President's message be translated to and broadcast in Arabic" because "there are over three million arabic speaking people, mostly voters, in the United States . . ." (Saleem A Al-Hatem to the President, January 3, 1938, *ibid.*).

32. *Ibid.*, OF 198-A. This Republican attack was brought to Roosevelt's attention by Carl Sievers, secretary of the St. Louis Association of German-American Democrats, who asked to have a message from the President to counteract the "bedtime stories" being published in the German-American press. Carl Sievers to Franklin D. Roosevelt, October 14, 1936, *ibid.*

33. See J. Joseph Boyle to James A. Farley, December 13, 1938; James J. Butler to Farley, November 23, 1938; and Lithgow Osborne memorandum sent by Farley to Franklin D. Roosevelt, December 16, 1938, *ibid.*, OF 300.

34. If Edward J. Ennis, general counsel of the American Civil Liberties Union, has his way, the Japanese-Americans should soon be able to exert an influence on American foreign policy toward Japan. Speaking before a recent convention of the Japanese-American Citizens League, Ennis asserted that "Americans of Japanese birth or parentage should claim the right to stand up and speak for the interests of Japan, just as some other groups of citizens speak for the interests of the countries with which they are connected by blood." *Saturday Evening Post*, December 1, 1956.

The First International Nisei Convention was held in Tokyo in October, 1957. Delegates came from numerous states, Hawaii, and Japan. The convention's principal resolution called upon the foreign-born children of Japanese emigrants to " 'express themselves on problems in United States-Japan relations.' It was for this purpose that the delegates decided to establish a permanent committee." Robert Trumbull, *New York Times*, October 26, 1957. T. P. Harada, executive vice president of the committee, in a letter to the author, February 2, 1958, said the convention was a "great success and recognized by both the United States and Japanese governments. Through this medium also we have gained the chance to express ourselves on problems in U.S.-Japan relations, which we consider very important for all concerned."

35. Republican National Committee, Research Division and All-American Origins Division, July, 1952. Copies in possession of the author.

36. *Reporter*, May 15, 1958, pp. 2-3. Harriman's action was described as "part of

an effort by the Democratic National Committee to light an election-year fire under a melting pot." Richard Amper, "Democrats Open Bid to Minorities," *New York Times,* April 28, 1958.

37. *Ibid.,* also correspondence between Mr. Amper and the author. See also Bone (above, note 28), pp. 61 and 89-93.

In 1963, Mayor Robert Wagner, chairman of the Democratic Nationalities Division, announced that the division would be known as the All-Americans Council, would expand its program, and would function throughout the year rather than only during campaigns. He explained that the party sought "to attract into the mainstream of our national political life the maximum number of Americans who speak a second language or, indeed, whose first language is foreign. . . . Of course, we hope to induce them to express their political wills through the Democratic party" (*New York Times,* April 14, 1963).

38. For example, in anticipation of the 1960 campaign, the Democratic Nationalities Division, under the chairmanship of Governor Williams and Senator Theodore Green of Rhode Island, invited "ethnic" Congressmen to participate in a meeting in November, 1959, for the purpose of discussing and drawing up possible platform planks. *Dziennik Chicagoski,* October 31, 1959, and *New York Times,* November 22, 1959.

39. At the 1960 hearings of the Republican Platform Foreign Policy Subcommittee, there appeared, among others, Dr. Lev E. Dobriansky, chairman, National Committee on Captive Nations Week; Charles Rozmarek, president, Polish American Congress; the Reverend V. Landamis, American Latvian Association; representatives of the American Friends of the Captive Nations; James H. Tashjian, American Committee for the Independence of Armenia; Dmytro Halychyn, chairman, Americans of Central and Eastern European Descent; Dr. P. Grigaitis, executive secretary, Lithuanian American Council; Michael Pizmak, vice president, Ukrainian Congress Committee of America; Clarence L. Coleman, Jr., president, American Council for Judaism, an anti-Zionist Jewish organization; representatives of American Zionist organizations; and Dr. Arthur G. Falls, an American Negro, American Committee on Africa.

40. U.S., Congress, Senate, *Brewing and Liquor Interests and German and Bolshevik Propaganda,* 66th Cong., 1st Sess., 1919, Senate Doc. 62, I, 465; II, 1465, 1569, 2834. See also Park (above, note 6), pp. 377-411.

41. Quoted by Moses Rischin, *Our Own Kind* (Santa Barbara, California: Center for the Study of Democratic Institutions, 1960). Chinese-American citizens have not been active in American politics. "If the group were larger," wrote Rose Hum Lee, "they would be pressed by the Democratic or Republican parties into their political campaigns." The number of their votes, evidently, is not large enough to swing any election. Nevertheless, according to Professor Lee, both parties during the last presidential elections "made gestures to gather all the votes they could in the large Chinatowns, especially San Francisco, through their Chinatown committees and followers." See Rose Hum Lee, *The Chinese in the United States of America* (Hong Kong, 1960), pp. 178-79.

42. Bone (see note 28), pp. 92-93.

43. Quoted by Rischin (see note 41).

44. *Dziennik Chicagoski,* November 1, 1958, and October 24, 1958. The election of thirteen Americans of Polish descent, one of them to the Senate of the United States, prompted a former member of the Polish parliament residing in London to send an open letter to the "American Congressmen of Polish origin" reminding them of the "Yalta Betrayal" and the failure of President Eisenhower to honor his campaign promises (*Ameryka-Echo,* December 7, 1958).

45. A typical example is the marking of October 11 as General Pulaski's Memorial Day. Proposals from Polish-American leaders and Congressmen with heavily Polish-American constituencies have been made annually since 1929, when Congress appropriated funds for the observance at Savannah of the sesquicentennial of Pulaski's death. In 1935 Congress passed Senate Joint Resolution 21 "authorizing the President to proclaim October 11 of each year General Pulaski's Memorial Day. . . ." The resolution was returned to Congress unapproved by President Roosevelt because, while Pulaski was distinguished, he "himself would not have wished to be singled out from his fellows and comrades for more honor than we can give to them all." The veto was overridden; the subsequent legislation was approved. Similar measures were successful in 1936 and 1937. In 1938, when Congress passed House Joint Resolution 622 for the same purpose, Secretary of State Cordell Hull advised Roosevelt that "serious consideration be given to the inadvisability of repeatedly giving approval to legislation of this character which, it seems reasonable to expect, will be introduced in Congress each year unless its sponsors are somehow discouraged in their efforts." The sponsors, however, were not discouraged. Pulaski Day has become an annual event. See W. B. Bankhead to Marvin McIntyre, January 20, 1939; Cordell Hull to Franklin D. Roosevelt, May 27, 1938; Samuel B. Pettengill to McIntyre, April 17 and 25, May 16 and 29, 1935, and June 18, 1936; Roosevelt to Lucien Maciora, January 28, 1941; and other material in file 1051, Roosevelt Papers.

46. In a letter to Democratic Chairman J. Howard McGrath, Leonard H. Pasqualicchio, National Deputy, Supreme Lodge, Order Sons of Italy in America, asked his assistance in securing President Truman's attendance at a forthcoming convention of the organization. "I want Mr. Truman to carry New Jersey and Pennsylvania in 1952! His presence at the convention will also help our candidate for Congress running on the Democratic Ticket in 1950." The next day McGrath wrote to Matthew J. Connelly, secretary to the President, enclosing communications from the Italian-American organization, reminding him "of the importance of this organization to the Democratic Party." Several weeks later Pasqualicchio wrote to Connelly saying there were several reasons President Truman should attend the convention. "First, there is a political reason." Leonard H. Pasqualicchio to J. Howard McGrath, July 13, 1949; McGrath to Matthew J. Connelly, July 14, 1949; Pasqualicchio to Connelly, August 3, 1949, Truman Papers.

CHAPTER III

1. Samuel Flagg Bemis, *The United States as a World Power* (New York, 1950), pp. 5-6.

2. Thomas A. Bailey, *The Man in the Street: The Impact of American Public Opinion on Foreign Policy* (New York, 1948), p. 22.

3. Germans living abroad, recalled Hermann Hagedorn, had "felt the need of a united and powerful Germany almost more than the Germans at home. A Britisher abroad was somebody; a Frenchman, an Austrian, a Russian was somebody; a Norwegian or a Dane was a man with a nation behind him. But what was a Hanoverian, a Saxon, a citizen of the free city of Lübeck or a subject of the Grand Duke of Sachsen-Coburg-Gotha?" Hermann Hagedorn, *The Hyphenated Family: An American Saga* (New York, 1960), p. 27.

4. John A. Hawgood, *The Tragedy of German-America* (New York, 1940), p. 52.

5. Carl Wittke, *Refugees of Revolution* (Philadelphia, 1952), pp. 217-18. Unlike the Irish-Americans, the German-Americans joined, as "charter members," the Republican party which began to form in the 1850's. In 1856, John C. Frémont, the

party's presidential candidate, announced that he favored giving the vote to immigrants after only three years' residence. The Republicans openly sought the approval of German-Americans, who had begun to be fearful of the southern Democrats' attacks on foreigners, by issuing the platform of that year in both English and German. They also subsidized German-language newspapers and even succeeded in converting some hitherto Democratically-oriented publications. By 1860 the Republican party had lost the association it had had in the German-American mind with temperance, Sabbatarianism, and nativist agitations; Lincoln had their support. See Hawgood (above, note 4), pp. 46-52; and Wittke (above), pp. 207-8. See also Donnal V. Smith, "Influence of the Foreign-Born of the Northwest in the Election of 1860," *Mississippi Valley Historical Review*, XIX (September, 1932), 192-204; Andreas Dorpalen, "The German Element and the Issues of the Civil War," *ibid.*, XXIX (June, 1942), 55-76; and Joseph Schafer, "Who Elected Lincoln," *American Historical Review*, XLVII (October, 1941), 51-63.

6. Wittke (see note 5), p. 352.

7. *Ibid.*, pp. 357-60.

8. *Ibid.*, pp. 352-57 and 360-64.

9. *Ibid.*, p. 355.

10. See Louis H. Bean, *How to Predict Elections* (New York, 1948), pp. 93-94.

11. William Weber, "Do the German-Americans Dictate Our Foreign Policy?" *Preussische Jahrbücher*, review in *American Review of Reviews*, XLI (March, 1910), 349-50.

12. Arthur S. Link, *Wilson: The Struggle for Neutrality, 1914-1915* (Princeton, 1960), pp. 20 ff.

13. James W. Gerard to Edward M. House, January 25, 1916, in Edward M. House Papers (Yale University Library, New Haven, Connecticut), 6/24. Cited hereafter as House Papers. Gerard to Woodrow Wilson, January 24, 1916, *ibid.*; and cable, Gerard to House, February 8, 1916, *ibid.*, 6/24A. In *Ambassador Morgenthau's Story* (Garden City, N.Y., 1918), pp. 404-5, Morgenthau wrote that the discussion of the German-American situation began with a statement which he presumed Zimmermann "thought would be gratifying" to him. Zimmermann spoke of how splendidly the Jews had behaved in Germany during the war and how deeply obligated the Germans felt. He continued, " 'After the war they are going to be much better treated in Germany than they have been.' " Then he asked, " 'Are you sure that the mass of German-Americans would be loyal to the United States in case of war? Aren't their feelings for the Fatherland really dominant?' " Morgenthau replied that he thought German-Americans regarded themselves as " 'Americans and nothing else.' "

14. Johann von Bernstorff to T. von Bethmann Hollweg, September 6, 1914, German Foreign Office Archives, quoted in Link (see note 12), p. 31. See also Ernest R. May, *The World War and American Isolation, 1914-1917* (Cambridge, 1959), pp. 175-77 and 34. Professor May suggests that in the early months of the war Wilson showed concern over the possibility of civil war and feared that the government was not "capable" of "putting down the German-Americans if they rose to help their Fatherland." "Owing to the large English and German elements in the population, government leaders assumed that the nation could never take part on either side without bringing on a civil war at home."

15. Link (see note 12), p. 161.

16. William J. Bryan to Walter H. Page, December 14, 1914, Page Papers, quoted *ibid.*

17. Johann von Bernstorff to the Foreign Office, January 12, 1915, German Foreign Office Archives, quoted *ibid.*

18. Woodrow Wilson to Robert Lansing, December 1, 1914; Hugo Münsterberg to Wilson, November 19, 1914; Lansing to Wilson, December 9, 1914, with enclosures; and Wilson to Lansing, December 10, 1914, U.S., Department of State, *Papers Relating to the Foreign Relations of the United States: The Lansing Papers 1914-1920* (Washington, 1939), I, 161-79. See also Link (above, note 12), pp. 161 ff.; and May (note 14), pp. 47-48.

19. See Link (above, note 12), pp. 22-23; and May (above, note 14), pp. 29-31.

20. Edward Grey to Edward M. House, August 13, 1915, House Papers, 6/63. British propaganda in the United States began in September, 1914, with the establishment of an official agency, Wellington House.

21. For German-American influence on the preparedness movement and neutrality policies see William H. Harbaugh, "Wilson, Roosevelt, and Interventionism, 1914-1917" (unpublished Ph.D. dissertation, Library, Northwestern University, 1954). For an excellent treatment of German-American activities during 1914-1915, see Link (above, note 12), particularly pp. 1-56 and 137-70.

22. Hawgood (see note 4), p. xviii.

23. Florence E. Gibson, *The Attitudes of the New York Irish toward State and National Affairs, 1848-1892* (New York, 1951), p. 14.

24. *The Letters and Friendships of Sir Cecil Spring Rice*, ed. Stephen Gwynn (Boston and New York, 1929), I, 66.

25. William D'Arcy, *The Fenian Movement in the United States: 1858-1886* (Washington, 1947), pp. 237-38.

26. Allan Nevins, *Grover Cleveland* (New York, 1933), p. 428.

27. George Osgoodby to Sir Lionel Sackville-West, quoted *ibid.*, p. 429.

28. Sir Lionel Sackville-West to George Osgoodby, quoted *ibid.*, p. 430.

29. Thomas A. Bailey, *A Diplomatic History of the American People* (6th ed.; New York, 1958), pp. 404-5; and Nevins (see note 26), pp. 429-31. This quatrain in which Cleveland explains his peremptoriness to John Bull appeared to the Republican *New York Tribune:*

"Believe me that I made him go
    For nothing that he wrote,
But just because, as well you know,
    I feared the Irish vote!"

Quoted in Bailey (see note 2), p. 96.

30. *Ibid.*, pp. 20-23.

31. Quoted in Bailey (see note 29), p. 449.

32. *Ibid.* See also Charles C. Tansill, *America and the Fight for Irish Freedom, 1866-1922* (New York, 1957), p. 113.

33. John Hay to John W. Foster, June 23, 1900, quoted in W. R. Thayer, *The Life and Letters of John Hay* (Boston, 1915), II, 220, 234. See also James W. Garner, *American Foreign Policies* (New York, 1928), pp. 23-24; and Bailey (above, note 2), p. 22.

34. Quoted in Garner (see note 33), p. 24.

35. Adam Mickiewicz's poem written to enhearten exiles after the Polish Revolution of 1830 was often quoted by Paderewski and is evocative of their mood:

"For a universal war for the freedom of nations
    We beseech Thee, O Lord.
For national arms and eagles
    We beseech Thee, O Lord.
For the independence, integrity and freedom of our country
    We beseech Thee, O Lord."

36. Randolph Bourne, *History of a Literary Radical, and Other Essays,* ed. Van Wyck Brooks (New York, 1920), p. 266. See also Hans Kohn, *American Nationalism* (New York, 1957), p. 162.

37. George M. Stephenson, "The Attitude of Swedish-Americans toward the World War," *Proceedings of the Mississippi Valley Historical Association,* X, Part 1 (1918-1919), 79-94.

38. Marcus Lee Hansen, *The Immigrant in American History* (Cambridge, 1940), pp. 208-9.

CHAPTER IV

1. Harley Notter, *The Origins of the Foreign Policy of Woodrow Wilson* (Baltimore, 1937), p. 217.

2. Ray Stannard Baker, *Woodrow Wilson, Life and Letters* (New York, 1927-1939), IV, 55.

3. Census, 1910.

4. Woodrow Wilson, *A History of the American People* (New York, 1902), V, 212-13.

5. *New York Evening Journal,* May 27, 1912, quoted in Arthur S. Link, *Wilson: The Road to the White House* (Princeton, 1947), pp. 383-90.

6. *Ibid.*

7. *Ibid.*

8. *Ibid.*

9. Woodrow Wilson, *A History of the American People* (2d ed.; New York, 1917), X, 98.

10. Carl Wittke, *The German-Language Press in America* (Lexington, 1957), pp. 245-48.

11. *Ibid.,* pp. 254-55.

12. John M. Blum, *Joe Tumulty and the Wilson Era* (Boston, 1951), p. 105; and Joseph Tumulty, *Woodrow Wilson as I Know Him* (Garden City, N.Y., 1921), pp. 189-91.

13. *National Party Platforms, 1840-1956,* comp. Kirk H. Porter and Donald Bruce Johnson (Urbana, 1956), pp. 195-96.

14. Quoted in Wittke (see note 10), p. 256. Twenty-five years later, just before America entered the Second World War, the chairman of the Steuben Society was to make a similar defense of German-American interests. "Americans of Germanic extraction do not want Communism, Fascism or Nazism, and they do not want British imperialism. They want Americanism." See p. 114.

15. Wittke (see note 10), pp. 256-57.

16. Theodore Roosevelt to the Progressive National Committee, June 22, 1916, *The Letters of Theodore Roosevelt,* ed. Elting E. Morison (Cambridge, 1954), VIII, 1071-72.

17. Daniel C. Roper to Edward M. House, October 7, 1916, Woodrow Wilson Papers, cited in Louis L. Gerson, *Woodrow Wilson and the Rebirth of Poland* (New Haven, 1953), p. 61 n.

18. Blum (see note 12), pp. 105-6.

19. *Ibid.,* pp. 107-9.

20. *Cincinnati Enquirer,* October 27, 1916.

21. Roman L. Modra to Woodrow Wilson, August 24, 1916, Wilson Papers, cited in Gerson (see note 17), p. 61.

22. Acting Secretary of the Interior Jones to Woodrow Wilson, March 30, 1916, Wilson Papers, cited in Gerson, *ibid.,* p. 62 n.

23. *Ibid.*, pp. 156-60.

24. Milada Paulová, *Jugoslavenski Odbor, Povijest jugoslavenske emigracije za svjetskog rata od 1914-1918* (Zagreb, 1925), quoted in Victor S. Mamatey, *The United States and East Central Europe, 1914-1918* (Princeton, 1957), pp. 117-18.

25. *Ibid.*

26. For the influence and activities of the Czech, Zionist, and other movements, see the next chapter.

27. In 1917 Paderewski numbered Polish-Americans at over four million. I. J. Paderewski to Woodrow Wilson, October 4, 1917, U.S., Department of State, *Papers Relating to the Foreign Relations of the United States: 1917, Supplement 2, The World War* (Washington, 1932), p. 763.

28. House was extremely susceptible to the compliments of Paderewski, who wrote his benefactor: "Words cannot express what I feel for you. It has been the dream of my life to find a providential man for my country. I am now sure that I have not been dreaming vain dreams, because I had the happiness of meeting you." I. J. Paderewski to E. M. House, December 22, 1915, in Edward M. House Papers (Yale University Library, New Haven, Connecticut). Cited hereafter as House Papers.

29. "I did not care to go into the interminable question as to who does or who does not represent a majority of the Poles." House diary, August 5, 1918, House Papers. See also John Dewey, "Autocracy under Cover," *New Republic*, XVI (1918), 103-5; Dewey to Woodrow Wilson, September 25, 1918, Wilson Papers, cited in Gerson (see note 17), p. 92 n.; Joseph Tumulty to Wilson, October 3, 1918, *ibid.*; Wilson to Dewey, October 4, 1918, *ibid.*; and *ibid.*, pp. 91-93.

30. House diary, May 10, 1918, House Papers.

31. House to Orlowski, January 15, 1931, *ibid.*

32. House diary, June 23, 1919, *ibid.*

33. A situation similar in some aspects occurred in Czechoslovakia. Thomas S. Masaryk's labors in the United States toward Czechoslovakian independence overshadowed the revolutionary contributions of Karel Kramar. Kramar's popularity, which had run high during the early years of the war, was eclipsed by Masaryk's by the end of the war. Kramar's influence was brought to a decline by the people's strong conviction that their independence had been won through Masaryk's efforts among Western powers. Though Kramar became the first prime minister of Czechoslovakia, he resigned his post in July, 1919, after having lost an election.

CHAPTER V

1. Georges Clemenceau, *Grandeur and Misery of Victory* (New York, 1930), p. 190.

2. George F. Kennan, *Russia Leaves the War* (Princeton, 1956), pp. 246-73. See also Charles Seymour, *The Intimate Papers of Colonel House* (Boston, 1928), III, 386-89 and 322. On January 2, 1918, after studying the December 29 Bolshevik appeal to the Allied peoples, written by Leon Trotsky, Lansing called Wilson's attention to the "horrendous" implications which a principle such as self-determination could have on Western political institutions and reminded him that the United States had denied the South this right in 1861. He concluded "that to make any sort of reply would be contrary to the dignity of the United States and offer opportunity for further insult and threats. . . ." Lansing's observation was evidently not, as Kennan points out, "wholly lost on the President." On January 3, Wilson told British Ambassador Sir Cecil Spring Rice: ". . . In point of . . . pure logic, this principle which was good in itself would lead to the complete independence of various small nationalities now forming part of various Empires. Pushed to its extreme, the principle would

mean the disruption of existing governments, to an undefinable extent. . . ." Less than a week later Wilson disregarded Lansing's warning and his own cautious assessment. See David R. Francis to Robert Lansing, December 31, 1917, U.S., Department of State, *Papers Relating to the Foreign Relations of the United States: 1918, Russia* (Washington, 1932), I, 405 ff.; Lansing to Woodrow Wilson, January 2, 1918, U.S., Department of State, *Papers Relating to the Foreign Relations of the United States: The Lansing Papers, 1914-1920* (Washington, 1940), II, 346-49; and *The Letters and Friendships of Sir Cecil Spring Rice,* ed. Stephen Gwynn (Boston, 1929), II, 423-24, cited by Kennan, p. 249.

3. See Joseph Stalin, *Marxism and the National Question* (New York, 1942); Frederick C. Barghoorn, "Nationality Doctrine in Soviet Political Strategy," *The Review of Politics,* XVI (July, 1954); and Edward H. Carr, *The Bolshevik Revolution, 1917-1923* (New York, 1951-1953), I.

4. One day before public announcement of the Fourteen Points, Wilson called Lansing to the White House and read him a draft of the address.

5. See Robert H. Ferrell, "The United States and East Central Europe before 1941," *The Fate of East Central Europe: Hopes and Failures of American Foreign Policy,* ed. Stephen D. Kertesz (Notre Dame, 1956), pp. 21-50.

6. Alfred Cobban, *National Self-Determination* (Chicago, 1947), pp. 20-21.

7. Thomas A. Bailey, *The Man in the Street: The Impact of American Public Opinion on Foreign Policy* (New York, 1948), p. 296.

8. Robert Lansing, *The Peace Negotiations: A Personal Narrative* (Boston, 1921), pp. 96-105.

9. Edward M. House diary, April 23, 1919, House Papers.

10. See *ibid.,* March 22, April 12, 19, 24, July 19, August 6, 1918; February 21, April 15, 18, 21, 29, 30, May 10, 13, 20, 21, 22, 24, 29, 31, September 20, December 29, 1919; and December 14, 1920.

11. *Ibid.,* February 18, 1919.

12. Arthur Hugh Frazier to Edward M. House, June 13, 1918, *ibid.*

13. Quoted in House diary, June 4, 1919, *ibid.*

14. U.S., Department of State, *Papers Relating to the Foreign Relations of the United States: 1919, The Paris Peace Conference* (Washington, 1942-1947), I, 44-45. The rationale for this Machiavellian policy, not dissimilar to Lenin's attempts to stir up nationalities in the interest of world Communism, was based on this reasoning: ". . . the more turbulent the subject nationalities become and the less the present Magyar-Austrian ascendency sees itself threatened with absolute extinction, the more fervent will become the desire in Austria-Hungary to make itself a fit partner in a league of nations. . . . By threatening the present German-Magyar combination with nationalist uprisings on the one side, and by showing it a mode of safety on the other, its resistance would be reduced to a minimum, and the motive to an independence from Berlin in foreign affairs would be enormously accelerated." *Ibid.*

15. U.S., Department of State, *The Lansing Papers,* II, 128; and U.S., Department of State, *Papers Relating to the Foreign Relations of the United States: 1918, Supplement 1* (Washington, 1933), I, 803 and 808-9.

16. Victor S. Mamatey, *The United States and East Central Europe, 1914-1918* (Princeton, 1957), pp. 263-64.

17. *Ibid.,* p. 130.

18. *Ibid.,* pp. 282-84.

19. See A. Whitney Griswold, *The Far Eastern Policy of the United States* (New York, 1938), pp. 223 ff. "There are numerous entries in Lansing's date book," observed Griswold, "from January to July, 1918, showing that intervention in Siberia was re-

ceiving his constant attention." *Ibid.*, pp. 232-33 n. See also Cordell Hull, *The Memoirs of Cordell Hull* (New York, 1948), I, 299; and George Kennan, *The Decision to Intervene* (Princeton, 1958), pp. 340-404.

20. *Ibid.*, pp. 360-62 and 391.

21. Robert Lansing, *War Memoirs* (Indianapolis, 1935), pp. 269 ff.

22. Woodrow Wilson to Robert Lansing, June 26, 1918, quoted in Mamatey (see note 16), p. 269.

23. See John S. Reshetar, Jr., *The Ukrainian Revolution, 1917-1920* (Princeton, 1952), pp. 329-30.

24. U.S., Congress, Senate, Committee on Foreign Relations, *Hearings, Treaty of Peace with Germany*, 66th Cong., 1st Sess., Senate Doc. 106, p. 838.

25. *The Public Papers of Woodrow Wilson*, ed. Ray Stannard Baker and William E. Dodd (New York, 1925-27), II, 244.

26. See Joseph Rappaport, "The American Yiddish Press and the European Conflict in 1914," *Jewish Social Studies*, XIX (1957), 113-28; and Rappaport, "Zionism as a Factor in Allied-Central Power Controversy (1914-1918)," *Early History of Zionism in America*, ed. Isidore S. Meyer (New York: American Jewish Historical Society and Theodor Herzl Foundation, 1958), pp. 297-325.

27. *Ibid.*, pp. 303-4.

28. See Selig Adler, "The Palestine Question in the Wilson Era," *Jewish Social Studies*, X (October, 1948), 304.

29. Frank E. Manuel, *The Realities of American-Palestine Relations* (Washington, 1949), p. 120.

30. Cyrus Adler, *Jacob H. Schiff: His Life and Letters* (Garden City, N.Y., 1929), II, 295-311. According to Chaim Weizmann, Levin immediately reacted by asking Schiff how he divided himself: "Was it horizontally or vertically? And if horizontally, exactly which part had he left for the Jewish people?" Chaim Weizmann, *Trial and Error* (Philadelphia, 1949), I, 62.

31. Adler (see note 30), 295 ff.

32. George Antonius, *The Arab Awakening* (Philadelphia, 1939), p. 263.

33. Rappaport, *Jewish Social Studies* (see note 26), pp. 118-19.

34. *Ibid.*, pp. 125-26.

35. Manuel (see note 29), p. 164.

36. *Ibid.*, p. 116. It is interesting to note that initially Morgenthau was reluctant to accept the ambassadorship. He was concerned that the post, where two Jews had previously served, was becoming a Jewish "plum," the awarding of which might be perpetuated as a sort of diplomatic "balanced ticket."

37. Memorandum of Henry Morgenthau's Secret Mission, June 10, 1917, in Robert Lansing Papers (Library of Congress, Washington, D.C.).

38. *Ibid.* See also U.S., Department of State, *The Lansing Papers*, II, 17-19.

39. Weizmann (see note 30), pp. 195-96. Balfour's play-acting during his conversation with the distraught Weizmann and his request that the Zionist leader stop the mission which he had previously approved was, in all probability, based on military considerations. A month after the Lansing-Balfour discussion, the British War Cabinet and Lloyd George had decided to use military means as the method to eliminate Turkey from the war. The disastrous military failures in March and April of Sir Archibald Murray, commander in Egypt since 1916, to control Gaza brought about his replacement by Sir Edmund Allenby. At the end of June, Allenby was ordered to direct the final offensive, with the expectation that Jerusalem would be brought to the British nation for a Christmas present. C. R. M. F. Cruttwell, *The History of the Great War, 1914-1918* (2d ed.; Oxford, 1936), pp. 610-11.

40. Weizmann (see note 30), pp. 197-99. See also *Felix Frankfurter Reminisces*, recorded in talks with Harlan B. Phillips (New York, 1960), pp. 145-53; Manuel (see note 29), pp. 155-58; and William Yale, "Morgenthau's Special Mission of 1917," *World Politics*, I (1949), 308-20. Morgenthau subsequently realized that he had been duped; his strong anti-Zionist stand noted by House and others may have stemmed from this incident.

41. Cited by Adler (see note 28), p. 312.

42. Cited by Manuel (see note 29), pp. 167-68.

43. Lord Balfour to Edward M. House, October 6, 1917, House Papers.

44. Manuel (see note 29), pp. 168-69. See also Chaim Weizmann to Louis Brandeis, October 10, 1917, House Papers.

45. Manuel (see note 29), p. 169. See also Edward M. House to Woodrow Wilson, October 16, 1917, House Papers.

46. Rappaport, "Zionism as a Factor in Allied-Central Power Controversy (1914-1918)" (see above, note 26, for the reference), p. 311.

47. Manuel (see note 29), p. 169.

48. *Ibid.*, pp. 176-78. See also Seth P. Tillman, *Anglo-American Relations at the Paris Peace Conference of 1919* (Princeton, 1961), pp. 219-28.

49. On January 28, 1921, William Linn Westermann, Chief of the Near-Eastern Division of the American Peace Commission, was asked: "Is not Palestine Arab in population, and is not Palestinian Zionism contrary to the idea of self-determination?" Westermann replied: "In Palestine there are six Arabs to every Jew, and the special privilege granted to the Jews there is contrary to the policy of self-determination," but he felt that the opportunity for a Jewish homeland "was bound to be helpful, rather than harmful, in the tangled situation in the Near East." When asked if a Zionist state were "a wise policy and safe for the peace of the Near East," he answered: "The Balfour declaration speaks only of a Jewish Homeland—not of a Zionist state. The Zionist movement and the independent state of Armenia were the two which promised the greatest good in the Near-Eastern situation." Edward M. House and Charles Seymour (eds.), *What Really Happened at Paris* (New York, 1921), pp. 466-67.

50. *New York Times* editorial, "By the Cellar Door," April 14, 1922. In 1922 the power of Lodge in his own state was considerably diminished. During the campaign it was necessary for him to ask Calvin Coolidge's aid. On Election Day his plurality was only 7,354 votes, but undoubtedly the Irish- and Italian-Americans figured in his victory, for each group believed it had cause, in his post-war activities, to be grateful to the aging Senator.

That same year the Balfour pledge was renewed and elucidated in the League of Nations' Palestine Mandate (Articles 2, 4, 6, 7, 11, 22, and 23).

51. There are many letters—some from private citizens, others from officials of states in which the Jewish population is relatively negligible—in the Truman Papers from Christian Americans urging support of a Jewish national home. For some examples see Andrew F. Schoeppel to Harry S. Truman, June 4, 1945; Wallace Conkling to Truman, October 5, 1945; Rose McConnell Long (Mrs. Huey P. Long) to Truman, October 11, 1945, in Truman Papers.

52. As early as September, 1945, this was well perceived by the executive director of the American Christian Palestine Committee, who reminded the administration of the assurance the Democratic party had given on carrying out the principles of the Balfour Declaration, which had been reaffirmed by the government in 1922, and then concluded, "The loss of Jewish support and Jewish votes coupled with the resentment of ten thousand clergymen in high places would be a serious matter for the party."

John Stanley Grauel to Matthew Connelly, September 21, 1945; and Grauel to Harry S. Truman, October 1, 1945, Truman Papers, 204.

53. Within a few days after Roosevelt's death, the new President received a great number of memoranda and letters from American Zionists and politicians informing him of the various promises and pledges which had been made by the American government. On April 18, 1945, Senator Robert F. Wagner of New York, having learned that his "good friends" Stephen S. Wise and Herman Shulman were to meet with Truman to discuss the Palestine question, forwarded an October 15, 1944, statement by Roosevelt, which he had been asked to convey to the Zionist Organization of America, that if reëlected Roosevelt would help to bring about the realization of the Jewish hope that Palestine be established as a free and democratic Jewish commonwealth. Wagner told Truman that after Roosevelt's return from Yalta, Roosevelt had issued a statement through Wise which read, "I made my position on Zionism clear in October. That position I have not changed and shall continue to seek to bring about its earliest realization." A July 2 letter signed by 54 Senators and 250 Representatives calling attention to previous American support for a Jewish national home and asking that "all powers of our Government be exerted toward the immediate fulfillment of that policy to which America is so deeply committed" was sent to Truman. In August, Wise and Shulman provided Truman with a "Memorandum on Palestine" which, among other things, traced the history of "The United States and the Jewish National Home Promise." In October, a somewhat similar memorandum for the State Department from the American Zionist Emergency Council was transmitted to the White House. At the same time Lessing J. Rosenwald, president of the American Council for Judaism, a small but vociferous anti-Zionist organization, indicated to Truman opposition to a Zionist state. In December, Senators Robert Taft and Wagner, in a cover letter for Senate Joint Resolution 112 which favored action "looking to the restoration of Palestine as a homeland for the Jewish people," detailed the antecedent promises and pledges and discounted the charge that the resolution "proposed to establish . . . a 'theocratic' state. . . ." Robert F. Wagner to Harry S. Truman, and enclosure, April 18, 1945; members of Congress to Truman, July 2, 1945; Wagner to Truman, July 3, 1945; "Memorandum on Palestine" by Stephen S. Wise and Herman Shulman, August 13, 1945; Leo R. Sack to Charles G. Ross, October 23, 1945; American Zionist Emergency Council memorandum on the occasion of the meeting of Abba Hillel Silver and Wise with James F. Byrnes, October 25, 1945 (not in file 204); Lessing J. Rosenwald to Truman, with enclosure of correspondence between Rosenwald and Cordell Hull, August 18, November 23, and December 5, 1945; and Wagner and Robert A. Taft to Truman, with enclosure, December 6, 1945, Truman Papers, 204 Miscellaneous.

54. Harry S. Truman, *Memoirs* (Garden City, N.Y., 1956), II, 160.

55. *Ibid.*, II, 157. See also chap. 11, II, 143-55.

CHAPTER VI

1. John Bartlett, *Familiar Quotations*, ed. Christopher Morley and Louella D. Everett (11th ed.; Boston, 1940), p. 700.

2. U.S., Congress, Senate, Committee on Foreign Relations, *Hearings, Treaty of Peace with Germany*, 66th Cong., 1st Sess., Senate Doc. 106, pp. 701-14, 757-903, 934-41, 947-79, 1041-66, 1091-1108, 1109-29. One Swedish-American, a self-alleged representative of the inhabitants of the Aland Islands in the Gulf of Bothnia, claimed that they did not wish to be under the jurisdiction of the Finns or Russians but preferred incorporation into Sweden.

3. "Republican opposition to the League, with a Presidential election in sight, was conditioned not so much on America's horror of Old World entanglements as on the presence of Old World entanglements in America." *New York Times,* April 14, 1922. The editorial was occasioned by Lodge's introduction of a Congressional resolution in support of the Balfour Declaration—an action which the *Times* believed to be a reflection of his concern over his reëlection.

4. Chester Bowles, *The New Dimensions of Peace* (New York, 1955), p. 291.

5. *Akron Germania,* July 2, 1920, cited by Carl Wittke, "Ohio's German-Language Press in the Campaign of 1920," *Proceedings of the Mississippi Valley Historical Association,* X, Part III (1920-1921), 469 n.

6. See Selig Adler, *The Isolationist Impulse* (London and New York, 1957), p. 88. See also "Help from the Hyphenates," *ibid.,* pp. 75-92.

7. Cited in Carl Wittke, *The German-Language Press in America* (Lexington, 1957), pp. 275-78; and Wittke, *Proceedings of the Mississippi Valley Historical Association,* X, Part I (1918-1919).

8. Edward M. House's reply when the German ambassador to Great Britain told him in July, 1923, that not unless the United States was in the League would Germany wish to join, reflected House's belief in the voting power of Irish- and German-Americans:

". . . I told him he was going at it the wrong way around. That if Germany became a member it would help those of us in the United States who wished our country to join to bring it about. In my opinion, there were about 25% of our population Irish and German born and their descendants, and with Ireland and Germany in the League, the German and Irish Americans would naturally desire the United States to become a member in order that Germany and Ireland might have a disinterested friend." Edward M. House diary, July 8, 1923, House Papers.

9. J. Joseph Huthmacher, *Massachusetts People and Politics, 1919-1933* (Cambridge, 1959), p. 23. See also "The Politics of Postwar Disillusion," *ibid.,* pp. 19-47.

10. Karl Schriftgiesser, *The Gentleman from Massachusetts: Henry Cabot Lodge* (Boston, 1944), p. 336 n.

11. Huthmacher (see note 9), pp. 23-26. See also Charles C. Tansill, *The Fight for Irish Freedom, 1866-1922* (New York, 1957), particularly pp. 369-96.

12. In the fall of 1919 the New York *Progresso Italo-Americano* collected one million lire for Gabriele D'Annunzio's filibustering expedition to seize Fiume. The money was sent to Benito Mussolini, who pocketed 480,000 lire to pay his armed *squadristi* before sending the balance to D'Annunzio. See Enzo Tagliacozzo, *Gaetano Salvemini nel Cinquantennio Liberale* (Florence, 1959), p. 234.

13. Huthmacher (see note 9), p. 21; Thomas A. Bailey, *A Diplomatic History of the American People* (5th ed.; New York, 1955), p. 667 n.; and Bowles (see note 4), p. 291.

14. *Gazzetta del Massachusetts,* May 12, 1919, cited by Huthmacher (see note 9), pp. 21-22.

15. *Ibid.*

16. The June 26, 1919, entry in the Edward M. House diary, House Papers, reads: "Gibson and I decided if we could get Morgenthau to head a commission to look into the condition of the Jews in Poland, we could right much of the misrepresentation and falsehoods that are being sent abroad. Gibson thinks the propaganda has been fostered by the Zionists in order to help concentrate favorable opinion upon the Zionist movement.

"After some persuasion, Morgenthau accepted, much to the consternation of the leading Zionists who know him to be unfriendly to their cause. . . ."

17. Huthmacher (see note 9), pp. 22-23 and 31-32.

18. Gordon Auchincloss to Edward M. House, August 9, 1920, House Papers, I-36.

19. John M. Blum, *Joe Tumulty and the Wilson Era* (Boston, 1951), p. 180.

20. *Boston Transcript,* October 15, 1920, cited by Huthmacher (see note 9), p. 32.

21. *Boston Transcript,* September 18 and 23, 1920, cited *ibid.,* p. 36.

22. *Toledo Express,* November 3, 4, and 25, 1920; *Cincinnati Freie Presse* and *Wächter und Anzeiger,* November 3 and 4, 1920, cited by Wittke (see note 5), 478-80. In the 1922 Congressional campaign a circular letter urged German-Americans of a Midwestern state not to vote for a Democratic Senator, because he had supported Wilson: "Two years ago the American people showed Wilson the door, mainly thanks to the united Germans. May the Germans of —— strengthen this political influence by keeping a good memory!" The Senator apparently drew a conclusion from his defeat; immediately after the election his speeches took on a violent anti-French cast. See Paul Scott Mowrer, *Our Foreign Affairs: A Study in National Interest and the New Diplomacy* (New York, 1924), pp. 118-19. By 1924 many German-Americans had turned against Harding. His administration was accused, as Wilson's had been, of antagonism toward German-Americans. The Steuben Society felt "the time was ripe for the re-entry of the German-Americans, as such, in politics and the support of the third party ticket." See James Wilford Garner, *American Foreign Policies* (New York, 1928), p. 27.

23. See John A. Hawgood, *The Tragedy of German-America* (New York, 1940), pp. 298-99; and A. Whitney Griswold, *The Far Eastern Policy of the United States* (New York, 1938), pp. 368-79.

24. Frederick Jackson Turner, *The Significance of Sections in American History* (New York, 1932), p. 42.

25. Nathan Glazer, "The Integration of American Immigrants," *Law and Contemporary Problems,* XXI (spring, 1956), 269.

CHAPTER VII

1. Charles A. Beard, "Giddy Minds and Foreign Quarrels," *Harper's Magazine,* CLXXIX (September, 1939), 337-51.

2. See Wayne S. Cole, *America First: The Battle against Intervention, 1940-1941* (Madison, 1953). See also Cole, "America First and the South, 1940-1941," *Journal of Southern History,* XXII (February, 1956); Paul Seabury, *The Waning of Southern Internationalism* (Princeton: Center of International Studies, Princeton University, 1957); Thomas A. Bailey, *The Man in the Street: The Impact of American Public Opinion on Foreign Policy* (New York, 1948), pp. 107-9 and 111-14; and Alexander DeConde, "On Twentieth-Century Isolation," *Isolation and Security,* ed. DeConde (Durham, N.C., 1957).

3. "Steam from the Melting Pot," *Fortune,* XXVI (September, 1942).

4. Carl Nicolay to Franklin D. Roosevelt, September 14, 1934, and October 8, 1934, with enclosures, Roosevelt Papers, PPF 441. The President's telegram and its reception by the United German Societies did not escape notice. The *New York Herald Tribune* gave a full account of the *heils* accorded Hitler and Roosevelt. The *Harvard Crimson,* student paper of Roosevelt's alma mater, reprinted the *Herald Tribune* article. Roosevelt was asked by its editors to comment on "the handclasp of solidarity" which he had received "from Fritz Thyssen and his Nazi bloodhounds." Henry Clay Laruer and Myron Kay Stone to Roosevelt, October 18, 1934, Roosevelt Papers, PPF 441.

5. John Tjarks to Franklin D. Roosevelt, October 2, 1933, Roosevelt Papers, OF 198-A.

6. Institute for Propaganda Analysis, "Axis Voices among the Foreign-Born," *Propaganda Analysis*, 4: 9 (July 24, 1941), p. 7, quoted by Alfred McClung Lee, "Subversive Individuals of Minority Status," *The Annals*, CCXXIII (September, 1942), 170.

7. Quoted by John Roy Carlson, *Under Cover* (New York, 1943), p. 116. See also Lee (see note 6), p. 171.

8. For example, the White House received a complaint concerning the conduct of Giacomo Ungarelli, Italian vice consul in Detroit, who, it was charged, sought to compel Italian-Americans' adherence to the Fascist government he represented. George W. Dean to Franklin D. Roosevelt, May 28, 1934, Roosevelt Papers, OF 233-A.

9. Adolf Hitler, *Mein Kampf* (Munich, 1933), p. 476, quoted in U.S., Department of State, *National Socialism: Basic Principles, Their Application by the Nazi Party's Foreign Organization, and the Use of Germans Abroad for Nazi Aims*, prepared by Raymond E. Murphy, Francis B. Stevens, Howard Trivers, and Joseph M. Roland (Washington, 1943), p. 69.

10. Leon M. Birkhead, reported by Institute for Propaganda Analysis, "The Attack on Democracy," *Propaganda Analysis*, 2: 4 (January 1, 1939), p. 1, cited by Lee (see note 6), p. 164.

11. See Frank C. Hanighen, "Foreign Political Movements in the United States," *Foreign Affairs*, XVI (October, 1937); "Nazi Agents in the U.S.," *Fortune*, XXII (October, 1940); "Voices of Defeat," *Life*, April 13, 1942; Clyde R. Miller, "Foreign Efforts to Increase Disunity," *The Annals*, CCXXIII (September, 1942); "Steam from the Melting Pot" (see note 3); Max Ascoli, "On the Italian-Americans," *Common Ground*, III (autumn, 1942), 45-49; "The War of Nerves: Hitler's Helper," *Fortune*, XXII (November, 1940); Lee (see note 6); and Joseph S. Roucek, "Foreign Politics and Our Minority Groups," *Phylon*, II (first quarter, 1941), 44-56.

12. Samuel Flagg Bemis, *A Diplomatic History of the United States* (3d ed.; New York, 1950), p. 12.

13. Colin Ross, *Unser Amerika* (Leipzig, 1936), quoted in Department of State, *National Socialism*, p. 182. The German legation protested the Dies Committee's recommendation in August, 1940, that Ross, as a German spy, be expelled from the United States. Ross denied the allegation. *The Goebbels Diaries, 1942-1943*, ed. Louis P. Lochner (Garden City, N.Y., 1948), p. 313.

14. Paul Strasser, Jr., "When Will Germany Receive a German-blooded Ambassador from America?" (Hamburg, September, 1933), quoted in Department of State, *National Socialism*, pp. 78 and 248.

15. *Ibid.*, pp. 93-130.

16. Gottfried Feder, *Das Programm der NSDAP* (Munich, 1933), p. 19, quoted in Department of State, *National Socialism*, pp. 68-69.

17. Quoted *ibid.*, pp. 115 and 99; Document 32-A, pp. 421-30; Document 24, pp. 308-13; and Document 4, pp. 178-82. By "the old American idea" Ross probably meant the confidence of the United States in its capacity to absorb ethnic groups. In 1940 he told Hitler that one of the main problems with which he had concerned himself on his research trips to the United States was how that country could be kept out of the war. Among other things, he informed the Führer that "although the American is gradually abandoning his belief that a national community can be created by education, independent of race and nationality (theory of the melting pot), nevertheless, any organization on the basis of nationality within the great American political community is still repugnant to him." U.S., Department of State, *Documents on German Foreign Policy, 1918-1945: The War Years, September 4, 1939-March 18, 1940* (Washington, 1954), Series D, VIII, Publication 5436, Document 671, 910-13.

18. Louis H. Bean to Franklin D. Roosevelt, February 12, 1941, Roosevelt Papers, OF 4351.

19. Samuel Lubell, *The Future of American Politics* (New York, 1952).

20. See *ibid.*, pp. 20, 21, and 22.

21. Bean's analysis here contradicts a passing remark of William L. Langer and S. Everett Gleason, *The Challenge to Isolationism, 1937-1940* (New York, 1952), p. 225: "The influence of foreign language elements, even the German, was much less marked than in 1914-1917."

22. A typical example quoted by Bean was from *Unser Amerika:* "Over 25 million Americans are of German stock (about every fourth white American). About 7 million Americans are German born or of German-born parents. More than 6 of these 7 million live in the 'German Belt,' i.e., the Northern States, from the Atlantic to the Rockies." Another was from *Der Auslandsdeutsche*, official organ of the German government's Foreign Institute in Stuttgart, which pointed out that "in Texas, in California, in the Broad Middle West or in the small farm cities of the North West, wherever *German* farmers have settled, *German* characteristics have been stamped. . . ." Still another was from a report by Norbert Zimmer, an official of the Low Saxon Research Bureau, which described 200 German-speaking settlements as a "possible to save" "half-sunken German *Volkstum.*" In its desire to alienate German-Americans from other Americans, the Nazi government was enheartened by such information.

The leading article, "German Youth in the United States," in the August 12, 1937, issue of the Württemberg *N. S. Kurier* contained these passages: "And these German-Americans, who for centuries have made nothing but sacrifices for America, who have made valuable contributions to the culture of the country, and who were too good-natured and honest to interfere with politics and to secure rights for themselves and their nationality, are now prepared for a final struggle. While preserving their national characteristics and their German world-outlook *they are prepared to incorporate themselves in the political life of America in order to be able to exercise a decisive influence on the formation of a new America* [italics mine]. . . .

"We want to lead the Germans in the United States, who have become partly alienated from their German home country and from German nationality, back to the great community of blood and fate of all Germans. . . .

". . . we want to organize the Germans in the United States, in order that their spiritual revival may be succeeded by economic recovery and political training." Quoted in Department of State, *National Socialism,* p. 130.

23. See Bean's report, "Research Project on the Influence of Nationality Groups on Election Returns," February 12, 1941, and attached memorandum, Franklin D. Roosevelt to Wayne Coy, William Bullitt, and Harold Smith, Roosevelt Papers, OF 4351. The report was sent by Roosevelt to Edward J. Flynn on March 3 and returned by Flynn on March 17, *ibid.*

A previous warning of the danger of Nazi and Fascist propaganda and suggested countermeasures had been brought to the President's attention by Mrs. Roosevelt when she forwarded to him a letter and memorandum from Hans von Hentig. Roosevelt sent them to Cordell Hull to "read and return." Von Hentig to Mrs. Roosevelt, November 3, 1938; and Roosevelt to Hull, November 16, 1938, *ibid.*, OF 705.

See also Samuel Dickstein to Roosevelt, October 17, 1933, with seven-page enclosure, "Confidential Committee [House Committee on Immigration and Naturalization] Print —Historical Sketch on Origin and Extent of Nazi Activities in United States," *ibid.*, OF 198-A; Bean, *How to Predict Elections* (New York, 1948), pp. 93-99; and Bean, Frederick Mosteller, and Frederick Williams, "Nationalities and 1944," *Public Opinion Quarterly,* VIII (fall, 1944).

24. Telegram, A. J. Sabath to Franklin D. Roosevelt, October 28, 1936, Roosevelt Papers, OF 300, Illinois.

25. Ernest L. Klein to Marvin McIntyre (abstract), November 2, 1936, *ibid.;* Frank K. Waldherr to Franklin D. Roosevelt (abstract), August 5, 1936, *ibid.,* OF 198-A; Erhard Mueller to Roosevelt (abstract), August 14, 1936, *ibid.;* Robert L. Soergel to James A. Farley, July 6, 1936, *ibid.,* PPF 441; and Jack Ingegnieros to Roosevelt (abstract), August 19, 1936, *ibid.,* PPF 1821.

26. See roster of division chairmen, under date of February 19, 1937, *ibid.,* PPF 603.

27. Telegram, Emanuel F. Schifanno, November 1, 1940, *ibid.,* OF 233-A.

28. Lena Stefani Butori to Burton K. Wheeler for forwarding to Franklin D. Roosevelt, June 10, 1940; and Wheeler to Edwin Watson, June 15, 1940, *ibid.,* PPF 200.

29. The 1940 Republican platform deplored Roosevelt's "explosive utterances." See *National Party Platforms, 1840-1956,* comp. Kirk H. Porter and Donald Bruce Johnson (Urbana, 1956), p. 390.

30. Alfred E. Beiter to Edward J. Flynn, October 1, 1940, *ibid.,* PPF 2532; Mark A. Bogart to Marguerite LeHand, October 24, 1940, *ibid.,* OF 233-A; Luigi Antonini to Miss LeHand, February 10, 1941, *ibid.,* PPF 7382; James A. Shanley to Franklin D. Roosevelt, July 9, 1940, *ibid.,* PPF 6735; and Roosevelt to Shanley (abstract), July 11, 1940, *ibid.,* OF 705.

31. Press release No. 31, Italian News Service, October 14, 1940, *ibid.,* OF 233-A.

32. Henry F. Pringle to William D. Hassett, with enclosures, March 13, 1943; and Hassett memorandum for files, March 15, 1943, *ibid.,* PPF 4617.

33. Memorandum, Edwin M. Watson to Franklin D. Roosevelt, October 9, 1944; telegram, Watson to Generoso Pope, October 12, 1944; and telegram, Pope to Watson, October 13, 1944, *ibid.*

34. See U.S., Department of State, *Documents on German Foreign Policy, 1918-1945: The Aftermath of Munich, October, 1938-March, 1939* (Washington, 1957), Series D, IV, Publication 3883, Doc. 527, 675-78; U.S., Department of State, *Documents on German Foreign Policy, 1918-1945: The War Years, June 23-August 31, 1940* (Washington, 1957), Series D, X, Publication 6491, Doc. 112, 125-26; and U.S., Department of State, *Documents on German Foreign Policy,* VIII, Doc. 431, 504-6.

35. U.S., Department of State, *Documents on German Foreign Policy, 1918-1945: The War Years, March 18-June 22, 1940* (Washington, 1956), Series D, IX, Publication 6312, Doc. 417, 550-51. *Ibid.,* X, Doc. 91, 101-02, makes reference to "the promotion campaign authorized by telegraphic instruction No. 666, of June 17." An advertisement such as that mentioned by Thomsen appeared in the *New York Times,* June 25, 1940.

36. U.S., Department of State, *Documents on German Foreign Policy,* IX, Doc. 493, 625-26.

Two others of Thomsen's "operations" among the Republicans are described in his communications to the foreign ministry. On June 27, 1940, he wrote, "I was able furthermore through a confidential agent to induce the isolationist Representative Thorkelson [Jacob Thorkelson of Montana] to have the Führer interview inserted in the *Congressional Record.* . . . This assures . . . once more of the widest distribution." The interview was that given by Hitler to Hearst Correspondent Karl von Wiegand which appeared in the *New York Journal-American,* June 14, 1940, and the German Embassy bulletin, *Facts in Review,* No. 27 (100,000 copies). *Ibid.,* X, Doc. 39, 39-40. On July 18, 1940, Thomsen wrote that a "fundamental speech" by Senator Gerald P. Nye of North Dakota incorporating many quotations from Sidney Rogerson's book, *Propaganda in the Next War*—a work apparently well-tailored to Nazi propaganda—

was printed in the *Congressional Record* and "distributed to 100,000 persons by the channel known to you." After lengthy negotiations, copies of Nye's speech, given in April, 1939, were sent "by the same channels to another 100,000 specially selected persons." Thomsen described the undertaking as "not altogether easy" and "particularly delicate" because "Senator Nye, as a political opponent of the President, is under the careful observation of the secret state police here [*der hiesigen geheimen Staatspolizei*]." *Ibid.*, Doc. 186, p. 243.

37. *Ibid.*, Doc. 91, pp. 101-2.

38. *Ibid.* See also *New York Times*, June 25, 1940. The advertisement was one sponsored by The National Committee to Keep America Out of Wars. It included statements from Senators Edwin C. Johnson of Colorado, Burton K. Wheeler of Montana, Rush D. Holt of West Virginia, Bennett Champ Clark of Missouri, and David I. Walsh of Massachusetts. A heavily outlined box in the lower right corner carried this message: "Write or wire to your Delegates at the Republican National Convention . . . to support a clearcut peace or anti-war plank. . . . Also write your Representative . . . to vote to keep America out of foreign entanglements and wars."

In July, General Friedrich von Bötticher, military and air attaché in the United States, and Thomsen reported, among other intelligences: ". . . a very trustworthy personage close to Lindbergh has asked me to inform German authorities that the wife of Commander P. E. Pihl, American Assistant Naval Attaché in Berlin, who is a sister of Willkie, has pronounced sympathies for Germany and might greatly influence her brother." U.S., Department of State, *Documents on German Foreign Policy*, X, Doc. 195, 254-56.

39. *Ibid.*, VIII, Doc. 129, 127-29.

40. See *National Party Platforms, 1840-1956* (see note 29), p. 390.

41. U.S., Department of State, *Documents on German Foreign Policy*, X, Doc. 190, 250-51.

42. *Ibid.*, Doc. 134, pp. 159-60. See also *ibid.*, Doc. 120, 133; and *ibid.*, VIII, Doc. 242, 268-70. The "40 Pennsylvania delegates" were not bought; the state delegation voted for Roosevelt. It is quite possible that Thomsen's report to his government exaggerated his role.

William Rhodes Davis was an American businessman "with long experience of dealing with German government agencies regarding the sale of Mexican oil." On September 15, 1939, he met with Roosevelt to inform him that he had had a message "from an associate with access to Göring that the latter hoped Roosevelt would use his influence" toward a mediated peace. Roosevelt said he could take no position unless such a proposal came through official channels. Davis subsequently submitted to Roosevelt two reports, dated October 11 and 12, concerning his talks with Göring on October 1, 2, and 3. See *ibid.*, 270 n.

Chapter VIII

1. "Steam from the Melting Pot," *Fortune*, XXVI (September, 1942).

2. See Everett V. Stonequist, "The Restricted Citizen"; Shotaro Frank Miyamoto, "Immigrants and Citizens of Japanese Origin"; Harold F. Gosnell, "Symbols of National Solidarity"; Carl Wittke, "German Immigrants and Their Children"; Edward Corsi, "Italian Immigrants and Their Children"; Clyde R. Miller, "Foreign Efforts to Increase Disunity"; and Otto Klineberg, "Race Prejudice and the War," *The Annals*, CCXXIII (September, 1942); and Morton Godzins, *Americans Betrayed: Politics and the Japanese Evacuation* (Chicago, 1949).

3. Harold B. Hoskins, "American Unity and Foreign-Born Citizens," *The Annals*, CCXX (March, 1942).

4. Department of State, December 10, 1941, quoted in Hoskins, *ibid.,* pp. 155-56.

5. After the United States entered the war, many of these became "rather inactive."

6. See also James F. Brown and Joseph S. Roucek (eds.), *One America* (New York, 1949), p. 397; and "Steam from the Melting Pot" (see note 1).

7. John F. Fahey to Franklin D. Roosevelt, July 31, 1940, Roosevelt Papers, OF 144-C. See also memorandum, March 23, 1943, *ibid.,* OF 705.

8. "Steam from the Melting Pot" (see note 1). In its June, 1943, listing of Italian-American publications, the Office of Strategic Services indicated those having pro-Fascist orientation before Pearl Harbor. It evidently found no traces of such leanings in 1943. In December, 1941, President Roosevelt received a telegram from the president of the Garibaldina Society of Los Angeles informing him of the society's resolution of endorsement. It concluded, ". . . The entire colony in Los Angeles is backing you to the fullest extent and we are working and praying for a final complete victory. . . ." Within a few days, Roosevelt heard from an aroused Italian-American who claimed, ". . . Gentleman sending telegram is . . . reactionary Republican follower of the enemies of our dear president and his policies. One of the many whose conscience hurts him now for his sympathy for Mussolini." Jerry Voorhis to Stephen Early, and enclosures, December 29, 1941, Roosevelt Papers, 233-A.

9. See U.S., Office of Strategic Services, *Foreign Nationality Groups in the United States* (Washington, 1943); "The Foreign Language Press," *Fortune,* XXII (November, 1940); Joseph S. Roucek, "The Foreign-Language and Negro Press," Brown and Roucek (see note 6), pp. 369-81; Roucek, "The Foreign-Language Press in World War II," *Sociology and Social Research,* XXVII (July-August, 1943); Yaroslav M. Chyz, "The War and the Foreign-Language Press," *Common Ground,* III (spring, 1943), 3-10; Thomas A. Bailey, *The Man in the Street: The Impact of American Public Opinion on Foreign Policy* (New York, 1948), p. 308; and Alfred Lee McClung, "Subversive Individuals of Minority Status," *The Annals,* CCXXIII (September, 1942).

10. See William W. Link, *"REPORT OF ACTIVITIES—RESULTS of Campaign for ELECTION* November 5, 1940," Roosevelt Papers, OF 463 and OF 463 A. In his report, Link, secretary of the Polish American Democratic Organization, described the methods used to win the Polish vote.

11. John Franklin Carter memorandum for Steve Early, August 21, 1941, *ibid.,* OF 463 A. Edward Flynn, chairman of the New York Democratic Committee, also recognized the importance of the Polish vote: "The Polish vote is tremendously important in the State this year, and if something could be done, it would be very nice." Edward Flynn to Marguerite LeHand, August 19, 1940, *ibid.,* 1051.

12. Edwin W. Pauley memorandum, and enclosures, December 14, 1942, *ibid.,* PPF 1820. See also Louis H. Bean, Frederick Mosteller, and Frederick Williams, "Nationalities and 1944," *Public Opinion Quarterly,* VIII (fall, 1944), which corroborates the findings of the Democratic National Committee and includes statistical tables indicating the "importance of the hyphen" in the 1940 election.

13. George H. Zator to Franklin D. Roosevelt, and enclosures, February 10, 1943; John F. Zielinski to Roosevelt, August 25, 1944; and Joseph Czyzewski to Mrs. Franklin D. Roosevelt, September 1, 1944, Roosevelt Papers, OF 463 A. See also Frank Nurczyk to Roosevelt, September 13, 1944; and Michael Pankiewicz to Stephen Early, and enclosures, November 4, 1944, *ibid.*

14. Telegram, Matty Radin to Franklin D. Roosevelt (abstract), October 18, 1944, *ibid.,* OF (abstract) 4070.

15. Celia Heller to Stephen Early, September 12, 1944, *ibid.,* OF 463 A.

16. Stephen Early to Paul Porter (abstract), October 31, 1944, *ibid.,* OF 4070. See

also George G. Sadowski to Franklin D. Roosevelt, October 21, 1944, *ibid.;* and Frank Kovarik to Roosevelt, and enclosures, January 3, 1945, *ibid.,* 144-C.

17. Documents "A," "B," and "C," November 14, 1944, *ibid.,* 3850.

18. See Charles Rozmarek to Edward J. Kelly, September 9, 1944; Rozmarek to Franklin D. Roosevelt, and enclosures, September 6, 1944; Francis Biddle to Roosevelt, and enclosures, September 28, 1944; Jonathan Daniels to Edwin M. Watson, and enclosures, October 11, 1944; and Biddle to Roosevelt, and enclosures, October 7, 1944, *ibid.*

19. See preceding chapter. For the effect of the 1944 Italian-American vote on American policy toward Italy, see Norman Kogan, *Italy and the Allies* (Cambridge, 1956), pp. 76-89. In the chapter "Italy and American Elections," Kogan ably and cogently pointed out how President Roosevelt, unable to ignore pressures from Italian-Americans, from Catholic circles, and above all from influential politicians like New York's Mayor Fiorello LaGuardia, made important economic and political concessions to Italy. These concessions, according to Kogan, were made over the protest of Britain and endangered the postwar settlement. "The key to this capriciousness can only be found in the elections of 1944. The pledges seem to have been made primarily for the benefit of the interested voters. Thomas Dewey was appealing to the Italian-American vote by charging that the administration was not doing enough for Italy. The Administration rose to the challenge."

20. E. Klein to James W. Gerard, transmitted to Franklin D. Roosevelt, October 24, 1944, Roosevelt Papers, PPF 977; Matt Pelkonen to Roosevelt (abstract), October 6, 1944, *ibid.,* OF 4070; Stephen Shumeyko to Roosevelt (abstract), October 13, 1944, *ibid.,* OF 463 A; Constantine A. Checkrezi to Roosevelt, November 2, 1944, *ibid.,* OF 4070; Charles P. Kal to Roosevelt, January 18, 1945, *ibid.,* OF 300; Gottfried Klueber to Roosevelt, October 16, 1944, *ibid.,* OF 4070. See also Anthony Grasso to Roosevelt, and enclosures, October 6, 1944, *ibid.;* Joseph J. Rinaldi to Roosevelt, October 13, 1944, *ibid.;* and Francis Biddle memorandum, October 6, 1944, *ibid.,* OF 233.

A concomitant resentment also occurred among exile governments, particularly the Czech, in London. See U.S., Department of State, *Foreign Relations of the United States: Diplomatic Papers, 1943* (Washington, 1963), III *(The British Commonwealth, Eastern Europe, The Far East),* 332-33 ff.

CHAPTER IX

1. The Progressive party polled over a million popular votes. The "Dixiecrat" or States' Rights party received the thirty-eight electoral votes of Alabama, Louisiana, Mississippi, and South Carolina, and one of Tennessee.

2. Arthur H. Vandenberg, Jr., with the collaboration of Joe Alex Morris, *The Private Papers of Senator Vandenberg* (Boston, 1952), p. 155.

3. *Ibid.,* pp. 313-14. Graham Hutton, in *Midwest at Noon* (Chicago, 1946), p. 313, said: "The stand taken by Senator Vandenberg of Michigan in 1945 on the United Nations Charter in the United States Senate called for more political courage than most foreign observers, and many Americans, realized. The 'Polish vote,' as it is still called, is a big hazard in Detroit and Michigan. . . ."

4. See following chapters.

5. Jack [John M.] Redding, *Inside the Democratic Party* (Indianapolis, 1958), pp. 147 ff. and 202-5.

6. "Activities of the *Nationalities Division* in the Election of *President Harry S. Truman* and *Vice President Alben W. Barkley,*" John M. Redding Papers (Harry S. Truman Library, Independence, Missouri). Cited hereafter as Redding Papers.

7. Redding (see note 5), p. 203.

8. "Activities of the *Nationalities Division*," Redding Papers; and Redding (see note 5), pp. 204-5.

9. "Activities of the *Nationalities Division*," Redding Papers; and Redding (see note 5), pp. 205-6.

10. "Activities of the *Nationalities Division*," Redding Papers.

11. *Ibid.*

12. The meeting of Truman, McGrath, Gazda, and Cieplinski took place August 12, 1948, and centered on three topics: the "importance of the foreign language groups," the "achievements among nationality groups," and the "strategy and tactics to gain the confidence and support of the foreign language population." After the meeting, Truman, "in the presence of Senator Barkley, Chairman McGrath, Senator Green and Attorney General Tom Clark, received 12 foreign language editors and political leaders who offered first hand knowledge of campaign strategy affecting their respective groups." *Ibid.*, and Redding (see note 5), p. 206.

13. Matthew J. Connelly to J. Howard McGrath, May 10, 1948, Truman Papers. This "unsuccessful" meeting did not deter Rozmarek from asking Truman to be the principal speaker at the opening session on May 29, 1948, of the second national convention of the Polish American Congress in Philadelphia. The President did not attend. Connelly even doubted the "wisdom of having the President send a message to this group."

14. "Knowing the great influence of the famous Polish painter, Tadé Styka, spiritual successor of the great Paderewski, in Polish and Slavic circles, *we succeeded in convincing Mr. Styka, in spite of Republican effort, to endorse President Truman.* President Truman's statement during the [presentation] ceremony referring to Woodrow Wilson's self determination plan for Poland as well as *Mr. Styka's endorsement proved of great value and was publicized many times in EVERY one of the 72 Polish language newspapers which carried more than 500 stories and pictures on this subject.* This reception was a turning point in the election campaign as far as Americans of Polish descent were concerned, giving us an unlimited source of publicity in newspapers, radio programs, speeches, etc." "Activities of the *Nationalities Division*," Redding Papers. See also *Nowy Swiat*, October 7, 1948; and Redding (see note 5), pp. 207-9.

15. J. Howard McGrath to Francis Myers, July 13, 1948, Truman Papers. See also Redding (note 5), pp. 209-10.

16. *National Party Platforms, 1840-1956*, comp. Kirk H. Porter and Donald Bruce Johnson (Urbana, 1956), p. 432.

17. Redding (see note 5), p. 210.

18. *Ibid.*, pp. 104-5.

19. *Ibid.*, p. 149.

20. See "Unsolicited Mail on the Palestine Question," Truman Papers.

21. Dorothy Thompson, "Why the Zionists Are Right," *Palestine*, II (February, 1945), Roosevelt Papers, 700.

22. *National Party Platforms, 1840-1956* (see note 16), pp. 403 and 413. The parties' competition for the Jewish vote was not lost on Zionist leaders. In the fall of 1945 the president of the Zionist Council of Essex County, N.J., warned Mayor Frank Hague of Jersey City that by "falling in with British trickery" the Democratic party was signing its death warrant. After indicating displeasure with the Truman and State Department policies toward Palestine, he pointed out that Dewey had been given a tremendous ovation at Madison Square Garden "from about sixty-five thousand Jews . . . the same Governor Dewey that probably would have been booed off the stage by a Jewish audience a year ago." Nathan H. Brodsky to Frank Hague, November

24, 1945, Truman Papers, 204. See also Hague to Robert Hannegan, November 26, 1945; and Richard R. Nacy to Matthew J. Connelly, December 3, 1945, *ibid.*

23. *National Party Platforms, 1840-1956* (see note 16), p. 432.

24. *The Forrestal Diaries,* ed. Walter Millis (New York, 1951), p. 347.

25. *National Party Platforms, 1840-1956* (see note 16), p. 453.

26. H. Bradford Westerfield, *Foreign Policy and Party Politics* (New Haven, 1955), pp. 227-39; *New York Times,* October 23, 25, 29, and 31, 1948. See also *The Forrestal Diaries* (note 24), pp. 346-47, 360, 363-64, and 441; and Redding (see note 5), pp. 148-50, 196, 215, and 253.

27. For a summary evaluation of the pursuit of ethnic voters by both parties see "Fight for Minority-Group Votes," *U.S. News and World Report,* September 10, 1948.

28. Based on correspondence between the author and Thomas E. Dewey, 1958. In 1958 Yarrow was vice president of the Free Europe Committee.

29. *New York Times,* August 18, 1948.

30. See also "Activities of the *Nationalities Division,*" Redding Papers, according to which McGrath established contact with Pope, "owner of the largest Italian language newspaper and foreign language radio station." The Nationalities Division was certain that "all Americans of Italian descent, being Catholic, were very much impressed by the conference of Senator Barkley with the Pope in Italy." A picture of the two was prominently displayed in *Il Progresso.*

31. *New York Times,* August 18, 1948. At his next press conference, August 19, President Truman opened with a prepared statement confirming the Knowles article. See Redding (note 5), pp. 216-21. See also *Washington Post, New York Herald Tribune,* and *Baltimore Sun,* August 20, 1948; J. Howard McGrath to the President, August 11, 1948, in J. Howard McGrath Papers (Harry S. Truman Library, Independence, Missouri); Luigi De Pasquale to McGrath, August 20 (with enclosure, Luigi Criscuolo to De Pasquale, August 19) and August 31, 1948, Truman Papers.

32. See pp. 30-31.

33. Redding (see note 5), pp. 221-22.

34. *Ibid.,* pp. 223-32, 259-62.

35. Samuel Lubell, "Who *Really* Elected Truman?," *Saturday Evening Post,* January 22, 1949.

36. This, apparently, was a reference to the Polish National Alliance and the Polish American Congress, both headed by Charles Rozmarek, who had declared for Dewey.

37. See p. 178.

38. The summary in "Activities of the *Nationalities Division,*" Redding Papers, signed by Senator Theodore F. Green, Antoine Gazda, and Mis (Michael) Cieplinski, stated categorically that "the vast majority of Americans of foreign descent voted Democratic in the 1948 election," citing wards, precincts, cities, and states which were newly Democratic or more strongly Democratic by large margins. See also "Facts How the Nationality Groups Supported President Truman," *ibid.,* and Redding (above, note 5), p. 262.

CHAPTER X

1. *National Party Platforms, 1840-1956,* comp. Kirk H. Porter and Donald Bruce Johnson (Urbana, 1956), pp. 436-47.

2. *Ibid.,* p. 429.

3. Fourteen years later, on June 6, 1952, Senator Everett M. Dirksen (Illinois) inserted in the *Congressional Record* Congressman Charles J. Kersten's (Wisconsin) address to the Conference of Americans of Slovak Descent, sponsored by the Slovak League of America, the title of which indicated the points Kersten stressed: "Inde-

pendent Slovakia Should Not Have Been Destroyed—Blundering Policies Responsible for Terrible Plight of Slovaks and Other Iron Curtain Countries—True Representatives of Slovak Nation Should be Heard and Recognized." U.S., *Congressional Record*, 82nd Cong., 2d Sess., XCVIII, Part 10, A3502-03.

4. The attitude of the Communist party of the United States then current was well delineated in the telegram sent to Roosevelt and members of Congress on September 11, 1939, by William Z. Foster and Earl Browder, chairman and general secretary of the party's national committee. "We wish to place on record our firm accord . . . against American involvement in the war. . . ." This, the leaders felt, corresponded with the President's ". . . expressed determination to exert our country's influence against extension of the warfare, especially as it involves the Americans. . . ." In the concluding paragraph, Foster and Browder called to Roosevelt's attention that United States policy was ". . . similar in most important respects to that . . . [of] the second most powerful nation, the Soviet Union. Both are neutral toward the rival imperialist ambitions and interests, both are deeply sympathetic to the peoples whose national independence is in jeopardy, both ardently desire and strive for an ordered and peaceful world, both wish to make the world safe for human culture, science, work and happiness." William Z. Foster and Earl Browder to Franklin D. Roosevelt, September 11, 1939, Roosevelt Papers, 463-C.

5. On December 7, 1941, at a banquet arranged by a small group of dedicated supporters of a Slav congress and attended by 1,400 Slavic-Americans, Attorney General Francis Biddle, who later was to denounce such "Communist fronts in no uncertain terms," addressed the group. The presence of Biddle "added prestige" to the gathering. U.S., Congress, House, Committee on Un-American Activities, *Report on the American Slav Congress and Associated Organizations*, 81st Cong., 2d Sess., 1949, Report 1951, p. 13. Harold Ickes, while Secretary of the Interior, also spoke at one Slav congress and read a message from President Roosevelt.

6. *Ibid.*, p. 1. The American Slav Congress was typical of the large network of Communist-front organizations which Soviet Russia brought into being "once the quarantine on the Soviet Union had been lifted in the fight against the Axis. . . ." Bernard Morris, in an able analysis of such organizations, said: "Successful initially in creating international organizations that included substantial non-Communist representation, the Kremlin soon saddled them with policy requirements which inevitably drove out the non-Communists and reduced the organizations to glorified paper mills, forms without substance, drums beating on the ears of a large, but captive, audience." Bernard S. Morris, "Communist Front Organizations," *World Politics*, IX (October, 1956), 79.

7. Cited in Edward J. Rozek, *Allied Wartime Diplomacy: A Pattern in Poland* (New York, 1958), pp. 174-75.

8. The American-Polish Labor Council was cited as subversive by Attorney General Tom C. Clark on December 4, 1947, and December 21, 1948.

9. Leo Krzycki to Franklin D. Roosevelt, March 21, 1945, Roosevelt Papers, 463-A.

10. Eugene Jasinski to James Barnes, April 9, 1945, *ibid.* For additional information on the activities of Communists within the American Polish community who endeavored to convince the State Department of Polish-American "support" of wartime decisions affecting the future of Poland, see Rozek (above, note 7), pp. 174-79.

11. William D. Hassett to Department of State, memo, April 6, 1945, Roosevelt Papers, 463-A.

12. L. Mlekowski to Franklin D. Roosevelt, February 26, 1945, *ibid.*

13. Committee on Un-American Activities, *Report on the American Slav Congress and Associated Organizations*, p. 17.

14. *Russky Golos,* August 25, 1946.

15. The meeting of the congress was held at the Manhattan Center, New York City, on September 20-22. The twelve major panels—Russian, Czechoslovak, Bulgarian-Macedonian, Croatian, Slovene, Polish, Serbian, Ukrainian, Carpatho-Russian, Youth, Trade Union, and Cultural—were held in the Center and nearby hotels.

16. Pirinsky was also national secretary of the Macedonian American People's League, an organization cited as subversive by Attorney General Tom C. Clark.

17. Evidently the White House became concerned over this meeting, particularly over Henry Wallace's support of the American Slav Congress. In the file on the American Slav Congress in the Truman Papers, there are many clippings from the American press which describe and analyze the proceedings of the congress, and which, among other things, call attention to "Byrnes' Name Booed, Wallace's Cheered . . ." and, as another stated, "Young Slavs in U.S. to be Wooed by Reds," September 26, 1946.

18. For a description of the activities of the Belgrade Conference see Committee on Un-American Activities (above, note 5), pp. 6-7.

19. Copy in the author's possession.

20. Krzycki called Tito the "Yugoslav George Washington," characterizing him as a "glamorous Hollywood figure, with a beautifully shaped head, immaculately dressed and refined in his manners"—the "undisputed idol of 15,000,000 Serbs, Croats, Slovenes, and Macedonians."

21. According to the Committee on Un-American Activities, a Milwaukee Polish language newspaper for February 6, 1946, attacked this invitation in the following manner:

"It appears that Krzycki will follow the Milwaukee Nazi (Eugene J. Buerk, who was deported to Germany in 1941 for recruiting Americans of German descent to work in German factories.) Many workers went (to Germany) and bitterly regretted it since. Krzycki wants Poland to be tied up with Russia as a Soviet puppet. Don't let any of you (Americans) betray the U.S.A. in behalf of Stalin." *Report on the American Slav Congress and Associated Organizations,* p. 33.

22. *Ibid.,* p. 30.

23. Harry S. Truman, *Memoirs,* II (Garden City, N.Y., 1956), 185.

24. According to Yaroslav Chyz, "Communist and Pro-Soviet Press and Organizations among the Ethnic Groups in the United States," Common Council for American Unity, 1950, there were 27 publications in 22 foreign languages and one in English that followed the Communist line in 1950. Their combined circulation was 147,549. It is significant that the circulation of the Communist *Daily Worker,* according to Ayer's 1950 *Directory of Newspapers and Periodicals,* was 23,400.

CHAPTER XI

1. *The Forrestal Diaries,* ed. Walter Millis (New York, 1951), p. 520.

2. Republican platform, 1952. See *National Party Platforms, 1840-1956,* comp. Kirk H. Porter and Donald Bruce Johnson (Urbana, 1956), p. 499.

3. See Republican National Committee, "The Margin of Victory in Marginal Districts," *Straight from the Shoulder,* III, No. 6 (1956). Twenty-eight million was a "rough approximation of first and second generation Americans in primarily industrial states." According to one ethnic adviser to the division, there were over 40,000,000 Slavic-Americans, representing 15,000,000 votes, and additional millions of "Americans of Italian, Mexican, Spanish, Portuguese, Rumanian, and Hungarian and other origin." See John J. Knezevich to Arthur Bliss Lane, January 22, 1955, in Arthur Bliss Lane Papers (Yale University Library, New Haven, Connecticut). Cited hereafter as Lane

Papers. Another correspondent estimated the Slavic-Americans represented 10,000,000 votes. Jack Cutler to Lane, September 20, 1952, *ibid.*

4. Lane retired from the Department of State on March 31, 1947. He was descended from William Bedford, second Governor of Plymouth Colony.

5. Arthur Bliss Lane, *I Saw Poland Betrayed: An American Ambassador Reports to the American People* (Indianapolis, 1948).

6. *Time,* September 22, 1952, p. 23, and *New York Times,* August 14, 1956. See also U.S., *Congressional Record,* XCVIII, No. 70 (April 25, 1952), A2626.

7. Lane to Earl T. Barnes, March 12, 1954, Lane Papers.

8. *Washington Times-Herald,* March 13, 1951. See also Lane to editor, *Times-Herald,* March 11, 1951; Elmer Davis to Lane, March 14 and April 8, 1951, Lane Papers.

9. Lane to S. Harrison Thomson, October 12, 1951, *ibid.*

10. Lane corresponded with Reinhold Niebuhr April 9 and May 24 and 25, 1954, *ibid.*

11. Lane's speech, Georgetown University Radio Forum, August 10, 1952, copy in Lane Papers. Compare this with the Republican platform of 1952, which said that the Republican espousal of liberation was one of the policies which "will inevitably set up strains and stresses within the captive world which will make the rulers impotent to continue in their monstrous ways and mark the beginning of their end." See *National Party Platforms, 1840-1956* (above, note 2), p. 499. See also below.

12. Lane to John Lodge, June 18, 1951, Lane Papers.

13. Lane to Barnes, March 12, 1954; to S. J. Skubik, January 23, 1952; to Herbert Hoover, January 23, 1952; Guy Gabrielson to Harold Stassen, January 24, 1952; and to Earl Warren, January 24, 1952, *ibid.*

14. Lane to Robert Taft, January 25, 1952, *ibid.*

15. Lane to Barnes, March 12, 1954, *ibid.*

16. Lane to Stassen, January 30, 1952, *ibid.*

17. Lane to Warren, March 10, 1952, *ibid.* See also Lane to Warren, January 11, 1952, *ibid.*

18. Lane to Dwight D. Eisenhower, April 8, 1952, *ibid.*

19. Lane to L. Corrin Strong, April 8, 1952, *ibid.*

20. Copy in the author's possession.

21. See Charles J. Kersten, "A Foreign Policy of Liberation for the 1952 Republican Platform," U.S., *Congressional Record,* 82d Cong., 2d Sess., 1952, XCVIII, No. 108, A4073-74; and Hugh A. Bone, *Party Committees and National Politics* (Seattle, 1958), p. 91.

22. Lane to Barnes, March 12, 1954, Lane Papers.

23. John Foster Dulles, *War or Peace* (New York, 1950), p. 136.

24. John Foster Dulles, "A Policy of Boldness," *Life,* May 19, 1952, pp. 146-60.

25. Republican platform, 1952. See *National Party Platforms, 1840-1956* (above, note 2), pp. 497 and 499.

26. Cutler to Lane, September 20, 1952; and Benjamin Mandel to Lane, August 15, 1952, Lane Papers. See also Lane to Gerald Keith, February 21, 1952; Harry A. Bullis to Lane, July 12, 1952; and Lane to William E. Dunn, March 11, 1952, *ibid.*

27. Nicholas T. Stepanovich, a friend of Peter II of Yugoslavia, wrote, "I talked to Joe Jackovics . . . and I'm convinced that Joe has a plan that can furnish the spark we need during the last few weeks of the campaign. I know that in dealing with leaders of foreign extractions many of them have sensitive feelings and must be 'handled with care.' I know that Joe knows their problem and whims and can be of great help." Stepanovich to Lane, October 10, 1952, *ibid.* See also Waldo J. Nielsen

to Lane, September 29, 1952; T. Bielecki to Lane, June 19, 1952; and Robert A. Vogeler to Lane, September 21, 1952, *ibid.*

28. A. B. Hermann to Iona McNulty, July 30, 1951; and Pat Calder to McNulty, July 9, 1951, *ibid.*

29. Waclaw Wusza to McNulty, July 20, 1951, *ibid.*

30. *Ibid.* See also Wusza to Lane, August 13 and 27, 1951; February 17, May 20, June 10, July 14 and 19, August 10 and 13, and September 17, 1952, *ibid.*

31. Lane to Adolf A. Berle, January 3, 1952; and to Wusza, January 28, 1952, *ibid.* Lane declined to recommend Wusza, because there were certain features of the National Committee for Free Europe with which he was not in "complete agreement," telling him to seek other sponsors. Lane to Wusza, March 23, 1953, *ibid.*

32. Material in the author's possession. See also publications of the Common Council for American Unity concerning foreign-language publications and radio stations.

33. Leroy A. Mullen to Lane, January 4 and 15 (with enclosure, Max Sherover to A. B. Hermann, memorandum), 1952; and Sherover to Wayne J. Hood, August 4, 1952.

34. *Human Events,* June 11, 1952, copy in Lane Papers. See also E. O. Militzer to Lane, November 13, 1952; and Cutler to Lane, September 20, 1952, Lane Papers.

35. *Human Events,* June 11, 1952, copy in Lane Papers; and Militzer to Lane, November 13, 1952, Lane Papers. See also Jan Wszelaki to Lane, November 6, 1952; Arthur E. Summerfield to Lane, August 1, 1952; and Lane's memorandum "Psychological Warfare and the Policy of Liberation," January, 1953, *ibid.;* and *Newsweek,* September 1, 1952, p. 7.

36. Wusza to Lane, July 14, 1952, Lane Papers.

37. Wusza to Lane, August 15, 1952, *ibid.*

38. Democratic platform, 1952. See *National Party Platforms, 1840-1956* (above, note 2), pp. 476 and 477.

39. *New York Times,* August 14, 1952.

40. *Ibid.,* August 26, 1952. Kersten used this part of Eisenhower's speech as a pre-amble to a series of House Concurrent Resolutions (114-20) which expressed Congressional hope for early liberation of the peoples of China, Bulgaria, Albania, Czechoslovakia, Hungary, Rumania, and Poland. For texts see U.S., *Congressional Record,* 83d Cong., 1st Sess., 1953, XCIX, Part 11, A3744, A3748, A3750, A3753, A3756, A3759, A3762, and A3765; and *ibid.,* Part 2, 1635-37.

41. *New York Times,* October 5, 1952.

42. *Ibid.,* October 6, 1952.

43. Lane to Barnes, March 12, 1954; to Leonard Hall, July 8, 1954; and to Mrs. Howard Coffin, July 23, 1954, Lane Papers.

44. *New York Times,* October 12, 1952.

45. Wusza to Lane, July 31, 1952, Lane Papers. See also *Chicago Tribune,* October 3, 1952.

46. *New York Times,* September 1, 1952.

47. Wusza to Lane, October 1, 1952; Francis J. Nahurski to Lane, November 15, 1952; and Lane to Wusza, November 20, 1951, Lane Papers.

48. List of directors in the author's possession.

49. Copy in the author's possession.

50. Enclosure, William DuRoss to McNulty, October 20, 1952, Lane Papers.

51. Knezevich to Lane, October 13, 1952; Mrs. Tony Whan to Lane, October 9 and 17, 1952; Karol Ripa to Lane, October 24, 1952; Vladimir N. Petrov to Lane, September 29, 1952; Sylwin Strakacz to Lane, October 2, 1952; Vincent J. Kowalewski

to Lane, September 24, 1952; David Keyser to Lane, September 6, 1952; and list of Lane's speeches, *ibid.*

52. *New York Times,* October 26, 1952.

53. Rear platform remarks of President Truman at Parkersburg, West Virginia, September 2, 1952, Truman Papers, Records of the White House Official Reporter.

54. Copy in the author's possession.

55. Democratic platform, 1952. See *National Party Platforms, 1840-1956* (above, note 2), p. 477. The section on immigration ended sententiously: "We will eliminate distinctions between nativeborn and naturalized citizens. We want no 'second-class' citizens in free America."

56. Truman Papers, Records of the White House Official Reporter.

57. RD-83, RD-76, and RD-77 (September, 1952), Research Division, Democratic National Committee. Copies in the author's possession.

58. See Michael J. Wargovich to John A. Danaher, November 5, 1952; Lane to Frank R. Barnett, November 19, 1952; to Keith, December 8, 1952; and Knezevich to Lane, December 4, 1952, Lane Papers.

59. See Lane to Wes Roberts, March 23, 1953, *ibid.* On July 22, 1953, Lane wrote Strong that he was convinced the continual emphasis on the repudiation of the Yalta Agreement brought "at least two million normally Democratic voters to the Republican side." Two months later he returned to his original estimate. "In 1952, 3,000,000 normally Democrat voters from these ethnic marginal groups voted for Ike, whose victory, if I am not mistaken, amounted to 6,000,000. A switch of 3,000,000 would have spelt a different story." Lane to Mrs. Peter Vischer, July 24, 1954, *ibid.* See also Republican National Committee, "The Margin of Victory in Marginal Districts."

60. Copy in the author's possession.

CHAPTER XII

1. James Burnham, *Containment or Liberation: An Inquiry into the Aims of the United States Foreign Policy* (New York, 1953), p. 228. It is significant that Burnham based his analysis on the interpretation of an Hungarian exile (Francis Honti) to which he added other "meanings," *ibid.,* pp. 219-30. In 1957, when liberation had been forgotten, he radically revised his ideas about it. See *National Review,* January 19, 1957.

2. Russell Baker, "Dulles Looks at Dulles' Policy," *New York Times,* April 28, 1957; and U.S., Congress, Senate, Committee on Foreign Relations, *Hearing, Nomination of John Foster Dulles, Secretary of State-Designate,* 83d Cong., 1st Sess., January 15, 1953.

3. Arthur Bliss Lane to Leonard Hall, June 18, 1953; and to L. Corrin Strong, July 22, 1953, Lane Papers.

4. Lane's memorandum "Psychological Warfare and the Policy of Liberation," January, 1953, *ibid.*

5. Lane to John Foster Dulles, January 7, 1953, *ibid.*

6. Lane's memorandum "Psychological Warfare and the Policy of Liberation," *ibid.*

7. U.S., *Congressional Record,* 83d Cong., 1st Sess., 1953, XCIX, Part 9, A121 and A1024.

8. *Ibid.,* Part 1, pp. 67, 68, 318, 435, and 756.

9. *New York Times,* February 4, 1953. See also Lane to George Creel, February 4, 1953, Lane Papers.

10. Lane to Creel, February 2 and 4, 1953; to Alexander Wiley, February 3, 1953; and Homer Ferguson to Lane, February 7, 1953, *ibid.*

11. U.S., *Congressional Record,* 83d Cong., 1st Sess., 1953, XCIX, Part 11, A3849.

12. Lane to Creel, January 30 and February 2, 1953; and Lane's memorandum "Psychological Warfare and the Policy of Liberation," Lane Papers.

13. *New York Times,* January 27, 1953. See also Lane to Creel, February 2, 1953; and Lane's memorandum of conference with Wiley, January 31, 1953, Lane Papers; U.S., *Congressional Record,* 83d Cong., 1st Sess., XCIX, Part 9, A149-51; and *ibid.,* Part 1, p. 390.

14. U.S., Congress, Senate, *Inaugural Address of Dwight D. Eisenhower,* 83d Cong., 1st Sess., 1953, Senate Doc. 9. See also *New York Times,* January 25, 1953; and U.S., *Congressional Record,* 83d Cong., 1st Sess., XCIX, Part 9, A380 and A605.

15. Lane to Arthur E. Summerfield, November 26, 1952; to John A. Danaher, December 15, 1952; to Thomas B. Cerajewski, December 16, 1952; to Nicholas T. Stepanovich, December 19, 1952; and memo to Karl E. Mundt, December 19, 1952, Lane Papers.

16. John Knezevich to Lane, December 4, 1952; and Waclaw Wusza to Lane, November 25, 1952, *ibid.*

17. Wusza to Lane, November 25, 1952, and March 4, 1953, *ibid.* See also translation of Wusza article, *Dziennik Dla Wszystkich,* January 29, 1955, attached to Wusza to Lane, February 7, 1955, *ibid.*

18. Lane to Bayard Ewing, February 16, 1953; to Carl Glazewski, December 16, 1952; to E. O. Militzer, December 10, 1952; and Stanley R. Pratt to Lane, January 13, 1953, *ibid.*

19. U.S., Department of State, *Bulletin,* February 9, 1953, pp. 207-11.

20. U.S., *Congressional Record,* 83d Cong., 1st Sess., XCIX, Part 9, 756 and 1344.

21. *Ibid.,* p. A614.

22. Lane to Dwight D. Eisenhower, February 5, 1953; and to Knezevich, February 16, 1953, Lane Papers.

23. U.S., Department of State, *American Foreign Policy, 1950-1955: Basic Documents* (Washington, 1957), II, Publication 6446, 1957-59.

24. *Ibid.,* p. 1958 n. See also U.S., *Congressional Record,* 83d Cong., 1st Sess., XCIX, Part 9, A820-21; and *ibid.,* Part 10, A1801. Senator Lyndon B. Johnson, Democratic minority leader, in his review of the first session, stated, "President Eisenhower's request that Congress join him in a condemnation of Soviet bad faith was buried in committee because the Republican members could not accept the language that he proposed." U.S., Congress, Senate, *Legislative Review: Eighty-Third Congress, First Session,* 83d Cong., 1st Sess., Senate Doc. 76. Senator William F. Knowland, Republican majority leader, did not allude to the request in his review of the first session. U.S., Congress, Senate, *Republican Congress: Seven Months' Progress,* 83d Cong., 1st Sess., Senate Doc. 75.

25. Lane to Creel, February 25, 1953; and to Leon Nicolai, March 23, 1953, Lane Papers.

26. *Human Events,* March 25, 1953, copy in Lane Papers.

27. Lane to Creel, March 27, 1953; to Wesley Roberts, March 23, 1953; and to Hall, June 18, 1953, Lane Papers.

28. *Human Events,* March 25, 1953, copy in Lane Papers.

29. See Samuel Lubell, "Who *Really* Elected Eisenhower?" *Saturday Evening Post,* January 10, 1953.

30. Lane to Creel, June 24, 1953, Lane Papers. See U.S., Congress, Senate, Committee on Foreign Relations, *Hearings on the Nomination of Charles E. Bohlen,* 83d Cong., 1st Sess., March 2 and 18, 1953. It was evident during the hearings that many

Senators had been influenced by Lane and James Burnham's writings on liberation. See also James W. Rosenau, *The Nomination of "Chip" Bohlen* (New York, 1958).

31. U.S., *Congressional Record,* 83d Cong., 1st Sess., XCIX, Part 10, A1801; and *ibid.,* Part 2, 2277 ff.

32. *Ibid.,* Part 11, A3917.

33. Lane to Danaher, July 1 and 6, 1953, Lane Papers.

34. U.S., Department of State (see note 23), pp. 1745-46.

35. U.S., *Congressional Record,* 83d Cong., 1st Sess., XCIX, Part 11, A3744, A3748, A3750, A3753, A3756, A3759, A3762, A3765; and *ibid.,* Part 2, 1635-37.

36. *Ibid.,* Part 11, A3849-50.

37. Lane to William DuRoss, March 12, 1954, Lane Papers.

38. Lane to Strong, July 22, 1953, *ibid.*

39. Lane to Paul Sapieha, July 28, 1953; to J. Paull Marshall, November 30, 1953; and to John Marshall, October 26, 1953, *ibid.*

40. DuRoss to Lane, March 3, 1954; and Lane to DuRoss, March 12, 1954, *ibid.*

41. Lane to Hall, July 8, 1954; to William Tonesk, February 2, 1954; Tonesk to Lane, February 14, 1954; and Wusza to Lane, July 21, 1953, *ibid.*

42. Lane to Mrs. Peter Vischer, July 24, 1954; Lane to Mrs. Howard Coffin, July 23, 1954; and DuRoss to Lane, July 14, 1954, *ibid.*

43. Lane to Stephen Gobozy, John W. Tauchen, Dean Biky, Knezevich, Blair Gunther, Ewing, Cerajewski, Nicolai, George Mardikian, Wusza, Charles Rozmarek, Thomas Peska, and Stepanovich, December 8, 1954, *ibid.* See also Lane to Mrs. Ogden Reid, December 10, 1954; Rozmarek to Lane, December 22, 1954; Lane to Petrov, November 24, 1954; to Antoni Sadlak, November 29, 1954; to Edward J. Bonin, December 8, 1954; to Francis J. Wazeter, December 7, 1954, *ibid.*

44. Lane to Hall, December 10, 1954, and January 11, 1955; Cerajewski to Lane, December 31, 1954, and March 3, 1955; Serge Belosselsky to Lane, March 24, 1956; Lane to Keith, March 16, 1956; Mardikian to Lane, December 10, 1954; Knezevich to Lane, January 22, 1955; and Petrov to Lane, December 15, 1954, *ibid.*

45. Lane to Gunther, February 10, 1955; to Hall, December 8, 1954, and January 31, 1955; to Knezevich, July 18, 1955; and Ewing to Lane, December 13, 1954, *ibid.* The only "bright hope" was the publication of the Yalta Papers, which some Republican leaders thought would "embarrass the Democratic party with minority groups in the large urban centers." See James Reston, "Yalta Disclosures Held up as Democrats Fight Move," *New York Times,* March 15, 1955.

46. Lane to Knezevich, July 18, 1955; Gunther to Lane, February 3, 1955; Lane to Gunther, February 10, 1955; to Mrs. Stanley Hawks, February 9, 1955; Lane's momorandum of conversation with Burton K. Wheeler, December 1, 1955, Lane Papers.

47. Memorandum attached to A. B. Hermann to Lane, February 13, 1956; Lane to Cerajewski, February 1, 1956; Rozmarek to Lane, February 2 and 7, 1956; Lane to Hermann, February 15 and March 8, 1956; to Hall, March 8, 1956; and Hall to Lane, March 13, 1956, *ibid.*

48. Lane to Keith, June 26, 1956; to Frank J. Lausche, April 23, 1956; and to Dulles, March 14, 1956, *ibid.*

49. Republican National Committee, "The Margin of Victory in Marginal Districts," *Straight from the Shoulder,* III, No. 6 (1956); and John Marshall to Lane, July 3, 1956, Lane Papers.

50. Lane to Hermann, July 6 and 19, 1956; Hermann to Lane, July 18, 1956; Lane's memorandum of conversation with Hermann, July 20, 1956, *ibid.;* and Lane to editor, *New York Times,* July 13, 1956.

51. *New York Herald Tribune,* July 31, 1956.

52. Republican platform, 1956. See *National Party Platforms, 1840-1956*, comp. Kirk H. Porter and Donald Bruce Johnson (Urbana, 1956).

53. Democratic platform, 1956. See *ibid.*, p. 526.

CHAPTER XIII

1. Copies of witnesses' statements made to Foreign Policy Subcommittee, Resolution (Platform) Committee, Republican National Convention, July 19 and 20, 1960, in possession of the author.

2. U.S., *Congressional Record*, 83d Cong., 1st Sess., May 20, 1953, XCIX, Part 11, A2779. From speech of Blair Gunther, censor, Polish National Alliance.

3. Florence E. Gibson, *The Attitudes of the New York Irish toward State and National Affairs, 1848-1892* (New York, 1951), p. 65.

4. John Rutherford, *The Secret History of the Fenian Conspiracy* (London, 1877), II, 242.

5. *Ibid.*, pp. 295-97.

6. Herbert Feis, *Churchill—Roosevelt—Stalin: The War They Waged and the Peace They Sought* (Princeton, 1957), p. 522 n. See also U.S., Congress, House, *Foreign Relations of the United States, Diplomatic Papers: The Conferences at Malta and Yalta, 1945*, 84th Cong., 1st Sess., House Doc. 154 (Washington, 1955), p. 677.

7. Norman Graebner, *The New Isolationism: A Study in Politics and Foreign Policy since 1950* (New York, 1956), p. 8. See also Samuel Lubell, *The Revolt of the Moderates* (New York, 1956), pp. 76-81.

8. Louis Wirth made the following observation shortly before the United States entered the Second World War:

"As during and immediately following the first World War a number of renascent European minorities, including the Czechs, the Poles, and the Irish, had drawn upon the moral and material support of their respective former compatriots in the United States, so today the conquered nations of Europe may well look to the immigrants they have sent to these shores to vitalize the struggle to regain their freedom from Nazi domination. While this will, of course, add to our strength in our national defense effort, it may also lead to a less rational formulation of our national policy, especially our war and peace aims, in the attempt not to offend the national aspirations of these various conquered countries and in the further effort to minimize the conflict between these various groups here." "Morale and Minority Groups," *American Journal of Sociology*, XLVII (November, 1941), 425 n.

9. At the 1960 Republican platform hearings Lev Dobriansky, Ukrainian-American leader, urged the party to strengthen its liberation promises, asking that it not be deluded by what he called "the myth of Soviet unity and power." To Dobriansky it made "little rational sense to hail the new states of Africa which have far less national sinews of historical continuity, geographical contiguity, religion, customs, language, mores, law, common experiences of war and peace, heroes and arts than the majority captive non-Russian nations in the U.S.S.R., and to overlook these nations situated at the very base of the enemy of the free world." Copy of statement to Foreign Policy Subcommittee, Resolution (Platform) Committee, Republican National Convention, July 20, 1960, in possession of the author.

10. *Nile's Weekly Register*, XX (July 21, 1821), 326 ff., cited in Foster Rhea Dulles, *America's Rise to World Power, 1898-1954* (New York, 1954), p. 6.

11. Samuel Flagg Bemis, *John Quincy Adams and the Foundations of American Foreign Policy* (New York, 1949), pp. 388-89.

12. William D. Hassett to Cordell Hull, May 18, 1936; Hull to Stephen Early, May

19, 1936; to Harold L. Ickes, May 19, 1936; and copy of speech, Roosevelt Papers, PPF 601. It is ironic that Hull, a disciple of Woodrow Wilson and an internationalist, should have felt it necessary to be concerned about movements in the United States directed toward the liberation of the homelands of ethnic Americans. For another instance of his attitude in regard to ethnic organizations, see p. 277, note 45, above.

13. Copy of speech in the author's possession.

14. Lithuanian- as well as Polish-Americans claim Kosciuszko as a "son" who "gave his genius and his sword to America in her struggle for independence." See memo submitted to the Senate Committee on Foreign Relations by the Lithuanian National Council. U.S., Congress, Senate, *Treaty of Peace with Germany: Hearings before the Committee on Foreign Relations*, 66th Cong., 1st Sess., 1919, Senate Doc. 106, p. 718.

15. Quoted by Thomas A. Bailey, *A Diplomatic History of the American People* (5th ed.; New York, 1955), p. 287, from *The Writings and Speeches of Daniel Webster*, ed. J. W. McIntyre (National ed.; Boston, 1903), XIII, 461, 426.

16. Barbara Miller Solomon, *Ancestors and Immigrants* (Cambridge, 1956), p. 56. Stung by recriminations and attacks from some Irish-American leaders, Lowell lost his balanced perspective and repeated Parnell's "distinction between 'the American people' and 'the Irish nation in America.'" *Papers Relating to the Foreign Relations of the United States* (Washington, 1882), p. 504. See also Florence E. Gibson (above, note 3), pp. 340-41.

17. "Steam from the Melting Pot," *Fortune*, XXVI (September, 1942).

18. *Ibid.*

19. Harry Schwartz reporting in the *New York Times*, January 27, 1957, and Sidney Hyman, "Mr. Dillon and the Fight for Foreign Aid," *Reporter*, March 20, 1958, p. 10. According to Schwartz, a "potent role" in the reversal in the Polish-American attitudes toward Gomulka was the "reports of several prominent Americans of Polish origin who visited Poland recently. These individuals reported that Mr. Gomulka had wide support among the Polish people and, that while economic conditions in Poland were very difficult, there was a newer and more free climate."

When Polish-American leaders came out in support of the Oder-Neisse line soon after Gomulka's rise to power, the Steuben Society of America adopted a resolution at its eighteenth national convention which, among other things, stated: "We maintain that it is un-American . . . for American citizens and representatives of American foreign language publications to meet with representatives of foreign governments in foreign capitals for the purpose of formulating policies to be executed on our shores, as was done at Warsaw, when the idea of 'Polonia' was conceived, which had for its purpose the conditioning of American public opinion to acquiesce in Poland's illegal acquisition of East Prussia, Pomerania, Silesia, and the Free City of Danzig." The resolution further noted "with dismay the bolstering of the Communist government of Poland with American tax dollars. . . ." *Sudeten Bulletin*, VI, No. 11 (1958), 252. Evidently this German-American organization felt that its activities urging support of a united Germany and the return of those German territories now under Polish control to a reunited Germany did not constitute "un-American" activities.

20. *New York Times*, January 27, 1957.

21. Yaroslav Chyz, "Communist and pro-Soviet Press and Organizations among the Ethnic Groups in the United States," 1950. Paper in the author's possession.

22. Rose Hum Lee, *The Chinese in the United States of America* (Hong Kong, 1960), pp. 428-30.

23. During the height of the 1958 crisis in Lebanon, which necessitated the dispatch of American Marines, the *Lebanese American Journal* asked its readers to "shower" the State Department, President Eisenhower, and Secretary of State Dulles with requests

"to stand firm" and with statements that the Lebanese-Americans were supporting them in the struggle against Nasser's United Arab Republic's attempts to control the "half-Christian and half-Moslem" state. The *Lebanese American Journal* also warned of "some of our Arabic speaking people" who "follow the UAR-Communist line regarding Lebanon." *Lebanese American Journal*, May 21, June 25, and July 16, 1958. In the editorial "Here We Go Again!," August 1, 1959, the same paper showed its concern over an article in the *Beirut Weekly* which had described some 500 Lebanese-Americans then in Lebanon as "Americans of ARABIC speaking descent" by stating: "First we're 'Lebanese'. Then we're 'Arabs'. Probably this week sometime we'll hear we're 'Syrians'. Then it will be 'Arabs' for two weeks more and finally in October we'll be called 'Lebanese' again. . . .

"And what is unfair to the governments abroad as well as to us is that Sado and Ansara [executives of the National Association of Federations of Syrian Lebanese American Clubs] claim they represent '500,000 Americans of Arabic speaking ancestry'." See also editorial, *Lebanese American Journal*, August 22, 1959. According to the *Oakland Tribune*, May 7, 1959, the State Department "endorsed" the third overseas convention of the National Association of Federations of Syrian Lebanese American Clubs, to which there were nearly 500 American delegates. In an editorial in the October 3, 1959, issue of the *Lebanese American Journal* came the warning, "We will declare a war against those who are trying to force a wedge between the immigrants and their motherland, Lebanon." It went on to attack those representatives of Lebanese societies who, speaking individually for the collective body without any authorization, extended "their cordial cooperation with the United Arab Republic," even asking Nasser to send instructors from Egypt for the emigrants' children.

24. George Kennan, *Russia Leaves the War* (Princeton, 1956), pp. 12-13. There are some, however, who believe "that a century and more of immigration has resulted in the enlightenment of American opinion about Europe." See "The Fabric of American Opinion on Foreign Affairs," *International Affairs*, XXVIII (1952), 147.

25. Arnold Toynbee, "La guerra missionaria," *Il Mondo* (Rome), October 20, 1959, pp. 3-4. I am indebted to my colleague, Professor Norman Kogan, for bringing Toynbee's remarks to my attention, as well as for his translation.

26. Harrison E. Salisbury, *New York Times*, October 22, 1957.

27. *New York Times*, July 10, 1959.

28. See Chapter X.

29. William J. Petrus to Franklin D. Roosevelt, August 13, 1942, Roosevelt Papers, OF 300, NY "V."

30. In an article analyzing causes for the defeat of a prominent Polish-American running for political office in Pennsylvania, *Ameryka-Echo* (November 15, 1959) urged its readers to prepare for the 1960 elections by joining with neighboring nationality groups favorably disposed to them. Bemoaning the disaffection of the younger generation, it concluded, "In time it will be difficult to ride the Polish-American horse, for the young generation does not speak Polish, it changes its name, leaves Polish parishes, and sends its children to foreign schools. Thus we lose much. Nevertheless, we still can have a political effect. Therefore, there is need to organize."

31. Lee (see note 22), pp. 425-28.

32. *Saturday Evening Post*, December 1, 1956.

33. U.S., *Congressional Record*, 86th Cong., 2d Sess., April 25, 1960, CVI, No. 74, 8015. The Logan Act reads in part:

"Any citizen of the United States, wherever he may be, who, without authority of the United States, directly or indirectly commences or carries on any correspondence or intercourse with any foreign government or any officer or agent thereof, with intent to influence the measures or conduct of any foreign government or of any officer or agent thereof, in relation to any disputes or controversies with the United States, or to defeat the measures of the United States, shall be fined not more than $5,000 or imprisoned not more than 3 years, or both" *(ibid.).*

Chapter XIV

1. Thomas A. Bailey, *A Diplomatic History of the American People* (6th ed.; New York, 1955), pp. 4-5. See also Julius Turner, *Party and Constituency: Pressures on Congress* (Baltimore, 1952), pp. 54-58, 98-127, 178-79; Frederick W. Williams, "Recent Voting Behavior of Some Nationality Groups," *American Political Science Review,* XL (1946); Louis Bean, *How to Predict Elections* (New York, 1948); Lawrence H. Fuchs, *The Political Behavior of American Jews* (Chicago, 1956); Louis Bean, F. Mosteller, and Frederick W. Williams, "Nationalities and 1944," *Public Opinion Quarterly,* VIII (fall, 1944), 368-75; Samuel Lubell, *The Future of American Politics* (New York, 1952); Donald R. Taft and Richard Robbins, *International Migrations* (New York, 1955), pp. 542-48; and Gabriel A. Almond, *The American People and Foreign Policy* (New York, 1950).

2. Thomas A. Bailey, *The Man in the Street: The Impact of American Public Opinion on Foreign Policy* (New York, 1948), pp. 15-18; Dorothy Thompson, "America Demands a Single Loyalty," *Commentary,* IX (March, 1950), 210-19; Oscar Handlin, "America Recognizes Diverse Loyalties," *ibid.,* 220-26, republished in another form as "Israel and the Mission of America," Handlin, *Race and Nationality in American Life* (Garden City, N.Y., 1957); Taft and Robbins, *International Migrations,* pp.547-48; Roy V. Peel, *The Political Clubs of New York City* (New York, 1935), p. 267; "The Fabric of American Opinion on Foreign Affairs," *International Affairs,* XXVIII (1952), 145; and speech delivered at the Czechoslovak Society of America Jubilee Banquet, March 7, 1959, St. Louis, Missouri, by Joseph Martinek, copy in possession of the author.

3. Copy of statement to Foreign Policy Subcommittee, Resolution (Platform) Committee, 1960 Republican National Convention, in the author's possession.

4. Interview with United States Senator, 1958.

5. James MacGregor Burns, "Professor in the Political Maze," *New York Times,* August 31, 1958.

6. *New York Times,* February 22, 1959.

7. In response to Representative Francis E. Walter's urging that the parties abolish their Nationalities Divisions, Democratic National Chairman John M. Bailey said, "Such an operation [as his party's Nationalities Division] will not be needed when American citizens of foreign descent are fully assimilated into political activities and other phases of civic activity in their communities. Until they are, I believe our Nationalities Division is performing a useful service." *New York Times,* January 27, 1962.

8. Johan J. Smertenko, "The Emerging Hyphen," *Harper's Magazine,* CCIII (August, 1951).

9. Charles P. Taft, "Campaign to Stop the Campaign Smear," *New York Times,* October 12, 1958.

10. In his 1942 appeal to President Roosevelt to support the nomination of Edward Vaczy for Congressman at Large, William Petrus, president of the Federation of Slovak Clubs of New York, supplied a characteristic *rationale* for the balanced ticket:

"In these crucial times when the Slavic Countries, Czechoslovakia, Poland and Jugo-Slovia, have been almost wiped out by the barbaric action of the psychopathic

Hitler regime, and the brave and courageous fight that the Russians are putting up . . . the sympathy of the world is with these Slav Peoples. . . .

"Nomination of Mr. Vaczy for the office of Congressman at Large would be timely at this psychological moment. It would encourage the Slavs, both here and in Europe, in their fight against our common enemy, by knowing that the most populated State in the United States had honored one of their own to the high office of Congressman at Large. The American Slav would definitely feel that they were not a forgotten People." William J. Petrus to Franklin D. Roosevelt, August 13, 1942, Roosevelt Papers, OF 300, NY "V."

11. Cited in Moses Rischin, *"Our Own Kind"* (Santa Barbara, Calif.: Center for the Study of Democratic Institutions, 1960).

12. The recent election of Edmund S. Muskie, a Polish-American, as Maine's United States Senator, is a good illustration of this. It is ironic that in states like Illinois, Michigan, and Connecticut, which have large numbers of Polish-Americans, the "balanced ticket" tends to preclude the nomination of a Polish-American for the Senate, whereas Maine, which has a number too small to weigh in the political formula, can send to Washington an able man such as Governor Muskie—the first Polish-American to sit in the upper chamber.

"Strange are the ways of our politics," editorially commented the *Dziennik Chicagoski* after Muskie's election to the Senate. "Here, in Chicago, where the Polish vote constitutes a strong bloc, we were not able, despite many endeavors, to elect a mayor from one of the leaders of the Polish community, while in the State of Maine, where there are almost no citizens of Polish origin, the governor for the last four years was Edmund S. Muskie (Marciszewski). . . ."

13. See Smertenko (note 8); Joseph P. Lyford, *Candidate* (New York, 1959); Duane Lockard, *New England State Politics* (Princeton, 1959); Louis Wirth, "Morale and Minority Groups," *American Journal of Sociology*, XLVII (November, 1941), 429 ff. The 1958 Rockefeller victory in New York, according to Leo Egan, "disproved a theory that voters of Italian origin would flock to the Democratic ticket because the Republicans had failed to name anyone of Italian extraction for state-wide office." *New York Times*, November 6, 1958.

14. *New York Times*, August 17, 1958; editorial, "Race and Politics," *ibid.*, August 10, 1958; and Ray Tucker, "The National Whirligig," *Berkeley Daily Gazette*, September 5, 1958.

15. Robert Bendiner, "De Sapio's Big Moment, or the Rout of the Innocents," *Reporter*, October 16, 1958.

16. *Ibid.* The slate envisioned by Bendiner may yet become a reality. In December, 1959, a national committee was formed, following a national congress of Indians, to elect to the U.S. Senate the first full-blooded American Indian. *Hartford Times*, December 16, 1959.

17. Following the selection of Senator John Kennedy of Massachusetts as "man of the year" by Polish-Americans in Chicago, the *Dziennik Chicagoski*, February 12, 1958, editorialized: "The Polonia of America, in the interests of Poland, needs friends. . . . men of influence . . . of authority in the high echelons of government. . . . Such men of authority Germans have, Jews have, not to mention the Irish and even the French. . . . Therefore, whenever an important citizen is found, who, without our attempts, turns to us in a friendly manner, it is imperative we show him gratitude and help him get elected.

"This, by the way, is exactly what we are doing . . . as far as Senator Kennedy is concerned."

18. Nathan Glazer, "America's Ethnic Pattern," *Commentary*, XV (1953), 407. See

also David Rodnick, "Group Frustration in Connecticut," *American Journal of Sociology*, XLVII (1941-1942), 157-66.

19. *Lebanese American Journal*, October 22, 1958. See also editorial in *Dziennik Chicagoski*, September 21, 1959, which commends to its Polish-American readers the example of the Jewish-American activities in behalf of Israel: "The solidarity of Americans of Jewish origin with the land of their forefathers and their sacrifice must produce surprise in everybody. They are not ashamed of their origin, they are not afraid lest this will not be liked by somebody. Their attachment is not expressed merely in words or by patriotic hurrahs, but concretely in the form of real and useful help to Israel. For this reason it is worthwhile to follow their footsteps."

20. Copy in the author's possession.

21. Harold B. Hoskins, "American Unity and Our Foreign-Born Citizens," *The Annals*, CCXX (March, 1942), 156.

22. Bailey (see note 2), pp. 15-18.

23. Even after Hitler's invasion of Norway, many Midwestern farmers of Norwegian descent remained isolationists. See Sigrid Undset, "Norway and Norwegian Americans," *Common Ground*, II (spring, 1942), 73-76.

24. Henry L. Roberts and Paul A. Wilson, *Britain and the United States: Problems in Co-operation* (London: Royal Institute of International Affairs, 1953), p. 28.

25. *The Letters and Friendships of Sir Cecil Spring Rice*, ed. Stephen Gwynn (Boston, 1929), II, 362.

26. U.S., *Congressional Record*, 85th Cong., 1st Sess., August 9, 1957, CIII, No. 143, A6523.

27. Richard H. Rovere, "Letter from Washington," *New Yorker*, August 29, 1959, p. 96.

28. The lack of professional achievement by contemporary ethnic leaders is becoming more evident. In response to a survey on how the younger Czech generation in exile conceives of its role, Professor Jiri Liska of the University of Chicago recommended that intellectuals who wish to take effective measures to influence American foreign policy become recognized leaders in their respective fields in order that their opinions would carry a greater weight—especially since they would then be less suspect as propagandizers. *Zápisník*, October-December, 1958. I am indebted to my colleague, Professor Curt Beck, for bringing this article to my attention, as well as for his translation.

29. Copy of #29348 in the author's possession.

30. A striking example of Roosevelt's skill in this maneuver is shown in the successful outcome of his trainside meeting during the 1944 campaign tour with Charles Rozmarek, who was supposed to have previously pledged Polish-American support to Dewey. "Rozmarek was touched by the President's gesture and replied, 'Yes, Mr. President, we shall stick with you to the end.'" Edward J. Rozek, *Allied Wartime Diplomacy: A Pattern in Poland* (New York, 1958), p. 324 n. See also Arthur Bliss Lane, *I Saw Poland Betrayed: An American Ambassador Reports to the American People* (Indianapolis, 1948), pp. 61-62.

31. Copy, including list of officers, in the author's possession. In the 1960 campaign the confederation, claiming to represent 18 million members of sixty-seven nationalities, called upon Presidential Candidate John Kennedy to drop his "appeasement and retreat" policy for Quemoy and Matsu. "U.S. ethnic groups cannot help recalling," it said, "that such defeatist policies are responsible for the Yalta betrayal, the China sellout, the Korean War, our failure to work out a serious and effective liberation policy, our amateurish showing in the propaganda war and the many

tragic blunders and retreats that have thrown Africa and South America to Communist subversion." *New York Times,* October 25, 1960.

32. *Ameryka-Echo,* July 27, 1958.

33. U.S., *Congressional Record,* 85th Cong., 2d Sess., August 22, 1958, CIV, A7658.

34. Copy in the author's possession.

INDEX

Adamic, Louis, 174

Adams, Charles Francis Jr., 4

Adams, Henry: on effect of immigration on homogeneity and culture, 4; mentioned, 5

Adams, John Quincy: views on intervention in foreign uprisings, 227, 228

Adams, Sherman: unwilling to distinguish among nationality groups, 217

Afro-American, 31

Afro-American party: attack by Cox on, 106

Akron Columbia: and 1920 presidential campaign, 102

Akron Germania, 101, 123

Albanian-Americans: organizations, 134; and Roosevelt, 141

Alessandroni, Eugene V., 156

All-Slav Congress: formation, 165

Altgeld, John Peter, 162

America First: foundation and purpose, 111

Americanism: in 1916 Democratic platform, 65, 68; and ethnic Americans, 100

Americanization movement: effect on political assimilation, 9-10

American Association of Foreign Language Newspapers, 38, 39

American Commission on Irish Independence, 82

American Communist party: endorses Progressive party, 163; attacks Roosevelt in 1940, 165

American Council for Nationality Service, 21

American Federation of International Institutes, 21

American Foreign Language Press Bureau, 123

American Hellenic Educational Progressive Association, 39, 159

American Jewish Committee, 87

American Negro press, 31

American parties: and ethnic Americans, 18, 59, 131; involvement in ethnic organizations, 21; and interest in Irish vote, 54; competition for ethnic vote during First World War, 60, 64-65; appeal to ethnic nationalism, 137, 140-41; modern appeals to ethnic vote, 244. *See also* Democratic party, Progressive party, Republican party

American party system: effect on ethnic nationalism, 10; and ethnic organizations, 12; and the ethnic vote, 18, 20; and ethnic pressures, 20; and Nationalities Divisions, 21

American-Polish Labor Council, 172

American Slav Congress: first meeting, 168-70; success of, 169-70; communist domination of, 170-71, 173; influence of on war conferences, 171-72; second meet-

ing, 173; attacks Truman's foreign policy, 174; aims, 176; supports Wallace, 176; mentioned, 13, 18, 124

Amerikai Magyar Nepszava: political advertisement in, 39

Ancient Order of Hibernians, 102

Anders, General Wladyslaw, 207-08

Anglo-American relations: and Irish-Americans, 47, 50, 54, 55, 56-57; and German-Americans, 47, 49

Anti-preparedness: during First World War, 60

Anti-Semitism, 9, 13, 105

Antonini, Luigi: on Italian-American vote in 1940 campaign, 125

Antonius, George: quoted, 88

Arab-Americans: and 1920 presidential election, 107

Arab League, 13

Arab nations: hostility to Zionism, 154

Armenian-Americans: and Lodge, 99, 104; and 1920 presidential campaign, 104-05; organizations, 134

Armstrong, O. K., 204

Assembly of Captive European Nations: formation and purpose, 22

Assimilation: successes in, xxiv; effect of 1920 presidential campaign on, 107-08

Auchincloss, Gordon, 105

Auslands-Organisation der NSDAP (AO): organization and purpose, 117

Austrian-Americans: organizations, 134-35

Austro-Hungarian Empire: reaction to Fourteen Points, 78; and Wilson, 78, 81-82; and Lansing, 81

Bailey, John M.: encourages appeal to religious vote, 246

Balanced ticket: outgrowth of machine politics, xxi; reasons for use, xxi-xxiii, 244-45; ethnic leaders' concern over, 241; encourages hyphenism, 244; results of, 245; and Irish-Americans, 245, 246; and religious vote, 246; objections to, 246-47

Balfour, Lord: and Lansing, 91; mentioned, 88, 92

Balfour Declaration: British motives for, 88, 89-90; formulation of, 90; reasons for delay, 90; and France, 90; and Brandeis, 90-91; Wilson's reaction to, 90, 93; impact on Zionism and Zionists, 90, 94; Lansing's objection to, 92-93, 94; House's reaction to, 93; statement of, 93-94; as war measure, 94; Lodge's support of, 94; and self-determination, 94; and Wise, 94; Wilson's public support of, 94; mentioned, 87, 88, 92, 95, 105, 154

Barclay, Colville, 91

Barnes, James, 172

Bayard, Thomas F., 55

311